THE MURROW BOYS

THE
MURROW
BOYS

**Pioneers on the Front Lines
of Broadcast Journalism**

Stanley Cloud and **Lynne Olson**

HOUGHTON MIFFLIN COMPANY
BOSTON ✦ NEW YORK ✦ 1996

For information about permission to reproduce selections
from this book, write to Permissions, Houghton Mifflin Company,
215 Park Avenue South, New York, New York 10003.

For information about this and other Houghton Mifflin trade and reference
books and multimedia products, visit The Bookstore at Houghton Mifflin on
the World Wide Web at http://www.hmco.com/trade.

Library of Congress Cataloging-in-Publication Data
Cloud, Stanley.
   The Murrow boys : pioneers on the front lines of broadcast journalism /
Stanley Cloud and Lynne Olson.
   p. cm.
   Includes bibliographical references and index.
   ISBN 0-395-68084-0
   1. Radio journalists — United States — Biography. 2. Radio journalism —
United States — History.   I. Olson, Lynne. II. Title.
PN4871.C56   1996
070'.092'2 — dc20   95-44939
[B]   CIP

Printed in the United States of America
QUM 10 9 8 7 6 5 4 3 2 1

Book design by Melodie Wertelet

Excerpts from CBS broadcasts are reprinted
by permission of CBS News Archives.

For our parents and children,
especially Carly, who had to live through it

Contents

1945 ✦ 1961

1961 ✦ 1992

Authors' Note

Before and during World War II, the great CBS journalist Edward R. Murrow assembled a group of radio correspondents who were later known as "the Murrow Boys." Who first coined the term and when it came into general usage are unclear; it was popular at CBS by the late 1940s. Others on the news staff considered it a sobriquet of honor, as did Murrow and the Boys themselves. Wrote former CBS correspondent David Schoenbrun in 1989, "At one point in the forties and fifties, . . . the 'Murrow boys' were not only number one, we were in a class by ourselves." The only problematic part of Schoenbrun's assessment, as we shall see, was his inclusion of himself among the happy few.

The first task facing anyone who sets out to tell the remarkable story of the Murrow Boys is deciding who they were, which is not as easy as one might think. William L. Shirer, for instance, never considered himself a Boy, because he never thought he was one of Murrow's protégés. Nor did the Boys themselves always agree on who should make the list; some excluded Cecil Brown, Howard K. Smith, and Winston Burdett on the grounds that they spent little or no time with Murrow in London during World War II; moreover, Smith and Burdett had not even been hired by Murrow. Thomas Grandin and Mary Marvin Breckinridge are rarely included, because their contributions have long since been forgotten and their brief association with Murrow and CBS ended before the United States entered the war. Finally, a few of the CBS correspondents whom Murrow hired, or caused to be hired, after the war — notably Schoenbrun — liked to think of themselves, and were often thought of by others, as part of the group.

The names we finally settled on are, in alphabetical order: Mary Marvin Breckinridge, Cecil Brown, Winston Burdett, Charles Collingwood, William Downs, Thomas Grandin, Richard C. Hottelet, Larry LeSueur, Eric Sevareid, William L. Shirer, and Howard K.

Smith. Collingwood, Downs, Hottelet, LeSueur, Sevareid, and Shirer were all hired by Murrow, worked with him during the war, and became his close friends and respected colleagues. Historical accuracy demanded our inclusion of Grandin and Breckinridge. Brown, though he resigned from CBS before the end of the war, is included because he was hired by Murrow and because his coverage in the Balkans and the Pacific theater was unique and brilliant. As for Smith and Burdett, although Murrow didn't hire them himself and saw little of them until peacetime, there is no question that he thought of both as part of his wartime team and treated them as such afterward. We confirmed this during extensive interviews with Murrow's widow, Janet Murrow, and for us that settled the matter.

During the war Murrow hired several journalists — including reporter Paul Manning, newspaper editor Charles Shaw, and magazine editor Willard Shadel — to augment CBS's staff in Europe. Although all three began as either part-time or temporary employees, they played important supporting roles in the network's war coverage. Yet they were not Boys. Manning went to work for the Mutual network, and Shaw became a television news director in Philadelphia. Of the three, only Shadel eventually became a full-time CBS News employee, but by his own bemused account he was never admitted to the charmed Murrow circle. Similarly, while several other postwar CBS correspondents — for example, Schoenbrun, George Polk, Daniel Schorr, and Alexander Kendrick — were outstanding journalists in their own right and personally close to Murrow, they did not have the same war-derived status as the Murrow Boys, and we have thus excluded them from our list.

The Boys' story of triumph and disappointment has all the sweep and drama of epic fiction. But there is no fiction here. There are no imaginary conversations or scenes, nothing that goes beyond the facts as developed in archival research, extensive reading, listening to old broadcasts, and scores of interviews, including many with the surviving Boys. Whenever we describe someone's thoughts, we have a primary source to support the description.

In short, *The Murrow Boys* is a wholly factual account of how legends are born and dreams die.

Stanley Cloud and Lynne Olson
JUNE 1995

We few, we happy few, we band of brothers . . .

— Shakespeare, *Henry V*

I would like . . . to tell a little about the boys who made up
[the] CBS crew during the war and how [they were] selected.

— Edward R. Murrow, *letter to Blanche Knopf about 1956*

THE MURROW BOYS

Prologue

On a fine fall afternoon in 1992, a memorial service for Eric Sevareid was held at the National Press Club in Washington, D.C. Some four hundred people attended. Among them were the luminaries of modern electronic journalism, including Walter Cronkite, Mike Wallace, Andy Rooney, Bernard Shaw, Sam Donaldson, Lesley Stahl, Don Hewitt, and Dan Rather. Carrying themselves with self-conscious pride in their own celebrity and wealth, the stars roamed the room looking for seats, greeting people they knew — and they knew almost everyone — with a wave, a handshake, an air kiss.

Whatever he had been when he began, at his death Sevareid was a luminary too. In the last decade or so before his retirement from CBS in 1977, he had become, with his mane of white hair, his pronounced jaw, his deep and ragged voice, a kind of totem of respectable opinion. Several times a week, on his evening news commentaries, he had tried to sell civility to a nation consumed with the passionate fires of race and Vietnam and Watergate. It was the totem who was remembered at his memorial service, not the young dreamer from Velva, North Dakota, not the adventurer he once had been, not the scourge of pompous generals and errant witch-hunters.

As a kid in Velva, Sevareid dreamed that someday he would travel far and then return to his hometown, and people would marvel at where he had been, what he had done, who he had become. Marvel they eventually did. For in 1937, when Eric Sevareid was a journeyman newspaper reporter, his head filled with radical political ideas, he boarded a freighter to Europe. Two years later he was hired by Edward R. Murrow as one of a small team of young, pioneering CBS radio correspondents who came to be called the Murrow Boys.

Sevareid and the rest of the Boys covered World War II and the postwar world for CBS, and in the process they invented broadcast journalism. "We had to create it as we went along," Sevareid once said. "There were no precedents. We had to create the tradition."

There were eleven of them altogether, but because of romance or professional pique, three dropped out early. There had never been a group of reporters quite like them before, and there never was again. Murrow once said during the war, "If I am remembered for anything, I want it to be for the people I have been able to persuade to work with me here at CBS. Without [them], I'd be nothing." The adventures they lived, the successes they enjoyed, the failures and disappointments they endured went beyond anything young Eric Sevareid had dreamed about back in North Dakota. "There was a high romance . . . a certain rapture about it that I never quite got over," he said.

Yet by the time he died in 1992 at the age of seventy-nine, most people, even many of his own colleagues, seemed to have forgotten all that about Eric Sevareid. He was just a rather stuffy old commentator who used to be on the evening news. And the Murrow Boys . . . well, hardly anyone remembered them at all.

✦

At the front of the room was a podium and a microphone. To one side, where the Sevareid family was seated, a quartet from the National Symphony Orchestra played softly. Dan Rather was the master of ceremonies, a role he relished; he had played it at Charles Collingwood's memorial service seven years earlier. Murrow and the Boys were Rather's idols. In the early seventies he tried to write a play called *The Murrow Boys*, but gave it up when he discovered, as Sevareid had discovered thirty years earlier, that he didn't know *how* to write a play. Rather had patterned himself after Murrow, Sevareid, Collingwood, and the rest of the Boys — as had most of the other broadcast journalists in the room, consciously or unconsciously.

They also liked to wrap themselves in the mantle of integrity that Murrow and the Boys had painstakingly woven out of the threads of their many battles with sponsors and network executives. Indeed, Rather donned the mantle so often in public that in 1987 Sevareid himself suggested he tone down the act a bit. "Rather is not Edward R. Murrow II," Sevareid wrote in a letter to Rather. Undeterred, Rather and CBS continued trading on the past, ignoring the inconvenient parts, such as the fact that Murrow and most of the Boys had been either forced out or sidetracked by the network's bosses.

Still, Rather *was* the voice of CBS News, and it was therefore not inappropriate for him to preside at Sevareid's memorial service. The trouble was that he didn't seem to have anything to say. At one point he told a lengthy anecdote about sharing a room with Sevareid in China that said nothing about Sevareid and only left his audience bewildered.

A little later Howard Stringer, the president of the CBS Broadcast Group and former head of CBS News, stepped to the microphone. Stringer, who in 1987 had presided over massive budget cuts that gutted the news division, seemed pleased to report that Sevareid "never talked about the good old days" to him (which was odd, because Sevareid often talked about the glory days of CBS News to other people).

Of all the speakers, only Richard Salant, another CBS News ex-president, seemed to appreciate the irony inherent in listening to modern TV journalists and executives extol Eric Sevareid. "The most important lesson that Eric taught us," Salant said pointedly, "was that, even in television, in the beginning was the word. Eric was the refutation of the mistaken notion that there must always be pictures, and that the cardinal sin is to show nothing but a talking head. . . . Perhaps today's television journalists, addicted to pictures no matter how irrelevant and distracting, might do well to recall that when Eric's talking head appeared on the CBS Evening News, that broadcast was dominant not only among the critics but also among the viewers."

When the service was over, those who had known Eric Sevareid best couldn't help wondering how the speakers had been selected. Said Don Hewitt, the executive producer of *60 Minutes*, "It was an awful service, one of the worst funerals I was ever at. . . . It was all a bunch of egos. They were all going to have their say there. They didn't care about Sevareid. They were going to use that [occasion] as their moment to make speeches." Some of Sevareid's friends, having had an advance look at the list of speakers, deliberately chose not to attend.

✦

One friend who did attend — an old man with hooded eyes, a crooked nose, and a wry grin — was ignored by the network stars. Many of them wouldn't have known who he was anyway. Larry LeSueur, then eighty-three years old, was the only one of the five surviving Murrow Boys at the service. LeSueur had known Eric Sevareid as well as or better than anyone in the room and had been Ed Murrow's close buddy during World War II. He, Sevareid, and Murrow had covered the Battle of Britain and the London Blitz together. LeSueur had also reported the siege of Moscow from behind *Russian* lines and had been with the second wave to land on Utah Beach at D-Day. He was an important part of CBS's history and of Eric Sevareid's life.

No one from CBS had bothered to inform him about the memorial service. A Washington resident, he just happened to read about it in the newspaper and decided to go on his own. As he listened to the speeches, he felt mounting sadness and irritation. "I didn't recognize Eric in them," he said afterward. "There was nothing about his essence. . . . It was a *production*. I thought: 'If this is what Eric was really like, then I guess I didn't know him.' There just wasn't anything about the Sevareid I knew. There was nothing about his *work* at all! It was all his later life. There was nothing about his career. Almost nothing about Murrow, and nothing at all about the Murrow Boys." LeSueur was sorry he had come. He left the National Press Club shaking his head and remembering how it had really been . . .

1937 ✳ 1945

✦ 1

The Voice of the Future

Larry lesueur and his Indian Scout were hurtling down New York's Henry Hudson Parkway at a speed, LeSueur admitted later, that should have satisfied anyone fool enough to ride a motorcycle in the first place. But young LeSueur, the wind whipping at his face, as usual wanted more.

He reached down and flipped open the carburetor latch. It was a trick he'd learned: if you force-fed air into the carburetor, you could get extra kick out of the Scout, which, even with its carburetor closed, was by LeSueur's reckoning a considerable cut above a Harley-Davidson. Now the supercharged Scout leapt forward like a horse under the crop, and LeSueur, trying to get where he was going that much faster, leaned over the handlebars to reduce the drag. This was more like it. He was *flying*. He *owned* the Henry Hudson Parkway.

As he approached a dip in the road leading under a bridge, with a steep rise beyond, he noticed that the other drivers were slowing down. Traffic was congesting under the bridge. LeSueur maintained his speed, roared down the incline, wove the Scout around one car after another, then started up the rise. Ahead lumbered a big green Pierce-Arrow. Now the always-cool-in-a-pinch Larry LeSueur was beginning to feel a small jab of concern. Time to rein in the Scout. But if he braked while the carburetor latch was open, the Scout would stall out below thirty miles an hour and probably flip. He reached down to close the latch, taking his eyes off the road for just a second. The next thing he knew, the gap between him and the Pierce-Arrow had vanished.

It was just a bump, not hard enough to do any damage to the car but hard enough to unseat LeSueur. There was a moment of weightlessness, followed by the sensation of a very heavy animal sitting on his chest. He was sprawled on the grassy verge of the highway, struggling to catch the wind that had been knocked out of him. His beautiful bright red Scout still lay in the middle of the highway on its side, its engine whining away, its wheels spinning uselessly.

As LeSueur recovered his breath and wits, he looked up. The driver of the Pierce-Arrow had pulled over and was walking back toward the motorcycle. The man turned off the ignition, yanked the bike upright, and guided it over to the verge. For a moment this unknown rich guy stood staring down at LeSueur, whose humiliation was compounded as he remembered he had on his father's beat-up, hand-me-down boots. With a patronizing look but without a word, the rich guy turned and strode back to his Pierce-Arrow.

It would be a while before Larry LeSueur got where he wanted to be.

✦

During the bleak years of the Depression, New York always seemed to be cutting Lawrence Edward LeSueur down to size. Little money, no opportunity for the adventures that had come so easily, according to family tales and legend, to so many Lesueurs before him (the S wasn't capitalized until Larry became a big-time war correspondent for CBS).

His father, Wallace Lesueur, had been a naval officer in World War I, then a journalist and foreign correspondent whose career included stints with the *New York Sun* and the *New York Tribune*. Between newspaper jobs he had been a press agent for various rodeos and traveling Wild West shows, including "Zach Miller's 101st Ranch." Larry was born in New York in 1909. The family, including his mother, Rose, and older sister, Margaret, lived in Chicago for a few years when Larry was a boy, then returned to New York. Wallace's father had been a publisher of a newspaper in Tama, Iowa, and had run the Indian reservation there; Larry grew up listening to his grandfather's tall tales of drunken Indians running amok. He loved those stories, just as he loved the summers he spent on the Lesueur family farm in Greencastle, Indiana, fishing and hunting and wandering wherever he pleased.

The adult Larry LeSueur would impress many people, especially women, with his urbane sophistication. But his roots and passions were deep in his grandfather's rural Midwest, a fact that went a long way toward explaining how he felt about life, his country, his work, and the world. At heart Larry LeSueur was a farm boy. He had little time or patience for urban angst. To him a person was who he was, and a creek was always a "crick." His love of open country and its pleasures made it difficult for him to leave the farm after summer vacations and go back to childhood life in the concrete landscapes of Chicago and New York.

Still, in the twenties, if a kid knew where to look, even New York City offered the odd bucolic delight. LeSueur fished and shot frogs with a BB gun where the Spuyten Duyvil Creek emptied into the Hudson River north of Manhattan. Best of all was the trapping. Often in the winters LeSueur would hop on a trolley near his home in Riverdale on the western edge of the Bronx, ride to Van Cortlandt Park, then trudge for miles, sometimes through heavy snow, to run his traplines from the northern reaches of the park into Westchester County. He trapped muskrats and an occasional mink, then skinned them and stretched and dried the pelts. The fur merchants in lower Manhattan seemed impressed every time this slim kid with the easy manner showed up to peddle fresh pelts. Larry LeSueur was, in fact, the first honest-to-God fur trapper most of the merchants had ever seen.

He grew up tough and resourceful, attending public schools in the Bronx, where fistfights and wrestling matches in barren schoolyards were a ritualized form of physical exercise for the combatants and a source of rough entertainment for their classmates. Many years later, about all LeSueur could remember of his time in elementary school was "fighting for survival or for dominance." There was little relief from the struggle until junior high, when he was admitted to the Speyer School, an experimental private school for boys operated by Columbia University. Even there, even as his writing and journalistic talents were being developed, he had to take his licks. Once he wrote an essay on New York City's last blacksmith for the school's literary magazine. It was so well written that his teacher said a twelve-year-old couldn't possibly have done it. When LeSueur insisted he had, his teacher slapped him hard across the face for lying. She never apologized, but a little later, when the school paper needed someone to cover a track meet, she suggested LeSueur's name to the editor. "He's a good writer," she said. That was the beginning of his career as a reporter.

He wanted to go to college and become a newspaperman like his father and grandfather. By the time he graduated from high school in 1927, however, that plan had become a pipe dream. His alcoholic father had died, and although Rose Lesueur had enough money to get by on (with the help of some odd jobs), there was not enough to finance college for Larry. He continued living with his mother in the Riverdale house and found a job as an office boy in the advertising department at Macy's. In two years he had saved enough to enroll as a commuting student at New York University.

Other students at the University Heights campus considered him a little wild. It was, after all, unlikely that many of them had been fur trappers, and none, as far as he knew, owned a motorcycle, not even a secondhand one like his beloved Indian Scout. Then there was Le-Sueur's famous schoolyard toughness, which, though he was soft-spoken, thin, and certainly no bully, led people to understand that it might be unwise to fool with him. At 143 pounds, he was the welterweight boxing champion of his freshman class. The next year he made the varsity boxing team and discovered he didn't have a lock on toughness. By his junior year, his nose had been badly broken (adding an additional touch of mystery to his dark face with the heavy-lidded eyes), and he was losing his enthusiasm for the manly art of self-defense. Then in one varsity match he was decked. Hard. He awoke, still on the canvas, unable to recall who he or anyone else was. When he finally regained his senses in the shower, he decided to hang up the gloves.

It was no great sacrifice. LeSueur had other, less physically punishing interests. He liked to read and was improving all the time as a writer. He decided to study English literature and became a frequent contributor to the campus literary magazine. Outside school he worked as everything from a car polisher to a waiter at Schrafft's. In 1932 he received his bachelor of arts degree and set out to find real work. But in that year the world did not appear to need another English major.

◆

New York was nearing the end of the corrupt, happy regime of Mayor Jimmy Walker. When the twenties were roaring, the dapper, fun-loving Walker had been an amusing diversion. But when the bread lines of the Depression began forming and people started selling apples on street corners, Walker became an intolerable embarrassment. New York elected Fiorello La Guardia to change things.

In the shadows of the recently completed Chrysler and Empire State buildings, LeSueur, like the throngs of other unemployed New Yorkers, tramped the streets, looking for a job. After months of searching, he was hired as an assistant to a private investigator. LeSueur spied on wayward spouses and prowled through stores to pick off shoplifters, many of them out of work. It was not, he said, "what you read about in mystery novels." It was "a nasty, sordid, mean job." So, Depression or no Depression, he quit.

After some more searching, he was able to return to Macy's, this time as a floorwalker, Saturdays only. It may have been a step up from gum-

shoe, and the floorwalker's requisite white carnation may have lent Le-
Sueur a certain follow-me-madam insouciance, but this was still not
what he had in mind for himself. There was nothing to look forward to
but a mind-numbing eternity of tending to peevish customers. Then
one Saturday an acquaintance approached him in the store.

"You can't do this all your life," the man said. "What do you really
want to be?"

"A reporter," LeSueur answered.

LeSueur's acquaintance said he knew an editor at *Women's Wear
Daily*, the newspaper of record, so to speak, of the fashion industry.
When the editor said he was willing to give LeSueur a tryout, LeSueur
didn't hesitate: he turned in his Macy's boutonniere. If *Women's Wear
Daily* didn't usually traffic in the kind of news that created journalistic
legends, and if the assignments weren't exactly in the adventurous tradition of the Lesueurs, at least he was moving in the right direction. In any
case he did not remain at *WWD* very long. In 1936, less than a year after
leaving Macy's, he was recruited by that rambunctious scapegrace of the
journalistic world, the United Press wire service.

✦

About this same time the policymakers at the Scripps-Howard newspaper company, which owned United Press, ordered their editorial writers to endorse the Roosevelt administration's proposal for a forty-hour
workweek. Among UP staffers, the irony was almost too delicious to
bear. A forty-hour workweek was unheard of at UP, and there wasn't the
slightest prospect that it would be heard of anytime soon. LeSueur, after
working ten hours a day or more, Monday through Friday, had to take
the Saturday-evening shift as well. When he finished, an hour before
midnight, the regular Saturday poker game was usually under way, and
LeSueur usually joined in. More times than he cared to remember, he
lost the entire $37.50 he'd earned that week.

Still, UP covered hard news, and it offered real opportunities for
adventure. If you were young, there was always a chance that you might
catch the eye of one of the newspaper bosses who used to watch the UP
wire carefully for signs of life and talent. They did so for a simple reason:
the skinflint, often slapdash wire service hired some of the most promising young journalists in the country. "UP got good kids, squeezed them
like oranges, taught them the trade, paid them nothing," recalled UP
alumnus Dick Hottelet. "Then they left, and UP picked up another kid

at fifteen dollars or so a week to do the same thing." Or, as Howard K. Smith, another former UP reporter, put it, "UP lived on the first years of a lot of journalists' careers."

Shrewd and unscrupulous editors have always taken advantage of the belief, held almost universally by reporters, that there is something more valuable than money — the chase, the hunt, the game, the beating of the competition. Nowhere was this belief held more strongly than at UP. The agency's young, aggressive reporters seemed to live on nothing but the adrenaline high that came from competition with their great, and by comparison rather regal, rival, the dominant Associated Press. If you got a few facts wrong, if the story wasn't quite complete, well, you'd do better next time; what mattered above all in the twenty-four-hours-a-day, seven-days-a-week, no-place-too-far, no-town-too-small world of the wire services was being first with the news. When you were, it meant that your agency's main clients, the big-city dailies — most of *them* in fierce competition with each other — were also first. A scoop measured in minutes, or even seconds, could thus bring a torrent of praise from headquarters.

Grouse as UP's youngsters did about their nineteenth-century work-house conditions, most of them loved the competition. It gave them more challenge and excitement than many had ever known before. But the combination of poker and low wages had nearly broken Larry LeSueur. Excitement was fine, but he needed to make more money. And one way to do that, he decided, was to moonlight some scripts for radio.

◆

At the time radio was barely out of its infancy. A little more than a decade earlier, most Americans didn't know what it was; now many couldn't imagine life without it. Social workers discovered that people who had lost almost everything in the Depression would sell their ice-boxes and other essentials before giving up their Atwater Kents or their Philcos. Radio became one of America's binding ties, all the more im-portant because of its immense reach. The isolated lobster fishermen of Maine had radio, at least, in common with the lettuce farmers of Cali-fornia.

Back in the 1930s, when Americans clustered by their radios to hear a prize fight or a presidential fireside chat, or to laugh at *Amos 'n' Andy* or Eddie Cantor, they became the first manifestation of what Marshall McLuhan decades later would call the "global village." Radio meant that people could instantaneously and simultaneously receive information from thousands of miles away. Or they could escape reality, forget for a while the low prices being paid for lobster or the bad lettuce crop or whatever else was wrong, and turn on the radio for pure entertainment. Best of all, after they bought a receiver (or built their own), this miracle of communication was free. Small wonder, in the midst of the Depression, that Americans developed a ravenous appetite for radio or that the people who worked in radio had to scramble ever more creatively to satisfy that appetite.

One tiny morsel for the maw was a show on the Columbia Broadcasting System's New York affiliate called *We, the People*, a series of sketches about American archetypes. In 1938 Larry LeSueur began submitting short scripts to the program's producers. After a few were accepted, he was pressed into service as the voice for some of his characters. His favorite was a fellow he called "the world-champion chump," a gullible soul forever being duped by con men on New York street corners, the kind of person who buys the dancing dolls that don't dance and the back-flipping toy monkeys that don't flip.

The producers of *We, the People* liked LeSueur's scripts and ideas but finally pulled the plug on his performing: listeners were beginning to recognize his voice, they said. He couldn't vary it enough to make his characters unique. LeSueur didn't complain; he was a reporter, not an actor. He began to explore other prospects in radio, especially in radio news, such as it then was.

✦

The only "newsmen" who counted for anything on radio in the early 1930s were the so-called commentators: mellifluous poseurs, for the most part, whose reporting consisted mainly of what they read in the morning newspaper or picked up from the wire services. To be fair, they were not hired to be reporters. The fledgling networks wanted them to purvey anecdotes and thoughts — controversial enough to attract listeners, safe enough to avoid lawsuits or government repression — in florid tones.

The two biggest stars in this burgeoning specialty were Lowell Thomas of the National Broadcasting System and the now-forgotten Boake Carter of the Columbia Broadcasting System. Thomas, said an NBC executive of the day, "had a million-dollar voice but not a nickel's worth of news." And Boake Carter? CBS's man was the quintessential commentator. An Irish immigrant born in Baku, Azerbaijan, he could roll his R's with the best of them. In some of his publicity photographs, Carter affected the look of an English squire — pipe, tweeds, jodhpurs, gleaming riding boots. He even managed to live a squire's life on an estate nestled in the rolling green hills outside Philadelphia, with a pool and stables and his own broadcasting studio. Sponsored by Philco, he was for a time America's most popular commentator. Experts estimated that two and a half million radios were tuned to his broadcasts every night. Newspapers and magazines treated him like a celebrity, and the Carter visage, with its trademark haughty expression, clipped red mustache, and prominent chin cleft, was nearly as recognizable as a movie star's. (Invariably missing from the publicity photos, however, was any point of reference that might reveal how *short* Carter was.)

There was just one problem: Boake Carter rarely ventured off his farm to discover what was happening in the world. He needed help in clarifying what was and was not important in the day's news. To fill that need, CBS asked United Press to install in Carter's house a special teletype connected directly to another teletype at UP headquarters in Manhattan. At the New York end a part-time "news consultant" would answer Carter's questions about the day's events and their meaning. The person UP chose as Carter's consultant was Larry Le-Sueur.

By the time LeSueur began consulting with him, the great man, though more popular than ever, was on the verge of self-parody. His colleagues suspected that sometimes he just made things up. As CBS announcer Robert Trout said, "Nobody ever had the faintest idea what he was doing, where he'd get his news." At one point, when Carter's sponsor, Philco, filed a patent-rights suit against Radio Corporation of America, Carter unblushingly supported Philco's case on the air.

Carter's critics derided his accent, his shameless shilling for his sponsor's products, his breathless, staccato delivery, his preference for Britishisms like "Great Scott," "by jingo" and "Cheerio." Clichés were his métier. In one memorable broadcast he used "war-torn," "dark shadow," "history in the making," and "the anvil of time" in just the first two sentences. He claimed to have attended Christ College, Cambridge, but there is no evidence that he actually did. He said his father had been a British diplomat, when the elder Carter had really been a worker for a British oil company in Azerbaijan. How, Boake Carter's critics wondered, could such an unschooled, untalented impostor hoodwink the American people into believing what he said on the air?

Among those wondering was the president of the United States. During Franklin D. Roosevelt's first and second terms, Carter, a right-wing isolationist, repeatedly denounced the villainies of the New Deal. To Carter, the risk of war came not from Adolf Hitler, then consolidating his power in Germany, but from what Carter dubbed "the World Savers' Brigade," led by FDR. Carter sneered and bullied and blustered and drove the New Dealers wild. "Croak Carter," Interior Secretary Harold Ickes dubbed him. When a fed-up James Roosevelt asked his father why he didn't respond to Carter's diatribes, FDR replied, "If the president or anyone else were to undertake to answer Boake Carter, he would have no time to act as executive head of the government."

New Dealers weren't Carter's only critics. William S. Paley, the upwardly striving young owner and president of CBS, didn't much care for him either. Paley, the son of a successful cigar manufacturer, was determined to achieve respectability for himself and the network he had purchased in 1928. He deplored Carter's lack of class, his raw-meat demagoguery. Yet Paley, never one to let principles stand in the way of income, did not intervene. The commentator's huge audience meant huge revenues for struggling Columbia.

CBS's older rival, NBC, had all the top entertainment stars from vaudeville and the concert halls — Eddie Cantor, Rudy Vallee, Arturo Toscanini — and a far more impressive array of sponsors. Paley and CBS were good at signing promising new entertainers like crooner Bing Crosby and the comedy act of George Burns and Gracie Allen, but once they established themselves, the performers (and their sponsors) tended to hightail it over to NBC. That left Columbia with public affairs and the news, which, for all practical purposes, meant Boake Carter. Until Paley could find some alternative, he would just have to grit his teeth and pretend that Carter was Walter Lippmann. If Boake missed an occasional broadcast because he wanted to go sailing on his sixty-foot ketch, Paley and the network had to live with it.

Aside from Carter, the meager remainder of CBS's news operation (then called the Special Events Department) was squirreled away in a seventeenth-floor corner of the network's headquarters at 485 Madison Avenue in New York. Paley did hire two serious and experienced newsmen to direct it: Edward Klauber, a former night city editor at the *New York Times*, became Paley's personal assistant (with duties that went far beyond the news operation); and Paul White, an old UP man, was made

CBS's news editor. But as late as the mid-thirties, the full-time staff of Special Events consisted only of White and his assistant, plus a secretary, and the mustachioed, baritone announcer Robert Trout, who, when he wasn't doing station breaks for *Jack Armstrong, the All-American Boy*, or opening the broadcast day with an organ reveille, read the news and described prizefights, ship christenings, and parades.

Amid such small-time competition, Boake Carter's ego expanded to heroic proportions. Evidently he came to think he could say absolutely anything. He supported Nazi Germany's claim to Austria in 1937, and his attacks on the Roosevelt administration grew ever more strident and unreasoning. The White House, tired of turning the other cheek, now resolved to take its revenge. Three government agencies began investigations of Carter, and there was serious talk in Congress of having him declared an undesirable alien. Administration officials encouraged the idea of a consumer boycott of Philco.

Under this pressure Philco surrendered, canceling Carter's contract in February 1938. Thousands of letters from outraged listeners persuaded General Foods to pick up the contract, but the reprieve turned out to be temporary. On August 26, 1938, Paley, who feared government regulation and interference almost as much as he feared bankruptcy, yanked Boake Carter off the air.

Political and economic pressures weren't the only reasons. The times were changing with stunning speed, and Carter expressed old ideas in an old and dying language. If he didn't sense how American opinion was shifting against Hitler, Bill Paley did. Even before Carter was shown the door, Paley, Klauber, White, and two CBS men in Europe had seen what Hitler was up to and in response had begun reinventing the very idea of radio news.

The two Europe-based employees were a young man named Edward R. Murrow, whom CBS had sent abroad in 1937 as "European director" (little more than a booking agent for broadcasts), and William L. Shirer, an itinerant, out-of-work American newspaperman whom Murrow had brought in to help. They were reporting Europe's rush to war in ways that not even newspapers — and certainly not Boake Carter — could match.

Reporting was the key. Fast, knowledgeable, experienced reporting based on firsthand observation, not just what Boake Carter or H. V. Kaltenborn or Lowell Thomas or anyone else back in the States happened to think. Murrow and Shirer had given CBS news a new voice —

a cool, rational voice that told of an approaching Armageddon. It was the voice of the future.

✦

Young Larry LeSueur, meanwhile, had grown weary of the United Press treadmill and his Boake Carter "consulting" job. He was aware of the changes taking place in radio news, had heard some of the early broadcasts by Murrow and Shirer, had devoured a book titled *I Found No Peace* by the legendary UP foreign correspondent Webb Miller. And now he knew where he wanted to be. He had to get to Europe, where the war was, where all the old assumptions and rules were changing, where men his own age were doing great and daring things. If his UP bosses wouldn't send him, and they wouldn't, he would go on his own.

And so, in the summer of 1939, Larry LeSueur took a leave of absence from United Press, packed up his things, said goodbye to his mother, and boarded a merchant ship, the S.S. *American Farmer.* His destination was England and — finally — adventure.

2

Murrow and Shirer

STANDING SIDE BY SIDE, they looked like a vaudeville comedy team: Murrow the elegant and sophisticated straight man, Shirer the dim and pratfalling sidekick. Rarely have appearances been more deceiving.

When the two men joined forces in 1937, Edward R. Murrow — who by the end of World War II would be the popular embodiment of the best in American journalism — was only twenty-nine years old and didn't have a day of real journalistic experience to his credit. But he was tall, lean, and likable, and there was genius in him, or at least startling precocity. And darkness, too. With his creased and troubled face beneath perfectly trimmed black hair, he already seemed middle-aged. He had piercing eyes and gleaming teeth (although neglect and incessant cigarette smoking would damage them terribly in only a few years). People always noticed Ed Murrow. He wore Savile Row pinstripes and had erased every vestige of his hardscrabble, dirt-poor origins in North Carolina.

Then William L. Shirer: though almost as tall as Murrow, he somehow appeared short and dumpy. He came from a relatively prominent, though relatively poor, Midwestern family. There was little elegance in Shirer, except for his mind and pretensions. He was only four years older than Murrow, but his sandy hair was already receding at an alarming rate, and what was left was wispy and ill combed. He wore a small, mannered mustache. His glasses were thick and metal-rimmed, and he had a blind eye (the result of a skiing accident in 1932) that stared disconcertingly through the right lens of plain glass. His off-the-rack jackets and trousers were rumpled, his fedoras dented in the wrong places, his shoes in need of polish.

When a photographer was around, Murrow knew how and when to

smile (and when not to); Shirer hadn't a clue. While Murrow's rich baritone was one of his many striking features, Shirer's voice was thin and reedy, and he droned in the flat cadences of his native Iowa.

Murrow strove to create a bon vivant's persona, but it was Shirer who actually loved and lived the good life, who savored fine food and wine, who appreciated and pursued (deep into old age) beautiful women. For Murrow, the farther he traveled from his rural origins, the more he seemed to want to return to his roots — or the more guilty he felt for not doing so. He was a man's man in an era when that meant hunting, fishing, smoking, drinking, and working, primarily in the company of male pals who knew how to take a joke and a punch in the shoulder. He was not an especially deep thinker or voracious reader. Shirer, on the other hand, was an experienced foreign correspondent who cultivated intellectuals. He despaired whenever he took Murrow to a fancy restaurant in Paris or Geneva and Murrow ordered scrambled eggs. Shirer found it almost quaint when Murrow chided him about his philandering. For Murrow, sex was hardly a compulsion. As for Shirer . . . once, at a party, he was asked to explain why, with his bald pate and blind eye, he seemed to be so attractive to women. Shirer smiled. "I try so much harder than all the rest of you," he said.

Despite their differences, or because of them, Ed Murrow and Bill Shirer were, for a few intense years, closer to each other than either would ever be to anyone else, wives and lovers included. Theirs was an extraordinary friendship, and when it shattered a decade later, the shattering would haunt them both for the rest of their lives. To be known as one of the Murrow Boys would eventually be no small honor at CBS and in the wider world, but Shirer wasn't just one of the Boys. In those turbulent years, he was Murrow's true and very nearly equal partner. The two of them did things that had never been done before and did them against all technical and human odds, often in spite of initially strong opposition from their bosses in New York.

Shirer shared Murrow's idealism, echoed his criticism of unearned privilege, and believed with him that a journalist should be a champion of the underdog. At the same time, they were intensely ambitious young men who yearned for admission to the clubs and salons that would establish their bona fides as persons of intellect and social standing. But how could they gain admission? As they set out together, Murrow and Shirer felt thwarted in their careers and wounded by the way radio news was then disparaged. "Murrow had fired me with the feeling that we might go places in this new-fangled radio broadcasting business," Shirer excitedly wrote in his diary after his first meeting with Murrow. They soon discovered that few others shared their vision.

◆

For most veteran foreign correspondents stationed in Europe at the time, "radio news" was an oxymoron. America's two largest radio networks — Bill Paley's CBS and David Sarnoff's NBC — had no reporters of their own crisscrossing the globe to find the news and relay it, with explanation and analysis, to the people back home. Instead, the networks had people like Murrow in London: functionaries whose job was not to report but to arrange broadcasts of various kinds — debates at the League of Nations, for example, or coronations, or the speeches of statesmen. Or, to cite a pre–World War II highlight of international broadcasting: CBS's live presentation in 1932 of a nightingale singing from England's Surrey woods. So successful was the program that America's radio editors voted it the "most interesting" of that not uninteresting year. One CBS executive, possibly overstimulated, declared the song of the Surrey nightingale "the greatest thing this company has ever done for Anglo-American relations."

Murrow had been transferred to London in 1937 to become CBS's European "director of talks." Before he left New York, he was advised that the broadcast of the nightingale was the standard by which his performance would be judged. Speeches were all well and good, but the nightingale was real entertainment. Try as Murrow might to think of himself as a correspondent, everyone kept bringing him back to earth. When he tried to join the American Foreign Correspondents' Association in London, his application was summarily rejected. "I wasn't even allowed to attend the meetings, much less become a member," Murrow recalled.

The association's rejection of Murrow was understandable: he clearly wasn't a foreign correspondent, and nothing in his background suggested he ever would — or could — join that elite fraternity. His real name was Egbert Roscoe Murrow. He was born April 25, 1908, in a 150-year-old house in Polecat Creek, a hamlet with no automobiles, telephones, or electricity. Egbert's parents were Quakers, although his mother, who had converted to Quakerism on her marriage, remained a closet Methodist all her life. His father, Roscoe Murrow, was an impoverished dirt farmer, a large, burly, good-natured fellow badly henpecked by his humorless, pious wife. Ed Murrow once remarked that when his mother answered the phone she refused to say hello, for fear of letting the name of the netherworld pass her lips. Expressions of love or affection did not come easily to her, or to her husband. Fun was usually frowned upon. "I never learned to play," Ed Murrow once said.

He was the last of three children, all boys. When he was five years old, the family sought to improve its lot by moving to Washington State, first to Blanchard, later to Beaver. Roscoe worked in logging camps and eventually became an engineer on short-line trains that hauled logs from the forest to the mills. By 1922 he had prospered to the point that the family could for the first time afford indoor plumbing.

Young Egbert grew up learning about the outdoors, especially hunting, and the virtue of hard work. He was driving a school bus when he was fifteen. During his later high school years and at Washington State College, he worked summers as a lumberjack. After being ragged about his first name by the loggers he worked with, he unofficially changed it from Egbert to Edward. In college he majored in speech under the gentle tutelage of Professor Ida Lou Anderson (who would write him letters of advice when he went into broadcasting), and he did some acting and debating. He was popular with other students and had the usual romances — the most serious of which led to an illegally aborted pregnancy. An excellent student, Murrow was deeply disappointed when he didn't make Phi Beta Kappa.

After graduation in 1930, he worked for the National Student Federation of America and, later, the Institute of International Education, primarily as an organizer of student conferences in the United States and Europe. He traveled to Europe three times and made a number of important new friends and contacts, including the prominent English socialist Harold Laski and a young American lawyer named Lewis F. Powell, who would later become a justice of the U.S. Supreme Court. In 1934 Murrow became involved in helping Jewish academics emigrate to America from an increasingly anti-Semitic Germany. That same year he married Janet Brewster, a pretty and lively young woman from a prominent but not wealthy Connecticut family.

For a time in the early 1930s, Murrow thought he might be headed for an academic career. When he was only twenty-six, he was offered the presidency of a small women's college in Illinois. But the offer was hastily withdrawn when the trustees learned he had lied about his age and had inflated his qualifications. He pulled the same stunt a year later when he was interviewed by Ed Klauber for a job at CBS. Murrow was twenty-seven at the time but said he was thirty-two, and he claimed to have majored in both political science and international relations. He also said he had attended the University of Washington as well as Washington State. The deceptions were never caught and probably wouldn't have mattered anyway. Klauber, who liked to bully people, found he couldn't bully Murrow and was duly impressed. In September 1935, Murrow was hired as director of talks. In April 1937, he was dispatched to London.

✦

His subsequent rejection by the foreign correspondents' association didn't discourage him; in fact, it only increased his determination. Later that year, when New York agreed to expand the network's European operations, Murrow decided to hire an honest-to-god foreign correspondent who would make the elitists at the association sit up and take notice. At the suggestion of Ferdinand Kuhn of the *New York Times*, he got in touch with Bill Shirer in Berlin, a veteran newspaper and wire-service correspondent who had reported from Germany, France, India, and points between. Going after someone as well known as Shirer was, Murrow knew, a gamble. But he liked to gamble. What he didn't realize, as he cabled Shirer in Berlin that summer of 1937, was that at that moment Shirer needed Murrow far more than Murrow needed Shirer.

The cable Murrow sent arrived in Shirer's Berlin office on a warm August night and lay unopened for hours. Shirer had put it aside because another cable, this one from his home office, had caught his attention first. Having read it, he lost interest in opening cables for a while. He couldn't believe it: the bastards at International News Service in New York had fired him! Professional that he was (and accustomed as he was to being fired), Shirer's first reaction was to finish the story he'd been working on before the cable arrived. Only then did he begin to hyperventilate. He rushed out of the office, desperate for air. Staggering along the banks of the river Spree, the Reichstag looming behind him, he felt a desperation he'd never known before.

A launch filled with merrymakers came toward him on the river, laughter and shouts filling the soft evening air. The passengers' light-heartedness only accentuated Shirer's misery. He was thirty-three years old and had, he thought, nothing to show for it. He had once tried to be a novelist and had failed at that, and now, even worse, he was a failed correspondent — fired three times in five years. A staff cut, they'd said in the cable. It was always a staff cut. That didn't make it any easier, especially with everything so tight. When he'd gotten the sack before, he'd managed to pick himself up and find another job, but because of the Depression, reporting jobs in Europe were becoming much scarcer, even with Hitler and Mussolini on the move.

So here was Bill Shirer in Berlin, surrounded by Nazis, his wife pregnant, and with nowhere to turn. Maybe he should head for New York — if he could borrow the third-class boat fare for himself and Tess. But stateside reporting jobs were scarce, too. Disconsolate, he headed back to his office, wondering how things could have gone so wrong.

♦

William L. Shirer had come to Europe from the Midwest twelve years before. He had been born in Chicago and, until he was nine, lived in the ferment, intellectual and otherwise, of that great lakeside city. As a child, he loved to listen to his parents and their friends engage in long, passionate debates about the monopolies' abuse of their workers, about the new educational theories of John Dewey, about the writings of Theodore Dreiser and Frank Norris. Shirer's father, Seward, was a U.S. attorney, a man with populist ideas who was never happier than when trying to break the power of Standard Oil or some other trust. Clarence Darrow was a frequent visitor to the Shirer home; Seward Shirer and Darrow were close friends, although in court they were sometimes on opposite sides. Seward was a stern disciplinarian, but what his son remembered most about him was his love of music, learning, and literature.

Shortly before Bill's ninth birthday, his forty-one-year-old father died suddenly of peritonitis. The boy was shattered: he'd lost the greatest influence of his life. Then, a few weeks later, his mother, Bess, with little money, moved Bill and his sister and brother to his maternal grandparents' house in Cedar Rapids, Iowa, the absolute antithesis of Chicago.

As he grew up, Bill Shirer came to detest the squeaky-clean, boring sameness of life on Cedar Rapids' tree-lined streets. Like many others his age, he'd grown up on *Main Street* and *Babbitt*, whooping with glee at the way Sinclair Lewis captured what Shirer considered to be the suffocating conformity and cultural sterility of his own Midwestern town. The worst of it, he decided, was his budding awareness that life didn't have to be like that.

From the beginning, Shirer made clear he would never conform to the mores of the world into which he had been thrust. He liked his quiet grandfather but considered his grandmother a sadistic old shrew.

One day, when she gave him a particularly hard punch, he said slowly, "Grandma, this is the last time. You're never going to do that again." She stared and asked why. His answer was a slap on the cheek and a push across the room that made her stumble over a chair leg and fall flat on the floor. Bill Shirer was unrepentant about what he'd done, and he remained unrepentant more than sixty years later. He had accomplished his purpose: his grandmother never hit him again. About her death in 1917, he wrote, "I was glad to see the last of her."

When it was time for Shirer to go to college in 1921, the family couldn't afford anything better than Coe, a small Presbyterian school in Cedar Rapids. He considered it an intellectual wasteland: two years of required Bible study, but no courses in philosophy, virtually none in foreign literature, and, in English and American literature, almost nothing after the Victorians. Nevertheless, Shirer managed to have a good time at Coe, chiefly by thumbing his nose at everything the college held dear. He joined a fraternity, learned to drink, and raised so much hell with his fraternity brothers that the Coe chapter was suspended for a year.

He became editor of the school paper and used it as a pulpit for blasting all things bourgeois. Labeling the English department "a Victorian swamp," he demanded more Sinclair Lewis, more Theodore Dreiser, more Edith Wharton, more H. L. Mencken. When Lenin died, Shirer wrote a tribute to the Bolshevik leader and took a shot at, among others, his hometown newspaper: "Lenin . . . cut a deep notch in history, the U.S. Chamber of Commerce, Secretary of State Hughes and the *Cedar Rapids Republican* to the contrary notwithstanding."

Upon graduation in 1925, Shirer wasted no time in escaping. Less than a month after receiving his diploma, he signed on to a 2,500-ton British freighter bound from Montreal to England. In return for his passage, he was required to feed and water a hundred head of cattle penned on the ship's main deck. He considered it a very small price to pay for his freedom.

The ship sailed in July. Shirer had told his fiancée, a young woman he'd met at Coe, that he'd be back in a couple of months, when his two hundred dollars ran out. She knew better; she knew he would never return. And she was, more or less, right.

When the twenty-one-year-old Midwestern provincial first arrived in Paris, the trousers of his three-piece suit ended well above his ankles, and hay, quipped his friend James Thurber, was still sprouting from his ears. On his first day, Shirer wandered around in a joyful stupor, saw the Seine, peered into Notre-Dame, visited the Louvre. He'd come to Paris, he wrote later, because he yearned for a place "where a man could drink a glass of wine or a stein of beer without breaking the law, where you could lead your own life, do as you please, get drunk or make love without Mrs. Grundy or the police or a preacher or teacher breathing down your neck."

At the end of the day, he sat on the crowded terrace of Le Dôme, had a glass of wine, and watched a bearded young man at a nearby table pull his female companion toward him, kiss the nape of her neck, then turn his lips to hers. The young Iowan was thunderstruck: he'd never seen anything like that in public before. Yes, he decided, this was the place.

Shirer's two hundred dollars lasted less than a month. He had looked for work but found none. On what he thought was his last night, he got drunk, hoping to wipe out the very thought of leaving. He had fallen in love with Paris, with its women and its ways. Now he would have to return, whipped, to stultifying Iowa. With the sun coming up, just hours before his train was to leave, he stumbled back to his *pension*. In his drunkenness he almost missed seeing an envelope that had been shoved under the door of his room. It was a note from the editor of the *Paris Tribune*, offering him a job. He went to work that same night.

Thus began what Shirer called "the happiest and the most wondrous years of my life." When he was an old man, his face would light up and his voice would resonate with a special timbre when he reminisced about those enchanted days in Paris. He earned only sixty dollars a month as a copy editor at the *Tribune*, an offshoot of Colonel Robert McCormick's *Chicago Tribune*. But that was more than enough to allow him to savor the city's delights. And he was not alone. "Never in the history of journalism," wrote an editor of the rival *Paris Herald*, "have so many men had such a wonderful time on so little money."

Shirer was neither the first nor the last Midwesterner to shed his provincialism and his inhibitions, not to mention his clothes, in the Paris of the twenties. But few could have enjoyed it more. On his afternoons off, he'd stop at the local bordello and have a glass of champagne with the girls. (This not-quite-believable, Toulouse-Lautrec-like imbibing was the only activity with the whores that Shirer would admit to later.) He went to parties at Isadora Duncan's apartment and fell hopelessly in love with the flamboyant aging dancer. Miss Duncan did not requite Shirer's affections, but he soon found someone who did — a married Parisienne named Yvonne, five years older and eons wiser, with whom he embarked on a deliciously hopeless affair.

For Shirer, the literary ferment in Paris was as intoxicating as the wine and the women. Over oysters at Pruniér or *choucroute* and beer at the Brasserie Lipp, he argued with Jim Thurber and his other *Tribune* colleagues about Hemingway and Fitzgerald, James Joyce and Ezra Pound, all of whom were laying claim to Paris at the time. One night Shirer even had the high honor and distinct pleasure of taking a drunken Scott Fitzgerald home and depositing him in bed. When Shirer's boyhood literary hero, Sinclair Lewis, held court at Le Dôme, Shirer drank in the words of the master. Like Thurber and practically everyone else on the *Tribune*, he wanted to become a writer, a *real* writer, not a mere newspaper hack.

In 1927 Shirer was promoted to the *Chicago Tribune*'s foreign staff. He had become a full-fledged foreign correspondent, and he emerged from his Paris cocoon to discover a world in turmoil. Assigned to report on Central Europe from Vienna, he found the once-dazzling former capital of the Hapsburgs in seedy disrepair. Even so, he enjoyed the music, the theater, and, of course, the women, all the while believing that the Viennese — indeed, all Europeans — were living in a frivolous dream world.

A year later Colonel McCormick ordered Shirer to New Delhi to report on Mahatma Gandhi's civil disobedience movement — a high point in Shirer's career. Afterward he traveled over the Khyber Pass to Kabul, to cover the installation of a new Afghan king. No foreign correspondent had been allowed to visit Afghanistan and its warring tribes for more than a year. Shirer's coup received page-one treatment in the *Tribune* and became the subject of a full-page *Trib* advertisement: "Only One Correspondent, a *Tribune* Man, saw Nadir Khan Become King!"

By now it was 1930, and Shirer was in love again, this time with a dimpled blonde Viennese barely out of her teens. Tess Stiberitz, the multilingual daughter of an Austrian civil servant, was beautiful, charming, and determined. After finishing her education in a Paris convent school, she had tried to get a job on several English newspapers by passing herself off as an expert on Viennese opera, which she decidedly was not. When she met Shirer, she was twenty (he was twenty-seven) and had become the Vienna correspondent of *Drama*, a London-based theater magazine. They were married on January 31, 1931.

America's Depression was becoming the world's, but when Shirer tried to write about it, he found the *Tribune*'s editors uninterested; the only stories they wanted were about Hitler and his power grabs. As a result, fewer and fewer of Shirer's pieces from Vienna appeared in the paper. He was nevertheless unprepared for the terse telegram he received from the *Tribune*'s managing editor in mid-October 1932: YOUR SERVICES WITH TRIBUNE TERMINATED TODAY.

Stunned, Shirer cabled for an explanation. His recent stories "had not been satisfactory to the management," came the reply. In truth, McCormick had responded to the Depression by ordering reductions in the foreign staff. Shirer was the third correspondent sacked that year, and he would not be the last.

When he couldn't find another job right away, he and Tess decided to take the thousand dollars he'd saved and spend a year in Spain, where he could write some magazine articles and maybe a novel. They had a wonderful time, but the writing did not go well. By January of 1934 they were down to their last pesetas. Then, on a cold, blustery day, Shirer received a cable from the *Paris Herald*, offering him a job on the copy desk.

Shirer had spent six years as a foreign correspondent, but now he had to start all over again. The only difference was that he was on the *Herald* instead of the *Trib*. Soon after his return to a less charming, grubbier Paris, the disillusioned Shirer realized that if he wanted to rejuvenate his faltering career, he would have to get to Berlin, where, he thought, every ambitious young journalist at the time ought to be. Finally, after only a few months with the *Herald*, he was offered a job in the Berlin bureau of Hearst's Universal wire service. He arrived in August 1934, just in time to cover Hitler's appearance at the Nazis' annual rally in Nuremberg.

In that quaint medieval city Shirer realized how completely and powerfully Hitler had begun to dominate his people. The Führer rode into town "like a Roman emperor," Shirer wrote in his diary, while his followers wound through the narrow streets, "an endless ribbon of bobbing torches," the air echoing with the sound of old German marching songs. It was, Shirer thought, like a scene from a Wagner opera.

For the next three years he tried to sound the alarm. He reported on Hitler's increasingly brazen violations of the Versailles Treaty — the reintroduction of conscription, the rebuilding of the Wehrmacht, the occupation of the supposedly demilitarized Rhineland. He documented the Nazis' suppression of political parties and trade unions, the abolition of free assembly and speech, the persecution of the Jews. He also exposed the Nazis' skillful attempts to manipulate international public opinion. In January 1936, on the eve of the Winter Olympics in Garmisch, Shirer reported that Hitler had ordered the removal of all anti-Semitic posters — "Jews Get Out" and the like. German radio accused Shirer of trying to torpedo the games; the front pages of the afternoon papers condemned him as a "liar," "cheat," and "German hater."

✦

By 1937 Shirer was in the top rank of foreign correspondents in Europe. He'd become good friends with the most famous of his Europe-based colleagues — John Gunther, Frank Gervasi, Vincent Sheean, Dorothy Thompson, and, most satisfying of all, Sinclair Lewis. And, after more than six years of marriage, Tess was pregnant. Life, Shirer thought, was finally fulfilling its promise.

Then, on August 14, he was informed that Universal was shutting down. Shirer was to join the Berlin bureau of Hearst's other agency, International News Service. Ten days later he received another cable. Headquarters had thought again. Shirer was out, fired.

After hours of walking along the Spree, feeling like an utter failure, he returned to his office. Only then did he open the second cablegram, from London. It read: "CAN YOU MEET ME ADLON [HOTEL] 8/27 FOR DINNER? MURROW, COLUMBIA BROADCASTING." Shirer had no idea what it was all about, and frankly he didn't much care. He had left America before radio amounted to anything, and he rarely listened to it in Europe. Still, if you're out of work, a free dinner is a free dinner.

When they met, Shirer at first dismissed the twenty-nine-year-old Murrow as just another handsome face in a custom suit — "what you would expect from radio . . . or even more from Hollywood." By the time they adjourned to the Adlon bar for drinks, though, he had revised his opinion. Murrow, he decided, was serious, intelligent, and sensitive, with warmth and a good sense of humor beneath his outward reserve. And he was an evangelist for radio. Murrow acknowledged that the new medium hadn't yet come into its own, especially where news was concerned. But it would someday, and he and Shirer could help make it happen. He was offering Shirer a job at the same salary INS had been paying — $125 a week.

"Is it a deal?" Murrow asked.

"I . . . I . . . guess so," Shirer said.

They celebrated over brandy. "Oh, there is one little thing I forgot to mention," Murrow said. "The . . . uh . . . voice."

CBS's New York executives were demanding a voice test before agreeing to Murrow's choice for the job. Shirer was thunderstruck. "So all depended not on my qualities as a foreign correspondent, on my intelligence, my experience — but on the voice God had given me," he wrote in his diary. "What a wacky business!"

Ten days later, practically paralyzed with nervousness, Shirer reported to a dingy room strewn with packing boxes in the government telegraph office in Berlin. The official German broadcasting studios were not available to CBS, he was informed, because German radio had an exclusive arrangement with NBC. But not to worry: he'd have a microphone and everything else he needed.

As it turned out, the microphone hung from a boom seven feet above the floor, and no amount of pulling and tugging would bring it down. The German engineer suggested that Shirer crane his neck and shout up into the mike, but that cut off his air and made his voice even thinner. With less than a minute until the broadcast was to begin, the engineer and Shirer frantically pulled over a piano packing crate, and the engineer boosted Shirer up onto it. Sitting on that rough wooden crate, with his feet dangling in the air like a ventriloquist's dummy's, trying desperately to remember the points Murrow had made about speaking over the air, Shirer fought back the impulse to burst out in hysterical laughter.

It was hopeless. His mouth was dry, his lips parched; when he started talking, his voice quivered and, more than once, jumped at least an octave. All he could think of was William S. Paley and the CBS vice presidents sitting there in New York, shaking their heads and agreeing that this Shirer guy was a disaster. Afterward, he went to an outdoor café and gulped down a double schnapps.

He didn't hear from Murrow for more than a week and was sure he'd been right about CBS's reaction. But Murrow finally called with astounding news: "The bastards in New York finally came through," Murrow said, using the stock phrase popular with all foreign correspondents when they refer to their home offices. "They think you're terrific."

Actually, the bastards in New York hated Shirer's voice and at first tried to prevent Murrow from hiring him. Paul White, the director of news and special events, was particularly opposed. The gruff White — beefy, boisterous, hard-drinking, his hair parted neatly down the middle of his large head — was a former UP reporter who loved news, card playing, and practical jokes, in about that order. White wanted to build up CBS news as much as Murrow did, but he wanted to do it on his terms, not Murrow's.

Four years earlier he had had his chance. In 1933 America's news-

paper publishers, dismayed by the increasing movement of big advertisers to radio, persuaded the three main news agencies, AP, UP, and
INS, to cancel their services to the radio networks. In response, CBS
gave White permission to create the Columbia News Service, a staff
of stringers and editors stationed at various points around the United
States. (NBC launched a much less ambitious service.) So successful was
White's operation that within six months the newspapers proposed a
truce. If CBS would drop its news service, the publishers would allow the agencies to supply short bulletins for radio — but only in late
morning and evening so that the newspapers could not be scooped. To
White's horror, Paley agreed. The deal, however, was patently unworkable and fell apart by the end of 1934. Soon thereafter the status quo
ante was restored.

With that, White's news domain shrank back to its earlier pitiful
size. When Murrow was hired as director of talks, White immediately
saw him as a potential rival — especially when Murrow was transferred
to London in 1937, just as talk of war in Europe was increasing. Now
White watched as Murrow began to expand his European operation by
proposing to set up Shirer as CBS's man in Berlin. Paul White knew an
internal threat when he saw one.

Having listened to the tryout broadcast, White decreed that Shirer
just wouldn't do — not with *that* voice. Murrow argued that White, as a
former newspaperman, should know better than to expect a golden-
throated announcer. War was coming. CBS needed someone who knew
the territory and spoke the languages — the hell with the quality of his
voice. Murrow wouldn't budge, and finally White caved. Ed Murrow
and Bill Shirer had become a team. And Murrow and Paul White had
fought the first skirmish of what would be a protracted struggle between
two proud and stubborn men — a struggle only one of them could win.

3

"We Take You
Now to London"

Shirer had been hired — but for what? Despite the furor over his voice, neither he nor Murrow was allowed to go on the air, though they asked repeatedly for the chance. As far as the executives in New York were concerned, the threat of war in Europe did not in any way alter the assignment of their European representatives: to arrange broadcasts and help overcome the advantage enjoyed abroad by NBC.

In the twenties the older, richer network had signed contracts with state-owned radio systems in most European countries, including Germany and Austria, giving NBC special access to the broadcast facilities in those countries. The name National Broadcasting Company confused many European bureaucrats. To them, *national* usually meant government-run, and they concluded that NBC was America's official network. General Sarnoff's European representatives did not consider it their job to clarify matters. That task fell to Murrow and Shirer.

It was a fierce, cutthroat game. Alarms had gone off at NBC when Murrow was first sent to London. Between 1937 and 1939 NBC's European representatives — Fred Bate in London and Max Jordan in Basel, Switzerland — were under orders to do everything they could to stymie Columbia. On March 16, 1937, NBC's John F. Royal, based in New York, alerted Bate that Paul White was soon to sail for Britain to help Murrow capitalize on the coronation of King George VI by drumming up a "publicity showing" for CBS. Bate must engineer a better showing for NBC, and in case he didn't understand the stakes, Royal spelled them out: "Don't let's be too ethical about the way we handle this show. . . . After the Coronation is all over we cannot have . . . Mr. Sarnoff yelling at us as to why we didn't get certain publicity."

Jordan — a German-born naturalized American and former INS reporter nicknamed "Ubiquitous Max" by his admiring competitors — was particularly determined to counter CBS's moves. After Murrow and

Shirer joined forces, Jordan showered his New York headquarters with status reports and proposals for new strategies. When Murrow and Shirer met in Berlin with Nazi officials in an attempt to break NBC's stranglehold on Rundfunk, the German broadcasting facility, Jordan made sure that "our . . . friends [in Berlin] pulled various wires." In a memo to Royal dated March 7, 1938, he fairly crowed about the results. "A major attack by Columbia against our contract with Germany — the worst and most determined so far — has been repulsed," Jordan wrote. Nazi officials had informed Murrow and Shirer that their government "had no desire whatever to discontinue the very satisfactory and pleasant relationship with NBC."

With competition like this, CBS's executives had little patience for the constant pleading by Murrow and Shirer that a good way to cut NBC down to size would be to let the two of them go on the air with their own reporting. The CBS brass wanted their European team to concentrate on breaking NBC's foreign contracts and on arranging attention-grabbing broadcasts. If CBS occasionally needed analysis of the latest news, some newspaper or wire service correspondent could be trotted out to provide it.

Shirer was especially furious about this policy. He'd be damned if he'd go hat in hand to some other reporter, who didn't know half of what he knew, who hadn't covered the stories he'd covered, and beg the reporter to go on the air over his own network! "So much for radio journalism!" he wrote at the time. "The idiocy of it staggered me." He would stay at CBS only as long as it took him to find another job that would allow him to be a serious journalist again.

✦

About this time CBS decided that the best place for Shirer wasn't Berlin but Vienna. After he and the pregnant Tess moved to the city of her birth, however, Shirer's frustration with his job became even more acute. Austria and its capital were one large tinderbox, and Hitler, determined to annex his homeland, was ready to put a match to it. The pressure and anxiety were too much for Vienna. Its economy was declining, its people disaffected; anti-Semitism was on the rise. In those early months of 1938, Shirer and Murrow tried again to persuade New York to allow them to report what was happening, but Paul White would have none of it. Concentrate on the job we hired you to do, White said, which at the moment consisted of arranging broadcasts of European children's choirs for a series of programs entitled *Columbia's American School of the Air.*

In February the Austrian chancellor, Kurt von Schuschnigg, capitulated to Hitler's demands that Austria lift its ban on the Nazi party and that von Schuschnigg appoint Nazis to key positions in his government. The capitulation was Austria's death warrant. Shirer asked CBS for fifteen minutes of air time to explain what had occurred. New York wasn't interested; Shirer was ordered to Sofia for a broadcast of the Bulgarian children's choir. Vienna was a cauldron of fear and intrigue, and Tess's baby was due. Even so, Shirer obediently packed his bags. "No foreign correspondent," he reasoned, "[ever] let his personal life interfere with his assignments, however asinine."

By the time he returned home from Sofia on February 26, the Austrian government was crumbling and Nazi gangs were rioting in the streets. Tess was in the hospital in desperate condition because of last-minute complications of her pregnancy. An emergency cesarean section had been necessary to save her life and the baby's. The doctor assured Shirer that the baby — a girl, Eileen Inga — was fine, and Tess would probably live. But it would be touch and go. Tess was terribly weak, and phlebitis had set in.

On March 9 the Austrian government made a last-minute attempt to save itself and the country by announcing a popular vote on the nation's future, to be held four days later. Even then, for Paul White, children's choirs took precedence. Shirer was dispatched to Belgrade for yet another broadcast in the series. He returned on March 11 to find that Tess was running a high fever; the phlebitis was resisting all medication. When Shirer walked into the hospital that afternoon, there was tension in the streets; when he left some time later, there was chaos. A Nazi mob was rampaging through the center of town, shouting "Sieg Heil, Sieg Heil," and the Austrian police were smiling and doing nothing. Some of the police even wore swastika armbands. The plebiscite had been called off, someone yelled. The chancellor had resigned. The Austrian army had been told to offer no resistance.

Austria was about to be swallowed by Hitler.

Shirer had the biggest story of his life, and he seemed to have it to himself: NBC's "Ubiquitous Max" Jordan, who had also been on hand for the crisis, was uncharacteristically out of town. This time Shirer wasn't going to listen to New York. He was going to report what he knew. He rushed to the Austrian state radio building, where men in

Nazi uniforms were hurrying about, brandishing revolvers. They refused to let him use a studio. After hours of arguing, Shirer was thrown out. Dejected, he returned to his apartment and was having his second beer when Ed Murrow called from London. He told Shirer to get on a plane to London. As soon as he arrived, he could go on the air — *go on the air!* — and give the first uncensored, eyewitness account of the Anschluss. Meanwhile Murrow would come to Vienna and cover for Shirer. "Don't let them tell you you're not supposed to talk," Murrow said. "The hell with that. Just go on, and I'm going to go on, too."

For Shirer, nothing was more important than this story, not even his critically ill wife. He tried but failed to get a message to her in the hospital and ended up leaving a note for the maid to deliver by taxi. Seventeen hours later Shirer was sitting in a British Broadcasting Corporation studio in London, earphones on, listening to the CBS announcer in New York say, "We take you now to London."

After six of the most frustrating months he'd ever known, Bill Shirer was finally, triumphantly, broadcasting the news.

But he wasn't first. Ubiquitous Max, on learning of Austria's fate, had hustled back to Vienna. While Shirer's plane to London was still in the air, Jordan had talked his way into the Austrian radio studio and had submitted his hastily typed script to the censor. It was Jordan, not Shirer, who broadcast to America the first eyewitness account of Hitler's takeover of Austria, censored though it was. By then Hitler himself had arrived in upper Austria, and Jordan added to his achievement by arranging to broadcast the Führer's speech to the Austrian people.

Despite his own breakthrough with CBS, Shirer was understandably disappointed. In all his later writings about the Anschluss, he never once mentioned Jordan's scoop. At the time CBS attributed it to NBC's special arrangement with Austrian radio. But Jordan pointed out that with the Nazis in charge, the NBC contract was null and void anyway. "If Columbia had only been on the job," he said, "they probably could have gotten the same treatment we did."

In New York, hearing of Jordan's broadcast, Bill Paley was frantic. Until the Nazi takeover of Austria, he had sided with Paul White in opposing any reporting by the network's employees in Europe. Reporting could easily lead to editorializing, to taking sides — and CBS was in enough trouble already with the Roosevelt administration, thanks to Boake Carter's off-the-wall pontificating. But the Anschluss changed Paley's mind. NBC was *trouncing* CBS! Paley got on the phone to Ed

Klauber, Klauber called Paul White, and White phoned Shirer, still in London. "We want a European roundup *tonight*," White said: a thirty-minute broadcast on European reaction to the Anschluss, with Shirer and a member of Parliament in London, Murrow in Vienna, and American newspaper correspondents in Paris, Berlin, and Rome. Nothing like this had ever been put together before. Shirer and Murrow had eight hours to do it.

It was insane even to try. Shirer had no idea how to pull it off, but he said yes anyway. For months he and Murrow had been after White to let them broadcast. Now they had their chance. Never mind that no one had ever done it. Never mind that it was five o'clock, London time, on a Sunday afternoon, which meant that all offices were closed and that all the technicians and correspondents and members of Parliament they would need were out of town, off in the country, or otherwise unreachable. Never mind the seemingly insuperable technical problems of arranging the lines and transmitters, of ensuring the necessary split-second timing. Never mind any of that. This was what being a foreign correspondent was all about. It was part of the code of the brotherhood: when the bastards asked if you could do something impossible, the only acceptable answer was yes. Shirer reached for the phone and called Murrow in Vienna.

And they went to work. Murrow persuaded the Germans to give him a phone line from Vienna to Berlin, which could relay his broadcast by shortwave to New York. Special lines were arranged for Paris, which didn't have an adequate transmitter. Newspaper correspondents were tracked down, two of whom had to get permission from their home offices, which they hoped would come in time. In London the phones jangled constantly; calls in four languages streamed in for Shirer. It was getting tight: with little more than two hours to go, he still hadn't located a member of Parliament, and one of the correspondents he'd found, Frank Gervasi of INS, reported that the Italians could not arrange his broadcast on such short notice. Shirer stayed cool. He told Gervasi to dictate his story to London and Shirer would read it for him. Then Shirer at last located Labour MP Ellen Wilkinson in the country, and she agreed to rush back to London. Fifteen minutes before the roundup was to go on the air, a breathless Wilkinson arrived at the BBC studios, and Gervasi was still dictating his piece to a stenographer.

Finally, on March 13, at 1 A.M. London time, 8 P.M. in New York, an exhausted Shirer put on his earphones and heard announcer Bob Trout say, "The program 'St. Louis Blues' will not be heard tonight." In its place would be a special report, a "radio tour of Europe's capitals, starting with a transoceanic pickup from London." Trout paused. "We take you now to London."

And Shirer was on.

An adrenaline rush had overwhelmed his exhaustion, but nothing in his soft, flat voice indicated either the excitement he felt or the crushing pressure he had endured over the last few hours. He was very professional, very calm. There was no hint that he knew he was making broadcast history as the primary organizer of the first CBS news roundup.

He opened by predicting that Britain would do little to stem the aggression of Hitler. The other correspondents and Ellen Wilkinson took their turns analyzing the apathetic reaction by European governments to Hitler's rapacity. As promised, Shirer read Gervasi's dispatch. Murrow, providing strong hints of greater eloquence to come, sketched a subtly sinister picture of a transformed Vienna: "The crowds are courteous as they've always been, but many people are in a holiday mood; they lift the right arm a little higher here than in Berlin and the 'Heil Hitler' is said a little more loudly."

Thirty minutes later the first European roundup ended, on time to the second.

A jubilant Paul White was on the phone to Shirer. The broadcast was a triumph, he said — "so much so that we want another one tomorrow night — tonight your time. Can you do it?"

Shirer didn't even pause. "No problem," he shouted over the transatlantic line.

With that first roundup, CBS and radio in general were on their way to becoming full-fledged news sources. Shirer and Murrow were largely responsible. The idea for a roundup had originated in New York, but Shirer and Murrow made it happen and made it work. They proved that radio was not only able to report news as it occurred but also to put it in context, to link it with news from elsewhere — and to do all that with unprecedented speed and immediacy. They set in motion a chain of events that would lead, in only one year, to radio's emergence as America's chief news medium and to the beginning of CBS's decades-long dominance of broadcast journalism. Nor was the justly famed CBS promotion department idle during this period. Within days of the Anschluss, it had produced a handsome brochure — "Vienna, March, 1938: A Footnote to History" — conveying the impression, according to *Scribner's* magazine, "that Columbia was omnipresent and omnipotent throughout."

Not even a visionary like Murrow could have foreseen all of this. But he and Shirer had seen some of it, and the barrier between them and the microphone had been smashed.

For the next five days Shirer thought about little but broadcasting. His wife, his new baby girl, and anything else beyond the story he and Murrow were covering were all but forgotten. He stayed on in London while Murrow, in Vienna, reported Hitler's triumphal arrival and the subsequent orgy of violence against the city's Jews. When Shirer returned to Vienna on March 18, Murrow met him at the airport. They adjourned to a bar off the Karntnerstrasse. Tired and depressed by all the hate he'd witnessed that week, Murrow didn't brighten until they started talking about their achievement. Then he smiled.

"Maybe now, my friend, we can go places," he said.

✦

The next morning Shirer visited Tess in the hospital. She was still in critical condition and had lived a nightmare in the past week. Her doctor, a Jew, had fled for his life; a Jewish woman across the hall had flung her baby and herself out the window when Nazi thugs started roaming the halls. As concerned as he was about Tess, however, Shirer still had other things on his mind. "On a personal and professional level, my whole life and work changed in the course of that dramatic week," he wrote later. Tess and the baby now took second place to Murrow and the unbounded vistas that had opened to both of them. Shirer and Tess "didn't have much of a life together," he said a few years before he died. "We used to say that it was a good thing because we wouldn't grow tired of each other. In retrospect, it was difficult."

Tess finally came home from the hospital, but only after a second surgery to remove some instruments that had been left inside her after the cesarean section. Shirer and Murrow had already agreed that when Tess was strong enough, the Shirers would move to neutral Geneva. From there Bill could cover Hitler's next move free of Nazi censorship. They left Vienna in June, but the Nazis did their best to make the departure difficult. At the airport, female guards ripped off Tess's bandages to see if any contraband was hidden beneath them.

Geneva had always seemed smug and stodgy to Shirer, but after the trauma of Vienna, it looked like paradise. Murrow flew from London to join the Shirers for a short holiday in nearby Lausanne, and for several blissful days they swam, ate, hiked, drank, and talked — talked, in this quietly beautiful setting, of the war they were sure was coming and of their need for more correspondents to help cover it. But how could they convince New York? The problem was that Paley, White, and the others, like most Americans, were losing interest again in foreign news as the Anschluss crisis faded. They had reverted to their normal preference for entertainment, and once again Shirer and Murrow were being dispatched to sign up European acts and attractions that Americans might find amusing. The news roundups were discontinued.

Then in September of that year Germany turned its gaze on Czechoslovakia. Hitler demanded that the Sudetenland, a mountainous industrial area that had been stripped from Germany after World War I, be restored. The Czechs refused, confident of their well-trained army and their mutual-defense treaty with the French. The rest of Europe, watching the standoff, seemed paralyzed.

On September 10 Shirer went to Prague to monitor the crisis. Before he left, he suggested to New York that he do daily five-minute broadcasts from there. At first White and the others refused, but finally they relented — if Shirer would promise to relinquish the time whenever there was not enough news to fill it. "My God!" he later wrote. "Here was the old continent on the brink of war . . . and the network was most reluctant to provide five minutes a day from here to report it!"

On September 12 Hitler spoke at Nuremberg, vowing to rescue the Sudetenland from Czech oppression. That ended New York's myopia. The news roundups were revived. Entertainment programs were interrupted with increasingly ominous bulletins: Nazis rioting in the Sudetenland, France mobilizing reservists, Germany moving its army into position, trenches being dug and gas masks issued in England.

For once, soap operas couldn't compete with the drama and excitement of what was happening abroad. Americans sat riveted to their radios, intently listening for the cues from CBS in New York — "Calling Edward R. Murrow" and "Come in, William L. Shirer" — then listening for the voices themselves, cutting through the shortwave whine and stutter and crackle. Murrow in London and Shirer, shuttling between Prague and Berlin, worked themselves to exhaustion, but the vicissitudes of shortwave broadcasting — poor fidelity plus frequent interference from weather and sunspots — could ruin the best plans and the best reporting in the world. For the first four days of the crisis in Czechoslovakia, every bit of Shirer's work turned out to have been wasted because of bad weather. It was a problem that would bedevil him and other radio correspondents throughout the war.

On September 30 Shirer was in Munich when the crisis was finally brought to its shameful conclusion and the leaders of Europe's two greatest democracies handed the Sudetenland to Hitler. The Munich sellout by the British prime minister, Neville Chamberlain, and the French premier, Édouard Daladier, came as a blow to Shirer in more ways than one. When he rushed to broadcast the text of the agreement, he was told by White in New York that Max Jordan of NBC had won again, reporting the pact's terms more than half an hour before Shirer. Shirer and CBS once more blamed NBC's cozy relationship with the state radio apparatus. Shirer maintained that Jordan had been given special access to the house in which the Munich conference took place and to the makeshift German radio studio in one of its rooms. In fact, Jordan did it all on his own. He slipped into the house with a young German radio broadcaster, who did have access, and was handed a copy of the agreement by a member of the British delegation just as the conference broke up.

Despite the second Jordan scoop, however, there was no question that overall CBS had outshone NBC, not to mention the other, smaller network, Mutual (ABC would not come along until 1942), in the days leading up to Munich and at the conference itself. An exhilarated Bill Paley, who stayed constantly tuned to CBS's coverage of the crisis, cabled Murrow and Shirer, COLUMBIA'S COVERAGE OF EUROPEAN CRISIS SUPERIOR TO ITS COMPETITORS AND IS PROBABLY THE BEST JOB EVER DONE IN RADIO BROADCASTING.

CBS's superiority lay not in scoops or in the hours broadcast, for all the networks were on the air twenty-four hours a day during the crisis. The CBS edge lay in the reporting and analysis by Murrow and Shirer and in the quality of the running commentary by H. V. Kaltenborn, who for eighteen days anchored in New York. Because of these men, radio news had finally came of age — and the broadcast journalist was born.

This new kind of journalist was no mere commentator or announcer. He was a full-fledged correspondent who did it all — reported, wrote, and spoke on the air. Thanks to the medium's speed and immediacy, and despite the problems of shortwave transmissions, the radio journalist had more impact than the print reporters who belittled him. In that era when all broadcasting was live, this new breed was not even hampered by editors or headline writers. He or (soon) she reported directly to the audience, beating the major newspapers by hours and reaching millions more people. *Scribner's* recognized the importance of the radio reporter in a major article on Murrow two months after Munich. Robert Landry wrote, "He has more influence upon America's reaction to foreign news than a shipful of newspapermen."

Over at NBC, however, the executives thought all this talk about radio correspondents was nonsense: slick promotional skills were the only edge CBS enjoyed, they said. NBC saw no reason to change the way it operated overseas: its men in Europe, including Max Jordan, would continue to arrange special events, and most of the news would come from print reporters hired as stringers for specific assignments. History has long since judged the wisdom of NBC's policy. By the time its executives woke up, it was too late: CBS was dominant in news and — capitalizing on the classy, responsible corporate image that news provided — would later take the lead in other programming as well. Murrow, Shirer, and those who followed helped Paley gain the prestige and credibility he had always wanted.

But that was for the future. Murrow and Shirer were too exhausted and depressed by what had happened in Munich to think much about potential fame and glory. Their main consolation was the company and support each provided the other: no one else could understand what it had been like. Their friendship had deepened in the past year and, although Murrow was getting the lion's share of the post-Munich publicity, Shirer's considerable ego wasn't battered. Murrow may have been younger, but he was the boss, Shirer agreed, and was better on radio besides. Shirer was the experienced European hand, the veteran correspondent, the one who spoke four languages. They almost perfectly complemented one another. "There was a remarkable chemistry of friendship," Shirer recalled a few months before he died. "He became my best friend." But it was more, even, than that. Said Shirer's Vienna-born daughter, Eileen Inga Dean, "Ed was the only close friend my father *ever* had."

✦

Shortly after Munich, Shirer and Murrow got together in Paris, a city which, after the French sellout of Czechoslovakia, had utterly lost its charm for Shirer. "It seems a frightful place," he wrote in his diary, "completely surrendered to defeatism with no inkling of what has happened to France." He and Murrow tried to get out of their depression by talking all night, tramping the streets, and downing bottle after bottle of champagne. Nothing worked. In time, Shirer noted, "even the champagne becomes sickening." They agreed that Hitler would soon strike again, in Poland. When he did, it would mean war — and there was no way they could cover that by themselves. The days of their exclusive partnership and friendship had ended. It was time for reinforcements.

✴ 4

The First Disciple

MORE AND MORE young American reporters were, like Larry Le-Sueur, heading across the Atlantic during the summer of 1939. They knew that in journalism, as in a number of other callings, war meant good jobs. News bureaus in London were hiring people to cover the Nazi advance, and Ed Murrow had let it be known that CBS was in the market for journalists who thought they could make the transition from print to radio.

But Murrow was more interested in talent, intelligence, and knowledge than in journalistic credentials. Indeed, the second person he hired, after Shirer, wasn't even a reporter, a fact that greatly agitated Paul White in New York. Murrow's insistence on Shirer, with his paper-thin voice, had been bad enough, even if Shirer had turned out to be a tireless worker with good instincts. But Thomas Grandin, the man Murrow installed in Paris in the spring of 1939, not only had a terrible voice, he had no journalistic experience at all. The thirty-year-old Grandin was a slim, bespectacled Ivy League intellectual from Cleveland. After Yale he studied in Berlin and Paris, then signed on as a resident scholar with the Geneva Research Center, an offshoot of the Rockefeller Foundation. He spoke fluent French and was an expert on French politics and government. But he had a pedantic manner — he used words like *expatiate* and *prognosticate* in his broadcasts — and a soft, high-pitched voice that White considered unmanly. As long as Grandin was with CBS, Paul White never stopped trying to get rid of him.

Murrow, whose own voice was perfect for radio, didn't give a damn how his men sounded. "He was always fighting New York on this business of voice and enunciation," said Bill Shadel, later hired by Murrow as a part-time CBS correspondent. "He loved to throw it in their faces."

For Murrow, Grandin's intellect and his understanding of France were far more important qualifications at a time when tension and turmoil were mounting in Europe. Hitler, having taken the Sudetenland, soon occupied the rest of Czechoslovakia, and the only countries with the power to stop him, Britain and France, did nothing. In Germany, Nazi-led mobs engaged in an orgy of violence against Jews, burning thousands of synagogues, looting and razing Jewish stores and homes, killing and raping. On one infamous night, November 8, 1938, dubbed Kristallnacht by the Nazis because of all the mere glass that was broken, more than eight hundred Jews had been killed or severely injured. Over time another twenty thousand disappeared into concentration camps. The rest of the world uttered only limp and feeble protests.

In July 1939 Paul White met with Murrow, Shirer, and Grandin in London. This was Shirer's first encounter with White, whom he thought was out of his depth as Columbia's director of news. "He could have lived a thousand years and never gotten the feeling for Europe, what Ed and I were up to," Shirer recalled as an old man. White expected the correspondents to produce a steady stream of reports, but he never seemed to consider the problems of travel or the physics of broadcasting. Whatever his failings, however, White knew a good story when he saw one. The trip to London convinced him that war really might be in store for Europe, and he set about helping to prepare for it, planning, with the European staff, which transmission lines and shortwave transmitters to use for reports from the front. White also agreed with Murrow's argument that the network's operation in Europe must continue to expand. And no sooner had the decision been made than Murrow placed a call to Eric Sevareid in Paris.

Sevareid was twenty-six years old at the time and only three years out of college. He was married and broke and holding down two jobs, one as a daytime reporter and editor for the *Paris Herald* at twenty-five dollars a week, the other as a nighttime copy editor with United Press at the same salary. He was almost unbelievably handsome, tall and rugged-looking, with a determined jaw and businesslike eyes that masked his shyness, insecurity, and numerous phobias. Sevareid was not what anyone would call a born war correspondent, but Murrow didn't seem to mind. What mattered to him was that Sevareid could write like an angel.

When Sevareid and his wife, Lois, had arrived in London from America two years earlier, Murrow was among the first people they met. Bearing a letter of introduction from a mutual acquaintance, the

Sevareids were invited to dinner at the Murrows' flat in Queen Anne Street. The two couples hit it off immediately. Sevareid was struck by Murrow's "extraordinary dark eyes . . . alight and intense one moment and somber and lost the next." The force and elegance of Murrow's words, his style, his startling self-assurance captivated Sevareid, who left London for Paris feeling he should write down everything Murrow had said over dinner. "I knew I wanted to listen to this man again," he wrote, "and I had a strong feeling that many others ought to know him."

Ed Murrow had found his first true disciple.

✦

For a lonely little boy named Arnold Eric Sevareid, the vast, bleak prairie that surrounded Velva, North Dakota, where he had been born in 1912, was a fearsome place. He often had nightmares about the nearby hills — which in his dreams became overwhelming prison battlements. So much about the place was menacing — the howling winds, the droughts, the locusts, the "frozen darkness of the winters when the deathly mourn of the coyote seemed at times the only signal of life." When he was four, he ran away from home and, for a brief time, became lost in the prairie; as an adult he could still recall the terror of being alone "in the eternity of nothingness."

Sevareid's mother, Clare, who hailed from the pleasant greenness of Iowa, hated North Dakota and passed on to her second son her "sense of having no identity in the world, of inhabiting by some cruel mistake . . . a lost and forgotten place upon the far horizon of my country." She had come to Velva with Sevareid's father, who, like many farmers of Scandinavian and German descent, had been lured by the rich soil and old-country climate. The son of a Norwegian immigrant, Alfred Sevareid prospered for a while in Velva, both as a farmer and as president of the local bank. He was a tall, stern, quiet man with strict Lutheran values, and he ruled like Yahweh over a home that, to his son, was "too full of rules" and "too empty of expressed love."

The emotional barrenness in the Sevareid home scarred young Arnie deeply (he didn't start calling himself by his middle name until after college). Reserved and repressed, he found it extraordinarily difficult, until late middle age, to demonstrate much warmth or affection. Reading was a consolation. He haunted the local library, devouring a book or more a day in the summer, learning and dreaming about far-off places like London, Paris, and Berlin.

His father lost everything when the bottom fell out of the wheat market in 1924, and Arnie's doubts and fears and insecurities were only heightened by the shame of his father's ruin. "It was pretty traumatic for a middle-class family to become very poor," he once recalled. "It's awfully hard to go down in your standard of living, and that kind of governed the atmosphere in our home for years, that constant grubbing to pay bills." Yet the experience hardened him; someday he would make everyone acknowledge that *he*, Arnie Sevareid, was important. When the Sevareid family moved to the larger town of Minot, Arnie would daydream about returning eventually to Velva in a white Panama suit and a chauffeur-driven white limousine. He would step from the limo in front of McKnight's drug store, a twenty-five-cent stogie in his mouth, and order three hundred ice cream cones for the townsfolk, who would smile knowingly and whisper, "I always knew that Sevareid boy would make good."

Soon the family moved again, this time to Minneapolis, where Alfred got a job as a cashier in a local bank. Arnie's years at Central High School provided him with few fond memories, although in his senior year he was named editor of the school paper. He mainly thought of school as an impediment to getting out into the world and proving himself. The summer of 1930, after he graduated, he and his friend Walter Port devised a spectacular first step toward that end.

Port was everything Arnie Sevareid was not, or so Sevareid believed: fearless, strong, athletic, and popular, especially with girls. Sevareid, though broad-shouldered and good-looking, thought of himself as physically awkward and lacking in courage. Determined to change, he agreed to join Port in an adventure so foolhardy, yet "so heroic in scope" (as Sevareid wrote many years later), "that I'm staggered to this day when I recall it."

The two young men, with their parents' apprehensive assent, decided to demonstrate that it was possible to travel by canoe from the Mississippi River up through Manitoba to Hudson Bay on the North Atlantic — a 2,200-mile journey through a complex maze of rivers and lakes, some never before charted. A photograph taken of them as they were about to depart shows the twenty-one-year-old Port, his fists on his hips, wearing an old fedora at an angle so rakish that if he tilted it one-tenth of a degree more it would roll off his head. Sevareid is in outdoorsman's garb, a small pipe between his teeth, with a cheerful, brassy expression that says, despite his internal doubts, "I cannot be beaten." He was seventeen.

The picture lied, at least where Sevareid was concerned: he was no outdoorsman. He couldn't drive a nail straight, couldn't chop firewood without gashing his shins, knew nothing about canoes like the second-hand one he and Port bought for the trip and which they christened *Sans Souci*. To prepare for the journey, Sevareid read handbooks on how to live in the forest.

The whole idea was crazy — going off into the wilderness with a used compass, some crude maps, summer clothing, a few weeks' food rations, and little real experience or knowledge. Perhaps because of the obvious dangers, Sevareid was able to persuade the editor of the *Minneapolis Star* to pay them one hundred dollars for a series of articles Sevareid would write and mail back to Minneapolis about the trip's progress. For an adventure that would come close to killing them both, Sevareid got what he craved: public attention and some money in the bargain.

It wasn't until they reached the northern end of Lake Winnipeg in Manitoba in early September, six weeks into their journey, that the real trouble began. Their maps were useless for the series of tiny lakes and rivers they had to navigate, some connected only by overland portages. In fog and drenching cold autumn rain, they got lost time and time again. Often they had to hack their way through portage trails so over-grown they couldn't find the path.

Frightened and cold, knowing winter was coming on and their food running out, they ran risks they could never have imagined. Instead of taking time to reconnoiter the many rapids they encountered, they simply and recklessly rode them, plunging through rocky gorges and over waterfalls. Their nerves were raw. One morning, after an argument over a dirty frying pan, they tore into one another — clawing and kicking, a fight that left both young men exhausted and Sevareid crying.

"I'm too young to die," he said to himself over and over.

The next day he and Port paddled nearly sixty miles. Just before dark, they spied a huddle of white buildings, the offices of the Hudson's Bay Company. Beyond the buildings a schooner rode at anchor. They had made it; they had gone from Minnesota to the Atlantic by canoe.

For Sevareid the odyssey had been a physical and psychological con-test between himself and his own fears and doubts — the first of many such contests — and he had endured. The *Star* printed his articles, and five years later Macmillan published his account as a children's book, *Canoeing with the Cree*. From then on, following in his and Port's foot-steps became a rite of passage for many young Minnesotans. Sevareid applauded those who sought to recreate the trip, although he could not resist pointing out that "now, they have equipment that's much safer and more comfortable."

After returning to Minneapolis, Sevareid got a job on the *Minneapolis Journal*, first as a copy boy, then as a cub reporter. Newspapering appealed to his idealism and his budding liberalism, but he soon discovered a harsher side of journalism. One evening the financial editor came into the newsroom, opened his locker, and dumped the contents into a suitcase. "I've been on this paper eighteen years, son," he said to Sevareid. "I've just been fired by a guy I used to teach where to put commas." Sevareid decided the only way to protect himself against such an end was to get more education. He enrolled in night classes at the University of Minnesota and envied the life that the full-time students seemed to be leading. Yet after only one semester, he decided to wander again and retest his courage.

This time he ventured alone to the California gold fields in the High Sierra. Among the grizzled miners with whom he worked that summer of 1931, the tenderfoot Sevareid was known, perhaps inevitably, as "Slim." He went to raucous parties in the miners' cabins, drank their home-brewed beer, was teased and taunted by the blowsy, middle-aged whores. Most of the miners never found gold in those played-out streams, but Sevareid admired them, just as he had admired Walter Port. They could fell trees and rebuild engines — they could do anything with their hands without reading a book of directions or studying a blueprint. They were everything Sevareid was not, everything he was sure he would *never* be. Still, he learned to swing a shovel and work a backsaw, and when he left in September, his chest was broader, his shoulders stronger, and in his knapsack was a tiny vial of gold flecks worth about eighty cents — the entire profit from his summer's work.

To get to California he had hitchhiked. Returning home, he rode the rails — and entered, briefly, the subterranean world of the Depression-era nomads who ate out of tin cans, huddled for warmth around camp fires, fought with fists and razors, had sex under blankets in boxcars. One night, as he waited for a train near Ogden, Utah, a large, burly man approached and asked if he'd like to come to his house for sandwiches. Sevareid walked down a lonely, dark road with the man, who suddenly stepped into a grove of willow trees and asked the kid if he'd like to earn a quarter. Sevareid fled. Later his companions asked how he could have been so dumb as to not recognize "a queer" when he met one.

Back home, Sevareid enrolled as a full-time student at the university. He was tougher now, more worldly. His months with the miners and hoboes had radicalized him, and soon he found himself caught up in the leftist revolt that swept U.S. campuses as the Depression deepened. Sevareid and other activists formed what they called the Jacobin Club and began a determined assault on the hegemony of fraternities over campus life. Within a couple of years the Jacobins had gained control of the literary and law reviews, the board of publication, and the student newspaper, the *Minnesota Daily*, which became their strongest weapon against the university establishment.

Appalled at the senseless slaughter in World War I and impressed with the leftist dogma of the time, Sevareid and his fellows became pacifists. With Hitler's power on the rise, they were "desperately anxious to keep America out of it." In 1934 Sevareid was among the hundreds who solemnly signed the Oxford Oath, pledging *not* to fight for God and country. That same year the *Daily* launched a campaign to end the university's policy of compulsory military training. Sevareid, by then a junior, wrote several stories about a brilliant philosophy student who had been suspended for refusing to attend Reserve Officer Training Corps (ROTC) drill classes. The stories created such a furor that university president Lotus Coffman was forced to reinstate the student. Then, on commencement day 1934, the board of regents voted to make military training optional.

It was a major victory for the Jacobins, but it came at a price for Sevareid. Labeled a "Red" by the ROTC department and vilified by some fraternity and sorority leaders, he was denied the editorship of the *Daily* in his senior year. He was shattered. Years later, when he wrote about his college days, all he recalled was "struggle, not so much the struggle of 'working my way through,' as the battle, in deadly earnest, with other students of different persuasion or of no persuasion, with the university authorities, with the American society of that time."

But in the midst of the struggle Sevareid found time for romance. During his senior year he married a tall, attractive law student named Lois Finger, the daughter of the university's popular track coach and granddaughter of a South Dakota congressman. Lois was as idealistic and politically active as her husband, but in other ways she was his opposite. Ebullient and vivacious, from a family that loved to talk and argue, she was an outstanding student and a gifted athlete who, according to family lore, once equaled a world record in women's low hurdles. At the university's law school she was one of only four women in the class of 1935. Shortly after graduation she easily passed the Minnesota bar examination.

Sevareid had little experience with women, but when he met this long-legged brunette with a rose in her hair on Washington's Birthday, 1934, he was immediately captivated. Two years older than he, she nudged him out of his shyness, made him feel important. "Our college romance was not the silent, hand-holding kind, but the animated-conversation kind," he once remarked wryly. "I conversed, mostly about me, while she looked animated."

That fall Sevareid and Lois eloped to Hudson, Wisconsin. They were married by a county judge, with another pair of eloping Minnesota students as their witnesses. After Sevareid placed a twelve-dollar ring on Lois's finger and they were pronounced man and wife, the judge turned to the other couple and said, "Well, you heard what I said to them. The same thing goes for you." The following May the Sevareids repeated their vows in a traditional ceremony before friends and family. Lois, who during Eric's senior year supported both of them as a social worker in St. Paul, never let Sevareid buy her another ring; her husband, not known for being loose with money, wrote, "I find this comforting, financially and otherwise."

After his graduation in December 1935, Sevareid went back to the *Minneapolis Journal*. He had developed a much harder edge and had become a dedicated union man. In college he had watched one day as the local police ambushed strikers from the Minneapolis Teamsters Union; fifty of the men had been shot as they tried to escape. It was then that Sevareid "understood deep in my bones and blood what fascism was." At the *Journal* he wasted no time in joining a newly organized chapter of the Newspaper Guild. The chapter's creation brought a new spirit of independence to the *Journal's* staff members, but Sevareid and others thought management would find some way to stamp out the union.

The blow came a year later. Sevareid had been doing rather well as a reporter. He had several scoops, including a page-one exposé of a local fascist outfit called the Silver Shirts. If the Guild's proposed new contract with the *Journal* was approved, moreover, he would receive a large salary increase. But management was keen on teaching the upstart union members a lesson. A few days after the contract went through, Sevareid made a minor error in a one-paragraph story. For that he was summarily fired. Several other union members soon followed him out the door and into unemployment.

When Sevareid's father had lost everything in Velva in 1924, he had moved on. Now his son decided to follow that example. He knew war was coming, and he had begun to realize that Hitler was making his Jacobin isolationism and the Oxford oath irrelevant. Sevareid wanted to get to Europe and did not want to wait until the United States entered the war. He hoped to see, before it was too late, those shining places — Paris, London, Rome — he had read about. And so, in the fall of 1937, he and Lois took a train to New York and, like Larry LeSueur and Bill Shirer and so many other American adventurers before them, they boarded a freighter, the S.S. *Black Eagle*, bound for Europe with a cargo of Virginia apples.

◆

"There is a smell in the continental cities," Sevareid wrote in his autobiography, "a wonderful smell that excites the blood." The seductive aroma was strongest in Paris, but with war approaching, Parisian gaiety had a certain forced quality. Café conversations might begin, as in the past, on the subjects of Picasso or Gertrude Stein or Hemingway, but now they ended on Hitler or Mussolini or Franco. The citizens of Paris could no longer ignore the mutilated young veterans of the Spanish Civil War and the shabby German and Austrian refugees who streamed into their city — reminders of how far Paris was from the days when Ernest and Scott were reinventing the novel and Gertrude was not reinventing the rose.

Eric and Lois Sevareid tried to see the situation as it really was. Lois became involved in a group working to get sick and wounded Lincoln Brigade volunteers out of Spain and back to the States. In the early mornings she and Sevareid often went to the Gare d'Austerlitz to help the dirty, haggard, red-eyed soldiers, some with missing limbs and eyes, off the trains. At night in their cold, clammy hotel room, the Sevareids listened, over cognac, to refugee writers, college professors, poets, and others talk about what Hitler was doing to their homelands and their people.

Still, the Sevareids were hardly immune to the charms of Paris. Eric, not yet the insightful sophisticate of his later years, was still a "big friendly country boy" when he met a twenty-six-year-old New Zealander named Geoffrey Cox, who was to become one of his closest friends. Cox, who'd been a Rhodes Scholar at Oxford and the Paris correspondent for the *Daily Express* in London, felt an instant kinship with the young man from North Dakota. "We were," Cox said, "two kids from the back of beyond, who found ourselves, quite amazingly, in the middle of things."

In Paris Sevareid shed some of his gloom, exchanged "Arnie" for "Eric," and got a job on the Paris edition of the *New York Herald*. The *Paris Herald* was not at all caught up in the war fever. During the Munich crisis the paper ran an ad headlined COME TO CZECHOSLOVAKIA. Almost all its local news was lifted word for word from the French press. Its news from America was largely invented. Sevareid had hardly been hired before he was promoted to city editor — mainly, he said, because he could type faster than anyone else. He also did some writing and reporting. On a good day he could turn out six columns of copy, and if the facts didn't make a good enough story, he, like the other *Herald* staffers, would invent some that did.

The paper allowed him to roam Paris and write about whatever amused him. In this congenial atmosphere his writing loosened up. Wit, grace, and style — sometimes a little too much style — began to enliven his copy. Describing a raucous exposition of surrealist art at the Galerie Beaux Arts, Sevareid noted that the decision of the police to shut the doors shortly after the exposition began was "like a spotted flag in front of a blue surrealist bull."

With war fast approaching, however, Sevareid was eager to do more than make up stories and craft elegant features about silly events. He took a part-time night editor's job with United Press, which, in addition to helping pay the bills, gave him a sense of being involved with serious news, even though he disliked the constant deadline pressure. UP was so pleased with his performance that its president, on a visit to Paris, offered him a full-time job.

While Sevareid was debating whether to accept, Ed Murrow called from London, asking if he'd like to try radio reporting. "I don't know very much about your experience," Murrow said. "But I like the way you write, and I like your ideas. There's only Shirer and Grandin and myself now, but I think this thing may develop into something. There won't be pressure on you to provide scoops or anything sensational." It was uncanny how Murrow knew the right thing to say when he was recruiting; he seemed to have divined how uncomfortable Sevareid was with UP's frenetic pace. All Murrow wanted, he said, were ideas and good writing. "Just provide the honest news," he said. "And when there isn't any news, why, just say so. I have an idea people might like that."

Sevareid was hooked for life. He accepted the offer and didn't even seem to mind the officious tone of a confirmation letter Murrow sent him on August 16, 1939, the day after their chat:

It is understood that we can dispense with your services if they are no longer required, and you, of course, will be free to terminate your association with Columbia, provided we are given reasonable notice. . . . Incidentally, the matter of terms of employment and the salary paid are normally matters of strict confidence, even between colleagues.

◆

Sevareid was frightened almost to the point of illness by the thought of speaking on radio. For the audition Murrow set up a closed circuit to New York, where Columbia's executives would be listening. Sevareid carefully wrote a story about a sensational Paris murder trial he had just covered. Two hours before his test, however, he learned that the broadcast would not only be heard by the executives but would be carried over the entire network. Terrified, Sevareid scrapped the trial piece and dashed off a story about French politics. When he sat down at the microphone, his hands were shaking so badly he was sure that listeners all across America could hear the rattling of his script.

Paul White and the others in New York couldn't believe it. Shirer and Grandin had only been bad. This guy was a true disaster. There were so many gulps and swallows and pauses and stumbles that you couldn't even understand what he was saying half the time.

After reporting New York's negative reaction to Sevareid, Murrow serenely added, "That's all right. I'll fix it. Quit your other jobs anyway and don't worry about it." Like a good son, Sevareid did as he had been told. And Murrow did fix it with New York. To ease the higher-ups' minds, he brought Sevareid to London for some training and arranged to put him on the air for a joint broadcast with H. V. Kaltenborn, then in London on a visit.

That was a mistake. Old pro Kaltenborn was never a shrinking violet, but his excellent commentaries during the Munich crisis had gained him a sponsor and a nightly program, which acted as a miracle growth hormone for his ego. Before his arrival in London that August of 1939, Janet Murrow wrote indignantly to her parents that the commentator had already instructed Ed to "arrange for him to see Mr. Chamberlain [and] Mr. Churchill . . . over the *weekend*!!! Who does he think he is?"

Among other things, Kaltenborn thought he was someone who didn't have to make room for young Eric Sevareid. When he finally relinquished the microphone to his would-be colleague, so little time remained that Sevareid was forced to edit his script as he was breath-

lessly reading it. It was another fiasco, and the humiliated novice broadcaster "would have resigned then and there," he wrote later, except that
he "lacked the courage" to tell Murrow he was quitting.

Actually, at that moment, no one dared say anything to Murrow, who
had been sitting across the table from Sevareid and Kaltenborn in the
BBC studio. Furious, Murrow stood up at the end of the broadcast and
stalked out, a pencil clenched in his fist. Sevareid followed him to the
elevator and saw the pencil Murrow was holding snap between his
fingers. Murrow's anger was aimed not at Sevareid but at Kaltenborn
and, by extension, at all the other self-satisfied bastards in New York.
Murrow was not going to let them stand in his way: Sevareid was going
to make it!

On August 23, 1939, Hitler and Stalin announced their mutual nonaggression pact. One day earlier Murrow had finally signed Sevareid.
With war coming, CBS needed correspondents right away, whether or
not they were born broadcasters. Sevareid never lost his mike fright —
"he was always on the verge of a breakdown when he saw a microphone," said Richard C. Hottelet — but it didn't matter to Murrow. In
his first week with CBS, Sevareid rushed back to Paris to help out the
beleaguered Tom Grandin.

◆

Hitler's diatribes against Poland became ever more shrill. It was the
Poles who were disturbing the peace of Europe, he ranted, the Poles
who were threatening Germany with invasion. Bill Shirer, who had
been alternating between Warsaw and Berlin, was bone-tired; so was
Murrow in London. They both had been broadcasting about the crisis
from noon until four in the morning every day for weeks. On top of all
this, they now had to deal with another of Paul White's power plays.

For some time the crafty White had been trying to goad Murrow
into making tactical errors. More than once, when Murrow suggested a
story, White would abruptly reject the idea, then change his mind so late
in the process that Murrow didn't have time to do an adequate job.
When Murrow failed to deliver, White would spread the word in New
York. Wrote the exasperated (and normally soft-spoken) Janet Murrow
to her family: "Fortunately, Ed's cables are all in order, and one day, I
hope he'll use them to show what a thick-headed snake our friend Mr.
White is."

White's latest gambit, with Europe about to go up in flames, was to
order Murrow, Shirer, Grandin, and Sevareid to do a broadcast of enter-

tainment and dance music from nightspots in London, Paris, and Hamburg. "They say there's so much bad news out of Europe, they want some good news," Murrow snapped to Shirer over the phone. The show, scheduled to be broadcast just as Germany was about to rape Poland, would be called "Europe Dances." Shirer was as angry as Murrow. "Can you imagine that!" he wrote in his memoirs. "Shirer and Murrow go bar hopping while Hitler gets ready to pounce on Poland!" Finally Murrow decreed, "The hell with those bastards in New York. It may cost us our jobs, but we're just not going to do it."

The sweep and pace of the war news protected them. In Berlin on August 31, Shirer listened on headphones to a German broadcast of the Nazi terms for peace in Poland and simultaneously translated for his American listeners. That night Germany shut down its long-distance phone lines. Shirer went to bed feeling completely shut off from the rest of the world. At six the next morning he was awakened by a call from Sigrid Schultz, the Berlin correspondent of the *Chicago Tribune*. "It's happened," she said. Germany had invaded Poland. World War II had begun.

✦

On that same late summer morning in Paris, Eric Sevareid sat at an outdoor café across from the Gare de l'Est, reading the morning papers with their huge black headlines — "C'est la Guerre!" He looked up to see a shoelace vendor hawking his wares as usual, a girl in the beauty shop across the way polishing the metal hoods of her dryers. Didn't these people realize that life would never be the same again? This time *c'est la guerre* meant more than the Gallic acceptance of the way things are.

When he crossed over to the train station and saw men pouring in, he began to understand. France had not yet declared war, but the men had been streaming out of the slums and tenements surrounding the station since dawn, most of them in work clothes, some with old oval army helmets hooked on their arms. Their red-eyed wives were there too, shuffling along in worn felt slippers. There were no military bands, no flags or bunting, no cries of "Victoire!" and "Vive la France!" There was no talk at all.

The men moved silently to the trains as if they'd been practicing for it since the last war. The morning papers might be filled with grandiose calls to patriotism, but in these blankly despairing faces Sevareid saw how France truly felt. "I thought," he broadcast a couple of years later, "that it must seem to them that they had fallen asleep in their uniforms, and the intervening twenty years was only a dream from which they had now awakened."

Later that morning Sevareid learned that France would declare war on Germany at five in the afternoon. He was the first correspondent in Paris, on radio or in print, to clear the story through French censors. Scheduled to broadcast at noon, he paced up and down the studio in a cold sweat, looking at the clock every two minutes. He'd been with CBS a little more than a week, and now he was about to scoop the world! Then, just before airtime his French engineer told him that New York had canceled his broadcast. Not knowing he had a scoop, Columbia wanted more from London, which had broadcast the British declaration of war that morning.

Sevareid tried without success to raise Murrow by phone and cable. In his fury he railed at his French engineer. Suddenly the engineer, his face a portrait of agony, burst into tears and shouted, "Get out! Get out!" What did it matter, he wanted to know, this nonsensical little scoop of Sevareid's? What did it *matter*? The engineer had received his call-up notice that morning. He had fought in the last war, had been wounded three times, had spent one year in a German prison camp. Now he must do it all over again.

Sevareid saw how foolish he was, he who didn't even *like* this sort of journalism. War wasn't slogans and rhetoric and military strategy, and it wasn't scoops. War was people and what happened to them. It was a lesson he would never forget.

Pictures in the Air

W E USED TO BE ABLE to telephone two or three times a day and write long letters. We met occasionally in Paris or Geneva." Now, Ed Murrow said from London, "that's all over."

A week after Germany invaded Poland and direct communications between England and Germany were cut off, Murrow was telling American listeners what this new war had already done to his two-year-old friendship with Bill Shirer. For a man of Murrow's reserve, it was an extraordinary public admission of personal feelings. He had been listening that September day to Shirer's report from Berlin, which preceded his own on Columbia's *World News Roundup*, and just blurted out how he already missed the little luxuries of peace, like being able to speak to Shirer.

"Other than official news broadcasts, his is the only voice from Berlin I'm likely to hear in a long time — and his voice reaches me by way of New York," said a wistful Murrow. He could only listen in on headphones now as Shirer did his broadcasts from Berlin to still-neutral America. Unable to chat with his friend, Murrow felt alone again. Evidently deciding he had bared enough of his soul for one day, he changed the subject: "You're probably not interested in my personal reactions when I hear [Shirer's] calm, cool voice from Berlin. So I'll give you the news."

In Berlin, Shirer felt the isolation even more keenly. He was cut off not only from Murrow but from so much else that he once took for granted, including Tess and their little daughter in Geneva, his other friends scattered throughout Europe, and, of course, the news, the real news, of what was going on in Poland and everywhere else. He could no longer get many foreign newspapers and magazines or easily listen to the BBC and other Western radio broadcasts. (The Nazis had promised death to any German caught listening to those frequencies, and foreign journalists weren't eager to test what the penalty might be for *them*.) Thus, except for what Shirer could pick up from other correspondents and diplomatic sources, most of the news he received had a distinctly Nazi slant.

As the Luftwaffe smashed Warsaw and other cities, the German papers blithely asserted that Poland was responsible for the slaughter of Polish civilians. When a German U-boat blew up the British passenger liner *Athenia*, killing more than one hundred passengers, the official Nazi line was that it was a provocation, that the British had sunk the ship themselves, hoping to pin the blame on Germany and thus encourage America's entry into the war. Whenever Shirer had to report such Nazi propaganda, he was tempted to tack on his own succinct commentary — "Bullshit!" On the *Athenia* story, he noted on the air that he was in no position to confirm the German version and was under orders from CBS to avoid giving his personal opinion.

✦

Objectivity — reporting the news without personal prejudice, opinion, or point of view — is in the subjective eye of the beholder. Was it "objective" for Shirer to suggest that Nazi propagandists were liars? Would it have been "objective" for a reporter to assert that Neville Chamberlain was a fool for trusting Hitler? Were respectable Western journalists "objective" when they played down Stalin's crimes after he joined the alliance against Hitler? If it is praiseworthy for an American journalist to point out when a foreign dictator has lied, is it praiseworthy for him to point out when an American president has? Is there a difference between "the truth" and "objective" facts? Journalists have been asking themselves these questions for as long as journalism has existed. In the end, they usually have settled on "fairness" as a better standard than cold-blooded, neutral, impossible "objectivity."

But objectivity had been a mantra for CBS news from the day in 1930 when Ed Klauber was hired as Bill Paley's right-hand man. Klauber's former employer, the *New York Times*, was a stickler for objectivity, and Klauber insisted on the same standard for the network's fledgling news department. Paradoxically, real conflicts over the policy didn't arise until the quality of CBS's journalists improved. Nevertheless, Klauber is credited with laying the ethical foundation for the eminent news organization that CBS later became. As Ed Murrow said in 1955, following Klauber's death, "If there be standards of integrity, responsibility and restraint in American radio news, Ed Klauber, more than any other man, is responsible for them."

It is significant that Murrow did not mention Bill Paley or Paul White in his tribute. They, too, espoused a policy of strict objectivity, but unlike Klauber, they seemed to equate objective facts with their own opinions. Paley often found it convenient to ignore the policy altogether. When Boake Carter was making huge amounts of money for CBS, Paley gritted his teeth and pretended not to mind his star commentator's right-wing animadversions. But as soon as the Roosevelt administration began threatening the network, Paley rediscovered his objectivity policy, rolled it up tight, and beat Carter over the head with it. Then, together with Carter's sponsors, he drove the commentator out the door.

Now it was 1939, and government was threatening again. After Germany invaded Poland, President Roosevelt reaffirmed America's neutrality. The administration could do little to influence what newspapers and magazines said about that policy, but radio, already regulated under the Communications Act of 1934, was different. Some New Dealers wanted to place the networks under total federal control. After all, this powerful new medium had not yet proved that it could be "responsible" in a war. What if the networks roused their audiences to such an extent that they propelled the country into the conflict? Should U.S. involvement eventually prove necessary, Roosevelt wanted to control the process, not leave it up to the likes of Bill Paley. Steve Early, FDR's press secretary, thus warned the networks to behave like "a good child" or else.

Bill Paley did not have to be warned twice. Suddenly he was more dedicated than ever to objectivity. He was a pure firebrand, though, compared to the executives at NBC and Mutual. So intimidated were they by the government's warning that they decided to get out of war reporting altogether. On September 8, 1939, NBC and Mutual halted all broadcasts from abroad, parroting the government's notion that more war news might create an uncontrollable groundswell in favor of U.S. intervention. Murrow and his correspondents already had a jump on their competitors. Now NBC and Mutual were leaving the field — voluntarily. By the time they regained their senses a couple of critical months later, CBS's dominance was clear.

But CBS war correspondents now had to abide by a new, stricter objectivity policy. The network's foreign reporters and New York–based newscasters must never reveal emotion or prejudice on the air, Klauber insisted. Above all, there must be no so-called editorializing. Germany's invasion of Poland provided an early test of the policy. Eric Sevareid, who had been reporting and broadcasting on the crisis twelve hours a day, seven days a week, heard his voice crack with emotion during one report. He expected to be reprimanded by New York, and he promptly was.

But the policy could not work. It did not take into account human nature or the astounding moral inequality between the sides at war. How could an honest reporter parrot the Nazi line about Poland? It wasn't possible to be morally neutral in this war, Murrow and his Boys felt, and most of them managed to make mincemeat of Klauber's objectivity standards.

Shirer used insinuation and irony to work his way around the network rules and Nazi censorship. When the German press insisted that the Poles were firing on their own capital city, Shirer reported in a bemused voice, "There was a headline that struck me tonight: POLES BOMBARD WARSAW. I thought it was a misprint until I read the story under it, which turned out to be an official communiqué of the German High Command." The fine print of the communiqué, Shirer noted, acknowledged that the Polish bombardment was actually aimed at the attacking German troops. A few weeks later he had fun with the German news report that a so-called shipping expert from America had confirmed that the British sank the *Athenia*: "We were told in the papers today that Gustav Anderson of Illinois — and Mr. Anderson is certainly the man of the hour here — had finally, in a sworn statement in Washington, decisively proved that Mr. Churchill and not a German U-boat had sunk the *Athenia*. For the German people, the *Athenia* episode is closed — Mr. Churchill sank the boat."

Shirer also used popular American slang to get some of his dispatches past German censors, who, in the beginning, had little knowledge of idiomatic American English. With this approach and with his use of inflection, he developed a kind of cult following among American listeners. Joseph C. Harsch, an old Berlin colleague of Shirer's, recalled "the marvelous way he had of sounding as though he were hinting at worse things than he was telling."

Although he preferred using indirection, there were times when Shirer couldn't quite disguise his passion. In late September he and other journalists watched the Luftwaffe bomb the virtually defenseless Polish town of Gdynia. German officers, he reported, "reminded me of the coaches of champion football teams at home, who sit calmly on the sidelines and watch the machines they created do their stuff. It was both tragic and grotesque. Grotesque that we should be watching the killing as if it were a football game."

Shirer managed to get such mild emotional reactions past the Germans, but they did not sit well with New York. Paley complained several times over the next few months that Shirer was becoming too anti-Nazi. "He and White thought I was stretching things to the limit," Shirer said shortly before he died in 1993, "but nobody could have lived in that country as long as I and not have hated [the Nazis]."

Aware of Shirer's hostility, the Third Reich was also aware of CBS's growing reach and influence, and was eager to use the network to trumpet Germany's defeat of Poland. During a trip by Shirer to the Polish front, the German broadcasting company offered him the use of a small mobile recording unit on the battlefield. By allowing listeners to hear the thunder of the panzers, the whine of dive bombers, he could bring the war home in a way his print colleagues simply could not match. But when Shirer approached New York with the idea, he was given a flat no.

Indeed, for most of the war, Murrow and the Boys pleaded to be allowed to record. Paley refused. Everything had to be live, he said, because that was the extra dimension radio offered — events as they were actually happening. Paley's real motive, as usual, was pure business. If he allowed recordings, singers and comedians might be able to record and distribute their own programs to local stations, cutting the networks out of the picture. Paley and other network executives preferred to keep *that* door firmly closed. Shirer thought the decision to ban recordings "was one of the most idiotic things that ever happened in the history of journalism." Murrow and the Boys would occasionally violate the ban — for example, by slipping recorded background sounds into their reports — but radio's war coverage was almost entirely live until D-Day.

✦

With the invasion of Poland and the formal declarations of war by the European allies, Americans became interested in European affairs again, even if the news came into their homes at the odd and unpredictable hours dictated by live coverage. News programs proliferated, yet listeners still couldn't seem to get enough of them. NBC and Mutual executives soon saw how wrong they had been to pull back from the continent and set about reversing their decision. So many news specials and bulletins were on the air that one CBS wag thought the standard program introduction should be changed to "We interrupt our news bulletins for one of our regularly scheduled programs."

CBS's New York–based news staff — librarians, researchers, writers, editors, commentators, and newscasters (who read the news but did not, as a rule, report it) — was growing even faster than Murrow's operation in Europe. But as a result the organization was developing two distinct personalities. On the one hand were Murrow and the Boys, intellectual adventurers who worked mainly abroad and who were becoming major international celebrities; on the other were Paul White and his staff in New York, anonymous craftsmen for the most part, few of whom received much public attention. Among the better-known New York staffers were elegant and knowledgeable newscasters like John Charles Daly (who would achieve his greatest fame in the 1950s as the urbane host of the CBS television quiz show *What's My Line*), Ned Calmer, and Douglas Edwards. There was also Elmer Davis, a veteran print journalist who distinguished himself as a CBS analyst before taking over the government's new Office of War Information in 1942. Taken together, the staff in New York, no less than the Murrow team, represented the modern face of a network that was fast burying both its own Boake Carter past and the competition.

The New York newsroom and studio were enlarged and expensively refurbished. Paul White's office was sleekly redone in beige, with glass walls so he could keep track of what was going on in the newsroom. No longer a neglected stepchild, CBS news was increasingly put on promotional display. One executive at another network groused that Columbia's setup had a "rather theatrical air . . . that undoubtedly makes it impressive to visiting writers."

The news operation was also impressing sponsors. As the popularity of news programs soared, advertisers fell over themselves to get in on the action. A few months after the war began, Columbia's twice-daily *World News Roundup* acquired its first sponsor, Sinclair Oil. Murrow soon announced that every time one of the Boys appeared on the program he would get a seventy-five-dollar bonus from Sinclair. Sevareid, typically, was troubled. "Ed, we are recording this great human story," he said. "Is it right to take money from this oil company?" Murrow fell silent a moment. "You'll get used to it," he said. And so they did.

✦

When Larry LeSueur arrived in London in the summer of 1939, among those he saw about a job was Ed Murrow. The two of them hit it off right away. Although Murrow was unable to offer a job immediately, he made clear that one would probably be available soon. He liked Le-Sueur's confident, easy manner and sense of humor and was delighted to learn of his experience with United Press and radio. Here at last was a print reporter with a strong and steady voice. For his part, LeSueur was as impressed as everyone else by Murrow's presence and eloquence.

LeSueur was in Paris a few weeks later, seeing the sights and meeting the girls, when the Hitler-Stalin nonaggression pact was announced. He returned to England on the next available boat to look for work. Walk-ing down a London street not long afterward, he heard a woman call his name. He turned around, and there was Kay Campbell, Murrow's di-minutive Scottish secretary. "Mr. LeSueur," she said, "Mr. Murrow has been looking all over for you. We've called every hotel in London." That very day Larry LeSueur became a CBS correspondent.

He lacked the tortured, writerly introspection of Sevareid, the expe-rience and drive of Shirer, the intellectual credentials of Grandin. Be-yond his radio experience, there was nothing special in his background to recommend him. Yet once again Murrow's judgment was acute. As the war spread, he would need more than a crew of intellectuals. He would also need tough, cool, brave journalists who were willing to put themselves in harm's way and come back with a story. All the Boys were capable of it, and all did it at one time or another. But LeSueur was different. He had no pretensions to being an "analyst" or a "commenta-tor." He was a reporter.

Murrow sent him first to Rheims, in the Champagne region of northeastern France. He was to cover the British army and air force units facing the Germans near the Maginot Line, the long necklace of concrete fortifications built between 1929 and 1934 that was supposed to stop any ground attack devisable by the mind of man. The cham-pagne was superb, the pilots' company delightful, but to LeSueur's great frustration, the news was all but nonexistent.

While Germany was bombing the Poles into submission, the British and French did nothing after declaring war except send a few token patrols across the Maginot Line, drop a few propaganda leaflets, dodge a few German fighters, fly a few reconnaissance flights over German territory, and shoot down a few German reconnaissance planes over French territory. France, with as many soldiers in uniform as Germany, and more reservists, chose not to fight. The conventional French wisdom was that it was best to sit tight and wait for Germany to commit the folly of attacking the unbreachable Maginot Line, with its eighty-seven miles of underground forts, barbed wire, pillboxes, tank traps, and guns.

◆

On a trip to the front, peering through binoculars at the Germans in forts on their own Siegfried Line, Eric Sevareid noted the relaxed air of the soldiers on both sides. They were acting, he reported, as if "nothing had happened and nothing would." To Sevareid, himself only twenty-seven years old, the soldiers seemed impossibly young. In a broadcast he said, "You have a feeling that all the schoolboys of Europe have been sent against each other."

All the schoolboys of Europe. He was getting it, this raw Midwesterner, whom Murrow had been tutoring about how to report for radio. Despite the still-dreadful monotone of his voice, despite his gulps and stammers and swallows and stumbles, he was getting it. It wasn't France versus Germany, it was schoolboy against schoolboy. That's what Murrow wanted: verbal pictures of the people in a drama that still seemed distant and incomprehensible to many Americans. Only by putting listeners in other people's shoes and other people's minds would the war begin to have meaning for them.

Murrow and the Boys were inventing an entirely new form of reporting as they went along, moving in on turf that had belonged exclusively to print. To be sure, as writers first and broadcasters second, radio was to them just another way of delivering their own written words. But now they were reporting and writing for the *ear,* not the eye, and that required a new technique.

What Murrow wanted was for the Boys to imagine themselves standing before a fireplace back home, explaining to the local editor or college professor or dentist or shopkeeper what was going on. But imagine, too, he said, that a maid and her truck-driver husband are listening at the door. Use language and images that are as informative and compelling to them as to the guests around the fireplace. Avoid high-flown rhetoric and frenetic delivery. Focus on the concrete, the specific, the telling detail. When he hired a thirty-three-year-old American socialite named Mary Marvin Breckinridge (the only woman to crack the fraternity of the Murrow Boys) and assigned her to Amsterdam, he told her, "When you report the invasion of Holland, or I report the invasion of England, understate the situation. Don't say the streets are rivers of blood. Say that the little policeman I usually say hello to every morning is not there today."

Pictures in the air were what Murrow wanted. He himself painted them brilliantly, as he would show again and again during the London Blitz. Never having been a reporter before, he threw out all the rigid, traditional rules of news writing. He and the Boys were calm and conversational, sometimes spinning their stories in the first person singular, just friends chatting with other friends. There was a closeness, a familiarity that few other reporters, on radio or in print, could equal. They created what Sevareid called "a new kind of pertinent, contemporary essay." He later wrote:

> Familiar, very American voices now brought faraway scenes and issues into millions of living rooms, giving, not just the bones of the news, not an editorial by itself, nor a descriptive "color" story by itself, but, in a very few minutes, putting it all in one package — the hard news of the day, the feel of the scene, the quality of the big or little men involved, and the meaning and implications of whatever had happened.

A good early example was provided by Larry LeSueur. During that wet, cold winter of what was called the "phony war," LeSueur, from an air base in Rheims, asked his listeners to put themselves in the place of a young Royal Air Force pilot he'd just interviewed. Flying reconnaissance missions over Germany, such pilots were among the few combatants who at that time were in any real danger. As LeSueur told the story:

> It still will be dark as you face the bitter wind off the airfield, grabbing that last puff on your cigarette, the last you may ever smoke. But you don't think about that because you're very young, with the feeling it always happens to someone else. . . . You're going up without protection of formation — alone. Moments pass. Underneath are the pillboxes of the Maginot Line. Moments more. There are the white tank traps that mark the Siegfried Line. Now your observer's camera is clicking steadily. It's beautiful up above the sunlit clouds. The smooth drone of your twin motors makes you happy. You feel like singing and then you do. Then out of the corner of your eye, you see four black dots, growing larger momentarily. It's an enemy patrol of German Messerschmitts. Your gunner has seen them too. You hear the rattle of the machine gun as you put your bomber in a fast climbing turn, but the Messerschmitt fighters climb faster. They form under your tail, two on each side. One

by one, they attack. A yellow light flashes in front of you. The first
fighter slips away while the next comes on at you. Again that smashing
yellow flame. Your observer falls over unconscious. Before you can
think, the next Messerschmitt is upon you. A terrific jolt. Your port
engine belches smoke. It's been hit. The fourth Messerschmitt is coming up fast now. Desperate, you put your bomber's nose almost straight
down. The air-speed indicator goes all the way around, to plus forty-
four miles per hour. The ground roars up at you. You pull out of the
dive. When your head clears, you hear your gunner say, "They left us at
ten thousand." . . . So back over the lines you limp on one engine. You've
done your job, come back with pictures. You force-land on the first
Allied airfield. That night, seated next to a hospital bed where your
observer nurses a scalp wound, you hear an enemy communiqué. A
British bomber was shot down over the lines today. Well, you puff a
cigarette and grin.

✦

If there was occasional action in the air, on the ground there was exqui-
site boredom, a fact that Eric Sevareid and Tom Grandin, reporting
from Paris, knew all too well.

One day, before leaving for the "front line" on the Rhine border,
Sevareid noted that the French lieutenant accompanying him had
brought along an Agatha Christie mystery, *Murder on the Links*, to help
him face the menacing enemy. The phantom combat that the British
troops called the "bore war" and the French called the *drôle de guerre* was
more than bizarre: it sapped men's bodies as well as their souls. In the
heavy snow and rain that winter, the French and British troops coughed
and shivered in uniforms that never dried out. They slept and ate and
kept watch in yellow clay dugouts whose walls oozed icy water. Hospi-
tals filled up not with combat casualties but with victims of pneumonia
and influenza.

To Sevareid the real phoniness of the war was less at the front than in
Paris, London, and Berlin, where people forgot about their troops and,
despite blackouts, quickly resumed their old occupations and pleasures.
The Paris Opera opened its season as usual, Sevareid told America, and
the French Institute, a gathering of prestigious scholars, met to discuss the views of Plutarch and Aristotle on zoology. In London, Murrow reported that the dance floors of the nightclubs were once again
jammed, that the theaters had all reopened, and that the war was now
barely making the front page of the papers. From Nazi Berlin, Shirer

told a similar story — theaters and revues sold out, cafés, bars, and nightclubs full, although American jazz was now *verboten.*

At one point Sevareid was even required by New York to go on the air with the editor of *Harper's Bazaar,* Carmel Snow, for her annual spring fashion broadcast from Paris. He found the assignment demeaning. No longer the naive Midwestern country boy, Sevareid was beginning to develop a sense of himself and his capabilities, a sense of purpose.

Things were changing for him in other ways as well. Until recently he and his wife had explored Paris and the rest of France together. Now Lois was pregnant, and Eric was preoccupied with the war. And his career. And himself. When Larry LeSueur came to Paris on weekends to escape the mud and boredom of Arras and Rheims, Sevareid would often ask him to stay with Lois while he went to the front. "When *I* would go up to the front, nothing ever happened," LeSueur recalled. "But Eric would come back looking exhausted. 'It's hell up there,' he'd say. Someone said he had a girl in [the town of] Nancy."

✦

The phony war couldn't last forever. Murrow wanted to put someone in neutral Scandinavia or the Low Countries, possible routes for Hitler on his way to France and England. His choice for the job was Mary Marvin Breckinridge. New York was getting used to Murrow's unorthodox hires, but this one was the most startling of all. Ed Klauber detested the very idea of women at CBS and had insisted that even his and Paley's secretaries be male. And there was an industry-wide prejudice against female news broadcasters.

Mary Marvin Breckinridge's background was about as far from the raucous world of journalism as anyone's could be. Tall and dark-haired, she came from a family that included tire king B. F. Goodrich (her maternal grandfather) and a former vice president of the United States, John Breckinridge (her paternal great-grandfather). As a debutante, Mary Marvin had even been presented to the king of England.

But she was no vacuous social butterfly. From her parents she had inherited a wanderlust and a love of adventure. She'd been to Europe three times before World War I and to Japan and China immediately after the war. Before enrolling at Vassar, she attended twelve schools in various countries and had not, as her mother always hastened to point out, been expelled from a single one of them. Unconventionality came easily to her. Indeed, to distinguish herself from a cousin also named Mary Marvin, she called herself simply Marvin.

She liked Vassar, but there were too many women there for her taste and not enough action. In the spring of her freshman year she tried to work off some of her restlessness by persuading a very reluctant friend to swim with her across the Hudson River, still flecked with ice. They made it — and nearly froze. Later Breckinridge found a less reckless outlet for her energy in the National Student Federation, which she helped found during her years at Vassar. This organization of American college students sought to enhance the peace movement by sponsoring international contacts among students. Breckinridge became president, a position that three years later would go to a young man named Edward R. Murrow.

When she graduated from Vassar in 1928 with a degree in modern history and languages, all Breckinridge knew about her future was what she *didn't* want to do: "I enjoyed parties and coming out, but I didn't want to make a whole life of it. I wasn't in a hurry to get married." She learned to fly a plane and in 1929 became the first woman from Maine (the Goodrich summer estate was in York) to obtain a pilot's license. Later she worked in rural Kentucky as a horseback courier for the Frontier Nursing Service, the first organization of nurse-midwives in the United States. The service, founded by her cousin (the *other* Mary Marvin Breckinridge), helped reduce the maternal death rate in that desolate Appalachian region by more than two thirds.

In 1930 Marvin's cousin asked her to study motion picture photography in New York so that she could make a fund-raising film about the nursing service. Marvin was game for just about anything. After taking private lessons with a movie cameraman, she made the film, riding more than six hundred miles on horseback and handling everything herself, including script, lighting, and hand-cranked cameras. The result, a touching documentary about not only the nurses but the proud mountain people they served, is considered a classic and is still shown at exhibitions featuring the work of women filmmakers.

Breckinridge liked the movie camera, but she liked the still camera even more. She took a one-year course at a New York school set up by master photographer Clarence White, and did extremely well. Photojournalism, she decided, was her calling. By the time of the Munich crisis, she was well established in the business, having sold articles and photographs to a number of major magazines. In July 1939 she decided she wanted to go to Europe. With assignments from *Town and Country* and other magazines, she sailed on the S.S. *Nieuw Amsterdam*, with a dressing case, two suitcases (one full of riding clothes and evening gowns), a hatbox, a typewriter, and a Rolleiflex. She planned to be gone six weeks.

While she was in Lucerne covering a music festival, Breckinridge learned that Hitler had invaded Poland. The festival was canceled, as were her other assignments. She decided the time had come to head for home, but in London she had second thoughts. "I had planned to take the first boat home if war should start," she wrote to her mother, "but it now seems foolish to run away from the most interesting thing that I could be doing on earth right now." She had no trouble lining up new magazine photo assignments. When her friends Ed and Janet Murrow asked her to dinner one evening, she told them about a picture story she had been assigned to do for *Life* on how an English village prepares for war.

"Why don't you come on the air Saturday night and talk about it?" Murrow said.

She did. After the broadcast Murrow asked if she'd like to spend the night in a London firehouse, interviewing the all-woman night shift, then do another broadcast about that. Again Breckinridge agreed, mostly because she knew her parents would be pleased to hear her on the radio.

Murrow didn't touch her script; the only instruction he gave was that she should pitch her voice as low as possible. It was a natural radio voice — strong, clear, and confident, with an upper-class American accent. In her firehouse broadcast she was cool and self-possessed. Only afterward did she learn that Murrow had asked all the CBS brass to listen in. Even if she had known, it probably wouldn't have made much difference. Unlike her male counterparts, Breckinridge never showed any nervousness about broadcasting.

After the firehouse report she headed for Ireland, where she'd been invited to ride with some friends in the nobility. Before she left, she volunteered to do a story for Murrow on Irish neutrality. Murrow liked the idea, and he liked the result so much that after the broadcast he offered her a job in Amsterdam. Breckinridge accepted but insisted on receiving an expense account large enough to allow her to live as comfortably as possible — a style of living that turned out to be, as she said later, "sometimes splendid, sometimes very uncomfortable." With the deal made, Breckinridge had a dogtag made (she felt it would be "unkind" to her relatives if she were killed and her body not identified), left her evening gowns and riding outfits with the Murrows, and was off for the Netherlands. Her only instructions from Murrow were: "Give the human side of the war, be honest, be neutral and talk like yourself."

The room clerk at the Carlton Hotel in Amsterdam asked how long she planned to stay. She wasn't sure, she said, perhaps just the weekend. She actually stayed six months, with several side trips to Norway, Belgium, and Germany.

Breckinridge was adept at taking complex issues and translating them into human terms as Murrow wanted. In a story on the Dutch refusal to discuss military cooperation with the British, she compared Holland to a popular fairy-tale heroine: "Holland is wearing her Little Red Riding Hood of neutrality, but she's a bit scared just the same as she goes through the wood. Even though the wolf may be far away, he might turn up at any moment, and the innocence of neutrality is no longer a safeguard."

In another broadcast Breckinridge persuaded the head of the Dutch Nazi party to tell her what he would do if the Germans invaded his country. "I would sit with folded arms like this," he said. At first the Dutch censors refused to approve the interview. When they finally did, it caused an uproar in the Netherlands. There were front-page headlines about potential treason and angry tirades in Parliament. (What the Dutch Nazi leader actually did when the Wehrmacht finally invaded was to flee across the border into Germany — just before Dutch police came to arrest him.)

Even the bastards in New York were forced to agree that Breckinridge was a success. "Your stuff so far has been first rate," Murrow wrote her in late December. "I am pleased, New York is pleased, and so far as I know the listeners are pleased. If they aren't, to hell with them!"

✦

As 1940 began, Murrow had had enough of his enforced separation from Bill Shirer. He cabled Berlin and instructed Shirer to meet him for a little rest and recreation in neutral Amsterdam. Dazzled by the lights and abundant food, delighted to be in each other's company again, the two friends behaved, as Shirer wrote in his diary, "like a couple of youngsters suddenly escaped from a stern old aunt or reform school." To Marvin Breckinridge it was like watching the reunion of a pair of old college friends who had been very close: "You could see how much they trusted each other."

Their exuberance was evident in the one broadcast they did together from Amsterdam:

Shirer: You have no idea what it's like to get into a city and see the streets all lighted up.
Murrow: What do you mean I've got no idea? I saw street lights, automobiles with real headlights, and lights pouring out of windows tonight for the first time in five months. It seems almost indecent to have all these lights about. As soon as we finish here, I'm going out and look at those lights again.
Shirer: When I got in last night and saw all those lights, I dropped my bags in the snow and wandered about the streets for half an hour. . . .
Murrow: Right now, Holland seems to me just about the nicest country in Europe.

They were supposed to talk about the war but couldn't keep their minds on it. Murrow ended the broadcast by saying, "Bill, let's go out and throw snowballs." Which is exactly what they did. Under a bright street lamp they engaged in a "mighty snowball battle," Shirer wrote. When it was over, his glasses and hat were missing. But that didn't matter — nothing could possibly matter that glorious night.

The two days in Amsterdam were a much-needed respite, but Shirer, sick of the cold, isolation, and evil of Berlin, yearned for even more time away. He persuaded Murrow to have Breckinridge replace him in the German capital for a few weeks while he escaped to Geneva to see Tess and Eileen. During her six weeks in Berlin, Breckinridge largely ignored Shirer's condescending advice that she handle "the woman's angle." She did do a few pieces on women and their roles in the war, but she also reported on the Nazi press, on a Nazi prisoner-of-war camp, on German reaction to talks between Herman Göring and U.S. Undersecretary of State Sumner Welles, and on local speculation that Italy might join the war on Germany's side.

She also borrowed some of Shirer's censor-evading techniques. When reading her script for the story on the German press, the censors deleted her assertion that the papers "allow no exchange of ideas and leave little to the reader's judgement." But there was no objection to her ending, in which she referred to the official Nazi newspaper, *Volkischer Beobachter.* "The motto of this paper," she said, "is freedom and bread." After a pause she added, "There is still bread in Germany."

Breckinridge proved better than Shirer at reporting on what the war meant to ordinary Germans. Avoiding his big-picture pieces, she talked of having tea in an unheated apartment with a German woman swathed in sweaters, fur coat, and overshoes; of going to a cocktail party where young girls chatted about the right color of nail polish to wear when their hands were purple with cold; of shopping at a food store whose shelves contained only a dozen cans of food — all solely for decoration. In a story on a school for the future brides of Nazi soldiers, she described a six-week curriculum that included housecleaning, cooking, and sewing, plus political theory and propaganda. On successfully completing the course, each young woman was presented with a personal copy of *Mein Kampf.*

The cold, dark winter days slipped by with no sign of an end to the phony war. But the British at least were beginning to bestir themselves. There were hints that the Royal Navy might try to cut off Germany's supply of Swedish iron ore, shipped to the Reich via Norway. In February a British destroyer intercepted a German supply ship, the *Altmark*, in Norwegian waters. There was a short battle, and the destroyer rescued 303 captured British seamen whom the *Altmark* had been carrying to Germany for internment. The *Altmark* was able to limp into a Norwegian port.

It was a major international story, with Germany accusing Britain of a blatant violation of Norwegian neutrality. Breckinridge braved a blizzard to get to Stavanger, where the *Altmark* was anchored. When she boarded the ship, the captain invited her to his cabin, gave her wine and cake, and agreed to an exclusive prebroadcast interview the next night. During that interview he contradicted the official line from Berlin and admitted the *Altmark* had been carrying guns. Suddenly the story became even more important.

Soon, however, two men from the German Propaganda Ministry arrived at the ship. The next evening, when Breckinridge asked during her broadcast if the *Altmark* was carrying guns, the captain said no. Breckinridge was furious, but there was nothing she could do.

Two days later Hitler ordered his High Command to complete plans for the occupation of Norway.

·✶· 6

The Fall of Paris

STANDING ON THE GERMAN SIDE of the Rhine, Bill Shirer looked across to France's celebrated Maginot Line. On his bank German children were playing in full view of the French troops loitering on the other side. Near the children, German soldiers were kicking around an old soccer ball. It was surreal, like a scene from some art film. Just a few hundred miles to the north, the Germans were bombing Norway — the phony war was supposedly over. But on this front, where everyone expected a pitched battle, Shirer could see only a vast panorama of bucolic peace.

Although he was covering the German troops, he wanted France and England to attack — and he managed to get hints of his attitude across to the American people. "What kind of war, what kind of game, is this?" he demanded in his first broadcast after visiting the front. The Allies, Shirer suggested, had let Germany get away with flagrant aggressions against Norway and Poland, where the Luftwaffe had bombed even rear-echelon communications facilities with impunity. Perhaps in those cases Allied inaction had some geopolitical justification. But what excuse could there possibly be for France's paralysis when its own territory was threatened — "here on the western front, where the two greatest armies in the world stand face to face [and] refrain completely from killing?"

The invasion of Norway and then Denmark in early April 1940 had happened so swiftly that most news organizations, including CBS, had no time to send in staff correspondents to cover the fighting. Frustrated and discouraged, Murrow, Sevareid, Grandin, and Shirer had to remain behind in their static posts, relying on firsthand accounts by part-time correspondents, or stringers. Shirer had tried to fill the gap with trenchant analysis and commentary. "Germany's self-appointed task of taking over the protection of Norway to safeguard its freedom and independence continued today," he said in one broadcast from Berlin. "Just exactly how she's faring is unknown."

That was not quite true. Thanks to Shirer, CBS had an excellent stringer in Norway named Betty Wason. Based in Stockholm, she had worked for radio stations in the Midwest and, after arriving in Europe, had been retained by Shirer to cover Scandinavia for CBS. One of only a handful of Western journalists who made it into Norway during the fighting, Wason did a good, gutsy job of reporting through April and May. Then she received a call from New York, instructing her to find a man to broadcast in her place. "My voice wasn't coming through," she recalled being told. ". . . It was too young and feminine for war news and . . . the public was objecting to it." New York's prejudice against women was reasserting itself.

Disappointed, Wason nonetheless followed orders. She found a twenty-four-year-old male freelancer named Winston Mansfield Burdett and taught him what she knew about radio reporting. Burdett was a summa cum laude Romance-languages scholar from Harvard who had been covering the war in Norway as a stringer for both the *Brooklyn Eagle* and a two-bit radio news service called Transradio. His voice at the time wasn't much better than Wason's (although it would soon develop into one of the most elegant and memorable in all of broadcasting). But at least he was a man, so Klauber and White could relax.

✦

In Paris the spring of 1940 was soft, gentle, and golden, a welcome relief from winter's bitter cold, but Eric Sevareid hadn't the time or inclination to enjoy it. His wife had gained one hundred pounds during her difficult pregnancy and was in danger of losing her twin babies. For three months Lois had to lie flat on her back. Her labor began April 25, and Sevareid rushed her to a maternity clinic in Neuilly. After several hours the doctor, his expression grave, told Sevareid, "I think it will go. For a time I was not so sure." One of the deliveries was breech, and Lois nearly died in the ordeal. Soon afterward, however, Sevareid learned that he was the father of healthy twin boys. Their combined weight at birth was thirteen and a half pounds.

Sevareid had little time to enjoy the moment. On May 9 he said goodbye to Lois, still in the clinic, and traveled south by train, en route to the French-Italian frontier in hopes of learning what Benito Mussolini and his Black Shirts were up to. Spending the night in the Provençal town of Valence, he was awakened the next morning by the

shrill of a siren and the sound of heavy boots thudding down the cob-
bled street. He rushed out of the hotel in time to see a shopkeeper
slowly write with white chalk on a blackboard outside his shop: "The
Germans . . . this morning . . . have invaded . . . Holland . . . Luxembourg . . . Belgium . . . They bombed . . . the Lyons . . . airport."

The war was here. Had German bombers reached Paris? What
about Lois? Sevareid caught the next northbound train and finally
reached the Neuilly clinic at midnight. The lights were off, the place
seemed completely deserted. Sevareid had to feel his way along the hall
to Lois's room, desperately afraid something had happened to her. He
found her in bed, looking frightened and lost. She hadn't been afraid of
the sirens, she told him, or the far-off explosions; what scared her was
knowing that everybody else — the nurses and patients — had left. And
there she was, alone with the twins, unable to walk, unable to do anything at all if the bombs came.

Sevareid took her and the twins to the apartment they shared in
Paris with Tom Grandin and his new wife, Natalia. Hardly pausing, the
two men then leapt onto the ferocious, relentless, mind-numbing treadmill that is twenty-four-hour-a-day crisis broadcasting. Not only did
they have to cover the news, write their stories, and submit them to the
censors (hoping that something like a usable script would emerge), but
then they had to race through the blacked-out city to the studio. And
sometimes, when they finally sat down in front of the microphone, they
would learn that the home office had given up and had ceased calling
into the void "Come in, Paris."

Hitler had taken full advantage of the glorious dry spring and the
eight months of Allied inaction. The Nazi blitzkrieg, tested and per-
fected during the Spanish Civil War and in Poland, was now cutting into
the very heart of Western Europe. Combining lightning air attacks with
artillery, infantry, and the terrible swift sword of the panzers, the blitzkrieg was a reinvention of the means of war. It crushed Luxembourg in a
day, Holland in five, and was well on its way to doing the same to
Belgium. Such pitiful French and British army units as had been thrown
into the fight were being pushed back so fast that only the English
Channel, if that, seemed likely to halt their retreat.

The censors in Paris allowed no news stories about what was really
happening at the front; instead the War Ministry prated on about "the
terrible German losses." Parisians were sure their proud army would
easily stop the hated (but not yet feared) Hun before he approached the
French border. And even if the Wehrmacht managed to make it that far,

it surely would be thwarted by the Maginot Line. So the Paris designers were showing their spring and summer collections as usual, the crowds were filling the grandstands at the Auteuil racetrack, and Maurice Chevalier, suspected by some of being a Nazi sympathizer, was entertaining nightly, his act followed by chorus girls who sang "We'll Hang Our Washing on the Siegfried Line."

Sevareid and the other foreign correspondents were not inclined to take the French government's word about the putative successes of its army: they wanted to see for themselves. After moving Lois and the twins to a small inn at Pontchartrain and arranging for a nurse to be with them, Sevareid left on a government-sponsored trip to the Belgian front. In the small French town of Cambrai, near the Belgian border, he was forced to take shelter in the hotel cellar while the concussions of bombs and artillery shells shook the walls. He had read about the war, written and talked about it, but now, for the first time, he felt the gut-wrenching terror of it, a terror that would haunt him for months. Sevareid, who had grown up doubting and testing his courage, had a new reason to doubt and test.

Nevertheless, his job was to see the front, and he and his colleagues made a serious effort to do so. They badgered the French press officers, who suddenly found it difficult to provide transportation from Cambrai. Suspecting that things were going poorly for the French, Sevareid decided to return to Paris. But before he went, he and other correspondents ventured over the border into Belgium. They didn't have to go far to find the war. The Germans, despite their claim that they bombed only military targets, had smashed homes and killed civilians in villages and towns all over Belgium.

Sevareid broadcast what he saw. Struggling to keep his voice calm as New York had ordered, he described two cars in a packed refugee train that had been ripped and splintered by bullets: "To a pilot, I suppose, a freight train is a freight train. It may carry women and children; it may carry troops. But even a pilot can tell what direction it's moving, and troops are not moving south." It was a unique kind of combat, he told his listeners, "truly a lightning war, a war of sudden sounds and flashing machines. It comes and is gone before you can move, and the men you rarely see."

With two other correspondents, Sevareid boarded a mile-long train packed with refugees and bound for Paris. But the train, instead of taking a straight route to the capital, veered west, repeatedly stopping along the way. Something was wrong. During a particularly long halt, several hours after the scheduled arrival time in Paris, Sevareid and his colleagues got off the train to escape its fetid air and stretched out on the grass. Soon they saw small flickers of flame in the distance and then, over the crying of children on the train, heard the sharp, nasty crack of artillery. They timed the intervals between the flickers and the sound, and suddenly realized what was going on — a battle was raging on their side of the border, somewhere near Sedan. The Germans had broken through to France.

When the train finally reached Paris, Sevareid called U.S. embassy officials, who confirmed that the Germans had pulled an end run around the Maginot Line. They had poured through the Ardennes Forest, crossed the Meuse River, and routed the weakly held French position at Sedan. When Sevareid tried to get the story out, however, he ran afoul of the French censors; he decided to put into operation a little scheme he'd devised months before in the event of precisely such a news blackout.

Back then he had sent a letter to Paul White with a crude code — a series of nonsense sentences, each standing for possible war developments in France: one sentence meant an Allied victory, another meant a major German breakthrough. He now cabled the latter sentence to White, hoping White would realize its significance and not just think that Sevareid had gone around the bend from all the pressure. In fact, that's what everyone at CBS *did* think for a while, until White remembered the letter and rushed to find it in his desk. That night commentator Elmer Davis went on the air to say that CBS had learned from a "usually well informed source" that the Germans had broken the main Allied defense line inside France. It was the first word the outside world had of the German advance.

✦

Suddenly Paris was like a deer caught in the glare of headlights, the terror-stricken people immobilized by the mechanized Nazi monster heading straight at them. Surely the French army would never allow the Germans into Paris! Surely there would be another miracle, like the one in 1918 at Verdun! But even as reality began to intrude, many blasé Parisians continued to sun themselves in the balmy late spring air, continued to sip apéritifs on café terraces as they tried to ignore the first sign of a war no longer *drôle* — the swelling river of refugees, many of them French, streaming into and through the city.

Sevareid and Grandin also found it hard to accept the truth, and their reporting echoed their false hopes. In one broadcast, Grandin reported that the Germans had been hampered by heavy air losses and that the "deeper the Germans drive into the country, the more determined the French become." Sevareid told his listeners that even if the unthinkable happened, even if "German motorized columns smash through the gates of the city, it's hard to believe that the French would abandon Paris without a desperate fight."

Where their families were concerned, though, they were taking no chances. Sevareid decided to send Lois and the twins back to the United States. He booked them a cabin on the S.S. *Manhattan,* sailing from Genoa. They said goodbye at the Gare de Lyon; then Lois, still weak from the delivery and carrying two wicker baskets, with diapers and a twin in each, boarded the train for Genoa. Ahead lay a long and arduous journey, including a dangerous ocean crossing. "She showed tremendous courage in doing all that," said Janet Murrow years later, "and I don't think she was ever given enough credit for it."

Grandin wanted to get his new wife, Natalia Parligras, out of France, too. Because she was Rumanian, she would be in considerable danger if the Germans occupied Paris. The mild-mannered and scholarly Grandin had fallen wildly in love with Natalia when they met at a Balkan foreign ministers' conference in Belgrade the previous February. A broadcaster for Rumanian state radio, she did not speak English, but that was no barrier to the multilingual Grandin, who proposed before the conference was over. They were married the day after it ended, and now she was pregnant. Grandin planned to take her to Bordeaux and put her aboard the S.S. *Washington* for America.

With their personal lives in turmoil, the two CBS men got some much-needed assistance from Marvin Breckinridge, who had left Amsterdam just two days ahead of the Germans. As soon as she arrived in Paris, she was pressed into service. But she would not be there long, for she had decided to marry a Berlin-based American diplomat named Jefferson Patterson. When Breckinridge sat in for Shirer in Berlin, she had renewed her long-standing friendship with Patterson, and the relationship had soon deepened. They planned to be married as soon as possible. In the meantime, Breckinridge did stories on the refugees streaming into Paris, on the city's pitifully inadequate civil defense plans, on the growing number of air-raid alerts. In her off hours she went to Lanvin for wedding-dress fittings.

As the crisis deepened, France's overwhelmed leaders were acting like petulant, quarreling children. "They talked the language of
party, special interests, of regional concerns," Sevareid noted, "but no
voice rose above the clamor to speak for France." Not even the new
premier, Paul Reynaud, one of the few French politicians to oppose
appeasement at Munich and an advocate of greater military readiness,
was able to stem the defeatist tide. On May 17 Reynaud named Marshal
Philippe Pétain, the eighty-four-year-old hero of Verdun, to serve as
deputy premier. More than slightly senile, Pétain was an architect of the
failed Maginot Line strategy and a high priest of defeatism. The Germans were already moving toward Paris when King Leopold of Belgium
capitulated to Germany and ordered his army to lay down its arms.
Five days later the Luftwaffe dropped more than a thousand bombs on
Paris.

Breckinridge figured it was time to leave. If she didn't set off for
Berlin immediately, she might not be able to get there at all. On June 5
she made her last CBS broadcast, an account of the impact of war on
a French farming village. Before boarding the train for Germany,
she cabled her resignation to CBS: FAREWELL COLUMBIA. HAVE EN-
JOYED WORKING WITH YOU.

Later she said that she had hoped to continue reporting for the
network after her marriage but that the State Department wouldn't hear
of it. Breckinridge — whose early feminism consisted of deeds, not a
coherent system of beliefs — gave in. She explained years later, "I didn't
want to kill off [Patterson's] career because I wanted to show off what I
could do."

A much different light is cast on Breckinridge's departure from CBS,
however, by Janet Murrow's contemporary personal correspondence. In
a letter to her parents dated June 11, 1940, she wrote, "Marvin has been
asked by the executive offices in New York to leave Columbia." The
letter went on to say that the executives thought Breckinridge had been
"too sensational" in her reporting about the refugees pouring into
France, a charge Janet Murrow found "sickening." New York, she
wrote, "cries for more sensational stuff all the months of the war. Then
when you can truthfully do a heartrending piece they get all scared
because the listeners in America might get all upset! . . . It's maddening
when the whole policy of the [CBS] people over here has been the truth
— and nothing but the truth."

Breckinridge's refugee reports were far from sensational. She made
American listeners understand what it was like for a displaced person to

arrive in a strange country, exhausted and bewildered, then dismount from overcrowded trains with

> baby carriages full of quilts, and bicycles with boxes tied all over them with bits of string. One little girl carried a black cat, and several families brought their dogs with them. . . . One woman, who arrived alone and looked less tired than the rest, was questioned by a little group of people: "What happened to my town? Was my home bombed?" Patiently she replied that she did not know. There was no news. Anxious friends waited in the station for train after train, and when their people did not arrive, they'd say to each other, "There's another train in half an hour. There's another train in half an hour."

There is little doubt that it was Breckinridge's sex, far more than any alleged sensationalism, that bothered New York. But she was Murrow's chum, so they couldn't just dump her as they had Betty Wason. Instead they let her know that she was no longer welcome. When she beat them to the punch by resigning to get married, the CBS publicity department, with breathtaking hypocrisy, sent out a flurry of press releases about her upcoming nuptials. Soon American newspapers were carrying headlines such as: GIRL REPORTER FOR CBS WEDS U.S. DIPLOMAT and FLEES FRANCE TO WED U.S. ATTACHÉ IN REICH and LOVE IN WAR.

Mary Marvin Breckinridge and Jefferson Patterson were married on June 20, 1940, at the U.S. embassy in Berlin. For the next eighteen years they traveled to diplomatic posts in South America, Europe, and the Middle East. They lived extraordinarily well: Patterson, an heir to the National Cash Register Company fortune, was even wealthier than Breckinridge. When he retired from the Foreign Service in 1958, they moved to Washington, D.C., where they took up residence in a home he had bought before the war, a splendid old mansion in the capital's exclusive Massachusetts Heights area. There Breckinridge slipped easily into the role of Washington grande dame. She said she never regretted leaving CBS, but she looked back with great fondness and pride on her six exciting months with Murrow and the Boys.

"I liked it more than any job I ever had," said the only woman who was one of the Boys.

✦

About the same time that Breckinridge departed for Berlin, Tom Grandin left with Natalia for Bordeaux. He assured Sevareid that he would return as soon as he put his wife on the ship. But when the S.S. *Washington* sailed, Grandin was on board. Shortly before departing, he had phoned Sevareid to say he was going, too. He had learned that Natalia, who did not have an American passport, would not be admitted to the States without him. Even so, his departure led to some grumbling among those he left behind. Janet Murrow thought Grandin had taken advantage of her husband's relaxed managerial style. Bill Shirer thought he had "turned chicken . . . instead of sticking with Eric Sevareid." Even New York, with no firsthand knowledge of the situation, chimed in. For some time afterward, Paul White spread the word that in his opinion Grandin had deserted his post under fire.

Murrow didn't agree. In 1941 he recommended Grandin for a government job in Washington. His departure from France seemed to Murrow "entirely justifiable under the circumstances." Later a grateful Grandin wrote to his former boss, "I cannot find words to express my deep appreciation of your kind and straightforward words in my behalf. They completely dispelled doubts that Paul White attempted to create by a one-man whispering campaign."

With Murrow's help Grandin won the job he had applied for — assistant editor of the foreign-broadcast monitoring service of the Federal Communications Commission. Later he was placed in charge of "confidential" government missions to Algeria, Tunisia, Italy, Egypt, Turkey, India, and England. In 1944 he was hired by the newly formed American Broadcasting Company and that June, on D-Day, the man who Bill Shirer and Paul White thought was "chicken" landed with the first-wave troops on blood-soaked Omaha Beach.

After the war Tom Grandin left ABC to became a sales executive. Later he was a rancher in Arizona. He and Natalia remained together until her death. They had three children.

In 1948 Ed Murrow received a telegram at his office in New York that read: YOUR BROADCASTS ARE SO EXTREMELY VALUABLE I CANNOT RESIST AGAIN TELLING YOU I THINK SO.

It was signed Thomas B. Grandin.

◆

The Germans were closing in on Paris. Rumors were spreading that Nazi spies were infiltrating the city. The French army, exhausted, leaderless, badly equipped, had given up. Some soldiers surrendered to the Germans; others, their uniforms in tatters, threw down their arms and limped back to their towns and villages and farms. It was a rout. Yet not a word came from the country's leaders. As late as June 9, when the government panicked and decided to leave the capital, it had made no arrangements for the evacuation or defense of Paris. The leaders merely sneaked out of town in the dead of night. What they left behind, in addition to the people, was chaos.

Under a thick, black shroud of smoke from burning oil reserves, Parisians stampeded out of the city on foot and in every imaginable kind of vehicle: cars, trucks, taxis, delivery vans, even pushcarts and hay wagons. The day after the government's flight, Sevareid decided to leave too. This was anarchy, and it deeply frightened him. In his final report from Paris, he tried to make as clear as he could, through the veil of censorship, that the city was doomed: "If in the next days, anyone talks to America from Paris, it won't be under the control of the French government."

With that report, America learned that Paris was about to fall. Then Sevareid and Edmond Taylor, an American journalist who had been enlisted to help out after Grandin's abrupt departure, climbed into the old CBS Citroën and, with Taylor's wife, began their own tortuous flight from the capital.

Smoke quenched the light of the moon and the stars. As the Citroën inched slowly southward in the endless line of escaping cars and wagons and trucks, there was nothing but blackness and the shuffling of the boots and shoes of refugees trudging along both sides of the road. To Sevareid they were like a "stream of lava flowing past, the unstoppable river which came from the unimaginable eruption somewhere to the north."

His own hegira ended in Tours, where the government had taken temporary refuge. Sevareid was enraged at the sight of the bearded old French senators dawdling over their three-hour lunches, chatting with their mistresses as if nothing had happened. "It was the time for defiance, for rally now, for embattled brotherhood, and yet the old habits prevailed." And they continued to prevail, even as the darkness that had begun seven years earlier in Germany blanketed the continent.

✦

Larry LeSueur was fleeing too. He had been with British troops in Belgium, but they were now escaping to the beaches of Dunkirk, pursued by German forces. Having bid farewell to the retreating Tommies, LeSueur had to find his way back to Paris. He walked out of Belgium and spent a night in a border shack with a lone Dutch colonial soldier who refused to abandon his post even after LeSueur told him his government had surrendered. The next morning LeSueur moved on, walking and hitchhiking the 150 miles between the Belgian border and Paris. He arrived just in time for the exodus.

LeSueur learned that a British troop train was leaving immediately for the south. As a correspondent accredited to the British forces in Europe, he was ordered to be on that train or face court-martial as a traitor. But he ignored the order and missed the train so that he could escort a young American woman friend and her mother out of the disintegrating capital. In a car hired from the Ritz Hotel, they made their way to Troyes, where the British army's headquarters had moved. LeSueur installed mother and daughter in a hotel room, then hurried on to Tours to lend a hand to Sevareid and, not incidentally, get a piece of the story that was now riveting the entire world.

But Sevareid didn't want any help. When LeSueur asked him if he could do a broadcast, Sevareid replied, Sure, how about the one at 2:30 in the morning? Oh, yes, and Sevareid was very sorry, but his hotel room just wasn't large enough to accommodate LeSueur.

Disgusted, LeSueur moved on to Blois and then to Nantes, where he was to catch a British troop carrier in the port of Saint-Nazaire. He hadn't had more than a nap or two in days, and all the hotels in town were full. Ever resourceful, he picked up a prostitute and offered to pay her to let him spend the night in the hotel room where she usually took her tricks. That was fine with the whore, but the man who ran the hotel, reasoning that she normally used — and paid for — the room an average of four times a night, insisted on quadrupling the normal rate. Too tired to argue, LeSueur handed over the money.

The next morning he started up the gangway of the troop ship, only to be told there was no more room on board. He hooked a ride on a British army truck going to Brest, where another ship was said to be waiting. While the truck was still on the road, a German dive bomber flew over the troop carrier LeSueur had been unable to board and dropped a bomb down her stack. The engine room exploded, and thousands of soldiers were killed. When LeSueur finally made it to Brest, he trudged wearily aboard the waiting ship and looked for a place where he could get some more sleep. A couple of days later he was safely back in England.

✦

After taking Paris, the Germans moved on toward Tours, tracking down the tottering French government like a bloodhound. Once again the leaders fled, this time south to Bordeaux, near the Atlantic. An hour after Sevareid left Tours to follow the government, German bombers smashed the city center to rubble.

For Sevareid and Taylor, Bordeaux was a blur of seemingly endless broadcasts, broken by brief catnaps in the Citroën. On the night of June 16, Sevareid received a tip that meant France was lost: Reynaud had resigned and Pétain was taking control. A list of new cabinet members in his hand, Sevareid raced through the streets of Bordeaux in the Citroën and out into the countryside, where a municipal shortwave transmitter was located.

Because they were so dependent on the technology of transmitting, radio people had to know more than print reporters about the available communications facilities. Sevareid had discovered the suburban transmitter on his own and had already arranged to use it if the need arose. But as he rushed up the steps to the studio, an NBC man named Paul Archinard was emerging. He had had the same tip and had already made his broadcast. Sevareid, angry and frustrated, asked Archinard what he'd said in his report, and the man from NBC replied, "Why, I told America, of course, that this is a war cabinet, to carry on the fight." He pointed to the list of cabinet members. "Look at all the generals and admirals."

He had *missed* the story! Sevareid ran into the studio, sat down in front of the microphone, and, speaking without a script, reported the change of government. Then he said, "Regardless of what you may have heard, this is *not* a cabinet designed to carry on the war." Sevareid's correct interpretation made him the first journalist to report that France had capitulated to Germany.*

The next day Pétain announced the surrender on the radio. Just as he concluded his statement, a violent thunderstorm shattered the air in Bordeaux. When it finally rumbled away, people emerged from their houses and shops, silent and transfixed. "They seemed somewhat stunned by it all," Sevareid broadcast after Pétain's announcement. "I

---

*The *New York Times* ran Sevareid's story on page 1, but with a typographical error that made mincemeat of it. The *Times*'s version said "This is *now* a cabinet designed to carry on the war," instead of "This is *not* a cabinet" (emphasis added.)

have seen no tears yet. It's all too sudden, too big and vast for them to comprehend just yet."

At that point Sevareid unilaterally decided to leave France. Without checking with Murrow in London or anyone else at CBS, he wangled passage on the *Ville de Liége*, a freighter of Belgian registry that turned out to be the *American Farmer* under a new flag. A year earlier she had carried Larry LeSueur to England for the beginning of his adventure; now she was taking a disillusioned and heartsore Sevareid away from the rot of the shining place he had dreamed about as a boy.

As the freighter, bound for England, steamed away from Bordeaux, Sevareid looked back at the thick black ribbon of refugees stretching for miles along the shore, people who had reached the end of the line and who could now only stare out at the lucky ones who were getting away.

◆

In Berlin, Bill Shirer was having lunch in the courtyard of the Adlon when he heard about the fall of Paris. The news fell on him like a hammer blow. When he was asked a short time later if he wanted to cover Hitler's visit to the French capital, his first impulse was to say no. But this was the story of a lifetime, and he felt he had to be there even if, as he wrote in his diary, it would be "the saddest assignment of my life."

Three days later his party arrived in Paris by car. The day was warm and silken, a day for enjoying a leisurely lunch on the terrace of Le Dôme or sailing toy boats in the pond in the Tuileries or strolling up the Champs-Élysées. But nobody was doing any of those things. Today everyone remained indoors. Today Germans were rumbling through Paris. As Shirer and some Nazi officers drove down familiar boulevards, the Germans, in high spirits, pointed out familiar landmarks. Shirer saw nothing but ghosts. Over here was the restaurant where he and the lovely, married Yvonne would often rendezvous, over there the café where he and Thurber and the rest of the *Tribune* crowd drank and laughed and debated the merits of Hemingway, Fitzgerald, and Joyce. Shirer gazed straight ahead: from the Arc de Triomphe, the blood-red swastika flag of the Reich fluttered in the gentle breeze.

After two days in Paris, Shirer picked up a tip from one of his German army sources that the armistice would be signed in the woods of Compiègne, north of Paris, where Germany had been forced to sign the humiliating surrender that ended World War I. Shirer rushed to Compiègne. There he discovered German army engineers tearing out the wall of the museum that housed the railroad car in which the 1918 surrender had been signed. The car, he was told, was to be moved to the exact spot where it had stood twenty-two years earlier.

The next afternoon, in a clearing surrounded by elms, oaks, and cypresses, Shirer watched the armistice participants arrive. First came Hitler, who stepped from his black Mercedes and stood briefly at the monument to France's 1918 triumph, then strode toward the clearing and the railroad car. The Führer's expression was grave, but Shirer noticed a "certain spring in his step." The French generals, their faces like marble, arrived and climbed into the railroad car. They listened, expressionless, as General Wilhelm Keitel began reading the terms of the armistice. Hitler did not speak. Finally, while Keitel was still reading, he got to his feet, shot his arm out in the Nazi salute, and left the car, his aides scurrying to keep up. Keitel continued reading.

The actual signing of the armistice was to take place the following day, but at breakfast Shirer learned that Hitler had ordered all correspondents, foreign and German, to be flown back to Berlin. Nuts to that, Shirer thought. He would damn well stay and, if possible, broadcast from Compiègne. Shirer, along with William Kerker, an NBC stringer, caught a ride to the surrender site with Shirer's army friend, who told them that Hitler had ordered all radio reports recorded in Berlin and held for later broadcast.

Minutes after the armistice was signed, Shirer sat in front of a microphone next to the German communications van and repeated over and over, "William L. Shirer calling CBS and NBC in New York, calling CBS and NBC from Compiègne, France." Shirer's army source had asked him to broadcast to both networks, and he agreed, even though he was sure his effort was futile. He went ahead anyway, not knowing if anyone was listening, glancing occasionally at his notes and describing without emotion the extraordinary events he'd witnessed that sun-dappled afternoon. He spoke for almost thirty minutes, outlining in precise and painful detail Hitler's humiliation of the French. As he finished the broadcast and relinquished the microphone to Kerker, who was to give further details, it began to rain. Shirer noticed that German engineers were already moving the railroad car.

"Where to?" he called to them.

"Berlin," they answered.

Shirer's report turned out to be the biggest story of his journalistic career. The next morning he learned that a technician in Berlin had thrown the wrong switch and sent his broadcast directly to New York.

At CBS they had picked up Shirer's call, and he had beaten everyone to the story, including the Germans, by nearly six hours. Hitler later ordered a full investigation. Shirer's army source hinted to him that the army had deliberately relayed his broadcast, because the High Command resented Hitler's effrontery at holding up such wonderful news. The victory after all was the army's, not the Führer's.

◆

Aboard the *Ville de Liége*, Eric Sevareid sat in the captain's cabin, listening apprehensively to the far-off burst of bombs, when someone flipped a radio on. He heard Bill Shirer's cool, flat voice from the woods of Compiègne. It was over now, really over. Emotions were running high everywhere. Yet all Sevareid felt was emptiness.

He lay in his bunk for much of the rest of the trip, overcome by the exhaustion of what he considered a personal defeat. His family had left, he had lost most of his personal possessions, and, far worse, he had cut and run from France without permission from CBS. He had practically killed himself to broadcast the story from Tours and Bordeaux, but the network had probably never received any of his broadcasts. He might not even have a job anymore. They'd fire him as soon as they found out where he was.

The thought of Ed Murrow in London bothered him most. Sevareid didn't think he could ever look Ed in the eye again, after all the faith Murrow had put in him.

When the *Ville de Liége* docked in Liverpool and Sevareid phoned Murrow to tell him what he had done, his fears and worries suddenly evaporated like the morning mist. "This is the best news I've had for a long time!" Murrow said. "We've all been in a sweat about you people. You know, you and Taylor have pulled off one of the greatest broadcasting feats there ever was. Come on to London. There's work to be done here."

Clapperless Bells

T O A B E M U S E D and still deeply troubled Eric Sevareid, the essence of what it meant to be English in that lovely and dangerous early summer of 1940 was captured by the bell ringers who kept practicing even after all the bells in all the steeples and belfries in all of bell-mad England had been rendered silent. The British government had decreed that no bells, church or otherwise, were to be rung for the duration of the war except in the event of a German invasion. All over England, clappers were removed to prevent false alarms. Shortly after Sevareid's escape from France, he reported watching English church-bell ringers in a small town who kept on pulling the ropes as if the silent bells still made wonderful music: "If I could tell you in a sentence, which I can't, why they do it, then I could explain in a sentence what distinguishes the British from their European neighbors. Imagine a rational Frenchman or National Socialist German ringing a noiseless bell."

After the panic and despair of France, Sevareid was beguiled by the legendary pluck of the British. But was pluck enough? England seemed certain to be Hitler's next target, and as Sevareid studied London's stolid and insistent normality, he remembered the screaming Stuka bombers, the relentless panzers, and he thought it was not. Nevertheless, Britain wasn't Hitler's simply for the taking. Before an all-out German amphibious invasion could occur, the Luftwaffe would have to confront the Royal Air Force and rid the skies of British planes.

The Battle of Britain was about to begin.

✦

It seemed the essence of unreality to cover the battle from the grassy, chalky, flower-strewn heights of Shakespeare Cliff above the Straits of Dover, with thirteenth-century Dover Castle brooding behind. But each morning at the siren's first wail, reporters strapped on their steel helmets and rushed from the seedy Grand Hotel and up the steep cliff, there to do the unreal. The show began — you could set your watch by it — at 8:30 A.M. every day. The German bombers and fighters would arrive first, buzzing across the channel like flies. Then the Royal Air Force would swarm up to meet them. Suddenly the air was full of planes, circling, dodging, diving — looking to Larry LeSueur as if they were on "a great roller coaster."

Now and then a plane plummeted, sometimes a white parachute drifted gently down. On the ground antiaircraft guns opened up with a hellish roar that you could hear for miles. It was over in minutes. Quiet would settle once again over the hillside, broken only by the drowsy buzzing of bees and the lapping of waves. Correspondents stretched out and napped in the warm sun, waiting for the next fight at 11:30, followed by another at 3:30 and a final one at about 7 P.M. Then it was back to the Grand's bar or the Maid of Honor or the King Lear for drinks.

Despite the courage and resourcefulness of the British Hurricane and Spitfire fighter pilots, the story of the Battle of Britain quickly lost its allure for many of the journalists on the cliff. Most saw the dogfights as a preliminary to a full-scale German invasion. That would be the *real* story! At one point in the two-and-a-half-month battle, Sevareid reported, three of his colleagues constructed a fake war monument out of a concrete slab and a tomato can with some wilted poppies in it. The sign on the slab read: "Here lie three pressmen who died of boredom waiting for the invasion, 1940."

What the reporters on the cliff were watching was, of course, a defining moment in the war. Thanks to British resolve, Nazi blunders, and British radar, Germany was unable to gain control of the skies over England, and Hitler had to postpone and eventually cancel the invasion, code-named Operation Sea Lion. Still, there were only so many ways you could describe a dogfight, only so many interviews you could conduct with the pilots, only so many statistics, so many British claims and German counterclaims you could report before you began repeating yourself. Besides, the air war was remote, impersonal. War was *people*, Murrow kept insisting. How could you tell America about these airborne British knights if you couldn't see their faces?

Formally, the Battle of Britain lasted from August 13 to October 31, 1940. But as September began, the frustrated Hitler and Reichsmarschall Göring, commander of the Luftwaffe, changed the subject. The Germans suddenly began hitting British cities with their heavy bombers in that prolonged reign of terror known as the Blitz. The first concentrated bombing attack on London occurred late on the afternoon of September 7. Now the war was no distant drama witnessed in bored safety. The victims weren't soldiers on the battlefield; they might be your vicar, your grocer, your next-door neighbor, your wife, your infant daughter, you.

In a sense the Blitz was what Edward R. Murrow had been preparing for since he arrived in Europe in 1937. Here was the perfect event for the new breed of radio journalists. It had immediacy, human drama, and *sound* — sirens, bombs falling and exploding, antiaircraft guns. Murrow had been arguing that the future of radio news lay in on-the-scene reporting, not in an announcer's reading wire copy in New York and not in Monday-morning quarterbacking by some commentator. He and the Boys who joined him in London were ideally positioned to prove his point.

Indeed, the balance had already tilted in Murrow's favor. Sometime between Germany's invasion of Poland and the start of the Blitz, the men in New York, overwhelmed by events and the sheer talent and energy of Murrow and the people he was hiring, retreated. Paul White would still exert a degree of administrative control over the European news operation, but the notion that Murrow and his Boys were, first and foremost, arrangers of broadcasts by other people was dead. In the terror of the Blitz, they tested the creative limits of their new freedom and power within CBS. And this time they weren't just standing on the sidelines. They were participants.

✦

September 7 was hot and sunny in London, another in that year's unusually long string of beautiful summer days. Larry LeSueur and Eric Sevareid were spending the afternoon at a public swimming pool just outside the city. Sevareid was floating in the pool when he heard the buzz of planes overhead. Looking up, he saw black crosses on the planes' wings. He scrambled out of the pool and, according to LeSueur, yelled, "Don't go into the water, Larry. You know it's noncompressible!" (A half-century later, LeSueur would laugh about the remark: "I still don't know what the hell he meant.") In a minute or so the sky over London was suffused with a fiery red glow.

LeSueur and Sevareid raced back to London. Using the brightest fires as beacons, they headed for the East End docks and overcrowded tenements. For more than a week the Germans had been sporadically dropping bombs on London, but the damage from all those raids combined couldn't compare with this inferno. In his broadcast that night, Sevareid told how flames swept through dockyards, oil tanks, factories, flats, sending towering pillars of black, oily smoke into the sky. Apartment houses lost their roofs and upper stories; a small church was completely blasted away.

"Good Lord, they just rained from heaven," an air-raid warden, his face black with soot, told LeSueur and Sevareid. "I'm just glad to be alive." Hundreds were killed in that first raid, thousands injured or driven from their homes. From a basement window two wardens carefully lifted a man's body out of the rubble. Under a blood-red moon, women, their faces vacant and dazed, pushed prams piled high with their salvaged belongings over the glass powder in the streets.

Beginning that evening, London endured fifty-seven straight nights of relentless bombing. As darkness fell, sirens all over the city would issue their deep quavering alarms, and for the next eight hours or more, Londoners would endure the hum of the bombers, the scream and roar of the bombs, the crash and thunder of the antiaircraft guns. Sometimes great landmarks like St. Paul's and the Houses of Parliament and Buckingham Palace were hit. Much more often the targets were flats and shops. When dawn broke, the city's residents would creep wearily from their foul-smelling underground shelters to see if they still had homes and neighbors.

Murrow and the Boys, working around the clock, surviving on coffee and cigarettes, wanted to get across how terrifying the lives of Londoners had become. Murrow implied both terror and courage by beginning each broadcast with his famous "This . . . is London" opening, delivered with a portentous pause between the first two words (suggested in a letter from his Washington State speech professor, Ida Lou Anderson), often with bombs exploding in the background. Another way of bringing the effects of the Blitz home to Americans was to describe in painstaking detail how people went about their lives as their world threatened to shatter.

In one broadcast Sevareid talked about the coming of evening in London, a city that smelled constantly of smoke.

People walk rapidly. They glance at their watches. If they stop to buy a paper, they stuff it in their pocket and hurry on. They run for darkened buses or stand in the middle of the street, impatiently whistling for taxis that go speeding by. Mothers are walking rapidly, pushing baby buggies, looking at the sky and thinking they're hearing a siren each time a car starts up in second gear.

Another time he described how firemen probed the rubble of an apartment house for bodies, while on the other side of the street, fruit peddlers resumed their trade. Holding up a bunch of ripe bananas, one peddler shouted, "The last one going, and it's cheap."

In a particularly notable program called "London After Dark," Murrow, LeSueur, and Sevareid, along with six other American and British journalists, reported on the nighttime sights and sounds of the city. In Trafalgar Square, Murrow kept silent for a moment, letting his audience listen to the air-raid siren in the background and to the muffled hum of traffic. Then he said, "I'll just ooze down in the darkness alongside these steps and see if I can pick up the sound of people's feet." Here was the Murrow method at its experimental best. He laid his microphone on the steps of St. Martin's-in-the-Fields church, picking up the click-click-and-grind of heels and soles on the pavement. "One of the strangest sounds one can hear in London in these dark nights," Murrow said, "is the sound of footsteps along the street, like ghosts shod with steel shoes."

From the Hammersmith Palais, London's largest dance hall, listeners heard the haunting strains of "A Nightingale Sang in Berkeley Square" before Eric Sevareid announced he was standing in the middle of a vast dance floor with more than a thousand dancers swirling around him. There had been an air-raid siren, but the orchestra leader said the band would keep playing if anyone wanted to stay. Only half a dozen or so left. "This is not Mayfair," Sevareid said. "Nobody comes here to be seen or to see. They come here to dance, for the pure pleasure of dancing. And any American who thinks the British are a phlegmatic race should see them dancing around me tonight. These shopgirls, these clerks, these workers, these people who make up the stuff of England, dance wonderfully well."

The next day the *Christian Science Monitor* said "London After Dark" managed to convey "a message which newspapers, even with the most brilliant reporting, photography and editing, cannot deliver." Belittling radio news was no longer so fashionable. Broadcasting's breathtaking potential had been realized in those "bright days and livid nights." No other medium could do what radio did, especially in the literate, intelligent hands of Murrow and his Boys. Even the newspapers were admitting as much now. "The men, the instrument, the moment were perfectly met," Sevareid later wrote. "It has never been quite the same since, [in] radio or television. . . . What counts is the word."

Murrow, who four years earlier had been snubbed by the foreign correspondents' association, was now the only London correspondent whom most Americans could identify by name. And now more than ever he was driven by a sense of purpose. As he wrote to a friend during the Blitz, "The thing that's most obvious is that if the light of the world is to come from the West, somebody had better start building some bonfires."

Listening to Murrow's reports was like hearing an old friend describe the threatened destruction of other friends and their entire world. Murrow's listeners trusted him. If he implied, as he did more and more often, that England couldn't go it alone, that America would have to join the fight, well, maybe he was right. In September 1940 a Gallup poll showed that only 16 percent of Americans favored providing more U.S. aid to Britain. One month later, as bombs fell on London, and Murrow and the Boys brought the reality of it into American living rooms, 52 percent thought more aid should be sent.

Thanks to CBS's new impact, Murrow became the most sought-after American in London. He dined with the Churchills, was courted by society hostesses, was invited to country house parties by aristocrats. The flat he and Janet maintained at 84 Hallam Street — just a couple of blocks from the BBC's Broadcasting House, where Murrow and the Boys went on the air — became a gathering place for generals, dukes, members of Parliament, and cabinet officials, as well as journalists. With Ed presiding, they drank and played poker and debated far into the night. Janet, as she pointedly said, was "kept busy providing food and drink."

The boy from Polecat Creek loved hobnobbing with the rich and powerful in the upper strata of the British class system. But the politics of the people he courted and who courted him were not necessarily his own. On the contrary, he became more and more committed to the liberal — the essentially American — notion that if this war was about anything, it was about the well-being and the future of ordinary people. War had a purpose beyond the defeat of Germany and certainly beyond the restoration of the status quo ante. The postwar world had to commit itself to the eradication of poverty, inequality, and injustice.

Most of the Murrow Boys shared that vision. They were dreamers and romantics, embarked on a quest for a better world. In the fiery hell of the Blitz they foresaw, among other things, the melting down of old class-ridden England and the forging of a new nation. Said Sevareid, "Men who had so suffered and achieved in common would no longer fear one another's clothes, accents, or manners but would regard one another in terms of true worth." It was a thoroughly Utopian vision. Years later Sevareid, famous, affluent, and somewhat disappointed, looked back on those terrible, wonderful days with a wistful fondness. They were, he said, "our Camelot."

✦

They seemed to have so much in common, Murrow and Sevareid. But try as Sevareid would — and he tried very hard — he was never as close as he wanted to be to the man he worshiped. Oh, he was invited to the Murrow apartment for dinner often enough, and he and Murrow would sometimes sit by the fireplace after the late-night broadcast, drinking Scotch while the ack-ack guns crashed in the distance and Murrow spun stories of the big rough Swedes he had known in the lumber camps. "In those moments," Sevareid recalled, "his laughter had the gaiety of boyhood."

For Sevareid, however, the moments were too few. He suffered with the knowledge that Murrow plainly preferred the company of a man who was, in most respects, Sevareid's opposite: the outgoing, tough, confident, and cool Larry LeSueur. And LeSueur took a certain pleasure in Sevareid's second-place status. He thought Sevareid had behaved badly by asking him to stay with Lois in Paris on weekends while Sevareid, dressed in riding boots and a uniform he'd designed himself, supposedly traipsed off to the front. And there was the incident in Tours, when Sevareid had refused to share the story. Their competition continued in London, and in one aspect at least — the rivalry for Murrow's attention — LeSueur was the clear winner. "Ed loved Larry LeSueur," Sevareid admitted. "Larry was terribly easygoing and relaxed and funny, and he was good for Ed, I thought. No, I was a much more uptight sort of fellow."

That was the irony: Sevareid was too much like Murrow for Murrow's taste — depressive, shy, and repressed. Every now and then Murrow would lapse into one of his famous "black" moods, would scowl and stare hopelessly at the floor and take another drag on that ever-present cigarette and not utter a word for as long as the blackness was upon him. "Ed is a sufferer," Janet Murrow used to say. He gravitated to those who could draw him out, make him laugh, argue with him. Larry LeSueur could do that.

LeSueur was "a marvelously ebullient, cheerful chap," said Geoffrey Cox of the *Daily Express.* "His success with the ladies was quite remarkable. He had the capacity to walk into any room, and the most beautiful girl would instantly gravitate to Larry." In that fall and winter of 1940, Murrow and LeSueur worked together, dined together, drank together late into the nights at Murrow's apartment, often with correspondents and editors from the BBC. LeSueur even moved in with the Murrows for a brief time after his own apartment was bombed. The frustrated young man from New York had come a long way in only a year. He and Murrow "lived each other's lives," he recalled. "I was very, very close to him."

Sometimes the two men would slip away before the evening bombing to play golf on a little nine-hole public course at Hampstead Heath with James Reston of the *New York Times* and other duffers from the journalistic community. It was a weird experience. The fairways were pitted with craters, and some areas were roped off because of unexploded bombs. If a ball rolled inside the ropes, it was considered an unplayable lie.

Theirs was a largely male world. Although the occasional female correspondent or researcher did manage to elbow her way into the circle, as a rule the male correspondents in London spent more time with each other than with their wives, girlfriends, or mistresses. Janet Murrow, for one, often felt superfluous. Murrow encouraged her to rent a house in the country, where she could live safely; Murrow and his pals would join her on weekends. She went along with this arrangement for a while, but the men rarely showed up. "They didn't want to leave the excitement in London," she said. She finally gave up the house.

Even in town she played second fiddle. During Murrow's frequent late-night bull sessions, when the whiskey was flowing freely and the cigarette smoke choked the very oxygen from the air, Janet was more often than not in bed. (She herself quit smoking forever during the Blitz because the windows had to be closed against the bombing, and the air inside became so noxious she could hardly stand it.) She was all the more appreciative on those rare occasions when Murrow asked her to do a broadcast, usually on some "woman's angle," for CBS. "I was finally being allowed to *talk* about something," she said. She had a good radio voice — melodious and deep — but Murrow seemed reluctant to put her on the air very often. "I think he doesn't want me to give him competition!" she confided in a letter to her parents. "He likes me to be busy and prominent and successful, but not in his line."

Murrow and Larry LeSueur often dined together at L'Étoile, a fashionable French restaurant not far from their studio in Broadcasting House. Even when the bombs fell uncomfortably close, Murrow insisted that they take the table beneath the restaurant's great glass skylight. Courage had become the most important standard by which one was judged in those terror-filled days, and Murrow went beyond even the stiff upper lip. He was constantly testing his courage, and he expected the Boys to do the same. LeSueur easily passed muster; Sevareid often did not.

A favorite story of Murrow's was about the time he and LeSueur were walking back to Broadcasting House from L'Étoile and the sirens began to wail and the bombs fell so close they could feel the ground shake. They walked on. Finally, with the bombs practically on top of them, they threw themselves to the pavement. "We were lying there, very foolish," Murrow said, "and Larry looked at me and said, 'You know, Ed, this can be dangerous.'" Murrow couldn't help but laugh. (According to LeSueur, that's not exactly the way it happened. "Actually, he was on the ground, flat out, and I was kneeling. I didn't want to get my suit dirty. . . . It's the only time I ever could look down on Ed.") .

Another time Murrow and LeSueur were trapped in a hail of bombs, and LeSueur — whose devil-may-care attitude was seen by some as a kind of absentminded obliviousness — was so bedazzled by the weird pyrotechnic beauty that he just stood there, gaping, while Murrow took cover.

"Get down, you goddamned fool!" Murrow finally bellowed. Only then did the transfixed LeSueur hit the pavement.

The CBS correspondents lived and worked in one of the most heavily bombed sections of London, a neighborhood of elegant Regency townhouses and small apartment buildings just south of Regent's Park. Looming over the neighborhood was the BBC's parabolic Broadcasting House, a magnet for German bombers during the war. The building, fortified by sandbags and more heavily guarded than 10 Downing Street, received only one direct hit during the Blitz. The many other German bombs aimed at it fell instead on the nearby buildings. CBS was bombed out of three offices in the neighborhood; the windows of a fourth were smashed.

One evening at his flat on Portland Place, directly across from the BBC, LeSueur was working on his script for the nightly broadcast. German bombers were particularly active that night, the antiaircraft guns so thunderous that he adjourned to the quiet subbasement of the BBC to finish writing. He had just arrived when he heard a tremendous crash. The building shook, bricks and beams fell, plaster showered down. The overhead pipes in the studio burst. A bomb had exploded on Portland Place, smashing LeSueur's apartment house and others around it.

As in France when he missed the troop ship, he had escaped death by minutes. But he didn't have time to consider his luck. The BBC ordered the building evacuated because of flooding water and sewage from the broken pipes, and LeSueur still had a broadcast to do. He grabbed his military censor, and together they found a cab to take them to another BBC facility. The bombing continued, and the shaken censor soon decided he'd had enough for one night. At a stoplight he bailed out. When LeSueur finally made it to the other BBC building, he was told he could not broadcast because he had no censor with him.

That was another story Murrow loved. So there was Larry in Broadcasting House, he told a colleague, "with bricks and beams falling all about his ears, and, worst of all, these pipes overhead busted, and — here's the payoff — one of them is a sewer pipe." Not long before the raid, Murrow and LeSueur had seen the Alfred Hitchcock movie *Foreign Correspondent*. They thought the ending, where the hero broadcasts in the midst of an air raid, tame. "Hollywood," Murrow said, "would never think of a sewer pipe."

How could the melancholy Sevareid, always in doubt about his own courage, possibly compete with such sangfroid? He was a better writer than LeSueur, and at least as good a reporter. But when it came to being hail-fellow-well-met, when it came to macho strutting and storytelling, Sevareid could only step aside for Murrow and LeSueur. He not only wasn't cool under fire, he was scared — really *scared* — when the bombs fell, and it didn't help when LeSueur joked that Sevareid's problem was that he didn't drink enough.

It was Sevareid's hope and dream that he could be as poised, "at least on the surface," as Murrow and LeSueur. Before Belgium that had been easy enough, because he didn't consider the possibility that something might actually happen to *him*. "Somehow I had had the idea that war correspondents were a privileged, unhittable species," he wrote. But when the Germans dropped bombs near his hotel on the Belgian border and, later, on the buildings of London, he realized no one was safe. "And God!" he said, "the terrifying violence of bombs nearby, how they stunned the mind, ripped the nerves, and turned one's limbs to water!"

Sevareid had tested himself so many times — on the canoe trip, in the gold fields, on the rails back to Minnesota — and had passed every test. Now, when it really counted and the prize was Murrow's favor, he failed. One particular evening stood out in his memory. He was in the lobby of a hotel, about to join Murrow for dinner in the dining room, when a small bomb hit the hotel roof. In the lobby plaster dust fell like snow, and water gushed from the ceiling. Sevareid hurried into the dining room, shouting, "Ed, I think we've been hit."

Murrow, "cold as ice," looked up at him. "No, that's at least as far away as Oxford Circus."

Murrow was annoyed, he could tell. "He thought I was being nervous." But, Sevareid insisted, "we *had* been hit."

Sevareid thought Murrow was "afraid of being afraid," and that may have been close to the truth. Murrow said he refused to take refuge in underground shelters, because "if I started doing it I'm afraid I might not stop."

In 1967 Sevareid said in a speech, "It was extraordinary, the command [Murrow] had of our hearts and allegiance. His frown, if you did badly, left you in purgatory; his grin of approbation handed you heaven for the day." During the Blitz, Sevareid found it harder and harder to win Murrow's approbation. While LeSueur and Murrow tried to outdo each other in courage, Sevareid crept cautiously along the sidewalks, flattening himself against walls when the screaming came closer and not infrequently "doing the last fifty yards at a dead run." He was spending more time in underground shelters, while the other two CBS correspondents occasionally watched raids from the rooftops.

A month after the Blitz began, Sevareid conceded defeat. He was sick and exhausted, and he hadn't seen his wife and the twins in some four months. CBS agreed to bring him home. He didn't want to leave — despite his fear and internal conflicts, he was exhilarated by his three months as a Londoner — but he felt he had no choice. In his final broadcast from London, Sevareid was surely talking about his own inner conflicts and self-doubt when he contrasted his departure from a dying Paris with his leaving a resolved and determined London.

Paris died like a beautiful woman, in a coma, without struggle, without knowing or even asking why. One left Paris with a feeling almost of relief. London one leaves with regret. Of all the great cities of Europe, London alone behaves with pride and battered but stubborn dignity. . . . London fights down her fears every night, takes her blows and gets up again every morning. You feel yourself an embattled member of this embattled corps. The attraction of courage is irresistible. Parting from London, you see clearly what she is and means. London may not be England, but she is Britain and she is the incubator of America and the West. Should she collapse, the explosion in history would never stop its echoing. Besieged, London is a city-state in the old Greek sense. Someone wrote the other day, "When this is all over, in years to come, men will speak of this war and say, 'I was a soldier,' 'I was a sailor,' or 'I was a pilot.' Others will say with equal pride, 'I was a citizen of London.'"

During the broadcast Sevareid could not hold his voice steady. Ashamed that he hadn't matched Murrow's coolness, he felt that what he'd said had been "filled with bathos, mawkish and embarrassing to all who heard it." When he was safely back in the States, however, people sought him out to tell him how deeply touched they'd been. A businessman who was driving when he heard the broadcast had to pull over to the side of the road for a moment to regain his composure; a professor of English told Sevareid that he had cried when he heard the broadcast in his bedroom and had had to bathe his eyes before going downstairs for dinner.

When Murrow drove Sevareid to Waterloo Station for the first leg of his trip home, Sevareid knew he would have to return, would have to come to terms with the fear that had vanquished him. He would have to regain Murrow's respect. And his own.

✦

Bill Shirer, too, was going home, driven not by fear or illness but by frustration and weariness, rage and ambition. Above all, ambition.

He was thirty-six years old, a fact he noted with dismay in his diary on February 23, 1940: "My birthday. Thought of being thirty-six now, and nothing accomplished, and how fast the middle years fleet by." He had always been haunted by the passage of time, by what he thought of as his failure to live up to his youthful dreams. For a while he and Murrow had been consumed with the task of creating a new kind of journalism. But after getting a start on that, the exhilaration — for Shirer anyway — vanished. He found himself submerged in the dreariness and lies of Berlin and struggling against the tightening vise of German censorship, all too aware that Murrow was capturing the attention of America with his vivid word-pictures of the Blitz.

At the beginning of the Battle of Britain, Shirer worked hard to present an accurate and fair view of what was happening in Germany. When the Nazis tried to persuade him to broadcast that an invasion of England was imminent, he refused because he had taken a trip to the English Channel and had seen no signs of German preparations. On the other hand, when the British claimed they had heavily bombed Hamburg in one of their first raids on German cities, Shirer reported that his tour of the port city revealed almost no damage at all. Throughout this phase of the war, both he and Murrow took pains to point out the widely divergent German and British claims of enemy bombers downed, implying to listeners that neither side was to be believed. "We're over here to try to get the truth if possible, a very difficult assignment these days," Shirer said dryly in one broadcast.

After Britain began bombing Berlin on August 25 — the event that prompted Hitler to order the Blitz — the Nazis launched a shrill propaganda campaign claiming that the bombs were intentionally aimed at women and children, while the Luftwaffe bombed only military targets in London. Somehow, on September 9, Shirer managed to say in a broadcast, "Many Englishmen probably didn't realize how many military objectives were hidden away in London." Another time, when the German censors forbade any mention that the Ruhr was being heavily bombed, he broadcast that contrary to British claims of having bombed Berlin, the city was so quiet that businessmen from the Ruhr went there to get some sleep. Shirer would not be able to get away with this sort of thing much longer.

The Nazis had begun to find censors who understood the nuances of American speech — the idioms, aphorisms, and special inflections that Shirer had used to such good effect. More and more, the censors were shredding his scripts until they made no sense at all. Arguing with them did no good, but he argued anyway. Once his script was so hacked up that he refused to go on the air. He learned later that a German radio official that day had cabled Paul White in New York: REGRET SHIRER ARRIVED TOO LATE TO BROADCAST.

When the British hit factories, gasworks, and railroads in Berlin, the censors insisted that Shirer report that the bombs had fallen far from any military or industrial targets. He could no longer use the words "Nazi" or "invasion" on the air. He couldn't call Germany "aggressive" or "militaristic" or anything else that might create an unfavorable impression in neutral America. He was forbidden to report bombing raids as they occurred, and, just in case a raid should begin while he was on the air, he was required to hold a small microphone next to his lips so that the roar of antiaircraft guns and the thud of bombs would not be picked up. Shirer had been reduced, he wrote in his diary, to "rebroadcasting the official communiqués, which are lies, and which any automaton can do. Even the more intelligent and decent of my censors ask me in confidence why I stay." When he complained about the censorship to Paul White, White cabled back: BILL WE THOROUGHLY UNDERSTAND, SYMPATHIZE CONDITION IN BERLIN BUT FEEL WE MUST CARRY ON WITH BROADCASTS EVEN IF ONLY READING OFFICIAL STATEMENTS AND NEWSPAPER TEXTS.

The hell with that, Shirer thought. If that's all New York wanted, the bastards could "hire a Nazi-American student for $50 a week to read that crap!"

At last Shirer advised New York that a friendly German official had told him the Nazis were building an espionage case against him. For this reason, if no other, he had to leave. "Ordinarily — and I was very conscious of this — you do not desert your post, especially in wartime," he wrote in his memoirs. "But I had no intention of letting the Nazis frame me as a spy." Joseph Harsch, who reported from Berlin for the *Christian Science Monitor* and who was a friend of Shirer's, doubted that the Germans were preparing any trumped-up spy charges. "I don't believe he was ever in any danger," Harsch said. "I don't believe he was ever really hassled. I think that was the result of his imagination. He wasn't all that much more critical of them overtly than any of the rest of us." Howard K. Smith, a future CBS colleague of Shirer's who at that time was reporting from Berlin for United Press, agreed. Shirer wanted to leave because he knew there was no future for him in Berlin, Smith said. "He could feel the pressure. They were cutting his broadcasts. He wasn't going to be a star anymore because his scripts weren't going to be very good. He got out of Germany at the right time."

The key was Shirer's diary. He had been keeping one, off and on, since childhood, but this time he was doing it with the idea of publishing. He had witnessed Hitler's rise and had recorded in his diary what he saw, heard, thought, and believed, censoring nothing and pulling no punches. If ever there was a time to share his musings with the world — and do it profitably — now was that time. Besides, his wife and daughter had already returned to the States.

Having received no satisfaction from Paul White about leaving Berlin, he went directly to Bill Paley, who agreed to an unpaid three-month leave so Shirer could work on a book based on his diary. CBS did not, however, promise him reemployment if he chose not to return to Berlin.

It wasn't much of a deal — in fact, it was quite a gamble — but it was better than getting fired. Smuggling the diary past Gestapo officials at the airport, Shirer left Berlin on December 5, en route to America.

◆

But first he would stop in Lisbon for a reunion with Ed Murrow. It had been almost a year since he and Murrow had romped like schoolboys in the Amsterdam snow. In Lisbon they spent seven days together, strolling on the sun-splashed beaches, drinking chilled white wine on café terraces, eating langouste at waterfront restaurants, trying their luck at the casino's gaming tables, hoping to revive the lighthearted fun of Amsterdam. It was impossible. Shirer was preoccupied with his book, and Murrow hated Lisbon. He saw intrigue and decadence and desperation everywhere they went. He was depressed by the sight of well-fed, well-oiled bodies on the beach, of Gestapo agents and British spies at the same roulette tables, of refugees gambling away their last marks or dollars or francs or pesetas, hoping to win enough for passage across the Atlantic.

Receiving word that the CBS office in London had been bombed and that NBC's bureau chief, Fred Bate, a friend, had been seriously wounded in the same raid, Murrow yearned to be back where he belonged. Amsterdam had been a respite. Lisbon was an ending. Shirer was opting out, breaking up a team, leaving behind the closest friend he would ever have. "Ed was annoyed at Bill for going home and cashing in," Larry LeSueur explained. "He never forgave him."

Just before Shirer boarded his ship, he and Murrow silently drank several glasses of brandy at a scruffy little open-air bar near the dock. When the ship's loudspeaker summoned the passengers, they walked over to the gangplank and shook hands. They struggled to speak, but there were no words. Murrow's eyes glistened with tears. Shirer boarded the ship. Making his way to the rail, he searched the waterfront for his friend.

But Ed Murrow was already gone.

✴ 8

A Taste of Fame

T HERE WAS a certain unreality, an impermanence, to this new business of radio journalism in faraway places. When you worked for a newspaper or wire service, the words you wrote would be set in lead type, then printed on paper in neat columns. And even if the newspaper wasn't printed in Europe, someone could send it to you later, and you could hold it in your hand and see your byline and read your story again and maybe paste it into a scrapbook.

But radio was live and thus ephemeral. At strange hours you went into a little room — they called it a studio, but that was just a high-flown name for a space not much bigger than a closet — and you sat down at a cigarette-burned table under a harsh light and read what you had written into a hunk of metal and wire called a microphone. And if the microphone and all the vacuum tubes and wires and cables and transmitters and relays worked, your voice somehow flew out into the air, bound for America.

If you were lucky, an engineer in the studio or in New York might tell you he liked what you had said. If your broadcast made it through all the technical and atmospheric obstacles, maybe one of your bosses would send you a note. And later you could, if you liked, read your script to yourself over a drink and pretend it was something really permanent or at least more finished than this piece of bad typing with pencil scratches on it. But with the nearest American landfall three thousand miles away, there was almost no sense that you had actually communicated with anyone or that anyone was even listening. You just cast your voice, your words, your thoughts into the air like tiny paper boats into the great raging Atlantic, and they vanished forever, as if they had never existed in the first place.

Eric Sevareid had felt this way when he broadcast from London, sitting before the mike in the BBC's stuffy little underground studio, rank with the essence of cabbage from the cafeteria down the hall. When Sevareid's voice spilled out into the void, it was heard, supposedly, by an audience numbering in the millions, half a world away. But he could never be sure, could never really imagine such a mass of people. Reality to Sevareid was the Londoners he saw on the debris-filled streets every morning, their faces stretched tight with the sleepless tension of the previous night's bombing. His work, he sometimes thought, was trivial and pointless.

✦

Sevareid returned to the States in the fall of 1940 aboard the Pan American Clipper, the huge Sikorsky-built amphibian that flew from Lisbon to Port Washington, New York, in twenty-four hours, more or less, and that offered its passengers, among other amenities, beds and a dining room. In New York, wracked with guilt about running out on Murrow and London, he nevertheless settled easily into the routine at CBS headquarters and began to see how little he and the other Boys understood about the business they were in, about radio's reach, its impact, its importance. The sheer power of the medium had grown phenomenally, and that power would have a radical impact on his life and the lives of his colleagues.

He clearly grasped this for the first time on a street corner in Manhattan shortly after his return from London. It was a warm autumn day. All the cars and taxis had their windows down. As Sevareid stood waiting for the light to change, he realized he could hear Larry LeSueur's voice. LeSueur himself was still in London, of course, dodging bombs with Murrow. Yet Sevareid could clearly hear that familiar, easy voice echoing through Manhattan's skyscraper canyons: Larry was broadcasting from the tight little cabbage-scented closet in the BBC basement, and at almost the same moment his voice was pouring out of the open windows of all these cars and taxis in New York City.

My God, Sevareid thought, *people* are *listening. Millions of them. Every day!* He realized radio was not just "a pantomime in an empty room." Standing there, Sevareid wanted to shout his discovery back to Murrow, LeSueur, and the others with all the passion of a convert: *They're out here, boys! They can hear you!*

And, he might have added, they can — with a little prompting from the ever-alert, ever-active CBS publicity office — make you a star.

✦

Three years earlier, when Sevareid had passed through New York on his way to Europe, he had been an overawed country boy, intimidated, even terrified, by this "unknowable, unconquerable place." Now, with the Depression finally ending, New York was a different city and Sevareid was a different person. For one thing, thanks to the way radio seemed to speed everything up — including the creation of fame — he was suddenly a celebrity.

From the moment he stepped off the Clipper, photographers tailed him, and newspaper and magazine writers clamored for interviews. The hacks and flacks had plenty to work with. There was Sevareid himself — tall and remarkably handsome, with little or no outward sign of the devils that beset him. And there was his lovely wife, Lois, who stood or sat beside him and gazed up adoringly as the flashbulbs popped. And there was the Sevareid story: the birth of the twins; the family's separation in Paris one step ahead of the Nazis; Lois's harrowing transatlantic crossing with the infants in her arms; Eric's thrilling flight just ahead of the German advance, broadcasting all the way to the south of France; his reports on the Battle of Britain and the Blitz.

The CBS publicity machine would have to have been utterly incompetent not to make something of the Eric Sevareid story. And the CBS publicity machine was anything but incompetent. In fact, it was — to the consternation of the other networks — the best in the business.

Bill Paley's press agents didn't even wait for Sevareid to arrive before they swung into action. Several months earlier, a swarm of reporters, photographers, and newsreel cameramen had been on hand when the ship carrying Lois and the twins docked in New York. The journalists invaded their cabin and followed the bewildered mother and her babies back to their hotel. As Lois and the twins made their way from New York to her widowed mother's home in Minnesota, small knots of people, total strangers, gathered to see them at every airplane stop. Finally settled in Minneapolis, where they would remain until Eric arrived from London in the fall, they found the reporters so persistent that Lois's indignant mother promptly locked the doors and took the phone off the hook.

After Eric and Lois were reunited, things became even crazier. Almost everywhere they went, the Sevareid name — and sometimes just Eric's voice — were recognized. New Yorkers wanted his autograph, his opinions, his company. This was the adulation he'd hungered for since childhood, and part of him took great delight in it — and would continue to for the rest of his life. At the same time, he found it overwhelming: he'd had no time and no means to prepare for it. Even if he *had* been prepared, he would have been uncomfortable. He liked going out on the town and being recognized, but he hated being approached by strangers. And deep inside, always, were his insecurity and the scorching knot of guilt that told him he hadn't earned and didn't deserve any of this.

Eric Sevareid felt he had left London a coward. It was difficult, though not quite impossible, to reconcile that feeling with the hero's welcome he received in New York. What's more, he often thought that those who cheered him could see right through him. "When people said, 'Why, you don't look at all as I had imagined,'" he wrote a few years later, "I had again this guilty feeling of being somehow an impostor under my own name."

He had been transported almost overnight from a London bomb shelter to the Manhattan social scene. Even without his guilt, it was an outlandish experience. One night he sat at a table in a nightclub, awaiting an audience with Walter Winchell, the renowned gossip columnist and opinion monger. A young CBS flack, whose only job was getting the network's stars mentioned in Broadway columns, was Sevareid's escort for the evening. "I'm like *that*, see, with Winchell, Runyon, all these guys," said the CBS man, crossing two fingers. "Took me just two years. What a country!"

The great Winchell had agreed to meet Sevareid at midnight. In the meantime Sevareid sat at his table and watched the sleek and confident men and beautiful, world-weary women, while the CBS publicity man downed highballs and saluted passers-by. One of them, a white-haired man whose boredom seemed infinite, grabbed a chair and sat down. "Tell him about London," the flack said to Sevareid. "Give him the lowdown on that Bordeaux thing." As Sevareid struggled to oblige, the man's narrow eyes circled the club, focusing on everyone but the radio correspondent. Then he jumped to his feet, cutting Sevareid off in midsentence. "Send the stuff to my office," he barked.

Losing patience, Sevareid asked the flack, "When does this Winchell character arrive?" The flack's eyes widened. "For Christ's sake, that was Winchell you was just *talking* to!" The next day Sevareid sent Winchell a written account of some of his experiences in France and England. A few days after that, Winchell, as was his occasional wont, turned the material into a column by "guest columnist" Eric Sevareid.

✦

It was hard for Sevareid to realize that many of his fellow Americans were simply not as interested in the events on the other side of the Atlantic as he was. He couldn't understand how New Yorkers could rush around their city, heedlessly following their daily routines, while England stood on the brink. When an ambulance or fire engine shrieked outside his hotel, he would sit bolt upright in bed, sweating, stomach churning, fighting the "hysterical impulse to scream out and order them not to make that terrible sound when there was no need."

On a lecture tour around the country, he found that people wanted more to be entertained than to be informed, and CBS's lecture brochure assured them that Sevareid would not disappoint. In breathless movie-trailer prose, the brochure reported he had "been within a hundred yards of German machine gun nests. . . . He will tell of a besieged Europe, and his story will have the authenticity that can only be acquired by a person who has lived through it." And the performing didn't end with the lectures. There were cocktail parties and receptions and suppers, mostly organized by local society women who valued charm above insight and information. Sevareid didn't like performing but did enjoy the attention, the fame, the extra money. And so he obliged.

He also entertained the idea of earning extra money by writing. In those days many journalists were frustrated novelists or playwrights or even poets, and most journalists, while generally paid better and more regularly than artists, worked for wages that were a long way from lavish. Sevareid's CBS salary, for instance, was $62.50 a week, plus whatever he picked up on the lecture circuit and from sponsored broadcasts. Thus, when a new acquaintance, an executive at Warner Brothers named Jacob Wilk, encouraged him to write a play about the Blitz, with the idea of turning it into a movie later, the young correspondent responded enthusiastically.

The only problem was he didn't know *how* to write a play. Wilk suggested he contact playwright Robert Sherwood, whom Wilk knew, for assistance. The suggestion was stunning in its presumptuousness. At that time Sherwood was perhaps America's most famous playwright. He had won two Pulitzer Prizes and would win his third that year with a war play of his own. The newly celebrated Sevareid was not deterred. The theme of his play would be "the moral regeneration of a whole society." The plot would involve the dissolution of class distinctions among the residents and employees of a London apartment house who spend each night together in an air-raid shelter. "There is something damn silly about class dignity," Sevareid wrote to Sherwood, "when you're in your pajamas and the house is shaking from the last bomb down the street."

Predictably, Sherwood begged off, and Sevareid, unable to find another collaborator, gave up on the idea. Maybe "moral regeneration" was too high-minded a theme for the period, or maybe Sevareid wasn't cut out for the theater. Besides, there was Hollywood to consider. Another Warner executive, Brian Foy, had given Sevareid a great title for a war movie — *Lisbon Clipper* — but Foy had no story to go with it. He urged Sevareid, as a recent passenger on the Clipper, to come up with a plot. Sevareid told a friend he was intrigued with the idea and hoped "to sell a picture story to Warners and to make a good sum on the deal."

The plot that the normally sober-sided, stone-faced Sevareid proposed, in a fifteen-page, double-spaced "treatment," involved an absurdly melodramatic romance between an American vice consul in Lisbon and a beautiful Czech actress who is pursued by the Gestapo. The heroine is also pursued by a young Czech refugee who is in love with her but in thrall to the Nazis. At the climactic moment the young man betrays his Nazi patrons and thwarts their attempt to capture the actress. She and the vice consul scramble aboard the Clipper and head to New York for a better life.

History does not record whether Sevareid ever submitted his treatment to Warner Brothers or whether he ever made a dime out of it. It is, however, interesting to note that just a year later Warner produced *Casablanca*, one of the most popular movies of all time, whose plot bore a certain loose resemblance to that of *Lisbon Clipper.*

In 1946, Sevareid, by far the best writer of nonfiction prose among the Boys, would write an autobiography of lasting historical and literary merit. He was well educated, thoughtful, and erudite, but he had a somewhat mercenary side, which underscored a dichotomy that increasingly characterized not only Sevareid but Murrow and the rest of the Boys: the urge to do right versus the urge to do well.

✦

Bill Shirer was also focusing on doing well. He returned to New York on Christmas Eve, 1940, to the same full-court-press publicity treatment that Sevareid had experienced two months earlier. SHIRER BACK FROM BERLIN, said the headline in the *New York Times*.

Older and more experienced than Sevareid and less given to introspection and guilt, Shirer gloried in the acclaim and quickly began to doubt the wisdom of returning to Berlin. So what if Paley and Paul

White were pressuring him? He didn't have time to worry about that now, not with every book editor in New York clamoring to publish his *Berlin Diary*, and every magazine editor, from *Time*'s Henry Luce to the *Reader's Digest*'s DeWitt Wallace, wanting articles from him. Book-publishing executive Kermit Roosevelt, Theodore's son, invited him to spend a weekend at the family estate in Oyster Bay. In the end, though, Roosevelt didn't get *Berlin Diary*. Shirer gave it instead to Blanche Knopf, the wife and partner of Alfred Knopf. But there was a problem, one that Shirer didn't discover until after he had edited his diary for publication. Alfred Knopf, who disagreed with his wife on practically everything, hated the very idea of Shirer's book and was infuriated that Blanche had paid a $10,000 advance, an impressive figure at the time. "Bill, it won't do," Knopf told Shirer. ". . . [You] can't get a book out of a diary. . . . A good book, Bill, has to have a beginning, a middle and an end."

Knopf wanted Shirer to dump the diary format, but Shirer, who could be extraordinarily stubborn, refused. A short time later he left on a lecture tour, almost as dispirited as when he first arrived in New York. He had been home for three months. His leave of absence was coming to an end, he was (as usual) running out of money, and now, although his book was in galley proofs, there was doubt that it would be published. Then, shortly before the end of his lecture tour, he received a telegram from Alfred Knopf: the Book-of-the-Month Club had chosen *Berlin Diary* as its July 1941 selection. Knopf dropped his objections. He would proceed with publication.

Berlin Diary was an immediate commercial and critical success. Within weeks it was at the top of the bestseller lists and eventually sold more than five hundred thousand copies. Reviewers lauded Shirer's forthright and sometimes passionate witness to the Third Reich's rise to power and its takeover of most of Europe. "It is a human as well as an historical document," said London's *Times Literary Supplement*. "Every entry in the diary grips, both for the matter recorded and for the manner of recording."

With his book's triumph, CBS finally agreed that Shirer could remain in the United States. Paul White came up to Cape Cod, where the Shirers were vacationing that summer, and offered a new contract, including an increase in Shirer's already substantial salary of $150 a week and a Sunday show of his own. In those days the sponsor of a news program paid the star an additional fee (sometimes as much as $1,000 a week) beyond the network's salary, and White assured Shirer that his program would eventually be sponsored. After fifteen years of scratching and scrambling, after being fired time and again, after coming to near-despair at the end of his assignment in Berlin, Shirer was getting just about everything he ever wanted — a book, a program of his own, money, fame.

He had left Europe — and Murrow — far behind. Never much given to looking back, he was not doing so now. But for a few minutes one warm summer evening at the Cape, his special bond with Murrow was revived with stunning intensity. He and Tess were driving along a country road, listening to the car radio, when they heard Murrow deliver a paean to Shirer and *Berlin Diary*. With feeling that seemed to well up from the depths of his soul, Murrow talked about the excellence of the book and the writer, about his friendship with Shirer, about how they'd been radio news pioneers together. While Murrow was speaking, Shirer pulled over to the side of the road, and after the broadcast he and Tess were so emotionally drained they sat there for several minutes, unable to move or speak. Later that summer an obviously lonely Murrow wrote to Shirer, "The job we did together gives me more pride than you can know. Since you left, much has gone out of the job for me."

Shirer valued his relationship with Murrow, but he enjoyed being out from under his friend's huge shadow even more. He discovered that he had his own following among radio listeners — not as great as Murrow's but still substantial. "He was a household name before *Berlin Diary* was published," said Joseph Harsch. "The book made his name just that much more important in radio news."

Before leaving Europe, Shirer had promised Murrow he would come to London in the fall of 1941 to pinch-hit while Murrow took home leave. In a letter that spring he repeated the promise. Perhaps sensing that Murrow wanted him back permanently, however, Shirer stressed that he would return only for the time Murrow was away. "The ignorance of this country about its enemy is titanic," he wrote, "and there is much good work to be done [here]." In the end Shirer reneged on even a temporary return to London. Things were going too well for him in New York, he thought; he would just stay where he was — where he was happy, where he had a name of his own, where he wasn't just one of the Murrow Boys.

Shirer had been all but flat broke when Murrow hired him in 1937. Now he had money and the perquisites of fame: a house in Bronxville; a nanny and maid; invitations to lecture; invitations to join New York's exclusive Century Club and the Council on Foreign Relations. Newspapers and magazines frequently carried stories about him (a story in *Time* was headlined SHIRER CASHES IN), and his name was in all the columns. For a $20,000 fee, he went out to Hollywood as a consultant for a war movie called *Passage from Bordeaux*. "There were times," he wrote later, "when I became rather pleased with myself and enjoyed the limelight, unmindful that in America, especially in broadcasting and papers, fame and notoriety are fleeting." His ego, never small, grew in the soft glow of celebrity the way a light-starved plant responds to the sun.

The principal victim of Shirer's egomania was his wife, Tess. She had given birth to their baby in a Nazi-occupied hospital in Vienna under the most trying conditions. She had run the CBS bureau in Geneva for no pay and no glory while Shirer reported from Berlin. With her toddler daughter, she had embarked on a frightening journey by bus from Geneva through German-occupied France to Spain, where she and Eileen boarded a ship for the States. Tess had endured so much. And now, just when it seemed that she and Shirer could have a normal life, the marriage was confronted with a new challenge. Her name was Tilly Losch.

Losch had been a prima ballerina in Vienna and later a headliner on the London musical stage. When Shirer was in his mid-twenties, he had seen her in a Noel Coward musical and had been instantly smitten. A friend suggested he go backstage to meet her then, but — oddly for Shirer — he was too timid; instead, he contented himself with clipping and saving newspaper articles about her.

More than a decade after he first saw her on stage, Shirer was in his office in New York one day when his old friend John Gunther stopped by. With Gunther were movie directors Frank Capra and Anatole Litvak — and Tilly Losch. Could they sit in on Shirer's broadcast that evening and then take him out for a drink? *Could* they! At "21" that night, he and Losch became engrossed first in conversation, then in each other. "I felt myself falling in love with her," he wrote years later. Soon his wife and his new mistress would each be pleading with him to give up the other. He refused — "In my foolishness, I thought both of them unreasonable."

"Bonnie Prince Charlie"

In LONDON, self-denial remained the order of the day.

Winter 1941 was bitterly cold. Coal supplies, always low, periodically ran out. Food rationing was tighter, clothing scarcer. The worst of the Blitz was over, but German planes still raided the city often enough to keep the strain in Londoners' faces. In that bleak atmosphere Ed Murrow looked around for someone to replace Eric Sevareid. He finally chose Charles Collingwood, a young man who outwardly seemed to be Sevareid's exact opposite.

Collingwood had not been the first choice. Murrow had preferred the elegant and talented Helen Kirkpatrick of the *Chicago Daily News*. But by now Ed Klauber was completely inflexible on the subject of hiring women. So CBS got Collingwood instead, a brash and handsome young popinjay, only twenty-three years old, who had worked less than a year for United Press.

At UP, Collingwood had covered the Blitz full-time. He sat in a little hut on the roof of the building where UP's offices were located, watching the London skyline with field glasses. Using a map of the city, he pinpointed where the bombs fell and phoned their locations down to the news desk. If some area was hit especially hard, Collingwood would grab his helmet and race through the streets to check the damage himself, often dodging shrapnel along the way.

He was thin and wiry, with curly blond hair and a glint of mischief always in his eye. And he dressed as if clothes were the most important thing on earth. It was hard to believe that only a few months earlier he had been a Rhodes Scholar, sipping sherry with black-robed dons and studying the intricacies of medieval law in the magnificent hush of the vaulted library at Oxford.

Starting his UP shift one day, Collingwood received a message that Ed Murrow wanted to have lunch with him at the Savoy. When Murrow, over drinks, mentioned the possibility of hiring him, Collingwood was uncharacteristically speechless. As he wrote to his parents, "I have been around here long enough to know that CBS could get any foreign correspondent in Europe."

So why did Murrow pick this inexperienced kid? First, he liked the contrasting elements he saw in him, especially his aggressiveness and courage as a UP reporter on the one hand and his academic bent as a Rhodes Scholar on the other. Murrow was glad to see that Collingwood hadn't yet been "contaminated by print," meaning that the young man hadn't been with UP long enough to be hobbled by the standard wire service formula of news writing. And it didn't hurt that Collingwood had worked one summer as a surveyor in a national forest. Murrow, who always took great (perhaps exaggerated) pride in his own summer logging-camp experiences, was impressed that Collingwood knew what a surveyor's chain was and — even better — actually knew how to throw one.

As it turned out, Murrow and Collingwood had quite a lot more in common than their experiences as former woodsmen. Collingwood, like Murrow, had a flair for the dramatic; indeed, he too had acted in plays in high school and college. Both had been high school student-body presidents and ROTC cadets. Beginning in their teenage years, both had worked hard, with almost Gatsby-like compulsion, to create an image for themselves, to try to look and sound older and more worldly than they were. And both were extremely good-looking — Murrow in a rugged way, Collingwood in a prettier, more delicate way. To BBC correspondent Pat Smithers, Collingwood "looked exactly like the dummy out of a rather good tailor shop window: impeccably dressed, with a collar too high for him, so that he looked as if he were about to choke. Very broad shoulders; crimped, curly hair. A very strange chap, we thought, to be a war correspondent. How wrong we were . . . how wrong we were."

Collingwood had a dazzling smile and a vague air of mystery and danger that worked wonders with many women, while others, men *and* women, found him too much the dandy. In fact, at their first meeting, Murrow had been put off by Collingwood's sartorial splendor, particularly his faddish orange argyle socks. Sensing this, Collingwood tried to hide the socks, tugging his trousers down and tucking his feet under the chair. Murrow obviously chose not to remember that when he was Collingwood's age and even older, he was a bit of a dandy himself. In

1935 he had arrived in London decked out in a boater and white flannels and swinging a cane.

But Murrow seemed to like Collingwood, argyles and all. Perhaps he understood that beneath the flash, this young man was another tortured and self-doubting soul who wanted someone to follow, someone to whom he could give unconditional loyalty. For despite Collingwood's apparent savoir faire and hint of recklessness, despite his good looks and his way with women, despite his clothes and his intelligence, despite his sense of humor and his courage, he was a man whose insecurities were probably even greater than Sevareid's. And, like Sevareid and others yet to come, Collingwood would find in Murrow an answer for his pain. "Charles idolized Murrow, absolutely," said his nephew, Harris Collingwood. "He just worshiped the guy. He thought Murrow was everything he could ever aspire to. I think the war and CBS news were what Charles had instead of a happy childhood."

Consciously or unconsciously, Murrow chose people who *needed* him. Most of his correspondents came from homes broken by death or divorce or were otherwise unhappy or uncertain in profoundly affecting ways. Most had distant, damaged, or nonexistent relationships with their fathers. Murrow wasn't that much older than they, but he was their surrogate parent, a kind of Peter Pan who wandered around Europe searching for talented lost children. When he found them, he scooped them up, promised them excitement and companionship, encouragement and protection, attention and guidance and (yes) love, not to mention pretty good pay. And what did Murrow get, besides a first-rate team of reporters? Said his old friend Michael Bessie, a well-known New York book editor and publisher, "Ed needed to be adored."

✦

Seen from the outside, Charles Collingwood's childhood shouldn't have been unhappy. He was the eldest of six children, the one, according to his sister Jean, "born with a silver spoon in his mouth." It wasn't that the Collingwoods were rich, for they weren't. But Charlie, as he was known then and later to family and friends, was a lovely, smart, talented little boy who excelled at everything. He was his mother's clear pet. Jean and the other children grew up hearing their mother ask, "Why can't you be more like your brother?" Said Collingwood's brother Tom, with whom Collingwood had a particularly tense relationship: "None of us were good enough for Charlie. The sibling rivalry surfaced very early."

Charles and his two brothers and three sisters grew up in Washington, D.C. Their father, Harris, was an official in the U.S. Forest Service. On the economic scale the family fell somewhere between middle class and poor. "There was always enough, but there was never plenty," said Tom, the second-born son. Still, there was a pervasive sense that somehow the family had fallen short. Harris Collingwood's wife, Jean, a proud, remote, and domineering woman, never seemed to tire of reminding the children that her father had been a state senator in Michigan and their father's father a judge. The children were taught to think of themselves as cultured gentility — a little down on their luck perhaps, what with the deprivations imposed by their father's pinchpenny civil-service salary, but gentility all the same.

Imbued with his mother's attitudes, Charles grew up feeling he deserved better. His parents' frugality was an embarrassment to him. The family lived in the capital's unfashionable Brightwood Park area, had makeshift furniture in their home, and drove used cars impounded from racketeers by federal agents and sold at auction. When the family traveled with Harris to business meetings, they stayed at cheap boarding houses, where Jean Collingwood would slip bread from the dinner table into her handbag. Harris bragged to his sons about how he would take his friends' hand-me-down suits and have them remade to fit his short, rotund frame at a fraction of what he would have had to pay for a new suit.

Sometimes, when Harris went on business trips to New York, he would take Charles along. They would stay in the cheapest room at a good hotel and meet friends in the lobby. While Charles's father was at his meetings, he'd send his son to the theater or the Metropolitan Opera. Having splurged, however, Harris would then turn tightfisted. Once, on the train coming home, he asked Charlie if he'd like some ice cream. When he said yes, his father pulled out the family's monthly budget and explained how little money there was. Charlie, said a member of the family, became "desperate to be able to spend money with abandon and unaccountability."

He began early. As a teenager he used whatever money he saved from part-time jobs to buy good-quality clothes and taught himself to wear them with flair. Each morning he would iron his slacks until they had a razor-sharp crease, then hang them up to preserve the crease. Only then would he tackle the rest of his morning chores. One of them — and a detested one — was to fix breakfast for the entire family. So it was a common sight in the Collingwood household to find Charlie in the kitchen in his undershorts, squeezing the orange juice or scrambling the eggs.

Another chore, which he hated even more than preparing breakfast, was baby-sitting for his brothers and sisters. But he made the best he possibly could of it. Sometimes, without his parents' knowledge or permission, he would drop his charges downtown at the National Gallery or some other suitable tourist attraction, then take himself over to the Library of Congress for a little dirty-book reading.

With a French-English dictionary open on the table beside him, Charlie would find and translate, read, and reread the erotic poetry of Baudelaire ("Lesbos, of sultry twilights and pure, infertile joy / Where deep-eyed maidens . . . toy fondly with the soft fruits of their nubility") and other racy French authors. He moved on from the French to Aristophanes (*The Clouds, Lysistrata*) and other Greeks, and then on to the best of Ovid and other Romans. Before graduating from high school he had become quite proficient in French, Greek, and Latin, linguistic skills he developed further in college.

When Charlie was in his teens, sex was a major preoccupation. One member of his family, who was close to him until he died, suggested that he may have experimented with homosexuality as a very young man. Others, including his brother Tom, thought he may have had bisexual tendencies, albeit thoroughly repressed ones. In any case, with his remarkable good looks and easy charm, Charlie was well aware of, and did not hesitate to use, the power he had over women.

He "would seldom be put in a corner that he couldn't wiggle his way out of," Tom Collingwood observed. But Charlie's precocious sophistication was mostly an act. Terribly insecure behind his self-confident facade, he analyzed himself relentlessly and mercilessly and usually found himself wanting. Boys in high school looked down on him, he felt, because of his good grades, his mediocre athletic ability, and his cynical wit. Many of his high school classmates "regarded me almost as a sissy," he wrote in a diary he kept during his college years. Girls, however, "never gave me any trouble," and it was through them that he took his revenge: "If another boy excelled in athletics or took some of my insufferability out on my hide, I could always take his girl."

Charles's insecurities grew in college. He wanted to be accepted by the other students, yet he found it difficult, perhaps impossible, to accept himself, to measure up to his own expectations. Little of this was apparent on the surface. Academically and physically, he thrived as a scholarship student at a unique institution called Deep Springs College, a two-year men's school in the isolated, sage-dotted foothills of California's White Mountains, just north of Death Valley. Founded on the Oxford tutorial system, Deep Springs had only twenty students and five professors. But it was no ivory tower. When the students weren't reading Proust and Plato or arguing about Nietzsche, they were working on the college's 420-acre ranch — branding cattle, fixing fences, tending hogs and chickens, bailing hay.

Collingwood could easily handle the rigorous study and all the hard work; what he had trouble coping with was his own self-hatred. When a classmate criticized him, Collingwood wrote in his diary with profound anguish, "Can't he see that I am so conscious of my shabbiness that I want to cover it with a fine cloak? . . . I know I'm not genuine and I hate myself for it. I know that I am superficial, shoddy. . . . I know I talk too much, irritate people, that nobody really knows me. I don't like it either. People are meat and drink to me, and to feel myself disliked, shunned, is the keenest pain I know."

Another time he wrote that the "egotistical and selfish and superficial side of me is the biggest defect in what might in many respects be a very admirable character. It is colossal, this complacent egotism. I am like a double entity, an alter ego. I see myself objectively . . . and I am disgusted, but I seem to do nothing to shake the awful, calculating, complacent self-love." He believed he was doomed to fail in anything he tried: "I haven't got the stuff, I won't make the grade."

As he often did, he turned to a woman for comfort and unquestioning approval. This time it was the wife of one of his professors, with whom he had a brief affair. "I love being loved," he confided in his diary. "I need women." When the professor's wife broke off the relationship, Collingwood agonized: "I have always had some woman to love me, try to understand me and it is a new thing and not wholly a pleasant one to be so lonely with no maternal, feminine bosom to confide in."

He never rid himself of his doubts, but for better or worse, he was able to bury them deeper inside as the years wore on. By the time he went to Cornell University for his last two years of college, he had toned down some of the traits that had irritated his fellow students at Deep Springs. Still, he had that urge to impress, to "posture a little bit," recalled Austin Kiplinger, who met Collingwood when they were both students at Cornell. And there were always people willing to be impressed. "I was in awe of him," said Bruce Netschert, who was two years behind Collingwood. "He was sophisticated and debonair, a true ladies' man. He had such an air of cool detachment, standing back, judging you."

Collingwood, Kiplinger, and Netschert lived at Telluride House, an independent institution associated with Deep Springs that provided free room and board to a select group of Cornell's top students. While Kiplinger became part of the nationwide liberal student movement of the thirties that earlier had swept up Eric Sevareid, Collingwood, a prelaw major, remained a neutral observer, "the philosopher king," as Kiplinger put it. Besides women, Collingwood's passions seemed to be confined to literature and drama; his only extracurricular activity was the Book and Bowl, the university's literary and drinking society.

Kiplinger was impressed with Collingwood's knowledge of the world. They were the same age, yet Collingwood, who had worked as a merchant seaman and forest surveyor during summer breaks, "knew about all kinds of things that the rest of us were just beginning to catch up with." In an English literature class, the students were assigned to critique a T. S. Eliot short story. Kiplinger missed the whole point of the story: the main character's homosexuality. Collingwood wrote a brilliant analysis of it. "Charlie got the point immediately," Kiplinger said.

Kiplinger was again outmatched by Collingwood's worldliness and his flair for the dramatic in 1939, when both were Rhodes Scholarship finalists. At their interviews they were asked to name a poet they particularly liked. Kiplinger made a safe choice, Robert Browning. Collingwood selected the old friend of his oversexed puberty, Baudelaire, then proceeded to recite one of the poems in French. "He wowed them," Kiplinger said. "I accused him of grandstanding, but it worked. He got the scholarship."

On July 1, 1939, two months before the beginning of World War II, Collingwood set sail for Europe, on his way to Oxford and away — finally, blessedly away — from his family. The rest of the world might have been focused on Poland, but for the next several months, Collingwood's entire universe was Matthew Arnold's "sweet city with her dreaming spires." Oxford was where he truly belonged, he thought. Among the things packed in his trunk, courtesy of his mother, were linens — a tablecloth and some napkins — so that he might set a proper British tea table. Collingwood delighted in being awakened every morning by his "scout," the manservant assigned to him by the university. He loved the parties and the sherry, the formal teas, the dances, the "very pukka formal dinners." In letters home he regaled his family with tales of his new friends, among them Hugh Astor and Sir Richard Percy, and of spending weekends at country estates straight out of *Brideshead Revisited*.

In his letters Collingwood included news of a special new friend he had made — a dark-haired Englishwoman named Barbara Stracey-Clitherow Blake but called Gracie. She was "related to half the peerage," Collingwood wrote. Unfortunately she was also married. Her husband was the scion of a wealthy Boston family, but the couple had separated. The affair quickly became serious, and for the first time in his young life, Collingwood lost interest in playing the field. Gracie took him to the races at Ascot, which he loved, because, as a member of his family put it later, "it was horse racing, it was society — all together in one world — and he could drink to his heart's content."

Still, much as he might have preferred to continue ignoring a world in flames, he was too intelligent and too aware to follow the example of many of his rich British friends. "The immediacy of the war is beginning to work on me," he wrote to his parents:

I am finding it harder and harder to care about medieval law with Armageddon coming closer and closer. . . . I am becoming more and more convinced that my place is not in Oxford. This is a sandpit for ostriches to stick their heads in and I am not an ostrich. People over here don't realize — and certainly they don't in America — what this war is going to mean, and what the world that comes out of it is going to look like. It is not going to be a world conducted by pale scholars, gorged with useless information, you can be sure of that.

Despite pleas from his family that he return home, he decided to move to London and become a journalist. "I cannot turn my back on this," he said in another letter. "It is a matter of simple integrity. . . . I cannot run away." During vacations from Oxford in 1939 and early 1940, he had filled in for vacationing staffers in the United Press bureaus in London and Amsterdam. When he left Oxford for good in the summer of 1940, UP in London immediately grabbed him for a full-time job.

Even with bombs crashing down around him — one badly damaged the little mews house where he lived — Collingwood remained enchanted by life in London. His letters home were filled with stories about how he dodged shrapnel to get to the Ritz for his nightly shot of bourbon; about taking Gracie to the posh Café de Paris nightclub, packed with patrons drinking champagne and eating oysters; about lunching with "old Lord Willingdon" at the Savoy; about finding six ruby Victorian wine glasses at an antique shop; about buying a Jaeger camel-hair coat that made him feel "like a real foreign correspondent."

As much as he wanted to be free of his parents, he remained in their thrall, financially and emotionally. Always broke, it wasn't until he went to CBS that he stopped asking his father for money. He also wanted his parents' approval, wanted them to be impressed with what he'd become and was deeply hurt when they criticized his free-spending ways and his frequent references to parties and drinking. At one point he wrote, "I wait for your letters and when they do finally come, they seem to be full only of objections, pious remarks and a high moral tone which seems completely irrelevant." He knew better than to broach some subjects: he included a lot about Gracie in his letters, but never mentioned that he had moved in with her after the Germans bombed his house.

When Murrow hired him in March 1941, Collingwood outlined for his parents the reasons he was so happy to get the job: the higher salary, the satisfaction, the prestige. "It's a new field with immense potentialities and Columbia is pioneering in it. From what I can learn, Columbia is doing a very responsible job — in many ways more responsible than the newspapers." His joining CBS also meant the beginning of true liberation from his parents. Henceforth, their place would be largely filled by Ed Murrow, who immediately labeled Collingwood "Bonnie Prince Charlie."

✦

Collingwood knew nothing about radio when he was hired, and Murrow used the sudden-immersion method to teach him. Collingwood assumed he would be able to observe Murrow and LeSueur at work for several days before he went on the air himself. But on March 24, his second day at CBS, Murrow phoned to say that he had an unexpected dinner engagement with the prime minister of the Netherlands. Would Collingwood mind sitting in for him on the late-night broadcast? Collingwood, who had a bad cold, gulped and said, "Sure." His throat hurt, his head was clogged, he had a fever, and he was scared as hell, but he wrote what he thought might pass for a script and headed for the BBC studio. Surely Ed, as he had promised, would get there in time to give him a pointer or two.

Murrow did not keep his promise. When he finally entered the studio, there were only seconds to go before airtime. He slipped into the seat across from Collingwood and waited. Collingwood started speaking into the microphone — his subject was inflation in London — and, all things considered, did a creditable job. His voice was loud and rather emphatic, but his script was knowledgeable and well written, and he sounded much more mature than his twenty-three years. When he finished, Collingwood was so glad he had made it through without a major gaffe that he forgot his sign-off. Murrow removed the cigarette from his mouth, leaned forward, and said into the microphone, "This is Charles Collingwood in London. Now back to Robert Trout in New York."

Collingwood asked how he had done.

"Oh, it was fine," Murrow replied. "Everything was fine."

Murrow's nonchalance was an act, of course. Before and during his own broadcasts, he suffered terribly, withdrawing from everyone and everything, sweating profusely, jiggling his leg like up and down. But with the Boys he affected a ho-hum air that impressed them all the more. Each time Collingwood completed a broadcast, he would ask Murrow for a critique. Each time Murrow said he'd done fine, just fine. Surely, there's something I'm doing wrong, Collingwood insisted. Finally, after about ten broadcasts, Murrow said, "These microphones are very good. You don't have to shout as though you were at the end of a long-distance telephone."

That was the extent of Murrow's advice. He didn't analyze his own broadcast style, and — apart from instructions about the kinds of stories he liked and the best way to tell them — he didn't much help the Boys with theirs. Collingwood watched Murrow dictate his broadcasts, listened to them, studied them, even parsed them. "You use short, declarative sentences, don't you?" he asked the master, trying to tease out the secret of his genius. "Do I?" asked Murrow. "I wasn't aware of that."

Collingwood said he wanted "to write like Ed and sound like Ed. I wanted to *be* Edward R. Murrow." But Murrow told Collingwood to be himself. "Ed told me the last thing he needed was another Ed Murrow in his life." Perhaps Murrow, the old speech major, declined to coach his bright young protégés because he feared they might eventually outshine him. Anyway, whether he liked it or not, most of the Boys, including Collingwood, imitated his understated, measured, highly personalized delivery.

Some even aped his appearance. When Eric Sevareid arrived in New York from London, the people at CBS were amazed at how much he imitated Murrow. "Eric dressed like Ed, talked like Ed, even pulled his fedora down like Ed," said Helen Sioussat, a former Murrow assistant. "On air he had that same terse eloquence." Once, when Sevareid came into the New York newsroom, Robert Trout, one of Paul White's boys, shouted, "Why, here's Ed Murrow in from London. Oh, excuse me, it's Eric. I thought it was Ed." Later Sevareid acknowledged that he imitated Murrow, although not on purpose. "We all did," he said, as if they couldn't help themselves.

✴ 10

Censored

As LONG AS A JOURNALIST and the outfit he works for are inconsequential, however inconsequentiality is measured, it's easy for them to believe in and stand for the verities of their craft: truth, reason, independence, freedom, and the like. But when the reporter becomes a celebrity, or when his reporting affects masses of people, or when he and his outfit start to earn large amounts of money, then the pressures mount to conform, to protect oneself, to protect one's income, to protect one's outfit, to avoid giving offense.

In 1941 all these conditions began to exist at once for Murrow and the Boys. The world was paying attention to them as never before, individually and as part of what was without question America's premier news network. Their responses to the pressures of this attention would form the core of the journalistic legacy they were creating.

Murrow and the Boys were hardly the first great stars of journalism. Newspapers had had their own stars long before, as had radio, with commentators like Boake Carter, H. V. Kaltenborn, Lowell Thomas, Raymond Gram Swing, and Gabriel Heatter, and gossipers and demagogues like Walter Winchell. But the people Murrow assembled and directed were the first electronic news stars who attained their stardom as bona fide, on-the-air reporters who had seen and lived the stories they covered. With their ordinary backgrounds and their lack of pretense (at least in the beginning), they were perfectly matched to the age of the common man and what would become the war of the GI. Their credibility, plus the size of their audience and the vast amounts of money at stake, gave them great power. They sought to exploit that power by interpreting and commenting on the news as well as reporting it.

"I am preaching from a powerful pulpit," Murrow wrote to his parents. In spite of various CBS directives on the need for objectivity, he and the Boys believed it was their duty and right to analyze the news.

That did not mean "editorializing." Editorials told people what to think. Analysis and comment gave them additional information and insight. But the Boys realized there were risks in this. The bolder and more successful they became, the more censorship they faced. At one time or another, virtually all of them engaged in some kind of confrontation with officials of foreign governments and the U.S. government, not to mention CBS executives in New York.

Like most journalists of the day, they welcomed the *principle* of military censorship on the Allied side. They supported the war and did not want to cause any breaches of security that might result in Allied deaths or jeopardize the success of an operation. They found, however, that because of the immediacy and influence of radio, they were subjected to much more rigid control than their newspaper colleagues. And, whether they were covering the Allies or the Axis, most of them did their best to get around what they considered unnecessary restrictions.

♦

In the spring and summer of 1941, Germany was striking everywhere at will. While its bombers still pounded London (albeit less frequently), its submarines wreaked havoc and death in the Atlantic and the North Sea, a new blitzkrieg was knocking over the Balkan countries like dominoes, and the Afrika Korps was threatening to seize all of the Middle East and North Africa. The story could no longer be told primarily from London and Berlin.

"We take you now to Ankara" became familiar words on the CBS morning and evening news roundups as Hitler postponed Operation Barbarossa (his plan for the invasion of the Soviet Union) so that he could first roll up Rumania, Hungary, Bulgaria, Yugoslavia, and Greece and gain access to their food, oil, and manpower. Ankara, the spy-riddled capital of Turkey and now an important listening post for news from the Balkans and North Africa, had moved into the spotlight. So had a new CBS correspondent named Winston Burdett, who had first worked for the network as the replacement stringer for the luckless Betty Wason in Scandinavia.

With his slight frame and sensitive face, his shock of wavy dark hair and sometimes dreamy air, Burdett looked more like Hamlet than a hard-bitten foreign correspondent. His ethereal air concealed many things, including an aggressiveness that caused the Nazis to kick him out of two countries. He had a knack for being in the right place at the right time, yet his personal history gave no hint of great journalistic talent. Indeed, prior to his arrival in Scandinavia in 1940 (on his own hook, he said), Burdett had been a rather lowly writer of culture and movie articles for the *Brooklyn Eagle.*

After replacing Wason, however, he had impressed both Murrow and the New York office with his reporting from Norway, where he covered a number of major battles and stayed behind to report even after the Wehrmacht cleared the British out. When German troops finally caught up with him, they sent him packing to Stockholm on the next train.

Later, staying ahead of the Nazi advance but never very far from the action, Burdett paid a call on Moscow, then pushed south to Rumania. There he reported on the Fascist government's collusion with Germany in its takeover of the country. Those reports led to his first expulsion by the Nazis. But before the order could be carried out, the twenty-five-year-old Burdett managed to get married. His bride was a pretty but overweight Italian journalist named Lea Schiavi, five years older than he, whom he had known for only about a month. They had met during a journalists' tour of Rumania when she noticed holes in his socks and volunteered to darn them for him. She spoke no English. An ardent anti-Fascist and suspected Communist, she had been in considerable trouble with Italian officials for her writings in left-wing Italian political and literary journals. Finally the Italian Fascists lifted her passport.

By marrying Lea, the courtly Burdett provided the security of his American citizenship and made it easier for her to travel. But chivalry wasn't his only motive. "My father was not a passionate man," said Richard Burdett, his son by a later marriage, "but he fell madly, passionately in love with this woman." Lea Schiavi was ebullient and full of fun and was adept at drawing out the reserved Burdett. "They seemed very happy together," said Farnsworth Fowle, a former CBS correspondent who knew and worked with them in Rumania and Turkey.

From Rumania, Winston and Lea moved to Yugoslavia. There the Nazi authorities revoked Winston's broadcasting privileges for reporting about anti-Mussolini unrest in Milan and other northern Italian cities. As the official pressure increased, so did the tensions. One night Burdett and *New York Times* correspondent Ray Brock, together with their wives, got into a wild barroom brawl with a bunch of Nazi toughs who had been taunting them. A short time afterward Burdett was expelled again. His next post was Ankara, where he arrived in mid-March 1941. En route he was promoted by Paul White to staff correspondent.

With war roiling all around Turkey, Ankara was a mecca for swarms of journalists and spies, who lent a boomtown atmosphere to the hot, dusty, ancient city on the Anatolian plain. These information hunter-gatherers — who have always had more in common than either camp likes to admit — preyed on one another constantly. Indeed, it wasn't always easy to tell who was the journalist and who the spy. Two fierce competitors among the journalists were Burdett and Martin Agronsky of NBC. Both worked day and night collecting information from diplomats, foreign agents, and anyone else who might have facts. Burdett and Agronsky were, a colleague said, "busy cutting each other's throats."

Not seven days a week, though. On Sunday afternoons the American and British correspondents adjourned to a local park, where they played softball and drank beer. Burdett, who pitched for the American team, struck Farnsworth Fowle as fun-loving and carefree, "very much part of the group." To others, including Agronsky, however, Burdett was withdrawn and mysterious. He seemed a pleasant enough sort on Sunday afternoons in the park, and he and Lea were good barroom company; certainly no one quarreled with Burdett's intellectual credentials. But there was something odd about him all the same.

At CBS all anyone knew was that Burdett did his job and did it well. "A lot of people have good second-class minds, like me," said Fowle, a former Rhodes Scholar. "And then you run into people like Winston, who have first-class minds, and you know the difference."

Burdett reported on the German invasion of Greece and on Yugoslavia's decision to capitulate. He used his Ankara listening post to piece together a picture of the anti-Fascist coup d'état in Belgrade and the Germans' overpowering response. It was all secondhand, however. Burdett, having been expelled from Yugoslavia, could not return to provide an eyewitness account of the Wehrmacht's unmerciful punishment of the rebels.

But Cecil Brown could.

✦

Brown had been hired by Murrow in February 1940 to cover Italy. Before that he had worked for INS, the Hearst wire service, and had moonlighted as an off-the-air stringer for CBS. A thirty-two-year-old Pennsylvania native, Brown thrived on adventure. When he was seventeen (six years before Eric Sevareid embarked on a similar odyssey), he and his brother had paddled a canoe four hundred miles down the Ohio River from Wheeling, West Virginia, to Cincinnati. Then Brown, like Sevareid, wrote a series of articles about the trip for his hometown newspaper. After his junior year at Ohio State University, he decided he needed a break from school; he stowed away on an ocean liner to South America and again wrote a series of articles about his adventures.

When he graduated from college in 1929, Brown shipped out as an able-bodied seaman aboard a freighter bound for the Mediterranean and the Black Sea. Returning to the United States, he decided to give journalism a try, working as a reporter for United Press and four different newspapers before returning to Europe in 1937. By the time he joined CBS, he had a reputation as tough-minded, energetic, and aggressive. A little *too* aggressive, some said. He had a terrible speaking voice — rough and raspy, with a noticeable lisp — but his fine reporting made up for it.

Tall and thin, with a beaklike nose and a toothbrush mustache that made him look a little like Basil Rathbone, Brown was thrilled to be a CBS correspondent — so much so that when an announcer in New York mispronounced his given name during his first broadcast, Brown didn't bother to correct him. The announcer rhymed Cecil with "vessel," as the English do, instead of with "diesel," as Brown normally did. He just shrugged and said his name the English way in his sign-off. He continued to pronounce it that way for the rest of his life.

On most matters he was not so nonchalant. Cecil Brown was one of those journalists who seem to need to fight and struggle in order to prove they are alive. He detested censorship and censors no matter what flag they represented. In Mussolini's Italy, Brown was fearless about taking on the people who wielded blue pencils. If he lost an argument with them, he would try to sneak something through. When Italy entered the war on June 10, 1940, he began his broadcast by saying, "Mussolini tonight sent the Italian people into the war. The Italian people did not want this war." When he tried to repeat those sentences in two subsequent broadcasts, the censors, having recovered their wits, refused to pass them.

Brown did not hide his disgust with Mussolini. He called the hastily mobilized Italian forces "a comic-opera army preparing for slaughter under the orders of a *Duce* with a titanic contempt for his own people." The Italian authorities, on discovering how much the truth can hurt, punished Brown on several occasions by suspending his broadcasting privileges. Then in April 1941, they kicked him off the air altogether and expelled him from the country for his "continuing hostile attitude toward Fascism."

When the action shifted to the Balkans, Brown arranged, with great difficulty, to get to Yugoslavia just in time for the German invasion. In a harrowing broadcast from Budapest one April morning, he described the beginning of the blitzkrieg: "the scream of Stukas, mangled bodies torn apart, streets spattered with blood." He told how the dive bombers streaked down over the Terrazia, Belgrade's main square, spraying it and everyone in it with machine-gun fire, and how the heavy bombers all but leveled Belgrade, Sarajevo, and other Yugoslav cities. This wasn't war; it was annihilation.

Brown had arrived in Belgrade only two days before the Nazis struck. After witnessing the carnage and seeing his own hotel blown up, he and several other correspondents managed to get away, following the routed anti-Nazi Yugoslav government on its doomed flight to Sarajevo. Always the German planes were close behind, swooping down on roads and villages, bullets from machine guns riddling cars and people.

Finally Brown left the group and fled with an American military attaché into the mountains, where they were found by German troops, arrested, and returned to Belgrade. Brown spent ten days under detention in that bombed-out shell of a city, watching from a hotel as tens of thousands of bodies were dug from the rubble. When the Germans were satisfied that he was an American correspondent and not a spy, they released him and threw him out of the country.

Brown's almost unbearably vivid eyewitness accounts of the destruction of Yugoslavia made him a true member of the Murrow team. After the Germans released him from custody in Belgrade, he proceeded to Budapest and returned to the air. Then he moved on to Ankara to rest a few days and to meet Winston Burdett before going on to his next assignment in Cairo.

Having endured Axis censorship, Brown was relieved to be able to report from the Allied side. Surely, under the benign supervision of the British authorities, he'd have no trouble getting out and reporting the truth about the war in North Africa. After only a couple of days in Cairo he discovered how naive that notion was.

A string of spectacular British victories over the Italians in Egypt and Libya had turned out to be merely a prelude to a terrible pounding being administered to the British forces by Field Marshal Erwin Rommel and his Afrika Korps. In March 1941 Rommel had rushed across the Mediterranean to rescue the Italian troops whom the British had swept out of Egypt and pushed as far west as Benghazi, Libya. By this time the British had captured the strategic port of Tobruk, only to learn that Prime Minister Winston Churchill had called a halt to the advance.

Churchill, in keeping with his misguided, World War I–era belief that the Balkans were "the soft underbelly of Europe" and thus the key to defeating the Nazis, ordered large numbers of British troops to Greece and Crete, where, as in World War I, they suffered disastrous defeats. This in turn emboldened Rommel to swoop down on the remaining British forces in North Africa. He forced them back from Benghazi, then laid siege to Tobruk (but would not actually recapture it for more than a year). In only ten days the Germans had regained almost all of the ground that the British had captured in three months.

In Cairo no one seemed very interested in the fighting. There were no blackouts, and at British headquarters the staff officers' gentlemanly pleasures continued as if sweet peace were regnant. There was polo on the greensward of the Gezira Sport Club, cricket at Mena House, whiskey in the afternoon at the mahogany long bar of Shepheard's on the Nile. Tommies who had actually collided with Rommel, who had perhaps lost an arm or leg, weren't especially welcome; they introduced an unpleasant note into all the pommy festivities. No more welcome were war correspondents like Cecil Brown.

When Brown was still assuming the best about British censors, he told them, in good Ed Murrow fashion, that he wanted to make the war real for Americans, wanted farmers in Kansas "to see and feel the desert sand, to understand what Suez means." The censors condescended to him. Later one of them referred to Brown as "the man who came out here to *dramatize* the war." Most of the time, though, Brown *couldn't* dramatize it, because the British military kept him bottled up in Cairo, where he began to clash more and more often with the censors.

Finally, almost two months after arriving in North Africa, Brown was permitted to go to the front, accompanying the Allied forces that captured Damascus on June 21. As it happened, however, that was the day Germany invaded the Soviet Union. Brown's first thought was satisfaction that some of the German pressure would be taken off Great Britain. His second was, "This will kill the whole Damascus story. America is not going to give a damn about Syria now."

✦

Still in London with Murrow, Larry LeSueur was restless again. The cure, he thought, might be a trip to Moscow. He wanted to see the great Soviet social experiment before the Wehrmacht dumped it onto the ash heap of history. LeSueur had long been fascinated by what Lenin and the Bolsheviks had done in Russia. He wasn't a communist or a socialist or, for that matter, much of anything politically. What appealed to him about the Soviet state was the sheer, monumental *adventure* of its creation — the sudden, radical rebuilding of a vast nation.

LeSueur desperately needed a new challenge. There was nothing much to report from London these days, except for Churchill's eloquent appeals for U.S. assistance and the odd air raid and, of course, the enduring courage of the British people. But these were old stories by now, and Murrow — with some help from Charles Collingwood — could handle them without LeSueur.

Murrow tried to talk him out of going. It was dangerous as hell, and the fighting would probably be over by the time he got there anyway — not to mention that Murrow, having watched Bill Shirer head for home, probably didn't want to lose the company of another close pal. But LeSueur prevailed. In October 1941 in Greenock, Scotland, as the Germans were closing in on Moscow, he boarded HMS *Temple Arch*, a rusty freighter laden with TNT, tanks, and boots for the Red Army and bound for the Siberian port of Arkhangelsk.

Even in the best of seasons and in peacetime, a voyage on a freighter from Britain to Arkhangelsk by way of the North and Norwegian seas can be arduous. In October, in a war, aboard an explosives-laden ship passing through submarine-infested waters, it can — if you survive — provide stories to tell your grandchildren. For LeSueur and everyone else aboard the *Temple Arch*, those bitingly cold, gray days were a mix of monotony and excruciating foreboding and fear. German U-boats used the Norwegian Sea as a hunting ground. The submarines lay in wait along the shipping lanes and picked off freighter after freighter carrying supplies for the Soviet Union, as well as many of the destroyers and minesweepers that were supposed to guard the freighters.

LeSueur and the two other American correspondents aboard the *Temple Arch* — Walter Kerr of the *New York Herald Tribune* and Eddy Gilmore of the AP — were pressed into daily service standing watch for submarines. They had to sleep in their clothes in case of a nighttime torpedo attack. When one of them nervously asked the captain how long the *Temple Arch* might stay afloat if a torpedo hit, the captain replied, "It's not a matter of how long she'll stay afloat. It's a question of how high she'll go."

After three nerve-racking weeks at sea, the ship finally made it to Arkhangelsk. But for LeSueur and his colleagues the adventure was only beginning. The local Red Army commander insisted he had no authority to allow them to proceed by train, as planned, to Moscow. In fact he hadn't even known they were coming. As LeSueur contemplated the prospect of returning to Britain the same terrifying way he had come, he decided to bluff. He pulled a scrap piece of paper from his pocket and waved it at the startled commandant.

"I have here a letter from Joseph Stalin," he shouted in English, "inviting us to Moscow to write about the great war effort of the Red Army. The American people want to know how the Red Army is fighting Hitler. Do you want to keep them from knowing, when Joseph Stalin says they can?" The commandant, deciding not to argue the point further, quickly picked up the phone. Within a couple of hours LeSueur, Gilmore, and Kerr were on a train to Moscow.

Assured by the conductor that the trip would take no more than a week, they boarded with their luggage, a teapot, and a week's worth of food. They had no rubles and spoke no Russian. They wouldn't have had even the food and the teapot if the captain of the *Temple Arch* hadn't suggested they take along some provisions. The train headed south toward Moscow, then inexplicably swung eastward, then south, then east again. Sometimes it stopped for hours. The journey stretched to two weeks and was well into the third, and still there was no end in sight. By this time the correspondents had begun rationing their nearly depleted food supply. When the train stopped, as it did frequently, they rushed out to the platform and traded with Russian peasants: a hairbrush or a piece of soap for a loaf of bread or a chicken. Soon, however, they would have nothing left to barter, and the weather had turned bitterly cold.

After seventeen days the train stopped for good. Stepping out into a chill wind, the passengers found themselves not in Moscow but in Kuibyshev, 530 miles to the southeast. And there they would remain, the correspondents were told, because Moscow was surrounded by Nazis. The train had traveled east to the Urals and Siberia, then back over the mountains to Kuibyshev, where the Soviet government, the diplomatic community, and foreign journalists had been moved.

Zdrastvytie, Amerikanskiye druzhya! Welcome to Kuibyshev!

Ferociously hungry, LeSueur headed straight for the dining room of the only hotel in town, the grossly misnamed Grand, where he ordered beef stroganoff. It was to be his first real meal in three weeks. But just as he was about to dig in, a British correspondent who had joined him at the table pointed at both their plates and bellowed to a waiter in his best Colonel Blimp imitation: "How many times have I told you to heat this?" To the utter astonishment and horror of the famished LeSueur —

poised with fork in hand to enjoy his first bite — the waiter whisked the plates away. An hour passed before they saw their food again. By then, LeSueur recalled, "I was at the end of my tether."

It took some time to understand why the resident foreign correspondents in Kuibyshev were always griping about their miserable living and working conditions. A freezing, three-week voyage through submarine-infested waters and seventeen days on a Soviet train with little food made Kuibyshev and the Grand Hotel look pretty good to LeSueur. It wasn't until he started working that he realized how impossible the situation really was.

Here the correspondents were, marooned, fighting with the censors and each other, while the battle for Moscow, the biggest story in the world at that time, was raging hundreds of miles away. The only sources of so-called news were official communiqués, which usually said nothing, and twice-weekly press briefings, at which the government spokesman deftly blocked every attempt to find out what was really happening. If, incredibly, someone did manage to uncover some news on his own, the censors killed it at once. LeSueur sent Paul White a telegram saying that the Soviets were treating the correspondents "like princes." The censors thanked LeSueur for his generosity. "I didn't tell them," LeSueur said, "that I meant like princes in the Russian Revolution."

Most American journalists who covered World War II complained, at one time or another, about censorship and the other official constraints imposed on them, but nowhere were those constraints more severe than in the Soviet Union. If the Russian front was the most important in the war and the worst reported, it was due in some measure to the totalitarianism of the Soviet government. Correspondents needed official permission to do almost anything — interview a general, talk to someone on the street, visit a school, factory, or home, travel anywhere outside the city, including, naturally, the front. Usually such requests were routinely denied, particularly if the officials feared that the story might give a negative impression of the Soviet war effort. (In one of his broadcasts from London, Murrow wryly observed, "The Russians consider the war too important a matter to discuss with foreigners.") The situation was bad enough in Moscow, before and after the German siege. But it was hell in the Kuibyshev cocoon. There, if a correspondent was lucky enough to get hold of a Moscow newspaper, it was at least three days old.

Kuibyshev had grown up on the site of a fort called Samara, built in 1586 to protect the Volga trade route. It soon became the terminus for trade caravans from China and India. In 1935 the Soviets officially changed the name from Samara to Kuibyshev and began to transform it into one of Stalin's new industrial centers. When Larry LeSueur and company were there, however, it seemed closer to the sixteenth century than the twentieth. Russia's provisional capital was a raw, crowded frontier town where drunks curled up in the gutters to escape the howling Siberian winds, and camel trains from Turkestan plodded through the snow-packed streets. Life in Kuibyshev sorely tested even the easygoing LeSueur, who was troubled by colds and dysentery throughout his six-month stay there.

In London news might have been sparse, but at least there were compensations: dinner at L'Étoile, drinks at the Savoy, golf with Murrow, parties, women. In Kuibyshev, there was dinner in the Grand's dining room, where the only dish available on its elaborate menu was the beef stroganoff, and endless poker games with disgruntled reporters. And there were — emphatically — no women. Aboard the *Temple Arch* LeSueur and Kerr had whiled away some of the harrowing hours talking about rumors they'd heard of beautiful young translators provided by the KGB. LeSueur's translator in Kuibyshev turned out to be a plump, middle-aged matron. At that he could count himself lucky. Walter Kerr was assigned a sixty-year-old Red Army veteran named Oskar.

LeSueur was the first American radio correspondent ever to broadcast "regularly" from Russia, or so the CBS publicity releases said. But the adverb stretched the truth a long way. Regularly? Half the time New York never received his broadcasts. Or it picked them up in midreport. Or he was cut off before he finished. Transmission snafus were nothing new to radio correspondents anywhere, but LeSueur and his CBS successor in Russia, Bill Downs, probably had the worst experiences of all. And that was on top of the hassles they encountered even before they *attempted* to broadcast.

LeSueur usually wrote his broadcasts in the early evening, then walked three miles down icy streets piled several feet high with snow to the censor's office. After doing battle there, he trudged back to the hotel to get some sleep. At 3 A.M. (7 P.M., New York time), with the temperature twenty degrees below zero or lower, he set off to the studio for his 4 A.M. broadcast — again on foot, since cars were scarce in Kuibyshev — the collar of his sheepskin coat pulled up over his nose and mouth against the stinging snow. It was a hazardous half-mile trip in the blackout. If he stayed on the sidewalk, he had to watch out for huge open sewer holes. If he walked in the street, he navigated over mountains of snow.

And what was the payoff? One memorable day it was a telegram from Paul White saying LeSueur's broadcasts had not been received for a month. Another time CBS announcer John Charles Daly in New York told listeners, "We are informed that, after a good deal of trying over some time, we may be able to get a direct report from Larry LeSueur in Kuibyshev." LeSueur's voice did come in, but it was barely intelligible in the buzz of static. Half a sentence into the broadcast, he was cut off.

When the Germans were turned back from the outskirts of Moscow, Russian authorities finally allowed the foreign correspondents into the capital again, and — wonder of wonders — allowed them to go to the front, or at least to get relatively close to it. Correspondents in Russia were never allowed to witness actual battles. Once the Russians had captured an area, the reporters were simply taken on a tour: a view of the battlefield and captured German fortifications, an interview with the victorious Russian general and some of his miserable German prisoners. If the correspondents were lucky, maybe they would get to hear actual gunfire — but always at a safe distance from the fighting.

Still, it was better than Kuibyshev, LeSueur thought, or would have been if his damned broadcasts had gotten through. When he finally got to Moscow and reported that the capital was still intact after two months of siege, New York didn't pick him up. Nor did they when he described his first visit to the front, although that time he managed to cable his script to New York — normally, sending a cable was about as difficult as broadcasting — and John Daly read it on the air.

The scene LeSueur described in that cable was surreal: frozen bodies of dead Germans, their arms stiff and reaching for the sky, and the blackened, charred skeletons of village huts set against a snow-covered backdrop of Christmas-card beauty. On another visit to the front, amid the abandoned German tanks, he came across empty champagne bottles jutting out of a snowdrift. "Reserved for the Wehrmacht," said the inscription on the labels. It was Pommery from Rheims, the same champagne LeSueur had drunk two years earlier with British flyers in France to help cope with the boredom of the phony war.

As the monumental Russian campaign seesawed back and forth throughout 1942, the correspondents shuttled back and forth between Kuibyshev and Moscow. They were never able to get near the besieged and suffering cities of Leningrad and Stalingrad. When LeSueur wanted to do a story on the battle of Stalingrad, the epic turning point on the eastern front, he had to rely on the testimony of an American observer pilot who had flown low over the smoking ruins.

✦

During his year in the Soviet Union, LeSueur was frustrated and sick, angry sometimes, and bored much of the rest of the time. Yet he found himself drawn to the Russian people, to the steel and fire they showed at Stalingrad, to their vitality and fierce love of "the motherland," a word that, in Russian and for Russians, means much more than "country," let alone "government."

When American and British correspondents were permanently relocated to Moscow in May 1942, LeSueur set up residence in the Metropole Hotel and made friends with several Russians who dared flout the official ban on consorting with foreigners. He even had a Russian girlfriend named Katya. He learned, he said, to judge people by their faces and thoughts, not by their shabby, worn-out clothes. LeSueur himself looked more and more like a Russian. He would keep the same shirt on for days, leave his suit unpressed for weeks, let his shoes get as scuffed as those of Russian workers. Though he was not at all ideological, LeSueur was profoundly affected by his experience in the Soviet Union, by his admiration for the way Russians managed to live life fully even in the midst of deprivation and repression. Now LeSueur understood the truth of the Russian aphorism "Have a heart and have a soul; all else is passing fashion."

He'd come to Russia to learn about the great Soviet experiment. What he had learned most about, however, was the warmth and limitless endurance of the Russian spirit. And quite a lot about himself as well.

11

Last Train from Berlin

To a great many germans, the thought of Russian endurance was almost laughable in the early summer of 1941. After a month's delay for the Balkans campaign, Hitler's troops had stormed across the Russian border in June. Victory, the Nazis were saying, would be Germany's by Christmas. But when the Russian offensive stalled that autumn and the British intensified their bombing of Berlin, German confidence ebbed, anger rose, recriminations began.

If Bill Shirer thought Berlin was bad when he departed for the States a year earlier, he should have seen it in the fall of 1941. Americans, whose government was still nominally neutral, were harassed on the street and in restaurants and sometimes beaten up. American journalists living in hotels were asked by nervous managers to leave. Phones were tapped, offices and homes watched. Newspaper stories and radio broadcasts were shredded by the censors. And German officials occasionally reminded correspondents of the arrest earlier that year of Richard C. Hottelet, a young American correspondent for United Press, on suspicion of espionage. "Hottelet is only the beginning," the director of the foreign press department told one reporter. "We'll get more of you soon."

Howard K. Smith, the new CBS correspondent in Berlin, remembered what had happened to Hottelet, for at the time they were colleagues in UP's Berlin bureau. Smith was at the office that March morning when Gestapo thugs burst in and turned the place upside down. Dazed, Smith could only wonder what it was all about. He received his answer from the ticker of the official German news agency, which spit out a story reporting Hottelet's arrest in his apartment a few hours earlier. Outside of the Gestapo, no one thought Hottelet was a spy. He was just an aggressive, courageous reporter who liked Germans but who, in his own words, "hated the Nazis' goddamned guts" and didn't much care who knew it. Clearly, the arrest was meant as a warning to other American correspondents.

After this incident the twenty-six-year-old Howard Smith felt especially vulnerable. At first glance the former Rhodes Scholar seemed the archetype of a courtly southern gentleman, with his tall, slim good looks, Louisiana drawl, and soft-spoken manner. But in fact he had been a hotheaded leftist rebel in school, and his experiences in Berlin under Hitler and the Nazis had not mellowed him. Suffering from a bad case of the "Berlin blues," he got into some serious wrangles of his own with the Nazis, yelling at officials, insulting the government's chief spokesman to his face. He even had some bitter arguments with Hottelet and other UP colleagues. For his own sanity, if not his safety, he felt it was time to leave Germany.

He quit his UP job in the spring of 1941 and applied to the German government for permission to leave. A few days later, still awaiting his exit visa, Smith entered a favorite bookstore and noticed that a window display for a volume of Russian short stories had vanished. With all the recent talk about the possibility of an invasion of Russia, Smith took the missing display as a sign that something was afoot. He canceled his plans to leave and asked CBS's Harry Flannery if the job Flannery had mentioned earlier was still open. It was.

Flannery, Bill Shirer's successor in Berlin, had been sent from the States a few months earlier by Paul White. A former announcer for a CBS station in the Midwest, he was not a good choice. Knowing little about Germany and not speaking the language, he was duped more than once by the Nazis. White conceded his mistake — which looked all the worse when compared to the success of Murrow's hires — and ordered Flannery to return home as soon as he could find a replacement. In that assignment, at least, Flannery was successful: he found Howard K. Smith.

✦

Smith, obstinate and headstrong all his young life, rarely hesitated to spit in the eye of authority. Born Howard Kingsbury Smith, Jr., in the dusty, rambunctious town of Ferriday, Louisiana, he angered his mother as a little boy by playing with black children in spite of her admonitions. It was one of his earliest rebellions. He had no use for the mossy traditions and customs of the decaying Old South, to which his father's family was so dedicated.

The Smiths could trace their aristocratic bloodlines back to 1640, when a forebear arrived in Virginia from England. Howard Smith's grandfather had been master of Lettsworth, a large plantation in Pointe Coupee Parish, Louisiana, a couple of miles from the Mississippi River. But the family's fortunes collapsed around the turn of the century, and the plantation was lost. Howard, the younger of two children, began his days in a tiny house just down the river from Lettsworth.

His father, Howard Sr., who had grown up on the plantation, never adjusted to the sudden decline. A charming, feckless, mild-mannered ne'er-do-well, he drifted from job to job until he became, for a time, a conductor for the Texas and Pacific Railroad. His wife, a beautiful half-Cajun, grew to have nothing but contempt for him, an attitude largely shared by his younger son and namesake. After three years in Ferriday, the family moved to Monroe, then to New Orleans.

Howard Jr. didn't care much for New Orleans. He found the city "sloppy" and "happy-go-lucky," like his father. By this time he was rebelling against just about everything: school, his family, the South. It wasn't until his junior year in high school, in the middle of the Depression, that he understood he was about to set out on the same road to nowhere that his father had followed all his life. It was time, young Howard decided, to change course. The decision led to a remarkable transformation: the sullen kid with bad grades ended up graduating from high school as valedictorian, class president, the school's track star, and the holder of a scholarship to Tulane University.

In college, despite his scholarship and a variety of part-time jobs, Smith was too poor even to buy books; he had to borrow them from classmates. Thin but muscular, he joined the track team, became a high-hurdles star and team captain. In 1936, at an all-South meet, he placed second only to Forrest Towns, who went on to win a gold medal in the 110-meter hurdles at the Berlin Olympics that same year. Before Smith graduated, he set a Tulane high-hurdles record that stood for forty years. As a senior he was elected president of the student body.

He was also a fraternity man, but when he recruited a fellow member of the track team, the fraternity turned the friend down because he was Jewish. The next year Smith chose someone "as Nordic as you can get," the son of a Norwegian sea captain and also a team member. Again the brothers said no, explaining that this fellow was the son of a working man. "My God," Smith exclaimed, "I'm the son of a working man who's *unemployed!*" That's different, they replied; you are a man of standing on the campus, and your father comes from a fine southern family. Smith walked out and never returned.

Fraternity life no longer held much appeal for him anyway. He was spending more and more time with members of a student socialist organization and trying to prepare himself to be a foreign correspondent. He learned French and German and won a summer scholarship to Heidelberg University offered by the German government. In May 1936 Smith graduated from Tulane with highest honors and a Phi Beta Kappa key; a few days later he was on his way to Germany, working his way across the Atlantic as a deck hand on a freighter.

He was astonished by Germany's rabid militarism and the world's uncaring response. The lectures he attended at Heidelberg were little more than Nazi propaganda. Smith returned to New Orleans in the fall, determined to get back to Europe as soon as possible and watch the upcoming drama play itself out. A Rhodes Scholarship the next year made that possible. He toured Germany for several months before taking up residence at Oxford. Even then he couldn't stay away from the country he despised; during term breaks, he rushed back to Germany to renew his anti-Nazi zeal. "Nothing made me hate Nazism, fear it and long to do some little things to destroy it more than a few long, deep breaths of its own atmosphere," he later wrote. During the summer before he enrolled at Oxford, he even landed in a Nazi jail for several hours after being caught at the German-Danish border with copies of an anti-Nazi newspaper he'd bought in Copenhagen.

It was a shock to go from the feverish, frightening belligerency of Germany to the placid otherworldliness of Oxford. Smith detested the very things that Charles Collingwood later loved — the afternoon sherry and tea, the formal-dress dinners, the soft and yawning certainty that nothing could ever intrude on this perfect upper-class world. At a party his first night, Smith drunkenly lectured several of his fellow students about the threat posed by Hitler. They laughed and haughtily scolded him for taking "the thing" so seriously. Shouting that they'd rue their smugness one day, Smith wobbled through the door. Once outside, he threw up.

Soon he discovered another Oxford, one composed of young Britons who felt the same as he. His friends for the most part were socialist and Marxist firebrands, all penniless, all passionately involved in the struggle against British appeasement. They were members of perhaps the most political generation in Oxford's history, the one that for better and worse shaped postwar England. Said ex-Communist Denis Healey, a close friend of Smith's at Oxford who later moved to the Labour Party and became England's chancellor of the exchequer, "It was a wonderful time to be young and there. The atmosphere was like the early days of the French Revolution."

An ardent member of Oxford's powerful Labour Club, an auxiliary of the Labour Party, Smith became one of its chief revolutionaries. He joined a small group of students who stole out before dawn to paint antigovernment slogans — "Chamberlain Must Go!" — in bold black letters on walls and pavements all over town. He joined protest marches in Trafalgar Square and before the Houses of Parliament. He picketed 10 Downing Street, wearing a sandwich board and shouting in unison with his fellow picketers: "Throw the rascals out!" He was breaking British law — he'd signed a pledge not to accept any employment, paid or unpaid — and he loved every minute of it. "It was the most fun I've had in my life, before or since," he said.

Smith was having so much fun that he all but abandoned his studies to devote himself to the Labour Club. At the end of his second year at Oxford, he was elected chairman, the first American to hold the office. He traveled around the country, planning demonstrations and parades, making speeches, organizing other university students. But with war fast approaching, he decided that university politics, even of the superheated Labour Club kind, were too tame. On the day war broke out, he got a job in United Press's London bureau and three months later was sent to Berlin. He had been there less than a year when he signed on with CBS.

◆

Smith was undaunted by radio writing and reporting. He had a good voice, with a soft and elegant southern accent, and his UP background had accustomed him to concise news writing. What's more, he knew how to provide the human details that Murrow liked so much. The problem was overcoming Nazi harassment and censorship. Smith was forbidden to go to the front. The typewriters at his office and studio had been taken away by the Gestapo, and he had had to borrow an antique one, with several keys missing, from a friend. Living conditions declined to the point that Smith thought he looked more like a German beggar than an American correspondent.

He stuck it out as long as he could, but as the German forces on the eastern front bogged down in their first Russian winter, he felt he wasn't coming close to telling American listeners the truth. By November Smith had once again come to the end of the line in Berlin. After a particularly heated confrontation with the censors, he called Paul White to inform him that CBS had been shut down in Germany but that the

Nazis would not let him leave. While the network and the U.S. government wrangled with the Germans, Smith had to sit tight — worrying that at any moment he might be jailed like Dick Hottelet.

As if things weren't complicated enough, Smith had also fallen in love with a nineteen-year-old Danish woman named Benedicte Traberg. She was a dazzling, dimpled, stubborn redhead who had been working as a researcher in the Berlin bureau of a leading Danish newspaper. They met in November, just as Smith was being declared persona non grata, and Bennie, as Smith called her, was about to leave for Stockholm to become a full-time correspondent for her paper. Smith proposed four days after they met. Bennie left Berlin less than three weeks later, traveling back to Denmark to get her father's permission to marry.

The Nazis finally gave Smith his exit visa on December 5 — not a moment too soon. That evening a German tipster who had earlier tried to warn Hottelet when the Gestapo was about to arrest him sidled up to Smith and whispered, "My dear Smith, if I were you, I would get out of Germany as fast as I could."

Two days later Howard K. Smith, drunk and bearing a train ticket for Bern, Switzerland, was escorted to the station by German friends and the few remaining American correspondents, all of them just as drunk as he. They continued the farewell party at the station, breaking open a bottle of precious champagne and singing, in four-part harmony, "Old Folks at Home" and "Lili Marlene." Smith was having a wonderful time — so wonderful that he decided, what the hell, he'd stay another day. His friends may have been drunk too, but they weren't crazy: they pushed him onto the train and waved goodbye as it pulled out of the station.

It was December 7, 1941. On the train to Bern, Smith was finally able to relax. Bennie was supposed to meet him there, and he looked forward to their reunion. He had no way of knowing that the authorities in German-occupied Denmark were about to refuse Bennie an exit visa or that the Japanese were about to bomb Pearl Harbor.

In Bern he was overwhelmed to find himself awash in city lights. The glow of the street lamps made him feel as "giggly as a thirteen-year-old girl in her first two-piece bathing suit." Wearing a threadbare suit and a dirty hat with a crooked brim, he walked the streets for hours, often not on the sidewalks but smack down the middle of the streets, grinning the whole way. *The lights! The lights!*

People who saw him must have thought he was crazy. They just didn't know! "Peace, brother; it's wonderful!" he wrote a few months later. "Peace is unbelievable. You cannot take somebody's word for it. You must spend two years in the Berlin blackout some time when you have nothing else to do, and then go to Switzerland suddenly, if you want to love Peace the way Peace deserves to be loved." Only when he returned to his hotel on that wonderful, light-filled December night did Smith learn that the Japanese had attacked Pearl Harbor and that all the American correspondents he had said goodbye to in Germany had been interned by the Nazis.

He had been on the last train from Berlin before the United States entered the war.

✦

Lights also blazed in Washington that night. Sitting in front of his microphone in the frenzy of the White House press room, Eric Sevareid watched other reporters rush in and out of the press secretary's office. He thought back on the strange, difficult year he'd just experienced and smiled. America was no longer on the sidelines. He felt justified. To-night was a good night.

He had been assigned to Washington after the publicity whirl that followed his return from London. Stunned by how reluctant much of the country seemed about American involvement, he had found Washington to be, if anything, worse. Washington, that "leafy, dreaming park," as Sevareid put it, that "clean and well-hedged suburb to the nation," was totally isolated from reality, unable to grasp the significance of the chaos spreading over the globe.

Sevareid despised the isolationist senators and congressmen he covered during hearings on U.S. aid for Britain. "Tobacco-chewing, gravy-stained, overstuffed gila monsters," he called them, "who, nestled in their bed of chins, would doze through other speeches, then haul up their torpid bodies and mouth the old, evil shibboleths about King George III, the war debts . . . and 'decadent France.'" Sevareid had fierce arguments with government officials, old friends, other journalists. He didn't understand how Washington reporters could be just as smug, as complacent, as insular as the people they were covering on Capitol Hill. Other reporters, in turn, thought Sevareid overwrought and arrogant. "Make way for the *com-men-ta-tor!*" someone once yelled when he entered the White House press room. "Make way for the ideology boy who sees all, knows all, and don't say *nuthin'!*"

In his broadcasts Sevareid was supposed to be "objective" and "neutral." But how could he be either when the future of the country and the world was on the line? Nearly every broadcast he made during his first year back in the States brought protests from directors of local radio stations and complaints from angry members of Congress about this "prejudiced propagandist" that CBS had sent to Washington. Paul White lectured him frequently about expressing his opinions.

In London, Murrow could go on the air and talk about what he called "the cause," about Britain's desperate need for American airplanes and the pilots to fly them, and then add, "This is not a personal plea to send American boys to die in the skies above Britain. These remarks have not been stimulated by an official source. I've been impelled to make them . . . because I've seen the faces of men who've come back from Dunkirk, Norway, and Greece, asking bitterly, 'Where are our planes?'" Though skillfully worded, this broadcast and others like it were Murrow's pleas for American help. Yet no one at CBS tried to curb *him*. Murrow was *sui generis*, a favorite of Bill Paley's. Besides, he was in London. It wasn't as easy for New York to criticize him there, since they didn't know anything about British policy, whereas *everyone* was an expert on U.S. policy.

In a broadcast on July 5, 1941, Sevareid questioned why journalists paid so much attention to the isolationists. "What weight," he asked, "shall be given the remarks of a minority whose responsibility in the decisions is only a fraction of those in power?" For Sevareid this was pretty mild stuff. But Paul White didn't think so. "The more I read [the broadcast], the less I like it," he wrote Sevareid. ". . . It seems to me that although many may be disgusted by the process, it is essential in a democracy that anyone and everyone should have his say at all times."

In a passionate, six-page reply, Sevareid said he wasn't arguing that the Burton Wheelers and Charles Lindberghs be silenced, only that reporters and editors should not treat both sides equally when they know "one side is utterly wrong and even lies." "After all, what is our training for? What are our experience and judgement and brains for? . . . There is no magic instrument to tell you where to draw the line. You have to put it up to your own professional soul."

White would have none of it. He responded, "I don't believe you have any more right to discuss private opinions in the guise of reporter than I would have to instruct CBS correspondents to plead for a negotiated peace."

With this exchange, the battle between Murrow and the Boys on one side and CBS management on the other was joined. The issue was journalistic independence and the chimera of soulless "neutrality" where the reporting of great issues was concerned. The battle would escalate in the years ahead. Before it ended, it would ruin great broadcasting careers and would turn colleague against colleague.

For now, though, there was a ceasefire. Sevareid did try to be a little more subtle and indirect, but he couldn't resist taking aim at America's absurdly inadequate preparations for war. In a broadcast on August 30, 1941, he noted that the government had prohibited the use of aluminum for banding the legs and wings of chickens. Poultry farmers were to send in all bands for reprocessing. "The new plan will save one hundred thirty-nine thousand pounds of aluminum," Sevareid mused. "How much airplane you can make out of that, I don't know."

✦

Ed Murrow was now taking his turn on the celebrity whirl, having returned to the States for a three-month break in November 1941. He was to do a national tour, then rest. At a banquet hosted by CBS at the Waldorf-Astoria, poet Archibald MacLeish paid eloquent testimony to the things Murrow had already accomplished in his war reporting: "You burned the city of London in our houses and we felt the flames that burned it. You laid the dead of London at our doors and we knew that the dead were our dead . . . were mankind's dead."

Among the notables on the dais with Murrow were Bill Paley, Paul White, Ed Klauber, and the network's other top news attraction, Bill Shirer. In the course of the glittering evening, did either Murrow or Shirer, young pioneers still in their thirties, ever look at the other and think about all the days and nights in Vienna, London, Munich, and Prague when they had struggled against some of the men with whom they were now sharing the head table and the applause? Murrow and Shirer had been so close then, and they still seemed the best of friends. The CBS publicity machine trumpeted their warm personal and professional relationship, and the company's publicity photographers shot dozens of stills of them together.

But there were strains in the relationship, tiny fissures that threatened to widen and deepen. Murrow resented Shirer's reneging on his promise to sit in for him in London. He disapproved of the way Shirer was profiting from his war experiences with his book and lecture tours. (The money Murrow made from *his* lecture tour that year went to charity.) In a letter to a friend, Murrow wrote, "One of my age cannot go about . . . making profits out of recounting the heroism of others, and then put the money in the bank." In another letter Murrow said he was "spending most of my time trying to keep my temper in check," seeing "so many well-dressed, well-fed, complacent-looking people" and hearing "wealthy friends moaning about ruinous taxation."

One day, talking with Shirer on the sidewalk outside Louis and Armand's restaurant after a few hours of drinking, Murrow couldn't quite contain his temper. He suddenly grabbed Shirer's battered old fedora off his head and threw it into the street, where a couple of buses and cabs immediately flattened it. "That old hat of Bill's got on my nerves," Murrow said later. "I told him that now, since he was in the money, he could afford a new one. I felt my trip home was a big success."

Murrow told that story often when he returned to London, and it always got a big laugh. But perhaps there was a darker reason for his impetuous shying of the hat. The truth was that Murrow didn't much *approve* of Shirer anymore. He also may not have been thrilled to learn that Shirer, the first person he hired, had in the past year become a major challenger to Murrow's position and prestige inside and outside the network. After all those drinks at Louis and Armand's, perhaps Murrow was trying to deliver a message: Don't presume too much, old pal. I'm *still* the boss. As if to underscore the point, Murrow the next day presented Shirer with a brand-new hat.

◆

Ed and Janet Murrow had been invited to have dinner with the Roosevelts in the White House on December 7. After the news of the Japanese attack on Pearl Harbor, Mrs. Roosevelt called to say the invitation still stood. The president did not dine with them, but the first lady said her husband wanted Murrow to remain afterward. A few minutes past midnight, Murrow was ushered into the Oval Office, where Roosevelt soberly sketched for him the magnitude of the disaster: the Pacific fleet decimated, 75 percent of the American warplanes in the Pearl Harbor area destroyed on the ground, thousands killed and wounded. That the president of the United States would confide all this to Ed Murrow alone on such a portentous night was a remarkable indication of the great distance Murrow and CBS had traveled in the four years since he had moved from New York to London.

It's possible that Roosevelt wanted Murrow to go public with the extent of the disaster — none of his remarks were placed off the record — but in the end, for reasons unknown, Murrow decided to keep the president's gloomy assessment to himself. Sevareid, however, was not so restrained. Through interviews with the high administration officials who hurried in and out of the Oval Office that night, he had learned the truth about Pearl Harbor, and while other radio commentators and reporters downplayed it, Sevareid went on the air and spelled out the reality. "It was the broadcast of Eric Sevareid in the evening that really set the wheels turning in American factories," Roger Burlingame, the biographer of Elmer Davis, wrote. "For the first time, he told the grim truth about Pearl Harbor: that the damage to the American fleet had been disastrous, that it would be impossible to exaggerate it."

A half-hour after his conversation with the president, Murrow joined Sevareid in the CBS office a few blocks from the White House. "What did you think," Murrow asked, "when you saw that crowd of people tonight staring through the White House fence?"

"They reminded me of the crowds around the Quai d'Orsay a couple of years ago," Sevareid said.

"That's what I was thinking. The same look on their faces that they had in Downing Street."

It was a look they both knew well. The look of a people going to war.

Sevareid and Murrow felt enormous relief: at last America was in it. There would be no going back. No matter what lay ahead, a great moral victory had been won even before the fighting on the battlefield began. That night Sevareid slept like a baby.

✦

A few days after Pearl Harbor, Paul White announced a new CBS policy. Where war coverage was concerned, there would be no further insistence on journalistic neutrality. "This is a war for the preservation of democracy," White wrote. "The American people must not only always be kept vividly aware of this objective, but of the value to every man, woman, and child in the nation of preserving democracy." As usual, CBS was following the government's lead.

It is doubtful that anyone, least of all Murrow and the Boys, disagreed with the new policy. But once again the executives in New York were dictating to the correspondents, and that could lead only to more trouble in the long and difficult months and years ahead.

12

Triumph and Misery

T HE DAY AFTER the Japanese attack on Pearl Harbor, Cecil Brown sent Paul White a cable from Singapore: OUT TOWNING FOUR DAYS SWELL STORY. The terse, colorful language of "cable-ese," invented to reduce the per-word cost of cables and telegrams before the verbose era of faxes, e-mail, and satellites, is now almost as dead as Latin. Brown, whom CBS had assigned to Singapore after Cairo, was saying he would be out of touch for four days, covering something interesting. For the sake of his job, he knew, it had better be interesting, because he was leaving his new island post just as the Japanese were closing in.

There had already been a light bombing attack, and Brown believed an all-out Japanese offensive was likely soon. But the British authorities were certain that their colony was impregnable. To prove it, they set up a four-day field trip for the ever-skeptical Brown and O'Dowd Gallagher, a South African reporter for the London *Daily Express*. The idea was for the reporters to see British sea power in action.

Sea power was the key to success in the war, said the British brass (ignoring the Pearl Harbor disaster). At that moment two of the Royal Navy's finest ships — the mighty battleship HMS *Prince of Wales* and her sidekick battle cruiser HMS *Repulse* — were swinging at anchor in Sinagpore harbor, about to get under way.

The *Prince of Wales*, which had helped attack and sink the German dreadnought *Bismarck* the previous May, was longer than two American football fields, with a maximum speed of twenty-seven and a half knots. Her main battery consisted of ten fourteen-inch guns. The *Repulse*, although she had yet to see combat, was no slouch herself. Forty-nine feet longer than the *Prince of Wales*, she was lighter by 10,250 tons and faster by two and a half knots. Her battery included six fifteen-inch guns. These two great ships had been dispatched to Singapore in late October by Prime Minister Winston Churchill (who had once been lord of the Admiralty) to show the flag and to impress — as how could they not? — the restless Japanese.

Great Britain, like the United States, was now at war with Japan. The *Prince of Wales* and *Repulse* were the only Allied capital ships between the Mediterranean and Hawaii. Brown and Gallagher had accepted the invitation to go aboard the *Repulse* for four days while she, the *Wales*, and four destroyers went hunting for the Japanese in the South China Sea.

In deciding to make the trip, Brown reasoned that if he stayed in Singapore, he probably wouldn't be able to get out a decent story anyway, no matter what happened. The British censors in Singapore were even worse than they had been in Cairo, and Brown's ranting only made them that much more intractable. Besides, the ships might well see action first. On board the *Repulse* Brown spotted a note from her captain, William Tennant, pinned to the bulletin board: FOR THE SHIP'S COMPANY: WE ARE OFF TO LOOK FOR TROUBLE. I EXPECT WE SHALL FIND IT. WE MAY RUN UP AGAINST SUBMARINES, DESTROYERS, AIRCRAFT OR SURFACE SHIPS. WE ARE GOING TO CARRY OUT A SWEEP NORTHWARD TO SEE WHAT WE CAN PICK UP AND WHAT WE CAN ROAR UP. WE MUST ALL BE ON OUR TOES.

The British naval force slid into the Straits of Johore in the early evening of December 8, just in time for a brilliant sunset that silhouetted wind-bent palms on the Malayan shore. When *Wales*, *Repulse*, and the destroyers entered the South China Sea, they headed north, paralleling the coast. The tropical heat was stifling, and Brown got very little sleep that first night. Next morning the skies had turned dark. There was rain and a rough sea, but the heat was, if anything, worse than it had been the day before. By this time reports had been received of Japanese ships and aircraft in the area. Then, late that afternoon, Captain Tennant's voice came over the ship's loudspeaker: "We are now being shadowed by enemy aircraft."

That night in the wardroom, Brown found the ship's officers in a blustery mood.

"Those Japs are bloody fools," said one. "All these pinpricks at widely separated points is stupid strategy."

"Those Japs can't fly," said another. "They can't see at night and they're not well trained."

When Brown cautioned against overconfidence, someone said, "Oh, but really, the Japanese are *not* very good."

After another restless night in the heat, Brown awoke on Wednesday at 4 A.M. A beautiful, sultry, partly sunny dawn would soon break, but the British navy was having second thoughts about the wisdom of this mission. The ships had already been spotted by Japanese aircraft, and, lacking air cover, they had been ordered back to Singapore. Seven hours later the *Repulse*'s loudspeaker squawked: "Enemy aircraft approaching — action stations!"

Standing on the flag deck, Brown squinted into the sky and could see twin-engine naval bombers heading for the *Repulse* — nine of them, stretched across the cloudless blue sky. For a moment they seemed so damned . . . *beautiful!* The ships' antiaircraft guns opened up, belching fire and smoke and terrible noise into the heavens. Soon the Japanese planes were directly overhead, and Brown, his mouth agape, stood looking up, unable to take cover or move. He could actually *see* the bombs falling toward him like "ever-enlarging tear drops." One hit the aircraft catapult deck twenty yards astern. He counted about fifty men killed.

"Bloody good bombing for *those* blokes," said a gunner.

Another wave of planes swooped in, this time with torpedoes. Brown watched the fish streak for the zigzagging ship. Vibrating with the crash and rumble of its own constantly firing guns, the *Repulse* managed to evade the torpedoes. The battle had hardly begun, and already the great ship's guns, firing round after round into the air, were so hot that the paint on them was blistering. The sweat-soaked crew, faces blackened with gunsmoke and soot and lit with excitement and a strange sort of "ecstatic happiness," shouted and cheered. Someone yelled, "Here they come again!"

This time there were twelve of them. They seemed to swoop in from everywhere at once, like vultures closing the circle. The planes strafed as they approached, and Brown could hear the bullets zinging through the air. He had moved to a position in front of a smokestack for a clearer view. As a plane passed overhead, he turned to follow its path to the other side and only then saw that a line of bullet holes had been drilled in the stack two feet above his head. Several gunners within his view lay wounded on the deck, but the *Repulse* again escaped serious damage. The once-clear sky was cluttered with ugly black puffs of ack-ack smoke. Bright orange circles of flame on the startling blue sea marked where Japanese planes had fallen.

With the stink of cordite in the air, Brown stood on a deck littered with rolling, blackened shell casings and slick with blood. He jotted his observations in a notebook and took pictures with a camera he'd brought. The *Prince of Wales* was also under heavy air attack, but the Japanese apparently were ignoring the escort destroyers.

Hearing a whine, Brown looked up: another wave of planes was coming straight at them. One dropped a torpedo less than a hundred yards off the *Repulse's* beam, then pulled up in a steep climb to safety. "This one's got us!" Brown heard someone yell. A crash on the port side, and he was thrown four feet across the deck. Another crash to starboard. The monstrous warship shuddered, then quickly heeled over like a close-hauled sloop in a stiff breeze. Brown pulled on a lifejacket but never managed to inflate it. As he moved about the canted deck, trying to find out what was happening and what he should do, he ran into O'Dowd Gallagher. They grinned nervously and wished each other good luck as Captain Tennant's cool voice came over the loudspeaker: "All hands on deck. Prepare to abandon ship. God be with you."

There was no panic and not much confusion. Lying on the edge of the eerily sloping and treacherously wet deck, Brown watched as men flung themselves into the oil-soaked sea. He saw a group of sailors carry a young lieutenant to the rail. The lieutenant had fallen down a hatch shortly after the *Repulse's* departure from Singapore and had broken his ankle. The men tied two lifejackets around him and pitched him overboard. Another group jumped too far astern and were sucked into the ship's still-churning screws.

Brown hesitated. He was sure he was going to die. What difference did it make if he stayed or jumped? Then he thought, *I cannot lie here and let the water come over me without fighting back somehow.* He slid five feet down the ship's listing hull and stopped again, continuing to take notes and snap photos. *There's no hurry*, he told himself. To jump into the water would only hasten the inevitable. From his precarious perch he could see that the *Prince of Wales* was also mortally wounded.

He looked at his watch, but it was no longer working. It had been smashed one hour and twenty minutes after the first bomb hit the *Repulse.* He clenched his left hand into a tight fist to prevent his loose ring from falling off. His wife had bought the ring for him on the Ponte Vecchio during their honeymoon in Florence, and he did not want it to go to the bottom of the sea, at least not without him.

As he felt the ship sliding out from under him, Brown knew he could wait no longer. He hurled himself twenty feet into the warm, choking, oil-clotted water. When he bobbed to the surface amid the debris, he gagged. Then the *Repulse* pitched suddenly upward, her bow pointed to the sky. Brown started to swim, trying to put as much distance as he could between himself and the dying ship. He turned to look back and saw her plunge beneath the waves. A half mile away the vast *Prince of Wales* was sinking, too.

Brown still had his fist clenched to preserve his honeymoon ring, his ruined camera still hung from his neck. Everywhere he looked he saw scenes from Dante. He saw men pulled under as the *Repulse* sank. He saw the young lieutenant with the broken ankle give up trying to swim, pull off his two lifejackets and, sobbing, toss them to men who didn't have jackets of their own. "Take them," the lieutenant cried. "I'm no good anymore." Then he sank. As Brown watched, a small table floated by. He climbed onto it and, almost too tired to think, let the current carry him.

Exhausted and retching, on the verge of unconsciousness, he finally felt himself being hauled aboard one the *Repulse*'s life rafts. Not long afterward he and the raft's other wretched passengers were rescued by one of the British destroyers. Brown's stomach was heaving, his hands shaking, but he went to work interviewing the other survivors of the Royal Navy's worst disaster of the entire war. Two of Britain's biggest and best fighting ships had been destroyed in less than two hours. More than six hundred fifty men lost their lives, and all because of a fantasy that the "Japs" would turn tail and run in the face of such might. Still ahead in the long, cruel Pacific war were such other monuments to that fantasy as Bataan, Corregidor, and the battle of the Coral Sea.

◆

In New York CBS officials learned from an AP dispatch that Brown had been on one of the two ships. They didn't know if he was alive or dead. Then a cable arrived from Brown. It began, I WAS ABOARD THE BATTLE CRUISER REPULSE WHEN SHE AND THE PRINCE OF WALES WERE SENT TO THE BOTTOM. Ecstatic, Paul White shot off a telegram: YOU MADE GOOD YOUR BOAST ABOUT WONDERFUL STORY CONGRATULATIONS. Another White telegram followed a few days later: COLUMBIA HAS TOLD YOUR BANK YOU DID ONE GRAND JOB, meaning that Brown had a thousand-dollar bonus.

Overnight he went from being one of CBS's more obscure correspondents to full-fledged celebrity. Bill Paley sent a congratulatory cable. *Newsweek, Life,* and *Collier's* wanted stories. Bennett Cerf, the publisher of Random House, and Blanche and Alfred Knopf wanted a book.

Among British officials in Singapore, however, Brown was regarded more than ever as a pluperfect pain in the ass. Since his arrival he had clashed repeatedly and bitterly with the British hierarchy — censors, generals and admirals, colonial officials. They cut his scripts to ribbons and even killed several outright, including one that declared: "Singapore society goes dancing almost every night, making money out of huge shipments of rubber and tin, and counting on the United States Navy to keep them from harm."

In Rome and Cairo, Brown had often railed against officialdom, but in Singapore he was a man possessed. He disliked the British and their attitude, which he summed up in his diary as "One whisky water, three gins, and jump to it, boy!" Many of his American colleagues (and even some British journalists) agreed with him, but they still found his behavior annoying. "He'd storm around and scream at everybody," recalled NBC's Martin Agronsky, who, having competed with Winston Burdett in Ankara, was now up against Brown in Singapore.

White dinner jackets were de rigueur in Singapore, and Brown dutifully had one made, then decided not to wear it until the war was over. "It makes me sick to see them being worn every evening at Raffles [Singapore's grand colonial hotel] while people in Britain are getting bombed," he said. He once took a young Chinese woman to dance at Raffles, knowing that her presence would infuriate everyone even more than his rumpled war correspondent's uniform.

Complaints about Brown finally led Paul White to send him a reproving letter:

> I do not feel that publicly or semi-publicly you have any right to criticize public officials in the language I derive you used. . . . From a number of returning correspondents who have been with you in Rome, Yugoslavia and Egypt, I frequently get this kind of good-natured comment concerning you: "Cec is a scrapper and a damn good reporter, but the trouble with him is that he feels everybody is out of step but him."

Even after the sinking of the *Repulse* and the *Prince of Wales*, dinner-jacketed men and evening-gowned women still danced and drank the nights away at Raffles. The lights of that lush and languid city still blazed. In spite of everything, some British military leaders even continued to think that the Japanese, now marching south from Thailand, would never penetrate the Malayan jungle opposite Singapore. So confident were they in this notion that they kept the city's guns pointed out to sea.

In fact, Singapore was virtually defenseless, a point that Brown kept trying — and failing — to get past the censors. Finally, in early January 1942, His Majesty's official representatives decided they'd had enough of Cecil Brown and revoked his credentials on the grounds that his reports might abet a fifth-column movement. CBS issued a strong protest, and the British information minister, Brendan Bracken, was sharply questioned about the matter in the House of Commons. Defending himself, Bracken declared, "It was felt that in the abnormal conditions prevailing, Mr. Brown's comments passed the bounds of fair criticism and were a source of danger."

In the end Brown had no choice but to leave Singapore and try to establish a new base for himself in Australia. At the Singapore airport, the military censor asked him to produce all his scripts, notebooks, and diaries. The censor glanced at them and then leaned close. "I know all about you, Mr. Brown," he whispered. "I hope you publish the whole story about Singapore. Publish everything about this country."

From Sydney, Brown tried again to describe the magnitude and imminence of the Japanese threat to Singapore. On February 12 he broadcast a particularly blistering indictment of British censorship and incompetence. "The tragic story of Singapore," he said, "is not all one of Japanese numerical superiority, fanatical courage and brilliant military scheming. The Japanese are at Singapore also because of what the British authorities failed to foresee, prepare for and meet at the crucial moment."

Four days later Singapore fell to Japan.

✦

While Brown was applauded in American editorials for his uncompromising criticisms, Paul White was uneasy. A month earlier, when Brown lost his credentials, White had advised him to keep quiet and work to get himself reinstated. The whole situation, White said, was "regrettable from the standpoint of Allied morale in America." Now, with CBS under pressure from both Washington and London to support the Allied war effort, White cabled Brown: SOMEWHAT AFRAID YOU UNWITTINGLY TAKING CRUSADING ATTITUDE YOUR BROADCASTS. CERTAINLY HAVE NO INTENTION GLOSS OVER INEFFICIENCY DISPLAYED BY ANY ALLY BUT FEEL IN VIEW SINGAPORE BAN GENERAL PUBLIC WILL FEEL YOU ARE PAYING OFF OLD DEBTS.

Brown said he would watch his step, and he more or less did, but he refused to abandon his anticensorship crusade. In late February, after it was announced that he had won the Overseas Press Club's award for best radio reporting in 1941, White urged him to say, in accepting the award, that it really belonged to all radio correspondents and that "freedom of speech, within the bounds of reasonable censorship, is one of the greatest guarantees of victory."

Brown took half of White's advice. In his acceptance speech, broadcast from Sydney to the club's annual dinner in New York, he did praise his radio colleagues: "It is a great tribute to the American radio correspondents that they have gone on insisting, persuading, fighting and winning in the job of doing factual reporting for America." But Brown was *damned* if he was going to put in a plug for censorship, "reasonable" or otherwise. So the speech, as he wrote it, went on to say that the correspondents were nevertheless "hemmed in by extraordinary pressures and intimidations in most foreign countries in which they operate." The audience didn't hear that part of the speech, however; it was cut by the Aussie censors.

A month later Brown returned to the United States, a hero and a star. He was given the full publicity treatment: interviews, lecture tours, mentions in columns. The book he wrote (for Random House) about his experiences, *Suez to Singapore*, soared to near the top of the nation's bestseller lists. When CBS's outstanding New York–based news analyst, Elmer Davis, left the network in mid-1942 to become head of the government's Office of War Information, Brown was given Davis's daily time slot from 8:55 to 9 P.M., one of the more lucrative commercial periods of the broadcast day. For Brown this was heady stuff after so many years of wire-service obscurity and laboring in the shadow of the other Boys. With his new program, he thought he was at last in a position to tell people what he thought.

✦

Although Murrow had hired Brown, they were never as close as Murrow and the other Boys were to one another. One reason, perhaps, was that Brown never worked closely with Murrow. The only other Boys about whom that could be said were Winston Burdett and Howard K. Smith, and even they, much as they loved and admired Murrow, were never bound to him in quite the same way that Shirer, LeSueur, Sevareid, Collingwood, and, soon, Bill Downs were.

In Brown's case, there was another possible explanation for Murrow's coolness. Overwrought and strident much of the time, Brown hardly fit the statesmanlike image that Murrow preferred. In a letter to Sevareid in Washington, Murrow dismissed *Suez to Singapore*, which was mainly a denunciation of British censorship, as a "mess." About the same time Severeid wrote Brown a note in which he said he found the book "fascinating" and "gripping." Nevertheless he chided the author for putting "too much stress on the squabbles with all the second rate officials." He continued, "Ed Murrow, Shirer and I (in Paris) all went thru the same kind of experience; we fought [censorship] consistently, but somehow none of us thought it was of world-shaking importance."

There was no sense of proportion about Brown, no sense of irony or humor. Murrow placed great value on those traits. If you had them, you could get away with a lot — even with being not quite as statesmanlike as Murrow.

Unlike Brown, Bill Downs had those qualities.

✦

In the late summer of 1942, when Larry LeSueur was becoming tired and frustrated after a year of covering the eastern front, Murrow began looking for someone to replace him in Moscow. Collingwood said they needed a "very good feature writer, someone to tell the anecdotes, give the flavor of life in wartime Russia, rather than just paraphrase communiqués." That, of course, was a backhanded slap at LeSueur. (As generous and charming as Charlie Collingwood was to most people throughout his life, he could be a devious competitor; this unfair little insult was just the first bud of what later became a full-flowered rivalry between him and LeSueur.) Bill Downs, in UP's London bureau, was just the man for the job, Collingwood said.

Downs did have a flair for feature writing, but he was above all a hard-nosed reporter, the kind who "got the story, got it first, got it right." He wore thick glasses with heavy frames. He was short and had an ample, powerful build, an abundance of dark hair, and a loud growl of a voice that when raised (as it often was) gave new meaning to the concept of wrath. But more than yelling, Downs loved to laugh. And drink. And tell stories. And argue. In roughly that order. He hated pomposity. When he first arrived in London, he entered a pub on Washington's Birthday and loudly proposed a toast to the man "who kicked hell out of the English army one hundred and fifty years ago." Bill Downs also had a fierce sense of integrity and honor. Ed Murrow took to him instantly.

Downs had grown up in Kansas City, and all he ever wanted to be was a reporter. His father, William Sr., was a Union Pacific railroad engineer, his mother a housewife with a third-grade education. During his father's long absences on the railroad, Bill — an only child for nine years, until his sister, Bonnie, came along — was doted on by his mother.

The family was never very poor. When business fell off during the Depression, the Union Pacific cut back on Downs's runs, but he always kept his job. Even so, Bill Jr. was expected to help pay for his schooling: two years at Wyandotte College and two years at the University of Kansas. One of his summer jobs was as a grain sampler, testing the quality of the wheat before it went to market. Downs had to climb to the top of huge silos and dive down into the "damn dusty stuff" and come up with a pint of sample wheat. It was a dirty, hot, dangerous job, but it helped strengthen Downs's already powerful physique. Later it turned out to have had another advantage: it was the kind of hard youthful work that always appealed to Ed Murrow.

In school Downs was sports editor of his high school newspaper and manager of the paper at Wyandotte College. At the University of Kansas, which he entered in 1933, he was, according to a college friend, John Malone, "the best and most prolific writer and reporter in the whole university."

In 1935 the campus paper, the *Daily Kansan*, went bankrupt. The next fall the newspaper's board appointed Malone publisher, and he in turn chose Downs as managing editor. Within a year the paper began to turn a profit, and it has operated successfully ever since. Malone gave most of the credit to the energetic, impatient Downs: "He was a great managing editor. He had the newsiest paper around, far better than the Kansas City papers." After college both Downs and Malone were hired by UP for its Kansas City bureau, along with another Kansan (and recent University of Texas dropout) named Walter Cronkite.

Downs was immediately tagged as a comer at UP. Within a few months, he was transferred to the Denver bureau and not long after that to New York. In 1941 he was given the wire service's plum assignment — the London bureau, the war. He loved the speed and immediacy of wire-service work, but when Murrow approached him about the CBS Moscow job in September 1942, Downs didn't hesitate. "Not only will it establish my name," he wrote to his parents, "but the work is easier and I believe has more future." Not to mention a seventy-dollar-a-week salary and an expense account.

First, though, he was supposed to undergo the pro forma voice test. It did not go well. Even Murrow called it "terrible" and told Downs to try again. This time, Murrow said, just go to Piccadilly Circus and come back with a story describing what you saw. On his return, Downs talked about two GIs leaning against a wall, admiring the passing parade of women, most of them in slacks. Suddenly one of the soldiers spotted an American Red Cross worker in a skirt. "Look, Willie," he shouted. "Ankles." Downs's growling voice didn't improve in the second test, but Murrow loved the story so much that he hired him anyway.

In November, after receiving a little radio training from Collingwood, Downs was deemed ready for Moscow. He set off, equipped with a new ankle-length, fur-lined leather coat and matching fur-lined flying boots for protection against the Russian winter. Although Downs found the assignment in Moscow no easier than LeSueur did, he managed to demonstrate that he was the equal of his seniors on the Murrow team. In late January 1943, after the Red Army's siege of Nazioccupied Stalingrad had finally forced a German surrender there, Downs and several other American correspondents were taken to see the ruins.

"Try and imagine," he told his listeners, "what four and a half months of the world's heaviest bombing would do to a city the size of Providence, Rhode Island, or Minneapolis or Oklahoma City." It was "utter and complete and absolute devastation." In a fifty-mile radius one could see only piles of bricks and rubble and corpses. Downs continued, "There are sights and smells and sounds in and around Stalingrad that make you want to weep and make you want to shout and make you just plain sick at your stomach."

✦

Charles Collingwood marked the third anniversary of the beginning of the war with a broadcast from London on what it was like to be English: "It's not a bit glamorous and seldom exciting. It has meant longer hours and less food and less sleep, and less, much less, fun." What was true for the English, however, was not necessarily true for Collingwood.

His work as a CBS correspondent, his association with Murrow, and his own charm and polish gave him increasing entrée to top government, military, and social figures in London. In letters home he regaled his parents with stories of dining with Lord Davies, lunching with Admiral Blake, chatting with Lady Churchill and Anthony Eden. But his biggest social conquest that summer and fall of 1942 may have been another American — the owner of the network that employed him.

In August Bill Paley had come to London for a month to see how CBS was faring under wartime censorship. He also wanted to become better acquainted with Murrow, who was now such a force both in London and back home. Paley had never before spent much time with his European news director, and in the course of that month together in London, they became close friends. Seeing the powerful, influential circles in which Murrow traveled, Paley for the first time really understood how significant a contribution the correspondents were making to his network's success. He was impressed by just about everything he saw — and not least by young Collingwood.

Paley quickly learned that he and Collingwood had several things in common, among them a love of women, high living, and art collecting. In the latter area, Collingwood was hardly in Paley's league. CBS's chief owned Cézannes and Matisses; Collingwood was just starting out with works by lesser artists — an oil by a minor French impressionist named Frédéric-Samuel Cordey, for example, and a watercolor by George Grosz. But Collingwood was just as passionate about collecting as Paley. As he wrote his parents, "I now have more pictures than I can conveniently hang, and I have several canvasses stacked in one corner of the living room which gives the place a pleasantly bohemian air. My collecting gives me a great deal of pleasure, and it keeps me out of trouble." It also helped make a friend of Bill Paley.

Not everyone in London was taken by Collingwood, however. His art collecting, his foppishness, his compulsive gambling and partying led some to consider him a dilettante, not serious enough to hold the Murrow banner. It would take Operation Torch for most of the critics to change their minds.

✦

In July 1942 the United States and Britain agreed on a joint invasion of technically neutral French North Africa, an operation code-named Torch. Both Roosevelt and Stalin would have preferred opening a second front in France, but Churchill — still enthralled with the "soft-underbelly-of-Europe" notion — insisted that the odds against a successful cross-Channel invasion of Europe were too formidable at that time. So Roosevelt came up with the idea of invading North Africa, kicking the Axis off the African continent and crossing the Mediterranean to enter Europe.

Torch would also strike Rommel in the rear and relieve the pressure on Britain's Eighth Army. Rommel, having snatched back the Libyan territory lost by the Italians to the British, had launched a major new offensive in January 1942, sweeping deep into Egypt and to within sixty miles of Alexandria. Finally the Eighth Army managed to hold him at El Alamein, some one hundred fifty miles from Cairo. Rommel had been stopped, but the Afrika Korps had not been destroyed. That was one of the objectives of Torch.

For American correspondents, the invasion was the biggest story of the war to that point. It would commit American troops to large-scale ground combat for the first time, and the three Allied invasion forces — one for Morocco, two for Algeria — would be commanded by American generals, including the flamboyant George S. Patton. Murrow assigned Collingwood, twenty-five years old and a combat novice, to cover this important story for CBS. "He took a hell of a gamble sending such a youngster to so important an invasion as North Africa," Collingwood wrote to Janet Murrow many years later. By now, however, such gambles were second nature to Murrow, and they almost always paid off.

The night before Collingwood left for Africa, he and Murrow went out drinking. As they stumbled back to Murrow's apartment in the blackout, both more than a little drunk, Murrow kicked over a garbage can and shouted, "By God, I envy you for going off! I wish I could go along with you!" The commotion woke Janet Murrow, who came outside and ordered them both to shut up and come in. They did, but only to have another drink.

Operation Torch was four days old by the time Collingwood arrived in Algiers on November 12, 1942. Radio coverage was given short shrift by the military when American and British assault forces came ashore at Vichy-held Casablanca, Algiers, and Oran; only newspaper correspondents were allowed to land with the troops. Algiers had quickly surrendered, but there was still light resistance by French forces in Oran and Morocco, all of which Collingwood and CBS missed. "We don't get in until everything is over," he complained in a letter to his family. "Generals think of radio as something like the tank or dive bomber — an incomprehensible device to be looked on with suspicion and treated with caution."

Wonderment at being in this exotic place soon overcame his pique. His first broadcast was a description of American soldiers' (and his own) wide-eyed reaction to hilly, white Algiers, with its minarets and crowded casbah, its veiled and barefoot women. In his initial naive excitement, Collingwood concluded that the taking of Algeria and its capital city meant the return of peace, justice, and prosperity for the country's citizens. Algiers, he said in that first broadcast, was a "friendly city, a happy city, a good deal happier, I think, than before we came."

He soon learned otherwise. Algiers was rife with suspicion, intrigue, and a sense of betrayal. The problem was that General Eisenhower had named Admiral Jean Darlan head of French military forces and the French government in liberated North Africa — Darlan, who had been Marshal Philippe Pétain's right-hand man at Vichy, who had collaborated shamelessly with the Germans in France, who had agreed to Nazi persecution of French Jews, who had ordered the mass arrests of Vichy opponents, who had supplied Rommel and his troops with food, trucks, and gasoline.

The Allies needed Darlan, Eisenhower believed, because he alone had the clout to order a truce and persuade the Vichy troops to lay down their arms when the Allies landed (which, despite fitful resistance, they mostly did). Eisenhower's main initial goal was to get across French North Africa with all possible speed and engage the Germans. His deal with Darlan helped accomplish that. But after agreeing to the truce, Darlan sent a message to the Vichy leader of Tunisia, declaring that the Americans "are our enemies, and we must fight them, alone or with outside help." With that the Vichy government in Tunisia opened the doors to German occupation, and a future battlefield was created.

The Eisenhower-Darlan deal betrayed a cynicism on the Allied side that tended to undermine the moral position of its leaders, notably Churchill and Roosevelt. How could Eisenhower give power to a man who, among other things, would not abolish the anti-Jewish regulations and other Nazi-inspired laws? After his initial excitement, Collingwood wanted to raise such questions in his broadcasts, but suffocating censorship made it nearly impossible to do so.

Then, on Christmas Eve, 1942, a twenty-year-old Frenchman named Bonnier de la Chapelle stood waiting outside Darlan's office. When the admiral emerged, de la Chapelle fired two shots from a revolver at point-blank range, killing Darlan instantly.

Like the other American correspondents, Collingwood found out about the assassination several hours before it was officially announced, but under the rules, no stories could be filed until the French released a communiqué. When one was finally issued after midnight, Collingwood and his radio competitors, including John MacVane of NBC, frantically pounded out their scripts, handing them to the censors page by page.

Once the scripts had been approved, the correspondents rushed to the transmitter and agreed on a coin toss to determine the order of broadcast.

It was the biggest story of Collingwood's short career, and he was determined to distinguish himself. But how could he, when the competition had the same story at the same time? Then he hit on a plan. "I don't care who goes first," he told MacVane and Arthur Mann, the Mutual correspondent. "You guys go ahead and flip, and I'll go last." Surprised at this unusual generosity, they agreed. MacVane won the toss and went first, followed by Mann. When it was Collingwood's turn, he took the mike and said, "This is CBS in Algiers. If anyone is hearing this signal, will he please call CBS collect in New York and say that Charles Collingwood in Algiers has an important story for them."

He repeated the message about fifteen times, while his rivals exchanged glances. What the hell was he up to? Why was he wasting all this time when they had already been on the air with the story? Finally, Collingwood said into the mike that he would begin his report in five minutes. Then he began a long, slow countdown.

He had figured out that the later his broadcast, the better chance it had of being received in full by New York. In Algiers, as in most of the Boys' wartime locales, it was impossible to talk directly to the engineers in New York. Because this broadcast was unscheduled, the chances were remote that the engineers would be able to pick it up in its entirety after a normal, quick countdown. Collingwood knew that Paul White had wisely put together an informal network of ham radio operators who would alert CBS if they picked up any unscheduled transmissions from correspondents. Collingwood had delayed his broadcast as long as possible to give CBS's engineers a chance to hear from the hams — and from his rivals.

The plan worked perfectly: CBS received his entire broadcast, while NBC picked up only a portion of MacVane's. And since the wire services and newspapers had severe transmission problems of their own that night, it was Collingwood who received all the attention afterward. His story and his byline were plastered across the front page of the *New York Times* and other American newspapers the next morning. Discussing his coup years later, Collingwood said, "It was due to no enterprise on my part. It was simply understanding the logic of the primitive communications." He was being too modest. In journalism "understanding the logic of communications" is another way of demonstrating enterprise.

Once again a Murrow Boy was the man of the hour. John MacVane was furious. Though first on the air, he had received no credit. When *Time* later published a piece about Collingwood and said he'd broken the story of the Darlan assassination, MacVane fired off a telegram to his home office asking why his scoop had been credited to someone else. *CBS's publicity department must have beaten us to the punch* was the reply. Doubtless that was true. CBS even had its own mini wire service to promote its accomplishments and transmit its scoops to other news outlets. But it was also true that MacVane had been outfoxed.

✦

Professionally, Collingwood came of age in North Africa. In his six months at the North African front, Bonnie Prince Charlie had transformed himself into a deeply insightful and informed correspondent. Through hard work, lavish use of his formidable charm, and the good French that reading Baudelaire had helped teach him, Collingwood cultivated an amazing array of sources, from officials in the pro-Vichy government to supporters of Charles de Gaulle. He picked the brains of his friends in the U.S. war intelligence service and in Algiers' persecuted Jewish community, which had developed a first-class intelligence network of its own. More and more often, newspapers in America and Britain were running stories by Collingwood that their own reporters were unable to match. Said *Newsweek*, "His broadcasts have created at least the illusion of uncanny insight; sometimes they have caught the turn of events days in advance of official releases."

Collingwood was first with the news of the summary execution of Darlan's assassin and with the news that French royalists had been behind it. But his main focus was on the continuing American support of Vichyites in North Africa. He wrote to his parents:

> We have perpetuated and tacitly supported a regime which is a reasonably accurate facsimile of what we are fighting against. Our excuse is that we must not interfere with French politics. I wonder whether we will enter Germany and say that we must not interfere with German politics. Either our leaders are too stupid to see that this is an ideological war . . . or they are too cynical to think it matters.

In his broadcasts Collingwood took special note of Eisenhower's appointment of General Henri-Honoré Giraud to replace Darlan. A brave military man but an incompetent political leader, Giraud was a rival of de Gaulle's. Once in power he maintained Darlan's policies and threw Gaullists and other critics of his regime into concentration camps. In one report Collingwood pointed out that several of those arrested had helped arrange the Allied landing in North Africa. He then quoted Giraud as saying that all the men detained were "engaged in making trouble." "That is doubtless true," Collingwood said. "There certainly are people in North Africa who are dissatisfied with things as they are."

He couldn't be as direct and forceful as he wanted to be, but he often managed to get his point across indirectly. "I honestly didn't try to evade censorship, but sometimes I'd get so upset at the news that I guess my voice was affected," he said after the war. Reporting in March 1943 that Giraud had finally agreed to relax some anti-Jewish laws, Collingwood said that the people of Algiers felt little had changed. "It still boils down to this: We have made permanent a regime which was just as willing to work with our enemies as it was with us, a regime that has never shown any notable enthusiasm for those principles which our spokesmen have repeatedly said we are fighting for."

As mild as Collingwood considered his broadcasts to be, Eisenhower regarded them as rabble-rousing. Summoning Collingwood to his headquarters one day, the general accused him of using censored material in one report. Collingwood denied it, produced his script with the censor's stamp, and noted that it was identical to the transcription the general had received. Eisenhower cooled down. Not long afterward, however, his aide, Major Harry Butcher, who had been a CBS vice president before the war and who was in the States on military business, paid a call on Bill Paley in New York.

"Bill, I hate to bring this up," Butcher said, "but you've got a fellow in North Africa, Charles Collingwood. He's a very nice young man but he doesn't really understand the politics of the thing, and he's been causing us a few problems. The boss [Eisenhower] would be very glad if you would transfer him somewhere else. He doesn't want to hurt his career or anything. . . . Maybe you could transfer him back to London or to some other theater."

Paley looked at Butcher and then fished around on his desk for a sheet of paper. It was the announcement that Collingwood had just received the highest prize in radio news, the George Foster Peabody Award, for his North Africa reporting. Paley read to Butcher the award committee's praise of Collingwood for using "the tools of inference, indignation and fact" to convey "to us through the screen of censorship an understanding of the troublesome situation in North Africa."

"Look," Paley said, "We're not unhappy with Collingwood's work. In fact, we're very happy with it. As long as we are, we're going to keep him in place. I don't care what the general thinks."

♦

With all the attention heaped on Collingwood, it was easy to overlook the other CBS correspondent in North Africa. Winston Burdett had in fact been there longer than Collingwood and had done the lion's share of reporting from the front, beginning in July 1942, when the British staved off Rommel at El Alamein. Burdett was glad to be in the thick of the action; it gave him something to think about other than the death of his wife. Three months before, in Soviet-controlled northern Iran, Lea Schiavi had been murdered.

In August 1941 the British and Russians had occupied Iran and divided the country between them. CBS reassigned Burdett at that time from Ankara to Tehran to cover the occupation. He had been there about six months when he was sent to India on temporary assignment. Lea remained behind in Iran. On a steamy day in April 1942 a friend came to see Burdett at his hotel in New Delhi with terrible news. According to that day's edition of the *New Delhi Times*, Lea was dead.

Burdett caught the first plane back to Iran and launched his own investigation. He found that Lea had been killed not far from the city of Tabriz, where the Soviet occupation forces had their headquarters. She and an Iranian woman friend had hired a car in Tabriz to take them to a Kurdish village; an Iranian army officer and a young Kurdish interpreter had accompanied them. Late in the afternoon, as they were returning from the village, the car was waved to a stop by two armed Kurdish road guards. The women in the car were asked if either was the Italian journalist Lea Schiavi. When Lea identified herself, a guard thrust his pistol into the car and shot her point blank in the chest. She died as the others rushed to get her back to Tabriz.

The guard who killed her was arrested, tried, and sentenced to life at hard labor. That was as far as the Iranian government was willing to go. Officials told Burdett they were sure his wife's murder had been a political assassination, but they didn't want to conduct a further investigation. It seemed clear that Lea's death *had* been ordered, but by whom? It could have been the Russians or Italians or Germans — German and Italian agents had been known to slip across the Turkish border into Iran — but why? Burdett finally concluded that Mussolini's agents must have been responsible, in revenge for Lea's outspoken anti-Fascism.

But there were other possible explanations, as he well knew. Lea Schiavi's death was as mysterious as the lives she and her husband had led. The mystery of those lives would not be solved until thirteen years later, when, near the end of the McCarthy era, Winston Burdett would finally reveal the secrets he kept.

✦

Later CBS assigned Burdett to Egypt, where Cairo's lively social life and the company of young European and American women coaxed him out of his grief. In the war zone General Harold Alexander had taken command of the British forces in the Middle East, and a little-known flag officer named Bernard Montgomery had assumed control of the British Eighth Army. With those changes in leadership and the Allied landings in French North Africa, the tide began to shift against the Afrika Korps. British forces, now vastly superior in number to the Germans, launched the second battle of El Alamein in late October, using air power and armor to force "Rommel's bomb-drunk army" (as Burdett described it in a broadcast) to begin its retreat from Egypt.

As the British pursued Rommel's troops, inexperienced Allied forces, fresh from the Torch landing, were being stymied by a separate German force in Tunisia. The deadlock was broken by Rommel, whose retreating Afrika Korps linked up with a panzer division and launched a counteroffensive. The German force smashed through Kasserine Pass, a mountain gateway to Tunis, and inflicted heavy casualties on the unseasoned and undisciplined American troops of II Corps who tried to defend it. It was the first major battle of the war in which the United States had taken part, and it ended in a resounding defeat. But Collingwood reported that "veteran soldiers say that troops learn more from a shellacking than they do from a victory."

To help guarantee that the proper lessons were learned, Eisenhower assigned Major General George Patton to command II Corps. Under Patton's brand of kick-ass discipline, the Americans rallied, and, with British help, forced Rommel back through the pass. That set the stage for the beginning of the end of the North Africa campaign. In April 1943 the British Eighth Army linked up with the American First Army and II Corps in Tunisia to form an unbroken Allied circle around the retreating Germans.

About this time Winston Burdett linked up with Charles Collingwood in Algiers. It was Burdett's first contact with his natty young colleague, and he found the experience bemusing. At one point Burdett received a note inviting him to dinner that night at the suburban villa Collingwood had rented for the duration of his stay in Algiers.

Arriving at the appointed hour, Burdett encountered a fabulous sight in the midst of a dirty and deadly desert war: the villa was perched like a castle atop a hill, and outside it stood Collingwood, silhouetted against a golden evening sky, dressed in an immaculate white dinner jacket (no Cecil Brown *he*), greeting his guests. During dinner, served by white-gloved servants, a dispatch rider drove up to the villa on a motorcycle. He rushed inside and dramatically handed Collingwood a cable from CBS New York, advising him he had been added to the broadcast schedule for that evening. Cool as ever, Collingwood asked Burdett to assume his duties as host, excused himself from the table, and in a few minutes batted out a story. Then, still in his dinner jacket, he hopped into the dispatch rider's sidecar and raced off over the nighttime desert hills into Algiers.

He was back in time for the cognac and cigars.

✦

Collingwood was never one to ignore his sybaritic instincts. In North Africa he was, among other things, official bookmaker for what was variously known as the "Eisenhower Cup," the "Camel Corps Stakes," and the "Poor Man's Futurity" — a race to see which correspondent would be the first to get his story from the typewriter to the wire. ("Growing up, Charlie would bet on anything," his younger brother Tom recalled. "'I bet that chipmunk is going to go up the tree,' he'd say.") He also pursued the young American and British women who served as military drivers and secretaries in Algiers. And throughout his stint in North Africa, he paid the strict and foppish attention to his appearance that had been his trademark since his teenage years and would continue for the rest of his life. Actress Kay Francis duly noted during a USO tour that Collingwood was "the only man in Africa who knows where to get a suit pressed."

On May 7, 1943, while the remaining Germans in North Africa were finally surrendering to the Allies . . . and while the Medjerda Valley near Tunis was being pummeled by hundreds of Allied bombers and guns . . . and while a tank battle raged nearby . . . Charles Collingwood of CBS and Bill Stoneman of the *Chicago Daily News* pounded stakes into the ground and played horseshoes! When they finished their game, still in the midst of a hellish din, they got into their jeep and, with Drew Middleton of the *New York Times*, drove off to cover the end of the

North African campaign. On the way they sang a song they had composed for the occasion: "South of Tébourba, down Massicault way."

In driving rain the correspondents followed behind the first Allied troops to enter Tunis. Though the fighting continued, thousands of ecstatic residents poured out of their houses and danced around the Allied jeeps and tanks. "People were crazy with joy," Collingwood later broadcast, "and we ourselves were a little light-headed at the thought of what it all meant that we had taken it — this mirage that had gleamed before us in the mud the long six months of last winter."

While the other correspondents filed their stories from the front and endured the usual interminable transmission delays, Collingwood hitched a ride in an American friend's plane to Constantine, where he knew there was a transmitter no one else would be using. Once again he was first, this time with an eyewitness account of the liberation of Tunis. Once again it was Collingwood's story, Collingwood's byline, on the front pages of American newspapers. "I don't think I have ever known a more completely satisfying moment than when I rode into Tunis," he wrote his family a few days later. ". . . It wasn't the cheering populace or the sudden realization of our own strength as much as it was the feeling that we had reached the end of a journey, that a dream had come true."

The end of a journey, indeed, for this pretty boy who had so distinguished himself in North Africa. He had silenced his doubters, had proved his true worth. Perhaps most important, he had won the respect and praise of his hero, Ed Murrow. In a letter to Eric Sevareid, Murrow described Collingwood's six months of work in North Africa as "one of the best jobs of foreign radio reporting since your stuff during the last weeks of France."

Collingwood had triumphed but was soon too sick to care — a bad case of gonorrhea, a CBS colleague later reported. He was shipped back to London to recuperate. It would not be the last time for him that misery would follow triumph.

✳ 13

The Sin of Pride

Having returned from Australia to New York, Cecil Brown was basking in stardom — basking entirely too much, if you asked some of his CBS colleagues. "Of all the people who came up in those days, he had the most swelled head of anybody," said Bill Shirer.

Shirer himself was not unfamiliar with the sin of pride, and in this case may have been guilty of a bit of old-fashioned envy as well. Brown had been given the best broadcast time of the evening, Elmer Davis's old 8:55 P.M. slot, now rechristened *Cecil Brown and the News* and sponsored by the Johns-Manville Corporation. Moreover, this relatively new Boy had been assigned to alternate with Shirer himself on the network's unsponsored 11:10 P.M. news and analysis program.

But if there was jealousy in Shirer's criticism of Brown, there was also truth. Like Shirer, Brown was lecturing and giving interviews about his war experiences. His book, *Suez to Singapore*, was a success. He had been awarded a clutch of prizes, including the Peabody and National Headliners Club awards, for his reporting from Singapore. He had hardly begun his new program before *Motion Picture Daily* listed him among the top radio stars of 1942, together with such notables as Bing Crosby, Arturo Toscanini, Dinah Shore, and Guy Lombardo. He was welcome at Manhattan's best tables and was making what was, for the Boys in those days, a fortune. In addition to his lecture fees and book royalties and regular network salary, he was pulling in a thousand dollars a week for the 8:55 P.M. program.

Some people are able to handle sudden fame, but not Cecil Brown. Looking back, even he admitted he had been rather unbearable. He had considered himself in "kind of a special category" at CBS, he said — "one of the first prima donnas." The left-wing magazine *The Nation* ran a blistering parody of his book, taking him to task for his unyielding opposition to wartime censorship and his general egomania. Written in the first-person-singular style Brown favored, the magazine's spoof had him saying: "I took my typewriter to a British store to get the capital 'I' renewed on Saturday afternoon. They told me it couldn't be done till Monday, because people stopped work on Sundays. What abject, nauseating nonsense. Don't they know there's a war on?"

Brown overestimated both his own importance and CBS's willingness to put up with him. Only six years had passed since Murrow had been sent to London. But in that time CBS had been transformed, thanks in no small part to Murrow and the news operation, into an institution; heaven help anyone who thought he was bigger than that institution or indispensable to it. Paul White and others had been trying to rein in Murrow and the Boys, with little success, ever since Murrow and Shirer first fought their way onto the air. But Brown wasn't Murrow or Shirer or even Sevareid. He was just tiresome, White and others thought, and he was getting out of hand.

It wasn't Brown's ego that bothered White so much. If ego were an issue, he'd have considered firing everyone on the payroll. It was Brown's "editorializing." The traits that had served the correspondent and CBS so well in far-off Cairo and Singapore — his independence, his resistance to censorship, his insistence on speaking out — were seen when he came home as annoyances at best and, at worst, as threats to the nation and the network (not necessarily in that order).

It seemed to White that "pale, frail Cecil Brown," as *Time* labeled him, preferred preaching to reporting. His analyses often contained dire warnings against complacency and selfishness in an evil and dangerous world, and he was emboldened to instruct U.S. leaders on how to do their jobs. And at times Brown simply went around the bend — as when he called for the wholesale, indiscriminate execution for war crimes not only of Japanese and German leaders but of ordinary foot soldiers as well.

Even his less extravagant opinions irked White. In the spring of 1942, for instance, on a two-month pulse-taking tour of the country, Brown larded his analyses with criticisms of American attitudes toward the war. At one point he said, "Today they are betting in Indianapolis that the war will be over this year, and, incredible as it may sound, they are betting nine-to-two that the war will be over by Christmas. . . . Such optimism is not justified by any of the facts, but a good many people in Indiana do not seem to be concerned with the facts." Nor was Brown persuaded that the Roosevelt administration's rosy picture of a nation united and ready to sacrifice was accurate. "It's amazing to a reporter recently back from countries fighting for their existence," he said, ". . . to find people who think gas restrictions a bit too irksome to endure."

Eric Sevareid had been making much the same point from Washington, also to White's displeasure. But Sevareid was close to Murrow and enjoyed a certain immunity that Brown did not. Almost from the moment he returned to the States, he felt White's wrath. Indeed, it wasn't long before White ordered the night news editor, Henry Wefing, to delete any opinions expressed in Brown's scripts. White even instructed Wefing to sit in the studio control booth and to cut Brown off the air if he departed from the edited script. Every time Brown sat down before his microphone, there was Wefing, looking for all the world like one of those military censors Brown hated so much.

By the summer of 1943, there were rumors inside CBS that Brown's sponsor, Johns-Manville, was also fed up with his liberal "editorializing." According to the rumors, the company's executives were particularly upset about his praise of a controversial Warner Brothers movie, *Mission to Moscow*. The movie had been more or less commissioned by the Office of War Information under Elmer Davis in hopes of increasing American support for the Soviet Union, Washington's new wartime ally. But the Johns-Manville people thought the screenplay went too far, glossing over such recent unpleasantness as Stalin's purges and the Soviet-German nonaggression pact. On August 24 Johns-Manville gave CBS thirty days' notice that it was exercising its option to drop Brown's program.

At the time Brown was out of town (without his CBS censor) on another lengthy national fact-finding tour. Broadcasting from Indianapolis and unaware that he was being dropped by his sponsor, he criticized President Roosevelt and Prime Minister Churchill, who had just concluded a summit meeting in Quebec, for failing to "dramatize what we are fighting for." Because of this failure of leadership, Brown said, "any reasonably accurate observer of the American scene at this moment knows that a good deal of enthusiasm for this war is evaporating into thin air."

It was a tough broadcast, but no tougher than others Brown had made. It expressed sentiments that Sevareid and Murrow, among others, had also expressed, although they had been more artful. But Brown's latest transgression came only a day after Johns-Manville's decision to withdraw its sponsorship, and it made Paul White *very* angry. White fired off a letter to Brown that was as strident as any of Brown's broadcasts, accusing him of the kind of defeatism "that would be of immense pleasure to Dr. Goebbels and his boys." Brown's entire report, White wrote, was "a statement of what Cecil Brown thinks, of what Cecil Brown would have done had he been President Roosevelt, disregarding the very obvious truth that the people did not elect Cecil Brown but did elect President Roosevelt." If Brown could not curb his personal opinions on the air, White said, CBS would be glad to release him from his contract.

Brown, now aware that he had lost his sponsor, hurried back to New York and into a meeting with White. He argued that his assertions about America's lack of enthusiasm were based on many interviews conducted over several weeks and were backed up by more than a thousand pages of notes. He pointed out that White had not once chastised him when he was CBS's correspondent in Rome for summarizing what he felt to be the attitudes of the Italian people. "You don't object to my having an opinion," Brown said. "You object because I'm not reflecting *your* opinion." Claiming he had been gagged, Cecil Brown resigned on September 2.

Immediately an impressive array of journalists outside CBS rallied to his side — no doubt to the surprise of White and others at the network who seemed to think this was an internal matter. Columnists and commentators from Dorothy Thompson to Walter Winchell denounced CBS; *Variety* said the network's thinking and philosophy were "threadbare." *Editor and Publisher* was more pointed: "We like our meat with salt. If radio cannot supply that salt [without worrying that it will] offend a few thousand listeners, an advertiser or two, or the Federal Communications Commission, it had better step aside now and leave the business of news to those who can handle it."

CBS's main pro-Brown antagonist was one of its own former commentators, H. V. Kaltenborn, who in 1940 had moved to NBC after many run-ins with White on the subject of objectivity. Kaltenborn had thought the network's policy ridiculous when he worked there, and nothing since had changed his mind. For one thing, he said, the policy was impossible to implement. "No analyst worth his salt could or would be completely neutral or objective. . . . Every exercise of his editorial judgment [by selecting one fact or one story over another, for example] constitutes an expression of opinion."

Kaltenborn charged, too, that CBS was hypocritical in enforcing its policy. He recalled how, when he was at CBS, Klauber would urge him to disguise his own opinions by attributing them to others. "Don't be so personal," Klauber would tell Kaltenborn. "Use such phrases as 'It is said. . .' and 'There are some who believe . . .'" That's exactly what Murrow and Shirer were doing now, Kaltenborn said, and unlike Brown, they were getting away with it.

Even the chairman of the Federal Communication Commission, radio's chief regulator, joined the chorus. CBS's wartime objectivity policy had been drafted back in 1939 because of Paley's fear of FCC punishment if his commentators stirred up public opinion against American neutrality. But in 1943 the commission's chairman, James Fly, sought to encourage a diversity of news and opinion on the airwaves. In a speech at the time of the Brown dispute, Fly noted that CBS's policy often forced its journalists to cite *other* people's opinions in order to make their own points. "The fact is," Fly said, ". . . that radio does have some of the most competent commentators and analysts on earth; and it would be a pity if the rules of the very medium which brings their voices to the people prevent their opinions from reaching the people."

CBS was unmoved. After Brown resigned, Paul White sent a memo to all editorial employees reiterating the network's objectivity policy and emphasizing his belief that they "were not privileged to crusade, to harangue the people or to attempt to sway public opinion." A short time afterward the memo was reproduced in full-page advertisements that CBS took out in New York and Washington newspapers.

What was going on here? If CBS didn't want to offend the government, and the government said that no offense had been or would be taken, why continue the crusade? One possible answer is that Paley, Klauber, White, and the others genuinely wanted their network to be free of opinion, analysis, and insight. Possible but unlikely. As Brown pointed out, and as the case history demonstrates, opinions per se were never really the problem; the problem was opinions with which the CBS brass, for one reason or another, disagreed. A more plausible explanation, therefore, was that concern about the government's reaction had been replaced by concern about the reaction of sponsors. Brown, opinions and all, almost certainly would have remained at CBS if Johns-Manville had kept paying the bills.

It was an early sign of the profound changes occurring at the network. Murrow and the Boys were becoming victims of their own success. During the war they contributed enormously to the increased popularity of radio, and that popularity made the medium irresistible to sponsors, who came to exert, through their advertising agencies, considerable control over the programs for which they paid. Commentators like Shirer and Brown, who appeared on sponsored programs, received more than $50,000 a year, compared to salaries of well below $10,000 for most regular radio correspondents, including most of the other Murrow Boys. But sponsorship came at a price. A sponsored journalist was subject to the whims, political and otherwise, of his sponsor and the ad agency; and sponsors, almost by definition, didn't like unpopular opinions that might cause people either to turn off their sets, and so miss the commercials, or to shun the sponsor's product in protest.

The newspaper ads CBS took out to trumpet its "objectivity" were probably aimed less at reassuring listeners than at reassuring advertisers. The liberal *New York Post* thought the network "was making a bid for new commercial sponsors, and through its [newspaper] advertising was taking steps to assure them it had not been promoting any one point of view." About this same time Walter Winchell, who often had good sources on such matters, reported in his column that CBS executives had met at the Union League Club with a group of wealthy business-men. The message from the advertisers, according to Winchell: "We spend a lot of money with CBS, money that is used to pay the salaries of commentators who voice opinions with which we disagree. Now, we do not say your commentators should agree with us, but we think CBS should hire reporters and analysts who give our side a break, too."

♦

With all the furor over Brown, little attention was paid to another CBS personnel change. This one also signaled a major reorientation of the network's approach to news and reinforced the idea that at Bill Paley's network, absolutely *no one* but Paley himself was indispensable. A month before Brown resigned, Paley had forced out his second in command, Ed Klauber. The original architect of the network's objectivity policy, Klauber had his faults. He could be hard-nosed, narrow-minded, and difficult, but he had always been the news department's champion, the one executive on whom the department could depend to preempt com-mercial programming for an important news bulletin or story. He had insisted on the highest editorial standards for CBS, and Ed Murrow, whom he hired, considered him the best editor he ever knew.

Klauber had come to CBS in 1930 from the *New York Times*. He had served Paley's needs back when the network was young and Paley was unsure of himself. These days, however, Paley was rarely unsure of himself, and he was tired of Ed Klauber. "[Klauber] and Paley just didn't seem to see eye to eye," recalled Frank Stanton, then the network's ace market researcher. Paley's choice as the new executive vice president was

Stanton's boss in the promotion and market research department, Paul Kesten: a newsman replaced by a pitchman. Slowly and rather quietly, Bill Paley was developing a new vision for his network — one whose implications would not be fully understood until after the war.

Certainly Murrow and the Boys did not fully understand the implications in 1943. Murrow was sorry to hear about Klauber's departure but was too preoccupied with the war to spend much time worrying about it. He was puzzled by the Brown controversy and wanted to know more, but for a while no one in New York responded to his queries. When he finally did receive a response, it was from Shirer.

In his letter Shirer hotly defended CBS and criticized Brown. (He had done the same thing publicly in an appearance at the Overseas Press Club.) He also predicted that Brown would try to make even more trouble for the network. Of course Shirer was hardly disinterested. He and Brown were competitors as well as colleagues, and Brown's resignation left the field open to him. As for White's latest restatement of the anti-opinion edict, both Murrow and Shirer agreed it was "a silly idea."

Murrow was concerned about what he saw as a growing intolerance on the part of the public, the government, sponsors, and the networks for truthful war reporting. As he wrote to a friend, "People seem to want to be misled, want to believe that things are going to be easy. . . . Any slight effort at realism is immediately labeled weariness, cynicism and pessimism. The result of this state of confusion and lack of faith is [my] recurring desire to stop broadcasting altogether."

He didn't stop, of course. How could he? He and Shirer were still on top. There was no reason to think things would change for Murrow and Shirer. Their names, almost as much as Paley's, were synonymous with CBS. They were, they thought, indispensable.

✦

When Cecil Brown resigned, less than two years after his adventure on board HMS *Repulse*, he was sure he would have little trouble finding a similar job at another network. "I was hot stuff," he said. "I was salable." He did manage to continue as a commentator, but he never found another slot as prestigious or influential as the one he had at CBS. He broadcast for Mutual from 1944 to 1957, then for ABC for two years, and for NBC for six years after that. In 1964 he became director of news and public affairs for KCET, the public television station in Los Angeles; he also did commentary for the station. And in 1966 he won the prestigious Alfred I. du Pont award for his "thoughtful, forthright opinions based upon many years of personal observation of, and involvement in, the major events of our time."

It was, in a way, a vindication for Brown and the rest of the Boys. What they had fought for against Paley, Klauber, White, and others, was not the right to "editorialize." That was a red herring. They didn't want to sell an ideology or a partisan view or persuade people how to think or vote. They wanted to draw conclusions about the stories they covered and present those conclusions to their listeners. They wanted to be more than conveyors of facts; they wanted to interpret the facts, place them in context, analyze them. They did not believe that all facts, or all ideas or actions, were equal, and in their reports they did not want to pretend they were. Murrow and the Boys weren't stenographers; they were journalists. They wanted, within reason, to make moral, ethical, and historical judgments, based on their knowledge and experience, and to share those judgments with the public.

✦

In 1946 Paul White left CBS in bitter circumstances and moved to San Diego. There he took a job as a commentator for a local television station, KFMB. Ironically, he also wrote and broadcast the station's editorials. In 1954, when Murrow used his *See It Now* television program on CBS to take on Senator Joseph McCarthy, *Newsweek* suggested that such a program would have been impossible a few years earlier, when White was crusading for objectivity. White responded with a telegram to *Newsweek*'s editors: "My nightly broadcast is proof that I no longer subscribe to that 1943 viewpoint. In that year I also thought that Soviet Russia was a valuable ally, that nuclear fission was impossible and that, after the war and with rationing and controls removed, steaks would be plentiful and cheap."

Return to Battle

Like cecil brown, Eric Sevareid saw little in America but complacency and selfishness.

When the United States entered the war, Sevareid was sure the country would shake off its pre–Pearl Harbor ennui and devote itself to the cause, as Britain had done in 1940. But unlike Britain, the United States was not under attack. "Life was easy," Sevareid wrote, "and getting more prosperous every week, and nobody believed in death." Americans needed to be roused from their torpor, he thought. Instead the Roosevelt administration had minimized the seriousness of Pearl Harbor and now was sweeping its mistakes under the rug.

Shaken when Eisenhower appointed the crypto-Nazi Darlan as wartime overseer of French North Africa, Sevareid began to fear that the ideal of a better postwar world would be sabotaged. The American military, with its sometimes strange taste in allies, he said, was "fighting against bodies, not ideas. . . . They would use any means, including individual Fascists and Fascist institutions, to aid them in their specific task, regardless of how the basic issues were muddied and the future placed in jeopardy."

What meaning could the war possibly have, Sevareid wondered, if it did not lead to justice and equality for the people now suffering its effects? "This is a political war, a great world revolutionary war," he said in an impassioned talk on the national radio program *Town Meeting of the Air,* "and not a breath of that is permitted to blow upon the minds of our soldiers. . . . We know that somewhere once, there was a great thing called the American Dream. Should we fail now to call it up again before our eyes, it will be lost forever."

This latest round of angst came at a time when Sevareid was thriving personally. CBS had named him chief of its growing Washington bureau, he was on the air several times a day, and, because his programs had sponsors, he was making considerably more money than he ever had in his life. Success, however, only deepened Sevareid's gloom. In Washington he felt himself a profiteer, "cut off from the solid work of America at war." He had managed to quell his old fear of being wounded or killed, and he wanted to be overseas again, "to see the war, be in the war, to know what men of my generation were going through."

The people who decided such things at CBS, however, were happy to have Sevareid where he was. In a letter to Murrow, he said he was so desperate that he was thinking about joining the army. Murrow gently suggested he might find himself "even more frustrated" there. Sit tight, Murrow advised, and he would try to persuade New York to send him abroad again. That was probably what Sevareid had wanted to hear.

In the end it was not Murrow but a mysterious fate that engineered Sevareid's return to war. In the summer of 1943 "a close friend of President Roosevelt's" (a man whom Sevareid never identified but who presumably was either in the government or acting on its behalf) summoned Sevareid to his office. Was Eric willing to go to China to see if he could get to the bottom of all the controversy swirling about the nationalist Chinese, their American advisers, and the Communist forces led by Mao Tse-tung? Sevareid was surprised by the request but readily agreed, provided he could go as an independent journalist and could report to the public anything he learned. The White House "friend" said that was exactly what he had in mind; anything he produced was bound to be an improvement on the cacophony of official, semiofficial, and unofficial voices that Washington was now receiving.

✦

In 1943 Washington's policy in China was in turmoil. The deputy commander of the China-Burma-India theater, U.S. General Joseph W. ("Vinegar Joe") Stilwell was at odds with the nationalist Chinese leader, Generalissimo Chiang Kai-shek. Stilwell wanted to build a thirty-division army to repel the Japanese aggressors. Chiang saw this as a threat to his control of the lackluster Kuomintang forces. The tension was only increased by Chiang's struggle against Mao and the Communists, who were also fighting the Japanese. Indeed, Stilwell suspected that Chiang, whom he considered corrupt and inept and whom he openly derided as "the peanut," was more interested in battling Chinese Reds than the imperialist Japanese. At the same time there was a bitter strategic debate going on between Stilwell and the Army Air Corps' General Claire Chennault, commander of the legendary Flying Tigers. Stilwell thought the war should be fought primarily on the ground; Chennault — and Chiang — favored air power.

And frantically stirring a noxious cauldron of pro-Chiang propaganda in the United States was the "China lobby," aided and abetted by Chiang's beautiful, brittle wife. Among the lobby's American leaders were two powerful editor-publishers — *Time*'s China-born Henry Luce and the castle-building prince of yellow journalism, William Randolph Hearst — whose reporters in China had to struggle against not only military censors but their own bosses' prejudices.

No wonder "a close friend of the president's" felt a need, in that summer of 1943, for an independent set of eyes and ears.

✦

On August 2 Sevareid found himself on a dusty airfield in a remote corner of northeast India, staring at a small twin-engine cargo plane. He, along with sixteen other passengers and four crew members, were to fly the perilous "Hump" over Burma and the towering Himalayas and into China. When Sevareid had persuaded CBS to approve and pay for his trip to China, he had not much considered how he would get there. Now, looking at this C-46, shimmering in the relentless heat, he was thinking hard.

Since his arrival in India, he had heard terrifying stories about the flying conditions and the loss of planes on the Hump run, established for the shipment of Lend-Lease supplies to Chiang. If the Hump sometimes conquered even solidly built planes, what would it do to a C-46 — the "flying coffin" — a plane that by most accounts was unsafe in any conditions? Sevareid's old fears from the days of the Blitz suddenly enveloped him again.

The plane took off uneventfully. On board as passengers were twelve American soldiers, two Chinese army officers, Sevareid, and two other civilians, one of whom was General Stilwell's State Department adviser, John Paton Davies (who would become a fall guy for Joe McCarthy and the China lobby during the postwar "who-lost-China" debate). The going was easy at first, and Sevareid started to relax. About an hour into the flight, however, a young corporal leaned over and shouted to him, "Know what? Left engine's gone out."

Sevareid's stomach tightened even as he tried to reassure himself that a C-46 could theoretically do as well — if that was the word — on one engine as two. A few moments later the crew chief rushed to the main door, removed it from its hinges, and began throwing out luggage. "All passenger baggage out!" someone cried. The roar of the plane's one good engine and of the air rushing past the open doorway was deafening. Breathing raggedly, Sevareid grabbed the beautiful new bag he had bought for the trip and tossed it out the door himself.

Seconds dragged by like hours. Surely the pilots would be able to keep this thing aloft! Then the door to the four-man crew's compartment burst open, and three of the crew grabbed parachutes from a pile by the radio operator's desk. Sevareid, who was already wearing his parachute but who had never in his life made a jump, froze in terror. His head was throbbing, and a great weight seemed to be pressing on his chest, making it almost impossible to inhale. "Oh, no, no!" he thought. "This can't happen to me, not to me!"

There was no warning. No order to jump was given — at least none that Sevareid heard. The other passengers just got up as if they knew what was happening and what they were supposed to do and, one by one, began hurling themselves out of the plane. Davies was among the first to jump. Sevareid hesitated.

He and two or three others were the only passengers left when the pilot rushed back toward them. He was shouting something, but *what?* Sevareid couldn't hear a word. At that moment the plane lurched to the left and plunged into a dive. Necessity overcame fear. Sevareid closed his eyes and dove head first into the rushing wind and the cold open air.

◆

His mind seemed to go blank, but he did remember to yank on his parachute ring. He felt a terrific jolt as the chute opened. Then he heard a voice shouting, "My God, I'm going to live!" It took him a second to realize that the voice was *his.* He opened his eyes and saw a fountain of orange flame erupting from the mountain below. The plane! He heard the voice again: "Dear God, don't let the fire get me! Please!"

The ground rushed up to meet him, and everything went dark. When he regained consciousness, he was in a panic. He struggled to get free of the parachute, beating frantically with his bare hands at the high brush and grass ensnaring him, then slipping and falling in his mad scramble up the hillside in the direction of the wreckage. He was sweating terribly in the heat. Trying to yell, he retched instead. Hysterical thoughts raced through his mind: *How will I live? Are there berries to eat? Can I make it out of here alone? No, that's impossible! But won't they search for the plane? They might not think I'm important, but surely Stilwell will order a search for Davies!*

He heard a shout and felt giddy with relief. At least he wouldn't die alone. Crawling toward him through the brush were the crew chief and a young sergeant, both with bloody faces. A few minutes later he and the other men found the radio operator, who had a broken ankle, and the pilot, who had fractured a rib. Recovered from his panic, Sevareid looked around at the dazed, listless men, most of them younger than he, and uncharacteristically decided to take charge. He bound the radio operator's ankle with a piece of parachute silk and led the men farther up the mountain to the still-smoking wreck.

There were no bodies visible and no signs of other survivors. They were in the remote mountains of northern Burma, amid tall brush and trees. As the men sat near the wreckage, trying to figure out what to do next, they heard the churn of an airplane's engines. Looking up, they saw an American transport directly overhead. Its wings dipped to signal that they had been seen. Screaming and shouting, the men ran to a nearby clearing, where the plane dropped a bundle containing knives, blankets, C-rations, a couple of rifles, cigarettes, and a note instructing them to remain at the wreckage until a rescue party arrived.

Moments later they heard a strange, rhythmic chanting. Sevareid grabbed a knife and watched as some twenty men, clad in black breech-cloths and armed with spears and knives, appeared from over a hill. They formed a semicircle around the Americans, and the chanting ceased. The silence was terrifying. Sevareid stepped forward, raised his palm, and said, "How!"

It didn't dawn on him until later how absurd it must have sounded. But these people, with their short bowl haircuts and tattooed arms and chests, didn't seem to mind. Maybe "How!" really was some universal word of peaceful intent. Anyway, the spears were jammed into the ground, there were smiles all around, and the white men were offered a bamboo pipe filled with a "very strong, very raw wine."

The tribesmen, who were Nagas, decided Sevareid must be the Americans' leader. Jumping from an airplane and living to tell about it had done something to Eric Sevareid, something very important, although at the moment he was still too shaken and sore to figure out exactly what it was.

The Nagas escorted the Americans to their village, a collection of fifty or sixty bamboo huts, some built on stilts for protection against animals and the monsoon rains. Soon the plane reappeared overhead, and Sevareid and his comrades ran back to the clearing to recover the additional supplies it had dropped. There was another note. "Do not go to the native village," it warned, "as they probably are not friendly."

Sevareid shrugged. It was too late now. Looking up, he saw the plane drop something else: three parachutes with men suspended beneath them. Tears in his eyes, Sevareid ran to the first man who touched down. He was Lieutenant Colonel Donald Flickinger, the surgeon at the air base in India, who had, with two assistants, volunteered to jump to the aid of the downed party. "Saw you needed a little help," said the cool Flickinger. Sevareid gladly relinquished his leadership role to the surgeon. Like Walter Port, Sevareid's youthful canoeing companion, Flickinger was the kind of man Sevareid deeply admired — "competent in the practical things of life." Men like Flickinger and Port are "completely normal [and] adjusted," Sevareid rather touchingly wrote later. "They don't worry half the night about something they said during the day or wrestle with their soul; they act, they live and then they die. We on the other hand are twisted up somewhere."

Flickinger had plenty of broken bones, sprains, cuts, and bruises to treat, but all those who had been aboard the C-46 were found alive except the young copilot, whose charred body was discovered in the wreckage. Under Flickinger's command, the Americans moved half a mile from the village to a clearing, where the Nagas erected three huts for them. The village chief wanted them out — for one thing, he was tired of all the parachute drops flattening his crops — and the men were just as glad to put a little distance between themselves and the villagers, who, it turned out, were among the fiercest head hunters in Asia.

A new note from the sky informed the party that they would have to stay put until rescuers could reach them by land. It might take a week or more. It turned out to be two — two weeks of apprehension that the Japanese might discover their position first or that the Nagas might decide to put some new heads on their pikes, two weeks of standing watch at night with carbines. But two weeks, as well, for the making of close friendships in extreme adversity, a kind of friendship Sevareid had never before experienced, not even on his epic canoeing trip as a teenager, the friendship of twenty men sitting around the fire at night singing and talking about women and Winston Churchill and food and democracy. Sevareid wrote in the diary he kept, "At such moments, I love it here, wouldn't be elsewhere."

When the rescue party arrived, it consisted of several dozen Nagas and two American soldiers, led by a tall, fair-haired young man with a cigarette holder drooping from his lips. He was Philip Adams, the British agent of the garrison village of Mokokchung, India, the "king," as Sevareid wrote, "of these dark and savage hills." Adams told Sevareid and the others he had hurried as fast as he could after hearing that some of the young warriors in the Naga village were planning a raid on their camp.

The party began a 120-mile trek through the mountains and back to civilization. The weeklong march was a much more difficult ordeal than the parachute jump: grueling days of marches of fifteen miles and more up and down steep mountain slopes, with Sevareid so exhausted that it sometimes required an act of will to put one foot in front of the other. Bleeding blisters the size of silver dollars. Severe sunburn. Even sunstroke. Almost collapsing and then watching with awe as his new friend, John Paton Davies, moved ahead and sang out, "Onward and upward with the arts — *Excelsior!*"

Finally they descended onto the flat plains of India, liquid in the stifling August heat. They rounded a bend in the road and saw jeeps and command cars and a crush of newsreel photographers, reporters, and officers ready to swarm around them. Sevareid turned and looked back at the "jagged blue lines of the mysterious mountains in which we lived." For a moment he experienced a "pang of unreasonable regret."

The front pages of newspapers across the country carried news of the crash and Sevareid's presence on the plane. For several days CBS did not know if its man was dead or alive. When the news finally arrived, the network clamored for his story.

Four days before his party reached civilization, Sevareid sent a dispatch from a mountain village, which he transmitted by hand-cranked radio. "Burmese jungle headhunters, every one a primitive killer, saved our lives when twenty of us leaped by parachute from a crippled United States transport plane into the mountains of northern Burma three weeks ago today," Sevareid reported. ". . . It was wild, savage country. We didn't know what kind of reception we would get. Some of the world's most primitive killers live in these mountains, so far away from civilization." He went on a little longer, then said, "Now I am so tired cranking this machine that I can send no more."

In his next dispatch he toned down the florid language and his implications of great peril: "I couldn't say that we have emerged from the jaws of death. There was hardship, but I couldn't honestly report that we suffered terribly. The truth is that many of us enjoyed the whole affair." Whether or not the others would agree on that last point, he was certainly speaking for himself.

✦

Sevareid's short stay in China proved a squalid anticlimax. Chungking, the wartime capital of China, was a sad, dismal, crowded place sprawled over a series of steep hillsides. The weather was cold and damp. A perpetual haze of grayish dust coated everything and made the air difficult to breathe.

Sevareid took up residence in an unpainted hostel that the Chinese had set aside for American correspondents. After a quick look around, he decided he "would be beside myself with loneliness and despair after six months here." His room had an unshaded electric bulb dangling from the ceiling and a lumpy bed with a coverlet turned dingy gray. In the courtyard chickens and ducks pecked the ground, and wild dogs scavenged. Showers were across a courtyard. The only toilet rarely flushed. The only telephone rarely worked.

The same went for the state radio transmitter. Sevareid lost far more confrontations with censors than he won, and only about 20 percent of his cleared reports got through. He would have to wait until he returned to the States, he decided, to present a complete picture of what he was seeing.

And what he saw was discouraging. Chiang's regime was, he thought, every bit as corrupt and repressive as Stilwell had said. Famine had devastated several Chinese provinces, and millions were dying of starvation because Chiang's army had looted the rice harvests. Sevareid broadcast an interview with an American famine relief worker, who described one district as a "huge graveyard" — bodies floating in ponds, arms and legs protruding from swamps, whole villages wiped out.

Only the Communists seemed to be trying to both help the peasants *and* fight the Japanese. "There seems little question," Sevareid wrote after leaving Chungking, "that the Communists have a fairly solid base of goodwill among the people in the North. They have done much to abolish age-old evils of landlordism and crushing taxes. They have given people their civil rights, nonexistent in the rest of China." Perhaps he should have been more skeptical about the kind of government the Communists might establish, but he was correct in concluding that China's postwar future belonged to them.

Sevareid remained in Chungking only a month. He didn't think he could have taken much more. He was tired and sick — dysentery had cost him thirty pounds — and he felt he had learned all he could.

◆

The Eric Sevareid who returned to Washington and his family after his trip to Asia was a far different man from the one who had left three months earlier. Geoffrey Cox, among others, was struck by the dramatic change: "Jumping from that plane and coping the way he did totally transformed Eric. He was much more filled out and confident, a chap greatly at ease with himself. That was, I think, the most profound experience in his life."

When Sevareid recalled everything that had happened, this chronic worrier and complainer who, as he himself said, could be driven to distraction by a hangnail or a mosquito bite, seemed astonished at the fortitude he had summoned: "It was interesting to find that you could walk along, go through the day's operation with flea bites having swelled your ankles to twice their size, with enormous blisters, with a sore shoulder, with sweat itching through your beard, with face and clothes unwashed . . . and take it all in stride."

On the professional level, his trip to China did not prove so successful. Sevareid soon discovered that while some important people were eager to have the truth, others were determined to bottle it up. A report of his findings, submitted in writing to the State Department, had no evident effect on U.S. policy and quickly disappeared into the files. What's more, despite the assurances he received from the presidential "friend," officials in the State Department refused to clear an article Sevareid wrote for the *Reader's Digest*. In it he asserted that the story of Chiang and his regime was the story of "Chinese revolutionary leaders grown secure and fat and callous . . . [of] a revolution betrayed and lost." He described the work of the China lobby as a "major deception of worldwide proportions."

Frustrated, Sevareid enlisted the help of as many influential friends as he could to persuade the State Department to clear his *Reader's Digest* article. Walter Lippmann even wrote a note to Assistant Secretary of War John McCloy, who promised to urge Secretary of War Henry Stimson to intercede. But the article remained on the spike. A reporter "must also be a politician and a wire puller before he is allowed to tell the truth," Sevareid concluded. "I am learning the hard way that one cannot write about war as the war actually, really, is while it goes on."

Despite his bitterness, Sevareid managed to enjoy himself back home. It was the second time he had been given the celebrity treatment, and this time he felt he deserved it. At a lunch in New York a magazine editor asked him to write an article on any subject he wanted, just so he could get "the Sevareid name" into his magazine. CBS featured him for two consecutive weeks on its popular entertainment series *Dateline*, which dramatized individual exploits and featured the actual participants as narrators. "Dateline: Burma!" the show's announcer proclaimed, as jungle drums thumped in the background. "With Eric Sevareid in person!"

How the world has changed for me! Sevareid thought.

Only once during this period was he brought up short. He walked into Paul White's office in New York one day to find White's desk "taken over by this extraordinary figure, a beautiful young man with golden curls." It was Charlie Collingwood, on his own triumphal American tour after his brilliant work in North Africa. Sevareid had left London before Collingwood was hired, and this was their first meeting. Collingwood put down the phone, looked at Sevareid, and said with a languid, aristocratic air, "Oh, the things I *do* for CBS."

All of Sevareid's hard-won confidence and assurance evaporated. He had "never felt more like a country bumpkin than in that moment."

◆

It seemed clear, in early 1944, that a monumental Allied invasion of France and a climax in the struggle for Italy were almost at hand. Sevareid, his blood up, decided to return to Europe and "see the end, to find out what had happened in the middle acts, and to try to gain a clue to the future of European civilization." And thus it came to pass, in March, that a reborn Eric Sevareid arrived in the pesthole of Naples, where he would witness the most tragically misguided campaign of the war and produce the best reporting of his career.

Naples became a symbol to him of all that was wrong with the Allies' Italian campaign and all the impure influences that were evident everywhere. The once-thriving port, in its incomparable setting above the Bay of Naples and the islands of Capri and Ischia, had been ravaged by its German occupiers and then, when the Germans withdrew, picked clean by the Allies. "A pigsty in Paradise," a colleague of Sevareid's called the city. Women in rags scrounged for food and drank water from stagnant ditches in the skeletal shadows of bombed-out apartment buildings; street urchins offered to sell their sisters for packs of cigarettes.

Meanwhile some enterprising rear-echelon American military officers were getting rich in Naple's thriving black market, while others were spending their plentiful free time at exclusive eating and dancing clubs or at the yacht club organized by the British around a fleet of requisitioned Italian boats. It was a very good life for the men who administered the war and ran its public relations, and for the Red Cross women who often served as their escorts. But for GIs on a few days' leave from the savage combat, there was no dancing or eating at posh clubs, no sailing in the bay. If they were lucky, they got a bunk in one of the miserable camps set up for "rest and recreation." They hated this campaign, this slaughter, they told Sevareid, and they particularly hated the generals and political leaders in charge of it.

When Allied troops had invaded Italy in September 1943, following the victory in North Africa, they had been assured by their generals that the drive up the Italian boot would be easy once the Italians surrendered. At that point the demoralized Krauts were supposed to simply vanish. It was all part of Churchill's grand strategy — strike at Germany through the "soft underbelly," keep the Russians out of Eastern Europe and, not incidentally, bolster Britain's imperial presence in the Mediterranean.

The Italians surrendered, but the Germans did not vanish. They dug in, occupying the mountains and hills of southern Italy behind the formidable Gustav Line, studded with pillboxes, barricades, and minefields. From those heights they mowed down Allied infantrymen, who also had to deal with rushing rivers and narrow dirt roads that turned into streams of mud with each chill autumn rain.

And the rain was followed by snow and freezing winds, as the American and British generals, Mark Clark and Harold Alexander, pressed their exhausted armies forward, inch by inch, through the late fall and winter. The GIs and Tommies did not have adequate clothing or food. They slept in wet foxholes. In the fall they had slogged into combat through knee-high mud, in winter through waist-high snow. Many developed such bad cases of trench foot that their boots had to be cut from their feet. Rotting flesh would come off with the boots.

This was the war to which Sevareid had brought a "deep desire to describe it as it truly was — its glories and brutalities, its achievements and stupidities, its misery and luxury." How naive he was, this reporter who had never seen real combat! In Italy there were fewer wartime glories and achievements than elsewhere, and even more brutality and stupidity. But Sevareid found that the brass weren't inclined to let the rest of the world in on the unpleasant truth. *You'll hurt troop morale*, he was told by the censors, but he — and the censors — knew full well that the troops were already demoralized and deeply cynical. *They* knew the facts. It was the people at home who didn't know. Indeed, Sevareid said, "Nothing bolstered a soldier's spirit more than evidence that the truth of the situation *was* being frankly told; nothing gave him more confidence than to know that *somebody* was aware of the things that were wrong." More than once Sevareid battled with censors, only to be asked by some GI: "Why don't you guys tell the truth once in a while?"

He tried, and sometimes succeeded. From Naples he reported:

Our armies do not advance, and so, inevitably, soldiers stationed here lose their feeling of fight. Desk officers keep regular hours, and some come to resent any intrusion of war. . . . With the top down and a cushion on the seat, a jeep becomes a passable roadster, and better-dressed girls are beginning to come out of hiding. Orchestras are put together, and suave, tail-coated waiters who served the fascists and Germans are just as suave and elegant now for us.

In another broadcast Sevareid described watching a recruiting film that extolled the pinpoint accuracy of American bombers. The audience of GIs fresh from the front hooted and jeered. There was a lesson here, Sevareid said: "Recruiting films should never be sent . . . where they can be seen by combat soldiers." Especially not soldiers who had witnessed the destruction of U.S.-controlled bridges and part of the U.S. Army's headquarters at Cassino by *American* bombers.

All winter long the Allied attempts to capture the German stronghold at Cassino, a major obstacle on the road to Rome, had been a bloodbath. The bombers had been called in to demolish the abbey, despite its priceless collection of art and artifacts, because it was presumed to be occupied by Germans. But the Germans weren't inside the abbey; they had surrounded it. After the bombing they quickly fortified the ruins and successfully repulsed several Allied assaults.

Just as nightmarish as Cassino was the Americans' attempted end run around the Gustav Line — their landing at the pretty beach resort town of Anzio, only thirty miles southwest of Rome, in January. Unopposed when he landed, the commander, General John Lucas, delayed moving his troops inland. Within days seven German divisions had sealed off the beachhead. From the surrounding hills, German artillery shelled Anzio day and night, and the Luftwaffe bombed and strafed at will.

It was, as Sevareid said in the first broadcast anyone made from the beachhead, like "living in a bull's-eye." He spoke from personal experience: as he rode in from the harbor at Anzio, two shells whistled over his jeep and blew to bits the truck just ahead of him on the road. Sevareid had left the safety of Naples for the Italian campaign's most exposed position, where any movement during daylight hours was considered suicidal. He was scared, but it was not the stomach-churning terror he had felt during the Blitz. His experience in Burma had taught him that he could control his fear, could remain calm as he slipped from the shell-pocked villa in which he lived to the makeshift radio studio in an equally battered villa nearby, knowing that the Germans might well have him in their sights.

Anzio had been a military miscalculation of the highest order, a point that Sevareid repeatedly tried to get across in his censored broadcasts. "The whole beachhead operation has mystified many people at home and not a few soldiers around here," he said in one broadcast. "The original Allied aim was based on the belief that a landing would break the Italian front. . . . Obviously, the combined chiefs of staff in Washington were quite wrong in that, as they were wrong last fall in their belief that the Germans would not give battle in southern Italy."

But Sevareid reserved most of his scorn for the commander of the U.S. Fifth Army, General Mark Clark. A tall, rangy man, Clark was also vain and arrogant. He had a personal photographer and nearly fifty public relations officers under his command, all dedicated to assuring favorable publicity for the general. Sevareid and other correspondents were told to refer to the troops as "General Mark Clark's Fifth Army," and news photographers were urged to take pictures only of the "good side" of Clark's face.

Clark wanted to be remembered as the general who liberated ancient Rome. Everything else, in Sevareid's opinion, was subordinate to that ambition. "No one in authority here claims that Rome itself has any military advantage for us," Sevareid managed to report in spite of censorship. "The usual statement is that the political or psychological value will be great. Why it will and just how it will pay off in that imprecise coinage has never been explained."

In May the Allies launched their big offensive, finally taking Cassino, breaking out of Anzio, and ripping through Italian villages and towns on their way north. Marching with the troops, Sevareid noted their casual unconcern as they passed through places they had razed. "For us invaders," he wrote later, "this is not a country but a map we are treading on, the picturesque farmers and their oxen like unreal painted figures on a scenic backdrop."

But it *was* a country, and it was being torn apart not only by the Germans but by the armies ostensibly sent to liberate it. Sevareid wanted to tell Americans about that. After an especially fierce battle had destroyed one town, he walked through the ruins and described "an awesome field of devastation, where trees had become splintered stumps and the leaves gone as though a cyclone had taken them." His eye was drawn to a remarkable sight in the midst of the smoking town: "one lovely rose bush, blooming and serene, and itself the only living thing." Always the Murrow-esque detail: in that small town a rose bush; in the rubble-strewn town square of Cisterna, the headless statue of a woman with "its attitude of shocked surprise"; elsewhere the "skinny horses stumbling ahead of the rickety carts" as peasants returned to their ruined villages.

"Home may just be a dusty pile of masonry, but it is their own and it is all they have," Sevareid reported.

◆

On May 24 Clark's Fifth Army linked up with the British Eighth Army, an event that Sevareid reported first, largely because his broadcast happened to have been scheduled for the same moment that the announcement of the linkup was released. Not knowing the circumstances, Paul White sent him a cable: CONGRATULATIONS YOU DID IT AGAIN YOUR STORY UPJOINING SOUTHERN ETANZIO FORCES UPPICKED EVERY PRESS ASSN WIDELY FRONT-PAGED. Sevareid, with admirable humility, cabled back: THANKS MUCHLY YOUR CABLE HOPE UNTOO MUCH PUBLICITY THIS BEAT, WHICH DUE ENTIRELY DUMB LUCK.

At first Clark and his army headed northeastward to cut the escape routes of German forces retreating from the south. Then, quite suddenly, the strategy was abandoned. "General Mark Clark's Fifth Army" was ordered to proceed west on a course straight for Rome. "There is a question whether the two aims [catching the Germans and liberating Rome] are compatible or mutually exclusive," Sevareid wrote in one of his scripts. Clark's censors cut that line.

According to the general's image-makers, the Fifth Army was "racing" toward Rome. Sevareid made clear this was just hype. Far from racing, the troops, in their soiled uniforms and with grime-covered faces, were physically and emotionally spent. "Even a triumphal march is exhausting, and they are numb with it," Sevareid said in one broadcast. "These things are real as we creep toward Rome."

On June 5, with Rome's liberation imminent, Sevareid fell into an exhausted sleep in a requisitioned villa just outside the city. He was awakened by the return to the villa of a haggard, red-eyed Winston Burdett, who some ten days earlier had joined Sevareid to cover the march to Rome. Burdett had sneaked into the center of the city, still occupied by pockets of Germans, and had just finished broadcasting his report of what he had seen. It was, wrote Sevareid later, "one of the most dramatic and beautiful broadcasts I have ever read," and it "would have been one of the memorable essays of the war."

Would have been, except that the operators at the Naples relay station had not been monitoring the transmitter and, once into the void, Burdett's words were lost forever.

✦

The next morning the Fifth Army marched into Rome. By the thousands, Romans poured out of their homes and mobbed the liberators, showering them with flowers, kissing their hands, almost dragging them out of their jeeps and tanks. Forty years later Burdett recalled watching Sevareid during this tumultuous victory procession. He looked so splendid, Burdett said, in his army correspondent's uniform, that beautiful Italian women were throwing themselves on his jeep, "evidently mistaking him for a general."

A few hours later one of Clark's press officers announced to the correspondents that the general would soon be having a press conference at the Campidoglio, Rome's city hall on the Capitoline Hill, with its sweeping view of the ancient city. When the reporters and newsreel cameramen dutifully presented themselves on the Campidoglio's steps, Clark turned to them in feigned surprise and said, "Well, gentlemen, I didn't really expect to have a press conference here. I just called a little meeting with my corps commanders to discuss the situation. However, I'll be glad to answer your questions. This is a great day for the Fifth Army."

That one comment summed it up, Sevareid thought in disgust — all that was wrong with this campaign. It was a great day for Mark Clark and his Fifth Army but "not apparently a great day for the world, for the Allies, for all the suffering people who had desperately looked toward the time of peace." As the cameramen took Clark's picture, he spread his map on the balustrade and posed as if he were pointing out something of interest to his commanders in the great vista below. Another correspondent muttered to Sevareid, "On this historic occasion I feel like vomiting."

The next morning a BBC correspondent rushed into the press room. "Eisenhower has announced the invasion of France!" he shouted. The typewriters stopped clacking. The correspondents stared at each other. Several, including Sevareid, sat back, took out cigarettes, and tossed their half-written stories on the floor. After all those miserable months slogging up the Italian boot, this was the payoff! D-Day had wiped them off the news map! Sevareid mused later that he and his colleagues were like "a troupe of actors, who, at the climax of their play, realize that the spectators have all fled out of the door to watch a more spectacular performance across the street."

Journalists, like generals, are not without egocentricity.

✦ 15

The Pleasures of War

DURING THE EXHILARATING FEW MONTHS before the invasion of France, Murrow and the Boys strode through London and Europe like lords of the realm, admired and respected by peers and heads of state, envied by younger journalists and would-be journalists who had discovered in them a new style of public and professional behavior, a new standard for success. "Spoiled we were," said Eric Sevareid, "by the privilege of the microphone, the pay, the quick notoriety; a few rotten spoiled, but only a few." The way the Boys dressed, the way they talked, the way they wrote, the way they broadcast, the way they thought — everything about them became touchstones for what journalists were supposed to look like and be. A young sergeant named Andy Rooney, a war correspondent with the army newspaper *Stars and Stripes*, thought they were "the big guys — I was in awe of them, all of us were."

The Boys parachuted out of crippled airplanes, leapt off sinking ships, went ashore under fire — and then, like medieval troubadours, told gripping stories about what they had seen and heard and felt and done. They watched Hitler's rise to power. Between 1939 and 1941 they covered the Wehrmacht's advances from behind *German* lines. They caught the very last train out of Berlin before the United States entered the war and were part of the great exodus from Paris as the Nazis approached. They were arrested by the Gestapo, endured months of deprivation in Stalin's Soviet Union. They dodged bombs in London and Singapore, U-boats in the North Sea, shells and bombs in North Africa, Italy, France, and Belgium. They stood up to generals, censors, government officials, and their own executives. Time and again they scooped their print competitors on some of the biggest stories of the war. They wrote best-selling books. Newspapers and magazines printed articles about them. They were scholars, swashbucklers, explorers, and interpreters, and they were responsible for turning radio in general and

CBS in particular into their country's primary source of on-the-spot news.

The Boys were clearly "the finest news staff anybody had ever put together in Europe," said Harrison Salisbury, head of UP's London bureau in 1944 and later a Pulitzer Prize–winning reporter and columnist for the *New York Times*. "They were all professionals, every single one of them," and their hiring by Murrow was "a magnificent achievement." In the view of Geoffrey Cox, "this was very much a gathering, not of a man and his followers, but of a *primus inter pares*. But, my goodness, what a level of *pares!*"

The only war correspondents in the same league with the Boys, said William Walton, a correspondent for *Time* during the war, were the reporters for Time-Life News Service and those with the *New York Times*. "We were the tops," said Walton, a close friend of Charles Collingwood's. "We knew it, and we didn't let anyone else forget it."

There was actually a little more room at the top. In addition to the Boys and Hanson Baldwin and Drew Middleton of the *New York Times* and Theodore H. White and John Hersey of *Time*, there were Hal Boyle, Wes Gallagher, and Ed Kennedy of the AP; Walter Kerr and Homer Bigart of the *New York Herald Tribune*; Quentin Reynolds of *Collier's*; Bill Stoneman and Helen Kirkpatrick of the *Chicago Daily News*; and Harrison Salisbury and Walter Cronkite of UP. And there were great photographers, most notably Robert Capa of *Life*. The difference between the Boys and the other top journalists who covered the war, however, was that the others were not famous beyond the journalistic, military, and diplomatic circles in which they all moved; their names were not household words.

In the category of celebrity-journalist, only the fabled Ernest Taylor Pyle of the Scripps-Howard Newspaper Alliance — Ernie Pyle, with his evocative coverage of "GI Joe" fighting in all the foxholes and on all the sandy islands of the war — rivaled Murrow and the Boys.

✦

The climax of the great drama that was World War II was at hand, and just about everyone had gathered in London, hoping to play some part in it.

If life was ever better, or would ever be again, it was hard for some people in London to believe — and life was good not in spite of the war but *because* of it. The invasion of Europe was just around the corner.

A feverish, nervous gaiety and pride gripped London as the mightiest armed force in history assembled in ports and towns all over England. The Boys who could get back from previous assignments — Larry LeSueur, Bill Downs, and Charles Collingwood — did so, and were promptly caught up, with Murrow, in London's carnival atmosphere. The others, to their regret, didn't make it to the party. Eric Sevareid and Winston Burdett were pinned down in Italy. Bill Shirer, who had planned to return to London for the Allied landing, was in a New York hospital, having his blind left eye removed because of an infection.

And poor Howard K. Smith was still stuck in Switzerland. Having fled from Berlin to Bern on the same day the United States entered the war in 1941, he had promptly found himself trapped. Neutral Switzerland was surrounded by Germany and German-occupied countries and airspace, so Smith, with the other Americans there at the time, could not leave their beautiful, boring haven until the Allies opened an exit corridor by either liberating Italy or France or defeating Germany.

In his first three months in Bern, while awaiting news from his Danish fiancée, Benedicte, Smith feverishly pounded out *Last Train from Berlin*, a book about his experiences in Germany and his hatred of the Nazis. The famed British socialist Harold Laski was so taken with *Last Train* that he wrote Murrow in July of 1942, asking how he could get in touch with the author to congratulate him. And, like all of the Boys' wartime memoirs, it quickly became a bestseller at home.

Meanwhile in Denmark, the German occupation authorities were refusing to issue Bennie an exit visa. After months of wrangling, her father, a prominent Copenhagen lawyer, appealed to Queen Alexandra, who interceded. But the visa that was finally issued was valid for only forty-eight hours, which made leaving nearly impossible; planes out of Copenhagen were booked solid for a month. Bennie, whose determination would become legendary in the years ahead, went to the airport anyway and managed to persuade a passenger to give up his seat. She flew to Bern, where she and Smith were married in early March of 1942.

Smith managed to turn in some solid reporting from Bern, which was a good listening post for news from France and other German-occupied countries. One of his best sources was Allen Dulles, who, as head of the Office of Strategic Services (OSS) network in Bern, was America's top spy in Switzerland. Barred by the Swiss from broadcasting for almost two years, Smith relayed what he learned by cable to CBS in New

York (and sometimes to *Time*, for which he worked as a stringer). He was among the first journalists to report on the activities of Tito, the mysterious leader of the Yugoslav partisans.

In late 1943, as the tide of the war began to turn, Swiss authorities relaxed their broadcasting ban, and an official nonchalantly advised Smith, "You know, you can telephone [New York] now." With that, CBS's man in Bern returned to the air. He soon learned, though, that there was a big difference between broadcasting and actually being *heard.* Technical snafus and atmospheric problems occurred frequently. Smith's carefully preserved scripts, some with hand-written notes and well-drawn doodles of pinup girls on the reverse side, record the frustration he felt when a broadcast was canceled or otherwise stymied. Read one such note: "UN-goddamned-DELIVERED#! To hell! with C.B.S. and the whole goddamned hemisphere!"

◆

For Larry LeSueur the hectic months before D-Day were a bittersweet time. His life had been turned topsy-turvy, and more than a year later it still had not righted itself completely. After his departure from Moscow in the late fall of 1942, CBS called him home for a quick celebrity tour. In New York he appeared as the central figure and narrator of a CBS weekly series called *An American in Russia,* based on his own observations and experiences. He gave speeches for the network and for Russian war relief, was invited to Paley's house and told to call the boss "Bill." And he too wrote a bestseller, *Twelve Months That Changed the World,* a book that Janet Murrow, for one, thought contained "a good bit more vodka and girls than would appeal to most people."

In New York, LeSueur also met and married — almost that fast — Joan Phelps, a twenty-nine-year-old Englishwoman. The bride was the ward of Sir William Wiseman, fifty-eight, who had been head of British intelligence in the United States during World War I and had become a wealthy New York investment banker after the war. Following their wedding in June 1943 and a honeymoon of less than a week, LeSueur returned to London at Murrow's request, expecting Joan to join him there soon.

As he worked with Murrow in London to help plan coverage of the expected invasion of the continent, LeSueur's mind was still back in New York with Joan. He talked about her constantly to Ed and Janet and proudly showed them photographs. "He can think of nothing else," Janet wrote to her parents. But she had doubts about the marriage, fearing that LeSueur had rushed into it too quickly and that the bride was "on the flighty side and used to a lot of money." "There'll be difficulties ahead," Janet wrote her brother.

Indeed. Only two months after LeSueur left New York, he was served with divorce papers. Instead of joining him in London as expected, Joan headed for Reno. There, as was standard in those days, she charged him with "cruelty," and on February 11, 1944, was granted a divorce. The next day she married Sir William, her aging guardian. LeSueur was stunned. Almost fifty years afterward he still found it difficult to talk about. He had no idea, he said, what caused his wife to dump him so abruptly, except that "she now had a title."

He didn't lack for consolation, however. At a party at St. James's Palace, he had been introduced to Priscilla Bruce, a tall, slim, twenty-four-year-old Scot who worked for British intelligence. She was married and so, at the time, was he. Still, there was no denying the mutual attraction. Bruce found LeSueur "very amusing . . . great fun." An affair followed, as LeSueur's divorce whipped through the Reno mill and as Priscilla took steps to obtain her own divorce. Two years later, in 1946, Larry LeSueur and Priscilla Bruce were married in Washington, both for the second time, both hoping for the best.

◆

After his year in Russia, Bill Downs had an even more difficult readjustment. Unlike LeSueur, whose trips to the Russian front early in the war were carefully controlled by Soviet authorities, Downs was a witness many times to the brutality and bestiality of the eastern front. "I've seen more bodies than I care to remember," he wrote his parents.

Stalingrad was first. Then Kharkov, where the Germans shot ten thousand Jews in the first couple of weeks of their occupation and let non-Jews die of starvation. Then Babi Yar, where thousands of Ukrainian Jews were killed. Then Rzhev, a small railroad town west of Moscow.

After the German occupation of Rzhev, only two hundred fifty people remained of the town's original forty thousand. Downs described how in one house he stepped over the body of an old woman, her face battered to a pulp. Near her were the bodies of her grandchildren — a nine-year-old boy and an eleven-year-old girl, both shot in the head. In another room lay the body of a second grandson, about fourteen years old, shot at least seven times. As Downs reconstructed it, the Germans had ordered all the women and children to go to the town's church. But the woman's older grandson was desperately ill with typhus, and she refused to move him. So the Germans killed them all on the spot, beating her to death for her disobedience and riddling the fourteen-year-old with bullets.

Downs was haunted by what he had seen in Russia. He told friends that "coming back . . . is something like stepping out of a St. Valentine's Day massacre into a Sunday school classroom." Over and over he described what he had witnessed but soon discovered that not everyone shared his strong feelings for the Russian people and the horrors they had experienced. Some looked at him curiously. Others expressed pity. Still others said he was a liar. On a lecture tour of the United States before returning to London, he even received an anonymous postcard calling him a Russian agent and threatening his life.

◆

By contrast Charlie Collingwood was having the time of his life. For him these were the glory days of the war. His exploits in North Africa had won him the respect of fellow journalists, which he craved, as well as the acclaim of London's social and power elite, which he may have craved even more. He was still living with Gracie Blake and was talking about marrying her once she obtained a divorce. But his attachment to Gracie did not prevent him from chasing other women and otherwise having a roaring good time.

In London's superheated preinvasion social whirl, with all the parties and poker games and nights on the town, Collingwood was in his element. The guest list for one of his dinner parties included the Murrows and Bill Paley, playwright Robert Sherwood, drama critic John Mason Brown, Ernie Pyle, Lynn Fontanne, and her husband, Alfred Lunt. Collingwood was the host, but it was Lunt, in London to appear with Fontanne in a Sherwood play, who actually cooked the dinner.

The suave Collingwood, now twenty-six, took to this sort of socializing with a preternatural ease that was the marvel of many of his colleagues. Walter Cronkite, in UP's London office, was a year older than Bonnie Prince Charlie but considered himself a "callow youth" beside this "debonair man of the world." Said Cronkite, "I was lucky to manage a beer with a broken-down GI in the evening. Charles dined with generals and royalty." Andy Rooney was, if anything, even more entranced. "I admired everything about Collingwood," he said, "and wished I was all that he was."

William S. Paley also joined in the poker and partying of London before D-Day. By this time Paley had received an army commission and was immensely enjoying himself outside the corporate confines of CBS. In 1943 he had gone to North Africa for the Office of War Information to set up Allied radio stations there and in Italy. In January 1944 he was assigned to General Eisenhower's staff in London as chief of psychological warfare broadcasting; among his subordinates, however, he was noted more for his love of pleasure than for his devotion to hard work. One night he attended a riotous, boozy stag party at Collingwood's apartment, which eventually spilled into the street. "Everything that happened that night was funny," Paley recalled years later. ". . . Everyone loved each other, and it was just a brawl, a great big lousy brawl, but it was one of those nights in my life that was very outstanding."

For Paley the romantic fatalism and hedonism of wartime London were especially appealing — he, at least, could eat, drink, and be as merry as he liked, with little chance that tomorrow, or anytime soon, he might have to die. As Harrison Salisbury noted, "Sex hung in the London air like the fog, its scent permeating every corner." Conventional morality had in many circles been laid to rest for the duration. "The normal barriers . . . to having an affair with somebody were thrown to the four winds," recalled Paley, whose marriage at the time was disintegrating. "If it looked pretty good, if you felt good, well, what in hell was the difference?"

The fever infected even Ed Murrow. Though he had never seemed much interested in women, he began a passionate affair with Pamela Churchill (later Pamela Harriman), the beautiful, auburn-haired daughter-in-law of the prime minister. Estranged from Winston Churchill's son Randolph, the bright and charming Pamela was known for her sparkling dinners and soirées. *Life* even went to her parties and once put her on its cover. "Ed was knocked off his feet by this absolutely glorious and desirable young woman. . . . She just bowled him over," said Collingwood, who had some trouble keeping his own feet under him in Pamela's presence.

Murrow was so serious about the affair that for a time he even considered divorcing Janet. But in the end he could not bring himself to do it and instead rather brutally broke off with Pamela. His decision stemmed primarily from guilt, a sense of responsibility, and his love for Janet, who, after eleven years of marriage, was pregnant.

It was a complicated time. Keeping things in balance wasn't easy — not for the often dark, dour, and moralistic Ed Murrow and especially not for the likes of such dedicated hedonists as Charlie Collingwood and

Bill Paley. They were three of the handsomest, most glamorous men in the city, and they were, a broadcasting colleague reported dryly, "very much admired by women."

✦

In late 1943 and early 1944, Murrow devoted much of his time to beefing up his staff and making preparations for D-Day. He hired several new people, only one of whom, Richard Hottelet, made it through the informal and rather mysterious process that determined who was and who was not a full-fledged Murrow Boy.

Among those who did not make it through was Charles Shaw, a former newspaper editor in Pennsylvania and radio newsman in Texas, who was the first of Murrow's new recruits in the months before D-Day. For Shaw it was like a dream. He was "among the giants . . . part of a legend." As he wrote in breathless wonderment many years afterward, "I was an Argonaut who had sailed with Jason, a knight who had sat at the Round Table with King Arthur, a Merry Man who had roamed Sherwood Forest with Robin Hood, one of the 'band of brothers' who had stood with Henry the Fifth at Agincourt." Shaw stayed with CBS, mostly in London, until 1946. He later moved to Philadelphia and became news director of a television station there.

Another Murrow recruit who didn't make it to the inner circle, although he had an excellent career in broadcast news during the war and for a couple of decades afterward, was Bill Shadel. Editor of the National Rifle Association's *American Rifleman* magazine (in the days before the NRA became the bare-knuckled lobbying outfit that it is today), Shadel had come to Europe to report on the war for the magazine. In 1944 Murrow retained him as a stringer.

And finally came Dick Hottelet. Although he was the last Boy hired, he was, from the beginning, a member in good standing of the brotherhood. He was already well known to Murrow when he came looking for a job in 1944. Only twenty-six at the time Murrow hired him, the tall, thin Hottelet was, despite a disarming smile and an elegant voice, an aggressive and sometimes abrasive reporter who refused to be intimidated by any official, Nazi or Allied.

Hottelet was also well known to another member of the Murrow team, Howard Smith. The two of them had worked together in UP's Berlin bureau from 1939 to 1941 and could barely stand one another. Hottelet, said Smith, "tended to treat people as though they were privates and he was the German lieutenant." Smith, too, could be didactic, and during their days together in Berlin, according to Hottelet, they were always shouting at each other. Personalities aside, they were also on opposite ends of the political spectrum in those days — Hottelet the most conservative of all the Murrow Boys, Smith the most liberal — and one never hesitated to let the other know when he was wrong. On one thing, however, they agreed: they were both avidly anti-Nazi. Hottelet, in fact, was the only American reporter singled out by the Gestapo for arrest and a prolonged term in jail.

✦

Hottelet's parents had emigrated from Germany to New York shortly before the turn of the century, and they spoke nothing but German at home. During the Depression, Hottelet's father lost his export-import business, and the family's standard of living plunged. They moved several times, always to a cheaper, more modest house. After he finished high school, Hottelet could afford to attend only Brooklyn College, a well-regarded urban commuter school, where he majored in philosophy. Like so many colleges and universities during the Depression, Brooklyn College was a hotbed of protest, with much of the agitation led by students who were either Communists or who pretended to be. But Hottelet protested against the protesters. At a student meeting called to plan a demonstration, he declared, "This is a lot of nonsense. What does this have to do with us?" The question was greeted by boos and catcalls, and Hottelet stalked out of the room.

When he received his B.A. degree in 1937, he had no job prospects and no idea what he wanted to do with his life. His father suggested he go to Berlin. He could take classes at the university there and live off the modest amount of money that remained in a blocked family bank account. With few alternatives, Hottelet took the suggestion.

In Berlin he lived with his father's cousin, a cultured and wealthy businessman who was opposed to the Nazis and risked his life trying to protect Jewish friends. Every Sunday morning the cousin would take the twenty-year-old Hottelet on tours of the city's museums and art galleries, explaining, teaching, showing — instilling in Hottelet what would become a passionate love of art.

After attending his first class at the University of Berlin, on the philosophy of Kant, Hottelet realized that the mission of German universities had shifted from education to propaganda. His professor, dressed in a Brown-Shirt uniform complete with Nazi armband, began the class by thrusting his arm into the air and shouting, "Heil, Hitler."

After trying several other classes, a disheartened Hottelet dropped out and began looking for work.

He had no particular desire to be a journalist but had heard that the United Press bureau in Berlin was hiring. He applied and was taken on as a stringer, then promoted to full-time correspondent. He was not quite twenty-one when he was assigned to cover German ground forces marching into the Sudetenland, and only twenty-two when he went along with the Wehrmacht on its quick march through Belgium and France. He followed the troops all the way to Dunkirk, where, from behind German lines, he watched sadly as the British retreated across the Channel.

Hottelet was a major pain in the Nazis' side almost from the beginning. Once he was arrested after sharply questioning Gestapo agents whom he saw loading Jews into trucks. Another time he spent an evening with a group of deported Jews in a pub on the German-Polish border. After phoning in his story, he was again taken into custody by the Gestapo, sent back to Berlin, and questioned. And in the fall of 1940, when a bomb went off during a Nazi party meeting in a Munich beer hall, narrowly missing Hitler, Hottelet, at the UP office in Berlin, telephoned the beer hall. In perfect German and his most arrogant *oberführer*'s voice, he shouted, "This is Berlin! What . . . is . . . *happening* there?"

The voice on the other end compliantly gave some of the details. Hottelet asked more questions and, to his delight, got more answers.

Periodically the man on the other end would ask, "But who are *you?*"

"This is *Berlin!*" Hottelet replied each time.

Finally a senior Gestapo officer came on the line and demanded his name. "This is the United Press of America," Hottelet confessed, "and we are calling to find out what happened."

"Get lost," said the Gestapo officer and hung up.

A report of this incident was probably added to the Gestapo's rapidly expanding Richard C. Hottelet file.

In the late winter of 1941, a German diplomat told him, "Dick, someone wants to turn over your apple cart." A few weeks later Hottelet was awakened at three in the morning by a loud pounding on his apartment door. He opened the door groggily to find two Gestapo agents.

"Get dressed," they said.

They hauled him down to Berlin's Alexanderplatz jail and charged him with espionage, specifically with sending German secrets to his girlfriend, an Englishwoman named Ann Delafield, who had worked in the British embassy in Berlin and now was in the British passport control office in Spain. Hottelet's arrest and confinement in a jail cell became a cause célèbre in the United States, but the Nazis resisted all official pressure for his release.

Frightened and lonely, Hottelet was kept in a tiny, unlighted cell at the Alexanderplatz jail for more than a month while Gestapo interrogators worked on him. They did not harm him physically but threatened to execute him as a spy. What frightened him most, however, was the possibility that the United States might enter the war against Germany while he was still in jail. In that case he would not be released until the war ended, if he lived until then.

In May he was transferred to the Gestapo's notorious Moabit prison, where he endured more interrogation. They asked him the same questions over and over, and he kept denying everything. His only diversion was reading books given him by his guards, including a tome on Japanese coal mining and a sentimental English romance. He devoured the romance, which took on a strange reality in the surreal world he was in. "I felt the pain, the frustration, the hopes of the characters in that book," Hottelet said. "It was a weird experience."

At last, in early July, a Gestapo officer strode into Hottelet's cell and told him to pack his things: he and Jay Allen, an American journalist imprisoned by the Vichy French, were being exchanged for two Germans taken into custody by the United States as spies.

Hottelet was given a warm welcome when he returned to the States. "To be treated as a conquering hero," he later remarked wryly, "the only thing you have to do is to survive." He married Ann Delafield and was assigned to UP's Washington bureau, but quit the wire service a few months later to join the Office of War Information. He was sent to London in August 1942, where he made broadcasts to German-speaking countries and wrote propaganda leaflets to be dropped over Germany. After a shakeup in OWI's London office, Hottelet resigned and was immediately hired by Murrow.

◆

As the most recent Boy hired, Hottelet expected to be given the worst assignments in preparation for D-Day. He was pleasantly surprised to discover that Murrow did not operate that way. Hottelet received the assignments he requested as long as no one else had staked them out first. If he wanted to cover the air force, and he did, Murrow let him do it, even though Murrow himself was then going along on a number of bombing raids over Germany.

Indeed, Hottelet was startled at the way Murrow seemed to go out of his way to court danger and death in the air. "If I went up in B-26s, it wasn't because I was driven," Hottelet said, "but because it was, unhappily, part of my job. Ed went up in those bombers because he was driven." Driven, in part, to prove himself again. Following the Blitz, Murrow had done little actual war reporting, staying behind in the backwater of London, envying the Boys who were on the line from North Africa to the South China Sea. By the end of 1940, he said after the war, his best reporting was behind him.

In all, Murrow flew twenty-five combat missions. In December 1943, as he was beginning preparations for D-Day, he received a note from Collingwood, who was briefly back in New York:

> That was a great piece you did on the Berlin raid. . . . [Paul] White was very upset before the show. Said you were crazy to have gone and all the rest of it. Swore that besides all the risk it was impossible to make a good story out of it. I told him that you had to go and that having gone it would be impossible for you to write a bad story about it. . . . After it was over I made the bastard buy me a drink as recompense for having been so stupid.

White and others in New York made clear to Murrow that on D-Day he was absolutely not, repeat not, to indulge in any of that kind of reckless daredeviltry. He was to remain behind in London, overseeing the invasion coverage, with Charles Shaw to assist him. The four radio networks had agreed to pool their reports because of the uncertainties of communications, and Murrow had been designated to supervise that effort.

The CBS assignments for the invasion broke down this way: Larry LeSueur would land with the U.S. infantry; Bill Downs would go in with British troops; Charles Collingwood and Bill Shadel would cover the navy; Dick Hottelet, the Ninth Air Force. Wistfully Murrow told the Boys how lucky they were to have such good assignments. And they *had* hammered the odds. Of the five hundred American correspondents in London before D-Day, only twenty-eight were chosen to accompany the invading forces. Of those, five were from CBS.

It was yet another indication of how much things had changed in the seven years since Murrow had been rejected for membership by the American Foreign Correspondents Association. And in 1944 Edward R. Murrow was elected president of the association.

✦

The Flying Fortress touched down at its home field near Lincoln, and Larry LeSueur breathed a relieved sigh — another bombing run successfully completed. During the seemingly interminable wait for the invasion of France, he had gone out on several missions. April had passed, then May. Now it was early June, and still no word. London was boiling with rumors: the invasion would be launched tomorrow . . . no, next week . . . no, next month. LeSueur, like everyone else in England, was sick of waiting.

As he left the plane, he noticed a jeep parked on the grass nearby. An army officer climbed out and, approaching him, loudly announced that he was under arrest. LeSueur was astounded. He hadn't done anything wrong and couldn't figure out what was happening. Ignoring his protests, the officer bundled him into the jeep and sped away, leaving behind the plane's equally astounded crew.

LeSueur's army escort took him back to his London apartment and ordered him to collect his bedroll and other gear. He was driven a couple of hours to a large enclosure surrounded by barbed wire, somewhere near Dartmouth. In the pen were several other correspondents, grumbling about being treated like cattle. Then it dawned on LeSueur: his arrest had been a sham to hide from the bomber crew the real reason he had been driven away. Designated correspondents were being rounded up all over England and were being taken, in utmost secrecy, to their embarkation points.

✦

At an air base north of London, Dick Hottelet was playing craps — and having the greatest luck of his life. He was not really a gambler, but in this game he was winning every pot, with runs he couldn't believe. Finally he was sitting on all the cash in the game. Hundreds, maybe thousands, of dollars were piled up in front of him, yet somehow he was scared and depressed. Tonight of all nights, just a few hours before he was to risk his neck covering a bombing run over France, he was having this incredible winning streak! It was not Dick Hottelet's style to be superstitious, but he regarded this as a warning that his luck was running out. Like the other CBS correspondents assigned to the invasion, he had been asked by New York to write his own obituary — just in case, they said. Hottelet wanted to make sure *his* obit stayed in the files. He started lending money to the other players, and before the game was over, he had lost everything.

"You can't imagine how happy and relieved I was," he said.

◆

In the predawn darkness of June 6, Hottelet climbed aboard a B-26. The plane was so heavily laden with bombs that it almost ran out of runway before lumbering skyward. As the night's blackness faded away, he looked down at the English Channel and sharply drew in his breath. There below, stalwart in the wind-whipped waves, was the mightiest armada in history — rank after rank of ships stretching as far as he could see, all bearing down on the beaches of Normandy.

Said Hottelet to Charles Shaw a few hours after his return to London, "If I had had to parachute out of the plane, I could have walked across the channel on the ships. . . . There were so many of them!" Five thousand, of every imaginable size and description: rusty tankers and freighters, hospital ships, channel steamers, attack transports, hordes of little shallow-draft landing vessels, minesweepers, battleships, cruisers, destroyers, and more.

Unchallenged by the Luftwaffe and encountering only light flak, Hottelet's Marauder and dozens of other bombers roared low over the eastern edge of the Cherbourg Peninsula in heavy gray rain clouds and dropped their bombs. The concussions shook Hottelet's plane. He watched sheets of flame erupt from the ground below, then become dull in their own mushrooming balls of brown and black smoke. The stench of explosives filled the plane.

Mission accomplished, the bombers turned back in the chill dawn, but not before Hottelet saw scores of white streaks in the water below — assault boats racing toward Utah Beach, the plumes of their wakes stretching out behind them.

The invasion of Europe had begun.

"Handfuls of France"

ALL LARRY LE SUEUR cared about, as he prepared to climb down a ladder from his heaving LCT into a smaller landing craft, was getting off this miserable tub and onto dry land. He would be in the second wave hitting Utah Beach, but at that moment he didn't care what the Germans threw at them. Anything would be better than the last forty-eight hours of bobbing up and down in the gale-swept English Channel, drenched by cold rain and crashing waves, listening to the retching and moaning of seasick soldiers from the Fourth Infantry Division.

The invasion had originally been set for June 5. LeSueur's ship was already in the Channel when word came that the landing had been postponed for at least a day because of the miserable weather, the worst in the Channel in twenty years. The larger ships returned to port, but the LCT LeSueur was on was too slow to make the round trip in time if Eisenhower gave the go-ahead for June 6; so they stayed out in the Channel, bucking and rolling. With almost everyone else seasick, including the galley crew, LeSueur volunteered to help the ranking officer on board, Colonel James Van Fleet, prepare dinner for all hands. But few of the men could get down the beans they cooked, and LeSueur wondered how soldiers so ill could possibly fight.

Now, clutching his typewriter and gas mask, LeSueur crouched in the bow of the landing craft as it made its way, along with swarms of other assault vessels, toward the beach. He was engulfed in noise — the shouts and cries of men, the throbbing of engines, the howl of the wind, the thunder of the navy's big battlewagon guns. Ahead great geysers of water were spouting up. LeSueur assured the frightened young soldiers that the shells came from the navy's guns. Then he realized they were from German shore batteries. Nearby boats were hit; others struck mines and exploded with terrible force. LeSueur saw helmets floating in the water.

When the LCT pushed up onto the beach and the door was low-ered, there was an instant of fear, anticipation, indecision. Then the troops dashed out and scrambled for cover. LeSueur and Robert Landry, a reporter-photographer for *Life*, headed toward the sea wall at the back of the beach. Panting hard as they emerged from the surf and struggled through the sand, they finally collapsed next to the wall, euphoric that so far they were unharmed. An army sergeant crawled over to LeSueur and, grinning, handed him a cigar. "Boy! We made it!" he said in a heavy Brooklyn accent.

Huddled against the wall, LeSueur and Landry could hardly take it all in. The sights and sounds of fighting were everywhere — noise, fire, death. But it was mild compared to Omaha Beach, where snafus and heavy German resistance were creating what appeared at first to be a disaster for the Americans. The battle for Utah Beach, by contrast, quickly took on a kind of normalcy. Strong tidal currents had carried the Fourth Division spearheads two thousand yards south of their assigned landing area. Coming ashore, the soldiers encountered relatively light German defenses. Already, as LeSueur and Landry watched, German soldiers were beginning to surrender. One, an immaculately dressed captain, blond and arrogant, refused to take cover with the rest of his men as German shellfire raked the beach. When Landry tried to take his picture, the captain turned away in disdain. A moment later he was cut down by his own guns.

What generals and writers call "light" defenses never seem very light to the soldiers trying to overcome them. The men on Utah were desper-ate to get off the beach and duck in under the range of the German artillery. With LeSueur and Landry in tow, they started pressing inland across a watery expanse that the Germans had flooded to hamper in-vaders. "The first tank to try to cross the swampland was hit by a German anti-tank shell," LeSueur reported in a broadcast. "A second tank fired one shot at the anti-tank gun and silenced it. We were on our way."

Later that first day LeSueur found himself advancing with about a hundred soldiers. Next to him was a chubby-cheeked kid, no more than eighteen years old, from South Carolina. He was carrying a flame-thrower and seemed to be tiring.

"My leg hurts," the kid said. "I don't think I can walk."

LeSueur was disdainful. "Hell," he said, "I'm older than you are and I'm going along all right. There's no dropping out *here*."

"Well, my leg hurts and I just can't go on."

Unable to hide his disapproval, LeSueur told the young soldier to sit down in a nearby ditch and he would look at the leg. He unfastened the kid's gaiter, pulled up his trouser leg, and discovered a shrapnel hole below the knee. He felt so guilty that in a broadcast several days later, he described the incident but failed to mention that he had initially suspected the young soldier of malingering. Instead he praised his courage and fortitude. "He had walked all day long with [the wound in his leg] and never complained," LeSueur reported, not quite accurately. "Those were the American soldiers on D-Day."

By late afternoon LeSueur and Landry had reached Sainte-Marie-du-Mont, where paratroopers from the Eighty-second Airborne Division were trying to dislodge some German snipers from the town's church steeple and other buildings. LeSueur watched a young paratrooper walk toward a house, rifle at the ready, shouting for the Germans inside to surrender. Several emerged, their arms in the air. At that moment a sniper in the steeple shot the American paratrooper. The bullet ripped through him, killing him instantly, and continued on to kill one of the surrendering Germans. Crouched behind old Norman stone houses, paratroopers lobbed grenades at the church, while in the streets several firefights raged. In the midst of it all a young French woman, heedless of her own safety, tended a dying paratrooper on the village green.

Not until evening was LeSueur finally able to sit down at his portable typewriter and put together an account of that amazing day. He had been the first correspondent from any radio network to land on D-Day, and the only CBS reporter to witness much action. He had a terrific story, the best of his career.

Following the instructions he had received from army press officers before the invasion, he made his way back to the beach under a jet-black sky — in the process nearly getting his head blown off by nervous young sentries. He handed his dispatch to the navy beachmaster, who was to put it aboard a ship returning to London. Anyway, that was how the system had been explained to LeSueur: file through the beachmaster until a radio transmitter is established. As the troops moved inland toward Cherbourg, LeSueur slogged back to the beach each night, past trigger-happy American sentries and stray German snipers, to turn his copy over to the beachmaster. As it happened, none of those dispatches, including the D-Day story, made it back to London. It was more than a week before LeSueur was able to broadcast, more than a week before he could tell listeners the great human story he had witnessed.

Before the invasion, in an interview with Ed Murrow, the chief American military press officer in London had promised CBS's listeners that when D-Day finally came, "at the first, earliest moment, you will hear the voice of your favorite war correspondent talking from the actual theater of operations." In fact, the military finally provided broadcast facilities only under heavy pressure. An exasperated Murrow blamed army red tape — and the military's desire "to hold broadcasting back so that it doesn't even enjoy the advantage of speed of communication." Of all the CBS correspondents covering D-Day, only Dick Hottelet, who endured a breakneck, stomach-churning car ride back to London after his bombing run, was actually able to tell America on June 6 what he had seen.

◆

In New York that day, Robert Trout introduced a recording made by Charles Collingwood the night before of interviews he had conducted with soldiers bound for the invasion. CBS had recently, and at long last, lifted the ban on recordings. For D-Day, hopes were high that a newfangled machine Collingwood had borrowed from the navy — one that used gelatinous tape instead of wire — would add immediacy to the coverage. The machine, big, clumsy, and unreliable, needed a technician to operate it, but the hope was that Collingwood, who had been assigned to cover the navy, would be able to capture the sounds of battle, plus his own and others' on-the-scene words and thoughts. If it took an extra day or so for the recordings to make their way back to London from the front, it would be worth it.

But London received no recordings or messages of any kind from Collingwood the day after the invasion. Or the next day. Or the next. LeSueur and Bill Downs also had not reported in. Bill Shadel had finally returned from his assignment aboard the cruiser *Tuscaloosa*, the navy task force command ship off Utah Beach, but the other three correspondents were missing. Murrow was almost beside himself with worry. Prompted by rumors that LeSueur was dead and that Collingwood's body had been seen floating in the surf off Utah Beach, he formally requested a search by the navy.

Then, late on the night of June 9, Collingwood returned to London. About the same time, the recording he had made on D-Day and given to the navy for shipment back to the CBS office also arrived — three days late, but no matter. There had been few recordings by correspondents who actually hit the beaches, and America was still eager for invasion news. That night and the next day CBS played Collingwood's recording again and again.

✦

Lugging his unwieldy recorder and trailed by a soundman, Collingwood had landed, like LeSueur, on Utah Beach, but more than ten hours after the first wave. He came in with a navy underwater demolition team aboard a small craft carrying half a ton of dynamite. Although the scene was less hectic than when LeSueur made his dash to the sea wall, Utah was still being pounded by German shellfire, a fact that Collingwood noted in his recorded broadcast with mild consternation, standing as he was in a boat filled with explosives. His legendary sangfroid was tested less by the German shelling, however, than by his attempt to interview a navy lieutenant on the beach. When he asked his name, the lieutenant laughed.

"I work for a rival network in New York City," he said. "Or I did."

"You did?" a flustered Collingwood repeated.

"I don't think I ought to ruin your broadcast."

But Collingwood recovered quickly. Ignoring the attempted brush-off, he asked, "How are things going on the beach?"

"Rugged, as a matter of fact," the lieutenant said, and proceeded to describe what was happening.

Most of Collingwood's broadcast was a straightforward account of the scene on Utah Beach as the sun was setting on D-Day. But he ended it with one of those poignant human details that were a trademark of Murrow and the Boys. He had told the sailors aboard his small landing craft that all he wanted to do when he landed was "pick up a handful of sand and say, 'This is France. I've got it in my hand.'" While he was broadcasting, the sailors approached him, their hands heaped high with sand.

"How does it feel?" Collingwood asked.

"Since I was born in France," one sailor said in an emotion-choked voice, "it has special meaning for me."

"We've got to save this," Collingwood said. "We've got to put it in a bottle." He turned back to the microphone: "All of the men are getting aboard, all of them with handfuls of France in their hands."

Collingwood took his own handful and let the sand run slowly from his fist into an empty soft drink bottle, which he then recapped and carried with him for the rest of the war.

◆

Despite the attention given to Collingwood's recording, it was Larry LeSueur who produced the most impressive invasion coverage for CBS, even if it did arrive several days late. He and Downs — and, briefly, Shadel — trudged and dodged with the troops across soggy Normandy. LeSueur captured the frustration and confusion of this unfamiliar hedgerow fighting, the exhilaration and relief of soldiers who proved themselves under fire, the joy of Frenchmen at being liberated.

The conditions were extremely difficult. There was no real front in much of Normandy. The famous Norman hedgerows — impenetrable, six-foot-high dirt walls topped with trees and bushes — made sure of that. As LeSueur reported, "This is a country with its defensive positions built in. The Germans just hide on one side of a hedge-enclosed field, and the open space in front gives them a field of fire for one hundred yards or more."

For the Allied troops the fighting was a series of quick, heart-stopping rushes across fields, from hedgerow to hedgerow, and sudden clashes with pockets of German troops. For correspondents the front was so poorly defined that as they roamed the countryside looking for fighting to cover, they ran the risk of stumbling onto fierce combat when they least expected it. "Your only clue to being too close to the front lines might be the sighting of bodies," said Bill Shadel. "If they were American dead, you knew you were too far forward."

Covering the endlessly shifting battles was only half the job. Once the radio correspondents had their story, they had to retrace their steps through the maze of hedgerow-enclosed fields, always on the lookout for snipers, and return to the landing beaches, where the mobile transmitter was still located. Most made the perilous round trip at least twice a day. (Print correspondents were able to send their dispatches back by messenger.)

Cherbourg was the first French city of any size to be liberated by the Allies. LeSueur affectingly described how its citizens, after gathering in the town square to pay tribute to French resistance fighters, suddenly broke into the *Marseillaise*. The stirring French anthem, LeSueur reported, was "sung for the first time [since the war began] by liberated

Thomas Grandin, Edward R. Murrow, and William L. Shirer (left to right) pose at Le Bourget in 1938. Grandin, the second correspondent hired by Murrow, suddenly resigned from CBS in 1940 to accompany his Rumanian bride to the United States. *Courtesy Inga Dean*

News broadcasting in the late 1930s was an almost exclusively male preserve until Murrow hired Mary Marvin Breckinridge, who had come to Europe as a photographer. He sent her to the Netherlands to cover the "phony war." *Courtesy Mary Marvin Breckinridge Patterson*

After graduating from high school at seventeen, Eric Sevareid (left) joined his friend Walter Port on a grueling 2,200-mile canoe trip from Minnesota, through Manitoba, Canada, to Hudson's Bay. *Courtesy Suzanne St. Pierre*

In early 1940 Ed Murrow, based in London, and Bill Shirer, based in Berlin, took a break in Amsterdam. The two young broadcasting pioneers get ready to ice skate with their new CBS colleague, Mary Marvin Breckinridge. *Courtesy Mary Marvin Breckinridge Patterson*

In 1941 Howard K. Smith was stationed in Berlin, where he met nineteen-year-old Benedicte "Bennie" Traberg, a Danish journalist, who would become his wife. Smith left Berlin only hours before the United States entered the war. *Courtesy Howard K. Smith*

Bill Shirer's wife, Tess, and their daughter, Eileen Inga, returned to the United States in the fall of 1940. Shirer joined them two months later and soon published his first book, *Berlin Diary*. *Library of Congress*

As Paris was about to fall to the Germans, Sevareid's wife, Lois, with their newborn twin boys, fled by train to Genoa, where they boarded the S.S. *Manhattan* for New York. *Library of Congress*

When Hitler accepted France's capitulation at Compiègne in 1940,
Bill Shirer was there for CBS, sitting in a clearing as the officials arrived.
The next day he reported the signing of the armistice. *Courtesy Inga Dean*

Murrow never quite forgave Shirer for leaving Europe during the war. When the two old
friends sat for a publicity photo in 1941, their relationship was already seriously strained.
Courtesy Bliss Collection / CBS Photo

Cecil Brown was aboard the British cruiser *Repulse* on December 10, 1941, when it and the battleship *Prince of Wales* were sunk by Japanese aircraft. Brown was photographed shortly after his rescue. *Library of Congress*

In August 1943 Sevareid (back row, fourth from left) was one of twenty men who had to bail out of a crippled C-46 flying over the famous "Hump" of the Himalayas. After nearly a month the survivors and a rescue team made their way back to civilization. *Library of Congress*

After escaping from Berlin, Smith was trapped in neutral Switzerland, reporting the war secondhand, until after D-Day. When the Wehrmacht retreated, Howard and Bennie were at last able to leave their Swiss haven, and he became a full-fledged war correspondent. *Courtesy Howard K. Smith*

After D-Day, radio correspondents found it even more difficult to transmit stories to the United States. But as Allied troops closed in on Paris, they captured a makeshift Nazi broadcasting studio, which Larry LeSueur puts to good use here. *UPI/Bettmann*

For most of the war, CBS and other networks refused to broadcast pre-recorded news reports, but by D-Day this policy was changing. Charles Collingwood (right) tests the recorder he will use to cover the Allied landing. Technician Gene Ryder observes. *Courtesy Molly Collingwood*

This picture of CBS's London-based D-Day team may be the closest thing there is to a formal portrait of some of the Murrow Boys. Front row, from left: Bill Downs, Charles Collingwood, Gene Ryder, Charles Shaw. Back row: Larry LeSueur, Ed Murrow, Richard C. Hottelet, Bill Shadel. (Ryder, Shaw, and Shadel helped with the invasion coverage but were never considered Murrow Boys.) *Courtesy Radio-Television News Directors Association*

Some members of the CBS D-Day team gather on a London sidewalk. From left: Richard Hottelet, Gene Ryder, Bill Downs, Charles Collingwood, and Charles Shaw. *Courtesy Molly Collingwood*

Hottelet with three captured German soldiers near the end of the war. *Courtesy Richard C. Hottelet*

Hottelet broadcasts under fire near Aachen in the winter of 1944. *Courtesy Richard C. Hottelet*

Hottelet interviews a survivor at the Buchenwald death camp. Years earlier, when he was a Berlin correspondent for United Press, Hottelet had been arrested and jailed by the Gestapo on trumped-up espionage charges. *Courtesy Richard C. Hottelet*

Paul White, the newsman who ran the CBS news operation from the early 1930s to 1946, talks by shortwave radio to the London bureau during the war. He designed the cue panel, known as "Paul's Piano." *Courtesy Radio-Television News Directors' Association*

After the war many of the top jobs at CBS News went to the Murrow Boys. Here Washington bureau chief Eric Sevareid checks the wires. *Library of Congress*

Charles Collingwood — "Bonnie Prince Charlie" — was a first-rate journalist who loved wine, women, gambling, fine clothes, and art collecting. In 1946 he married movie actress Louise Allbritton. *Courtesy Molly Collingwood*

Charles Collingwood at the 1948 Republican convention in Philadelphia, which was the first convention to receive television coverage. *Courtesy Molly Collingwood*

Bill Downs, the often unheralded workhorse of the Murrow team, married Rosalind Gerson of the CBS News staff. Here they are touring the port of New Orleans. *Courtesy the estate of Mr. and Mrs. William R. Downs*

Murrow enjoys a broadcast by Howard Smith (left) and Larry LeSueur, possibly from a hotel room during one of the 1948 political conventions. *Courtesy Howard K. Smith*

In 1950 CBS radio launched a program known as the year-end roundup. A great success, it became an annual event, called *Years of Crisis*. Murrow presided, joined by most of the original Boys and a few other correspondents. Gathered for the second radio broadcast are (from left) Murrow, Hottelet, Ned Calmer, Smith, and Winston Burdett. *Courtesy Howard K. Smith*

Ed Murrow and Larry LeSueur on assignment in Korea. On an earlier trip Bill Downs met Murrow at the airport and shouted, "Go back! It's not our kind of war!" *Courtesy Larry LeSueur*

When *Years of Crisis* moved to television, many of the same correspondents participated. In 1955 the group included (from left) Collingwood, Calmer, Burdett, Sevareid, Bill Costello, LeSueur, David Schoenbrun, Smith, Hottelet, and Murrow. The young man next to the camera is Don Hewitt, later the creator and executive producer of *60 Minutes. Courtesy Bliss Collection/ CBS Photo*

Winston Burdett testifies in 1955 before the Senate Internal Security Subcommittee. Burdett had joined the Communist Party as a young journalist working for the *Brooklyn Eagle*. In his testimony he identified other journalists who had been Party members. *UPI/Bettmann*

Howard K. Smith moderated the first debate between John F. Kennedy and Richard M. Nixon during the 1960 presidential campaign. Here the candidates and Smith prepare to go on the air. *Courtesy Howard K. Smith*

Sevareid and his second wife, Belèn, in Acapulco, about 1970. *Courtesy Belèn Sevareid*

Sevareid married Suzanne St. Pierre, his third wife, in 1979. *Courtesy Suzanne St. Pierre*

Collingwood (center) made many trips to Vietnam to cover the war. On the right is young State Department official Richard Holbrooke, who in 1995 would become the Clinton administration's lead negotiator in Bosnia. *Courtesy Molly Collingwood*

Frenchmen in the free capital of Normandy and sung with such a feeling of life and warmth as has not been heard in France for four years." A cry of "Vive de Gaulle!" then thundered throughout the square. "'Vive l'Amerique!' and 'Vive l'Angleterre!' followed with enthusiasm, and the first mass meeting of liberated Cherbourg was over."

Throughout that long and humid summer, LeSueur devoted most of his reporting to the young American soldiers picking their slow, bloody way across Normandy. After the liberation of Cherbourg, he sketched a vivid word-picture of how the troops' hard-won victories had improved their confidence and morale.

Men are shaving again. They are polishing their boots. Makeshift clotheslines of underwear, shirts, and socks dangle in the breeze. Men have once more found sewing kits, and you can see them industriously patching their uniforms. Every American soldier had a secret feeling that the American army was invincible. The only thing they weren't sure of was themselves. Now they know that they themselves have been tested under fire and made the grade. American troops who have never been under fire before suddenly have found themselves victorious veterans.

✦

Shortly after Cherbourg, Collingwood returned to France from London to cover the fighting. At that point a long-smoldering rivalry between him and LeSueur flared up and would continue until the end of the war. Neither ever liked to talk about it, although many friends and acquaintances were aware of it. Both men were ambitious and eager to get on the air, and there may have been competition over who was closer to Murrow. LeSueur, by now a CBS veteran, also considered himself a better reporter than Collingwood and may have felt a bit envious of all the attention lavished on his likable but rather affected junior colleague.

While LeSueur spent all his time with the troops and bedded down on dreary cots in makeshift press camps, Collingwood and Bill Walton of *Time* took up residence in a spacious villa outside Cherbourg, along with Major John Palfrey, an Englishman who had been appointed chief of Cherbourg's Allied police force. "Both Charlie and I wanted to live as little in a press camp as possible," said Walton. They had three servants, whose salaries Collingwood put on his expense account, and a plentiful supply of whiskey and cigarettes, commandeered by Palfrey from a former German supply dump outside Cherbourg.

By day Collingwood and Walton covered the war; by night they threw boisterous parties. Their house became the social center of Cherbourg. Among those who bunked with them at various times were Ernest Hemingway, *Life* photographer Robert Capa, and Time-Life's London bureau chief, Charles Wertenbaker. The house was normally so full of guests that when Bill Paley showed up unexpectedly one day, he was relegated to a cot in the attic — "and was very happy to get it," Walton recalled.

After three weeks Collingwood and Walton had to give up the villa. By then the Allied forces had moved too far away for them to make the trek back to Cherbourg every night. But they always managed to find what they considered suitable accommodations as they made their way across northern France. In August they moved into a fine old hotel in recently liberated Mont-Saint-Michel, along with Wertenbaker, Capa, Hemingway, and *New Yorker* writer A. J. Liebling. After a hard day of covering the fighting around the nearby port city of Saint-Malo, the correspondents would return to a splendid dinner prepared for them by the *patronne*, complete with vintage wines that had been kept hidden from the Germans during the occupation.

As the summer wore on and the Allied advance across France picked up speed, Collingwood and Walton were often in the vanguard. On at least one occasion, they actually found themselves *ahead* of the first elements. They were on their way to Orléans to join up with a column of Major General Jacques Philippe Leclerc's French Second Armored Division when they drove through a small town that had not yet been liberated. The few Germans still there were no longer in a mood to fight. So they surrendered — to Walton and Collingwood. The delighted townspeople asked the correspondents to make a victory speech from the balcony above the town hall. "Charles was very happy to comply," said Walton. In his excellent French, "he was quite flowery and gave them just what they wanted — 'Vive la France' and the whole thing. There was cheering, clapping, a lot of shouting of 'Vive l'Americain!'"

In Orléans, Collingwood served as interpreter and liaison between the French underground and the officers of the American force that had just liberated the city. "Moving with a force like this is heady wine," Collingwood reported from Orléans. "Everyone has an enormous, exhilarating sensation of power. You feel you can go anywhere, do anything. 'Get me enough gasoline up here,' an officer said, 'and I'll go straight through to Coblenz.'"

Or at least to Paris.

✦

Generals Dwight Eisenhower and Omar Bradley (the commander of American ground forces in northwestern Europe) had no plan at first for the immediate liberation of Paris. Their intent was to bypass the city, which they considered of little strategic importance, and roll on with all possible speed toward Germany and the Siegfried Line. But that was before Roger Gallois, a French Resistance leader, showed up at Bradley's camp on August 21 and pleaded with the general to take the French capital.

The Parisian Maquis had risen up against the German occupiers but now were nearly done for. If the Allies did not come to their aid, Gallois said, hundreds of thousands of Parisians would be killed. Furthermore, the German commander in Paris, General Dietrich von Choltitz, was under orders from Hitler to destroy the city before surrendering it to the Allies. Von Choltitz didn't like the order, but he intended to carry it out. He sent word through Gallois that only the Allies' speedy arrival could stop him.

Bradley was convinced and, with Eisenhower's approval, ordered Leclerc's Second Armored Division, French citizens and colonials all, to head for Paris. Leclerc, who had vowed three years earlier to be the liberator of his country's capital, was delighted, as were the swarms of American correspondents anxious to cover what they knew would be one of the most dramatic stories of the war.

Unaware of the sudden shift in plans, one of the reporters most keen on covering that story was on his way back to London for emergency dental work. Larry LeSueur, who had broken off a front tooth a few days earlier on stale K-rations, had been assured by General Courtney Hodges, commander of the U.S. First Army, that Paris would not be freed for at least another two weeks. One of the last radio correspondents to broadcast from a defeated Paris back in 1940 (both he and Sevareid claimed the distinction), LeSueur was intent on being the first American to broadcast from a liberated Paris in 1944. But there was no way he could continue to broadcast with this damned broken tooth: when he talked, he *whistled*. As he left for London, he was sure he would be back in plenty of time to make that first broadcast and beat his main rival for the honor, Charlie Collingwood.

Collingwood had other ideas. Informed by General Bradley of the Resistance uprising and the decision to move on Paris, he vowed *he* would be first with the story. But first he had to figure out a way to bypass the always uncertain broadcasting facilities. He hit upon an ingenious, if thoroughly unethical, solution. He would see to it that his story was ready and waiting in London when the liberation occurred. Then it could be used when the first flash came through that Allied troops had entered Paris.

That night Collingwood sat down and wrote a detailed and emotional account of an event that had not yet happened:

The French Second Armored Division entered Paris today after the Parisians had risen as one man to beat down the German troops who had garrisoned the city. It was the people of Paris who really won back their city. . . . Every hand was raised against the enemy. For the first time in this war, the inhabitants of a city have wrested it from the enemy. Paris would have fallen into our arms [anyway], but every American soldier in France would rather have had it this way. Paris, the queen of cities, fell to her own citizens . . .

When he had finished typing it, he recorded the story on his tape recorder, then slipped recording and script into a military press pouch for London. He had outwitted the system. Now he had only to await the payoff.

Two days later, on August 23 just before midnight, the pouch arrived by courier plane in London and was delivered to the CBS office. Someone at CBS read Collingwood's report to a London-based military censor and dispatched a backup copy to the censors' office. Then, in what Allied headquarters later called a "pure but serious" error, the censors — apparently (and erroneously) assuming that the story was true and that their counterparts in France had already passed it — approved it for transmission.

Dick Hottelet was on duty in the CBS London office when Collingwood's copy was handed to him. As he started to read it, he thought, *My God, Paris has been liberated! Charlie's there and he's broken the story!* He grabbed the phone and called New York, where it was now nearly 7 P.M. on the 23rd. Meanwhile, something equally bizarre had happened: the BBC had interrupted its regular programming to tell listeners to stand by for an important announcement.

"Paris has been liberated," an emotional voice finally declared. "I repeat, Paris has been liberated." There were no details, no on-the-scene reports. Just the bulletin.

But that was all Hottelet needed to read the story on the air. Collingwood had a worldwide exclusive — the first eyewitness account of the liberation of Paris. In New York CBS interrupted its programming and switched to London. "The first American correspondent to enter Paris," the network trumpeted as it later played Collingwood's recorded version over and over into the night.

America, and much of the rest of the world, went wild. People danced in the streets, car horns blared, newspapers put out extras with Collingwood's story emblazoned across the front page under huge headlines. Opera singer Lily Pons sang the *Marseillaise* to a crowd of twenty thousand in Rockefeller Center. In Washington, President Roosevelt called the news "an ebullient passage of total victory." In London, King George congratulated General de Gaulle, and thousands cavorted around Nelson's column in Trafalgar Square.

Larry LeSueur was decidedly *not* among the celebrants. He had been in a dentist's chair in London when he heard the news. His heart plummeted: he'd missed the whole thing! Once his tooth was repaired, he dashed from the dentist's office and caught the next military flight to France.

In Paris, where ten thousand German troops were still engaged in bloody combat with Resistance fighters, and in nearby Rambouillet, where dozens of impatient correspondents were holed up waiting for the march on the capital, Collingwood's story and the BBC's bulletin were greeted with astonishment, then fury. What the hell was going *on* here? Arriving in Rambouillet, LeSueur was quick to debunk his colleague's putative scoop. In his first broadcast after his return to France, he reported:

> Paris has *not* yet been entered by Allied troops. The French Second Armored Division is still outside the city, held up by diehard bands of German anti-tank and mine fields and small groups of German tanks. . . . Correspondents returning from a vain attempt to enter the city this afternoon reported that at least fifteen tanks are barring the way twenty miles west of the French capital.

It was a fiasco, the mother of all mistakes, and few, if any, of Collingwood's colleagues were appeased by the explanations that he, CBS, the military, and the BBC offered. Collingwood's unlikely account was that he had been told by army press officers that his story would not be released by censors in London until Paris was actually liberated. Any material that proved erroneous would be deleted at that time. But neither the script nor the recording carried a "hold-for-censorship" message, and the censors — unaccustomed as they were to editing fabricated news stories — failed to check the facts. According to a CBS statement, the network's London bureau assumed it *had* been censored.

As for the BBC's mistake, its information had come from Colonel André Vernon, head of the Resistance information office in London. Vernon had intentionally written a false news bulletin — but not a full story — that Paris had "liberated itself," and he had sent it to the BBC without going through censorship. He had done it, Vernon said later, to put pressure on the Allies to liberate Paris as soon as possible.

The humiliation and embarrassment all around were enormous. Ed Murrow, standing stoutly — and wrongly — by his man, assigned the entire blame to the military press officers and censors. Said Murrow, "We were just doing our best — we thought it was right at the time — and take such comfort as we can from the knowledge that nothing we did, or that SHAEF [Supreme Headquarters, Allied Expeditionary Force] didn't do, endangered the life of a single fighting man." It was a rather fatuous defense.

Collingwood, who loved living on the edge and who perhaps had come too far too fast, had badly overreached himself this time. He had fabricated a story, which, even after Paris *was* liberated, turned out, not surprisingly, to be riddled with errors. Yes, the Resistance did rise up, as he had predicted. But the French fighters would not have been able to free the city without the help of the Allied troops.

Andy Rooney, who had so admired Collingwood before this, was amazed that CBS didn't fire his hero. The disillusioned Rooney never forgave Collingwood for disappointing him. Most people, however, found it difficult to stay angry with Bonnie Prince Charlie for very long.

✦

On the beautiful, sunny morning of August 25 — the feast day of Saint-Louis, the patron saint of France — Leclerc's Second Division finally did reclaim a delirious Paris. Throngs embraced and kissed the soldiers as they marched and rode by. Glasses of champagne and cognac were handed to them. People climbed up on the moving tanks, threw flowers and food, waved handkerchiefs and flags. "Vive Leclerc!"

they shouted. "Vive de Gaulle!" Above all, "Merci! Merci!" High above the crowds, the great bells of Paris — in Notre-Dame, Sacre-Coeur, Sainte-Chapelle — rocked the city with their joyous peals. Even gunfire from German snipers and sporadic duels between Allied and German tanks failed to dampen the celebration.

In front of the Scribe Hotel, headquarters for the Allied press corps, the street was crowded with dozens of young women in flimsy summer dresses. They kissed and hugged every male journalist in sight. Watching them, Ernie Pyle turned to a group of correspondents and said, "Well, all I've got to say is that anybody who doesn't sleep with a woman tonight is just a goddamned exhibitionist."

But at least one reporter that night had his mind on other things. Larry LeSueur slipped over to Rue de Grenelle, where a clandestine Free French radio station had been operating under German noses, and sat down before the microphone. He had done it! He was about to deliver the first American radio report from a liberated Paris! Never mind that he had not submitted his piece to a censor as required. He had tried to find one at the Scribe, but none had shown up yet, and he'd be damned if he'd wait any longer. He was going to be first with this story and *hang* the consequences!

"Paris is the happiest city in the world tonight," he said into the mike. "Paris has been scarred by its liberation, but it bears its scars proudly. It was not an open city this time. Shortly after seven o'clock tonight, General de Gaulle was in Paris for the first time in four years. The cheers that filled Paris left no doubt in anyone's mind as to de Gaulle's popularity. Tonight, all Paris is dancing in the streets."

He had recruited several other correspondents, including one from UP and another from the BBC, to go with him to the station, because, as he said years later, "I didn't want to be the only goat [when the military discovered the evasion of censorship]." All of them had sent their stories by the time John MacVane of NBC rushed into the station waving his own account, which bore the censor's clearance stamp. Rehearsing his piece before he went on the air, he began, "This is the first broadcast from liberated Paris." Overhearing him, another correspondent broke the bad news: LeSueur and the others had already filed.

"But that's impossible," MacVane protested. "My script was the first one through censorship!"

"Censorship?" the colleague snorted. "Who cares about censorship *tonight?*"

Poor MacVane — outsmarted by Collingwood in North Africa and by LeSueur in Paris! "At least," he wrote later, "I had the cold comfort of moral satisfaction."

Morality and ethics were not in great supply that week in Paris, however, and transgressors went virtually unpunished. LeSueur and the others received two-week suspensions from SHAEF — a slap on the wrist. In fact, a little time off in Paris didn't seem like punishment *at all* to LeSueur. It was great not to have to work, to be able to amble around that glorious city, drinking and eating in its cafés, accepting the thanks of its grateful citizens, ogling the bikini-clad women at the pool in the Bois de Bologne (the first bikinis LeSueur had ever seen). Finally SHAEF realized its mistake and put LeSueur on a plane to London, where he would serve out the rest of his suspension in rather more dour surroundings.

But he had no regrets. None at all.

✦

Charlie Collingwood, in contrast, was lying low. Like the other correspondents, he and Bill Walton had come into Paris with Leclerc's division and witnessed the delirium of the city's liberation. But at first Collingwood stayed away from the scene at the Scribe and from the radio station on rue Grenelle. Instead he and Walton drove up to Montmartre with its disreputable cafés and nightclubs.

They stopped in front of a hotel and went inside to find rooms, leaving their army driver in the jeep. While talking to the manager, they heard a commotion and looked out the window to see their driver surrounded by women — what appeared to be Montmartre's entire population of whores. As Walton later recalled the scene:

> They had come streaming out of every café, and they were all jumping up and down, screaming and shouting. Charles said, "We'd better go out and see what's going on." We got back in the jeep, and one very forward woman gets up on the hood of the jeep, raises her skirts up — she had dyed her pubic hair red, white and blue. She did a dance. All the other girls were making fun of her, saying, "Clarice will do anything." All of them wanted us as customers. There were hundreds of ladies, and hardly another man in sight. . . . Skip to the morning. I leave my room and go down the hall to Charles's room. He is out on his balcony in a scarlet silk dressing gown — he'd had it in his knapsack all

the time — talking and laughing with women as far as you could see in the square outside. Having the time of his life, just talking and laughing. *That* was Charles.

Nothing could mar such a splendid morning for Collingwood, not even the events of two days before. He was in Paris. He was adored by the ladies. It was heaven itself.

✳ 17

Victory

For HOWARD SMITH the liberation of France meant he could at last leave his refuge in Switzerland and do some real war reporting. During his two and a half years in his Bern listening post, Smith had made valuable contacts and uncovered some good stories about what was happening in the occupied countries. But he was tired of reconstructions. He wanted to witness events again — so much so that, even before the Swiss border was reopened, he and Bennie sneaked out of the country in search of a story in Nazi-occupied France.

As Allied troops were closing in on Paris, the Smiths entered the French border town of Saint-Julien just a few hours after its liberation by the French Resistance. The Maquis lent them a captured German command car, and for the next three days they traveled to half a dozen newly freed towns and villages. The last stop on their tour was Annecy, the capital of France's Haut-Savoie Department, about twenty miles south of Geneva. The town's buildings were festooned with bunting, and its people marched through the streets, laughing, cheering, crying, and singing the *Marseillaise*.

Late that night the Smiths were sipping soup at a café when gendarmes burst in through the front and back doors and grabbed Bennie. As Smith sprang up to help her, two gendarmes jammed pistols into his gut and barked that he was under arrest. Outside the Smiths were ordered to stand against a wall, while a growing crowd of townspeople screamed insults and taunts at them. A Maquis pointed a Tommy gun at Smith's chest and yelled that it would give him "infinite pleasure" to shoot both of them right there in the street. A gendarme pulled the man away, and the Smiths were marched through the dark streets with their hands high in the air and submachine guns at their backs. *My God*, Howard Smith thought, *it's like the French Revolution!*

Taken to Maquis headquarters, Howard and Bennie were placed in separate rooms, interrogated by gendarmes, and accused of being Nazi agents. When Howard produced his American passport, one of his interrogators threw it back at him. A forgery, he said. After two hours of grilling, Smith was close to despair. Suddenly the door of the room was flung open, and a young man in a khaki coat strode in. He yelled at the gendarmes, demanding to know who had appointed *them* judges. Turning to Smith, he bowed and said, "Monsieur, in our ardor to free our country and create a new France, we are arresting everyone whom we fear is with the enemy. We have caught many of our enemies. Unfortunately we have also caught some of our friends, like you."

The Smiths wasted little time returning to Switzerland.

In early September, with the German occupation of France collapsing everywhere, they decided to move to Paris. It would not be an easy trip. Bennie was pregnant, and the still somewhat unsettled military situation forced them to go by car to Lyon, then hitch a flight with a U.S. military cargo plane to Paris. For more than seven hours, in a driving rain, they waited on the tarmac at the Lyon airfield for an empty flight. The plane that finally took them north encountered heavy turbulence, and Bennie became airsick. After flying at treetop level to avoid German fire, the plane landed fifty kilometers north of Paris, and the Smiths caught a ride to the French capital in an open jeep, drenched once more by heavy downpours. By the time Bennie and Howard arrived in Paris, she felt wretched and looked worse.

The Smiths proceeded to the Scribe Hotel, where, lacking reservations, they hoped to talk their way in. From a house phone in the lobby, Smith rang Charles Collingwood's room. The ever-ebullient Collingwood told them to come right up.

When he opened his door, the Smiths — rumpled, rain-soaked, and disoriented by the change from drab, neutral Bern to romantic, bustling, anything-but-neutral Paris — were overwhelmed. Standing before them in the doorway was a vision of such opulent decadence that an act of will was required for them not to gape.

Charles Cummings Collingwood, draped in Chinese red silk pajamas, was puffing languidly on a cigarette set in a six-inch ivory holder. He looked to Smith like a "twentieth-century replica of an eighteenth-century Beau Brummel." On the bed behind him the Smiths could see a young woman, very French, very pretty, very blonde. A couple of Collingwood's recently purchased Picassos hung on the walls. All things considered, Bennie, still a little nauseous, her hair looking like wet straw, felt as if she'd been dragged in from the gutter by some starved cat!

Collingwood grandly ushered them in, bid them sit, inquired about their journey. Smith, tired but anxious to get to work, asked how one went about getting SHAEF press credentials to cover the war. Collingwood seemed suddenly distracted. He said he had a slight touch of the flu this *particular* evening but promised to see about the credentials in the morning. *First things first, though. Let's get you two kids a place to stay.* He picked up the phone and spoke in French. Minutes later the Scribe's management had found an available room in the overbooked hotel. The bedazzled Smiths said they had imposed enough for one evening. As they were leaving, they saw the young woman run her fingers through Collingwood's wavy blond hair. They shut the door quietly behind them. Bern was never like this!

The next day Collingwood, evidently recovered from the flu, arranged for Smith's press credentials. A process that normally took days was accomplished by the bonnie prince, with his usual excellent contacts, in under an hour. Smith wanted to get to the eastward-moving front as soon as possible, but wondered if he could make a few broadcasts from Paris in the meantime. Collingwood said he and LeSueur would be happy to share slots on the CBS Paris broadcast schedule with him. As a matter of fact, this week's schedule from London was overdue. When it arrived, Smith would be worked into the lineup.

But Collingwood didn't receive the scheduling cable. Puzzled, he telephoned London. The office there insisted the cable had been sent, and so it had. Smith learned later that LeSueur had intercepted it and done all the broadcasts up to that point in the week himself, without telling his colleagues. For Smith it was a rather rude introduction to the concept of teamwork held by some of the Murrow Boys.

When he finally did break into the broadcasting rotation, Smith got another taste of LeSueur's competitiveness (or anyway of his sometimes quirky sense of humor). Smith had just finished a broadcast one morning when LeSueur told him that Bill Paley was in town and wanted to meet him. Flattered, Smith said he had to return to his hotel and get spruced up; he hadn't had a chance to shave before he came over to do the broadcast. LeSueur told Smith not to worry, that Paley didn't mind if people hadn't shaved. So Smith dutifully hustled over to the George V, where Paley was staying, and discovered he was the only unshaven guest at an elegant luncheon in the Paley suite. "I looked," Smith said, "like a bum."

In general, rivalry had replaced fraternity among the Murrow Boys, at least in Paris. Some of them, particularly Sevareid, would reminisce in later years about what they had meant to one another. Ed Murrow aside, however, legends rarely seem all that legendary to their contemporaries and peers. There was a reasonable degree of genuine friendship among the Boys, and each had enormous respect for the others and pride in what they had collectively accomplished. Yet these knights quested mostly alone. They were rarely, if ever, in the same place at the same time, and as far as is known, there are no photographs of the entire group. The "team" was a collection of individualists — talented, highly motivated men, each interested in advancing his own career, each chasing his own stories, each competing for a finite amount of airtime.

Indeed, they took pride in their individualism. "There was a great feeling about it, a sense of intoxication," Dick Hottelet recalled. "It was *your* job, *your* voice, *your* report. That didn't happen in any other work." Or as Murrow put it, "No one in New York can rewrite or change our material. We say what we see, and no one can insert lurid adjectives or qualifying phrases." The degree of their freedom was remarkable. "We had no budget," Murrow recalled. "Nobody gave orders. New York asked us only to find the news, try to report it and keep our heads." In these circumstances collegiality suffered. "We all had big egos," Hottelet said. "We all wanted to be the star. The only one who could have managed this team of horses with any success was Ed Murrow."

✦

As the Allies pushed the Germans back, the competition among the Boys only intensified. There were so many fronts, so many stories, so many reporters! The Boys had to compete not only with each other and outside rivals but with CBS reinforcements sent over periodically from New York — announcers and newscasters like Bob Trout, Ned Calmer, John Charles Daly, and Douglas Edwards. Nor did they any longer enjoy the luxury of spinning out the carefully crafted, colorful details of a story for three or four minutes. Now their slots on the morning and evening news roundups were two minutes, tops. The Boys were seeing the future.

The evening roundup was the real prize, because the sponsor paid a correspondent fifty dollars every time he appeared on it. Bill Shadel discovered the hard way just how valued the prize was. When he was hired, Murrow urged him to try to get on both the morning and evening roundups as much as possible so that listeners back home would start recognizing his name and voice. He tried but was rarely able to get on the evening program. Finally Kay Campbell, Murrow's secretary, explained to Shadel that other correspondents often persuaded the boss to bump him from the schedule and put them on instead.

✦

It was much easier to get on the air if you hung around Paris or London, covering the war secondhand, than if you got involved with some lost battalion in the boondocks. If you actually went to the front in France or the Netherlands or Belgium or Germany, there was a better than even chance that your story would never be heard. Even in London and Paris, atmospherics, line breaks, and power outages regularly disrupted broadcasts. In the field, where transmitting facilities were marginal at best, a correspondent often felt he was, as Smith put it, "carefully writing a script and dropping it in the nearest manhole, and that was the end of it."

After broadcasting one day from the front, CBS reporter Farnsworth Fowle received a cable from New York saying, QUALITY GREAT LAST NIGHT. WHICH WAVE LENGTH USED? Fowle laughed at the absurdity of the question. "As if I had any idea. There they were, sitting on Madison Avenue, with absolutely no understanding of our crude pioneer setup."

It was particularly frustrating for a broadcast reporter to witness a dramatic battle and fail to get it on the air, only to discover later that a colleague in Paris had done the story based on some official briefing or handout. "At times," Ed Murrow said near the end of the war, "broadcasts are like big fish. Most of the big ones get away, just as most of the good broadcasts never get through to the States."

Both LeSueur and Collingwood, their rivalry as intense as ever, succumbed at first to the professional and personal lures of Paris. But in the fall of 1944 LeSueur left Paris and for the rest of the war alternated between London and the fighting in Germany. Collingwood mostly stayed in Paris. "I like the city and I like the life," he wrote his parents. "There is always something to look forward to . . . friends to see, an exposition, a part of the city I haven't got around to revisit yet, a shop where they say there are some nice things, a gallery where there are some good pictures." Not to mention large-scale expense-account partying with the elite of Paris.

Collingwood's social life had always been important to him; now it assumed a grander dimension. "A new Charles was born in Paris," said Bill Walton. "He was invited to very fancy soirées, with roomfuls of famous people. It was a world he found terribly fascinating. Charles began to get very fine feathers in Paris."

He kept his room at the Scribe but stayed most nights at the Lancaster, a smaller and more elegant hotel on the Rue de Berri, along with many of his D-Day buddies, among them Walton, Charles Wertenbaker, and Bob Capa. Collingwood had become particularly close to the dark and handsome Capa, perhaps the best-known photographer of World War II, whose own professional and personal adventures were the stuff of legend. If Murrow was Collingwood's surrogate father, Capa was the older brother he never had — a rakish older brother, irresistible to women, who lived a very fast life. The two were having a wonderful time in Paris, so much so that when Collingwood's London love, Gracie Blake, proposed to join him, he discouraged her from doing so "until things get a little more normal over here."

Beyond partying, womanizing, and art collecting, Collingwood began to overindulge in another favorite avocation that would later force him to give up some of his cherished paintings. He had always enjoyed gambling, whether at cards or on the horses, but in Capa's company he started playing for much higher stakes. At the Longchamps racecourse, at the casino at Enghien-les-Bains, or in poker games with pals, Collingwood was betting what for him were astounding amounts. "I have been having a very bad time at poker," he confessed to his parents in a letter in early 1945, "and in the last month have lost a sum which at one time I would have been very happy to have had for a year's salary."

To make good his debts at one point, he had to sell one of his prize Picassos and borrow money from CBS, although he managed to make a small profit on the sale of the painting. To his parents he was philosophical (and pretentious) about it all: "It is a good thing to be able to say about civilization that in its moment of stress, perhaps the only sure and stable international value (except for gold) are paintings, this civilization's greatest intellectual and spiritual achievements."

Collingwood would have occasion to consider the value of art many times in the future. Over the years he had to sell off most of his collection, worth hundreds of thousands of dollars then and many millions today, to pay his gambling debts.

✦

After Paris the veterans among the Murrow Boys were content for the most part to let their newer, hungrier colleagues, who had not yet made big names for themselves, handle coverage of the fighting. It was not an entirely altruistic gesture. The veterans had been through a great deal and may have felt they had beaten the odds enough for one lifetime. In early October, Eric Sevareid landed with the U.S. Seventh Army on the French Riviera and followed the troops north through the Rhone Valley. But when they finally bogged down in the dense, heavily mined forests of the Vosges mountains, Sevareid, fed up with "the wretched army mess and bone-chilling cold," decided to leave. Before returning to London, however, he managed a feat that temporarily lifted his spirits. On September 1, 1944, he, Carl Mydans of *Life*, and Frank Gervasi of *Collier's*, set out to find Gertrude Stein, the famous American writer and collector of art and people.

Ever since the German invasion of France in 1940, Stein, a Jew, had been in hiding with her longtime companion and lover, Alice B. Toklas, in an unknown location. What had become of them was one of the war's minor mysteries. Sevareid and the other searchers, acting on reports that Stein and Toklas were somewhere in the upper Rhone Valley, found them, after a day's drive, in a small chateau in the village of Culoz. Gertrude Stein had been liberated!

"I always knew they would come," she said. "I always knew that war correspondents would be here. I never doubted it for a single moment." She and the men talked for hours, Stein demanding to hear the latest gossip about Hemingway, Thornton Wilder, and Alexander Woollcott (she didn't know Woollcott had died the year before). Two days later Sevareid, having fetched Stein from Culoz to the Seventh Army's press camp, interviewed her on the air. "What a day is today," she said, adding with a typical flourish, "that is, what a day it was day before yesterday. What a day!"

A short time later Sevareid packed up and headed back to London by way of Paris. He did not return to the front again until the Allies were well inside Germany. As he left he was typically unsatisfied, feeling that he had failed to describe what soldiers go through, what battle was really like. In one broadcast, he delivered what he called "a kind of confessional":

Only the soldier really lives the war; the journalist does not. He may share the soldier's outward life and dangers, but he cannot share his inner life, because the same moral compulsion does not bear on him. The observer knows he has alternatives of action; the soldier knows he has none. Their worlds are very far apart, for one is free — the other, a slave. This war must be seen to be believed; but it must be lived to be understood. We [journalists] can tell you only of events, of what men do. We cannot really tell you how, or why, they do it. We can see, and tell you, that this war is brutalizing some among your sons, and yet ennobling others. We can tell you very little more. War happens inside a man. It happens to one man alone. It can never be communicated. That is the tragedy — and, perhaps, the blessing. A thousand ghastly wounds are really only one. A million martyred lives leave an empty place at only one family table. That is why, at bottom, people can let wars happen, and that is why nations survive them and carry on. And, I am sorry to say, that is also why, in a certain sense, you and your sons from the war will be forever strangers.

Sevareid was always very proud of that broadcast. It brought more mail than he had received for any other broadcast up to that time.

♦

From the fall of 1944 on, the bulk of CBS's battlefield reporting was done by Bill Downs, Dick Hottelet, Howard Smith, and part-timer Bill Shadel. Downs was in the field most of the time, covering some of the fiercest battles of the war and having serious problems getting his reports on the air. Some felt he did not receive the attention and respect he deserved at CBS, that the network was taking advantage of him by keeping him so much in harm's way. In one letter home Downs himself complained that he was the only CBS reporter covering four armies: the Canadian First, the British Second, and the American Ninth and First. "I keep telling the office it's stretching me pretty thin."

By all accounts, Downs was an excellent reporter; some people, including Bill Shadel and Paul White, thought he outshone the other Boys. "He was the best damn reporter of the whole works, absolutely the gutsiest guy in the world," Shadel said. Paul White, not perhaps the most objective witness where the Murrow Boys were concerned, told a colleague that Downs was the only one he would trust to cover a four-alarm fire back home. Late in the war Murrow wrote to a friend, "It's interesting to see these boys I helped develop. Some get money-mad, others want fame, and some, like Downs, go on just doing their job."

With his explosive delivery and booming voice, Downs was not very good on the air. Nor was he an elegant writer. He wasn't handsome and glamorous like his better-known colleagues, didn't pal around with generals and politicians. He was Murrow's Ernie Pyle, more at home with the troops and his correspondent buddies than with celebrities, more at home at the front (despite his increasing abhorrence of war) than at the rear.

He was the first correspondent into Caen after it was liberated, having run a gauntlet of German mortar and artillery fire to get there. "I'm giving up the idea of being the first anywhere," he wrote his parents later. In another letter he said, "I get shelled or mortared frequently and have become adept at hitting the ground faster than it takes to blink an eye." And, after the liberation of Brussels: "I have been kissed so often that I almost wear a permanent blush of lipstick. I have refused enough wine to float a battleship. Never have I seen such joy."

The euphoria lasted only until September 17. Until Arnhem. An overconfident Field Marshal Montgomery had ordered his paratroopers to drop behind German lines and capture several bridges crossing the Rhine. Near the Dutch town of Arnhem, the paratroopers were met by an overwhelming German force ordered by Hitler to defend and, if necessary, destroy those same bridges. The battle lasted more than a week. One day, in the thick of it, Downs and Walter Cronkite of UP dove for cover in a ditch as dirt and rocks tumbled over them. Downs tugged at Cronkite's sleeve. "Just think," he shouted. "If we survive them, these will be the good old days!"

Of the more than ten thousand Allied troops who fought at Arnhem, more than seven thousand were killed, wounded, or captured. It was a major Allied defeat, and it threw Downs into a severe emotional tailspin. Since his months in the Soviet Union, he had borne witness to little but killing. Needing a rest, he returned to London and bunked at Ed Murrow's apartment. He found it hard to sleep and was tormented by nightmares. The indifference of many Londoners only made matters worse. He wrote home again, "After watching men die like they did, and then to come back and suddenly realize that people behind the lines were carrying on as if nothing had happened, got me down."

He soon pulled himself together, though, and returned to the front.

✦

Assigned to the U.S. First Army, Dick Hottelet was the first CBS correspondent to enter Germany. When American troops besieged Aachen, just inside the German border, Hottelet was on hand to deliver a memorable broadcast. Using a recorder, he captured the jarring blast of shellfire and the rattle of machine guns, as the Americans engaged the Germans in ferocious house-to-house combat. Taking refuge in the top story of a building, Hottelet leaned out a window and reported on the fighting raging in the street.

"Right down below us," he said in an unnaturally high, strained voice, "the houses still are in German territory, and if anybody is leaning out a bay window and draws a bead on this recorder, you will probably never hear it." Just then the sharp stutter of submachine-gun fire could be heard. "Right now, Lieutenant Walker's men are facing down the tree-lined street," Hottelet explained. "They've located a suspicious-looking building and are starting to fire rounds at it."

It wasn't analysis or interpretation and he hadn't written a script. He just peered out the window and described what he saw. But his dramatic report was an early example of what radio could do in the field, now that the ban on broadcasting prerecorded material had been lifted. Hottelet's listeners might imagine themselves in Aachen, in the thick of the fight — see the smoke and the dust, hear the guns slamming, feel the fear and tension of the troops. Under the ban such broadcasts were possible only when transmitters were readily available; now they could be done from almost anywhere.

But using a recorder had its own hazards, as Larry LeSueur found out when he tried to capture the sounds of a skirmish between American and German troops in a German forest. The generator powering Le-Sueur's recorder made so much noise that it drew German fire on his position. As LeSueur stood there holding his mike high in the air, bullets whizzed past his head and the GIs with him hit the dirt. Somehow he escaped intact. When he got back to the press camp, he excitedly replayed the recording. He couldn't believe the results: the gunfire that had turned his insides to jelly a few hours before sounded like popcorn popping! He never used the recorder again.

✦

A couple of weeks later Howard Smith, with the Ninth Army, returned to Germany and contrasted the arrogant country he had left on December 7, 1941, with the desolate one he found now: "On the roadside lie skeletons of streamlined gray Wehrmacht cars which careened to conquest over every highway in Europe. Now they lie, belly to the sky, burned out and red with rust from the autumn rain. The whole desolate scene is one of crushed power."

But Germany's might was not yet completely exhausted, as Downs, Smith, and Hottelet would soon learn. On December 16, in fog as thick as cotton batting, Hottelet drove from the Belgian town of Spa to the headquarters of the Fourth Division in the Hurtgen Forest. Harried officers there greeted him with astonishment. "For Christ's sake, don't you *know?*" one asked. "The Germans have been attacking us since this morning!"

"Holy Jesus!" Hottelet cried. He rushed back to Spa, managing to stay clear of the massive German force that had just broken through U.S. lines. His was the first news report of the beginning of the Battle of the Bulge, the western front's largest and fiercest battle. In a desperate final attempt to turn the tide, the Germans, using every available soldier, attacked from the rolling, heavily wooded Ardennes region of Belgium. They caught the Allies, mostly Americans, totally by surprise. Protected by heavy snow and fog, which prevented Allied air strikes, the Germans punched deep into Belgium, creating a "bulge" in the Allies' overextended lines and threatening Antwerp, the principal Allied supply port in the area.

For almost three weeks the Americans desperately and gallantly resisted. Covering the fiercest stages of the Battle of the Bulge for CBS were Hottelet, with the U.S. First Division, and Smith, with troops from the Eighty-second Airborne, who struggled through hip-deep snow while German shells ripped through the treetops all around them. In one broadcast Smith described what it was like to be a target: "A [German] rocket screams you an eight-second warning before exploding, an artillery shell one and a half seconds, and a mortar — well, a mortar doesn't scream at all. It just plops down next to you and explodes."

The tide began to turn in late December. Elements of General Patton's Third Army, having wheeled smartly north from France, relieved the German siege of the 101st Airborne at Bastogne, and, as the weather cleared, American planes were able to bomb German positions again. In early January, Montgomery, who had been under pressure for days to counterattack, finally did so. With that the war in Europe was, for all practical purposes, over.

❖

In March the greatest air fleet in history — 3,500 gliders and transports, hundreds of bombers and fighters, and some 14,000 American and British paratroopers — roared across the Rhine. Code-named Operation Varsity, it was also the largest mass airdrop of the war. Ed Murrow and Eric Sevareid had come from London to help cover this monumental event. Murrow, Downs, and Hottelet were in the sky with the paratroopers, Sevareid and Smith on the ground with the Ninth Army. Looking down from a P-47 fighter, Downs felt as if the entire east bank of the Rhine were on fire. "Honest to God," he said in a broadcast later that day, "those paratroopers stepped out on a carpet of flame you could walk on."

Hottelet was in an unarmed B-17 with reporters, photographers, and other observers. As the great, lumbering bomber swung over the drop zone, he saw puffs of ack-ack explosions around them but was more interested in the thousands of blue, red, yellow, and khaki parachutes blossoming over the German heartland. The war had begun with a German blitzkrieg against defenseless Poland; it was ending with this breathtaking Allied airborne assault on Germany. No matter how tired or bored or traumatized a person was by the long war, he would have to be dead to the currents of history not to be stirred by this sight.

But the war had not yet ended. With a loud shudder Hottelet's B-17 was hit by antiaircraft fire, then hit again. Flames erupted from its engines, its interior filled with smoke. The fire, Hottelet saw, was "eating a larger and larger hole in the left wing like a smoldering cigarette." He pulled off his flak suit and buckled on a parachute. He didn't want to jump at all — he had always had a fear of falling — and he especially didn't want to jump *now*. The plane was still on the German side of the Rhine; even if the territory below wasn't in German hands, it certainly was a battlefield. But the pilot managed to keep the plane aloft, its left wing blazing, until he could nudge it back across the river.

There was no longer any choice; Hottelet and the others aboard the B-17 had to jump. As he fell, Hottelet pulled his ripcord, felt the sharp jerk of his parachute opening, watched France coming toward him, and at last tumbled — bruised but otherwise unharmed — into a cow pasture. There soldiers from the British Second Army found him and plied him with tea and whiskey. Dazed and aching, sporting the beginnings of a radiant black eye, he bundled up his parachute and hitched a ride in an army truck, trying to find a radio transmitter.

At the Ninth Army press camp, Eric Sevareid was in the radio van, broadcasting his own story about Operation Varsity, when his young CBS colleague appeared in the rear door, looking like unshirted hell, still clutching his parachute to his chest, and shouting that he had a great story and had to get on the air immediately. Accounts differ about Sevareid's reaction. Sevareid said he moved aside and let Hottelet have the mike — "ruined my broadcast, but he got on the air." Larry LeSueur said Sevareid told him he simply refused to yield the microphone.

Years later the always diplomatic Hottelet could no longer recall for certain whether Sevareid had let him go on the air or not, but no Hottelet broadcast for that day could be found.

♦

The Boys' lives had been transformed by this war, but by the end of 1944 they were profoundly tired of it — tired of the risks, the grind, the killing, tired of the way it was dragging on when it should have been over. They were tired, too, of racing from press camps and transmitter sites to the front and then having to turn around and race back, averaging as much as two hundred tough, dusty miles a day. "I literally bumped one jeep to death," said Howard Smith in a broadcast. "Piece by piece, it fell apart. Finally, I had it towed to the side of a burned-out Sherman tank. . . . I left it there and hitchhiked to the front."

Tempers were short, nerves frayed. When Murrow was deciding whether to assign Smith and Hottelet to Germany to cover the end of the war, Sevareid advised against it. "It will be a disaster," he said. "They don't speak to each other. When they do, they fight." About the Boys, Murrow wrote to his wife, who was in the States at the time: "They are all unhappy, feel they haven't enough air time."

Several were sick. LeSueur had been hospitalized briefly in London after recurring bouts of dysentery. Downs, still suffering from battle fatigue, also had gastrointestinal problems. Sevareid, always a bit of a hypochondriac, went to a doctor to find out why he was feeling weak and lethargic. The doctor told him he was physically fine, Sevareid wrote in his notebook, but that he was a "low blood-pressure type, [who] will never have the robust energy of other types who feel on top of the world every morning. I will complain of feeling lousy all my life, [the doctor] says, which will probably continue to the age of 80 or so [a remarkably accurate prediction]. He suggests that a couple of whiskies a day would . . . stir me up a little."

The Boys had discovered that reporting a war, like fighting one, involved long, dull stretches interspersed with brief periods of extreme excitement and danger. Now everything seemed anticlimactic. "In the old days when it really mattered whether one thing happened instead of another, the war was exciting, the end full of meaning," Collingwood wrote to his parents. ". . . Maybe when it is over things will be important again. . . . We'll be making the world then instead of tearing it up." In London, Sevareid found ennui everywhere. "Where every man and woman was a hero, heroism was a bore," he wrote. "Where men of all known tongues had swarmed, the lingering Americans were a bore. . . . War itself was a bore."

Once the center of world attention, London had become a backwater. Beginning one week after D-Day and continuing for almost a year, Germany fired guided missiles — first the jet-propelled V-1 buzz bombs, then the much larger and deadlier V-2 rockets — at England and Antwerp, killing almost as many English people as had been killed in the entire Blitz. Yet even this new terror, these harbingers of worse weapons to come after the war, didn't seem to hold much interest for the rest of the world. London, said Sevareid in a broadcast, "is like a once-smart hotel gone seamy and threadbare after an interminable convention of businessmen. . . . The exaltation of danger is gone."

◆

Had anything been gained after all the deprivation and suffering of the last six years? Would the more just and equal world that Murrow and the Boys had envisioned in the early years finally emerge? The dream seemed almost foolish now. "Some of us have the impression that the high hopes, the determination to improve the social and economic conditions that characterized the dark days of the war are beginning to fade a little," Murrow declared in a broadcast. "In other words, that the old order may not have changed as much as we thought it had."

After Greece was liberated in the fall of 1944, Winston Churchill dispatched British troops to fight the Communist-backed Greek guerrillas, who earlier had played a key role in the resistance against Germany. In a broadcast Sevareid said British leftists were convinced that the prime minister "has already reverted to the old Tory Churchill and is leading the British ruling class back into its old battle against popular and socialist movements wherever he can fight them."

From the tone of his report, it seemed clear that Sevareid, the most outspoken of the Boys throughout the war on the Allies' failure to live up to their democratic ideals, shared the leftists' opinion. After the Yalta Conference in February 1945, however, when Churchill and Roosevelt effectively handed Poland over to the Soviet Union, he saw another kind of sellout. "The Poles," he said, ". . . face the prospect now of seeing their nation's whole future decided, without the prior consent of the many thousands among them who have fought the Germans these five long years."

◆

In Italy, American troops and officers were behaving more like conquerors than liberators. While millions of Italians went homeless and hungry, American occupation officials caroused in luxury hotels, allowed black-market corruption to flourish, and enjoyed the hospitality of socialites who just months before had lavishly entertained the Germans. In one brilliantly scathing broadcast, Winston Burdett described the wartime "trials" of a rich American expatriate in Florence:

> We have visited the estate of the Marchesa Torrigiani, formerly Lucy Davis of Worcester, Boston and Philadelphia. She spoke to us with feeling of her hardships, with butter and coffee so expensive, and as many as nine German officers in her salon at one time. But, she told us, the German commander in Florence was a nice man. He gave her a driving permit. The greatest outrage occurred when her chauffeur deserted his post to become a Partisan leader. He wants his old job back now that the fighting is over. "But," said the marchesa, with the firmness of a lady whose great-grandfather had had something to do with the Boston Tea Party, "I'm taking him back on probation only."

✦

Even before he entered Dachau with the U.S. Third Army, Larry LeSueur saw bodies everywhere — hundreds of them in trenches along the road leading to the camp. The German guards, panicked by reports of the approaching Allies, had forced prisoners to dig their own makeshift graves and then shot them. More bodies spilled out of a freight car parked on a spur line to Dachau.

Inside the death camp bodies were neatly stacked in piles. The still-living inmates were small, frail, skeletal wraiths who, if they moved at all, moved with the slow and spectral stealth of those who know all too well how short life is. They were so weak that they had to ask some GIs to help them hang a couple of Nazi guards who had tried to escape. The GIs, LeSueur noted, were more than happy to oblige.

Between 1941 and 1945 Murrow and the Boys, like most of their journalistic colleagues, provided little coverage of Hitler's attempt to exterminate the Jews. For one thing, once the United States entered the war, details of the Holocaust were not readily available. Certainly there is no evidence that CBS deliberately avoided the story. Indeed, prior to Pearl Harbor, Shirer, Smith, Hottelet, and other Berlin-based journalists had risked the wrath of their Nazi censors by reporting the Third Reich's early repression and subjugation of the Jews.

In any case, those CBS reporters who saw the death camps in 1945 as Hitler's Germany collapsed — LeSueur, Hottelet, Downs, Shadel, and Murrow himself — were overwhelmed. After visiting Buchenwald, Murrow described his first stunned look at the emaciated, ragged scarecrows who surged around him and Bill Shadel at the main gate of the camp. In the distance were the "green fields . . . where well-fed Germans were ploughing," but in the camp were naked, bruised bodies "stacked up like cordwood outside the crematorium; the terrible stench; the piles of gold teeth and human hair, the lampshades of human skin." Murrow concluded, his voice taut with barely repressed fury: "I pray you to believe what I have said about Buchenwald. I have reported what I saw and heard, but only part of it. For most of it, I have no words."

When he returned to London, Murrow told Dick Hottelet there were twenty million Germans too many in the world. Hottelet, who despised Nazis but fiercely loved his parents' homeland, was appalled. "You should be ashamed of yourself!" he barked at his mentor and boss. "He knew I meant it," Hottelet said many years later, "and he took it in very good part. Devoted as I was and respectful as I was, I wasn't going to echo his sentiments in that regard." For once Howard Smith agreed with Hottelet and effectively argued on the air that the Allies should seize the opportunity to remake German society.

At that time, however, with the war still being fought and the full extent of Nazi atrocities still being learned, most of the Boys shared Murrow's sentiments. Bill Downs told friends after a horrific visit to Auschwitz that he felt like shooting the first German he saw. Before the war was over, he bought an Oskar Kokoschka watercolor, a clown with a grotesque grimace of a smile. At the bottom of the painting was the inscription *Liberté, egalité, fratricide*. "That in a nutshell summarized my dad's attitude about the human race," said Downs's son Adam.

"By the time the war ended, all our idealism was gone," Downs said later. "Our crusade had been won, but our white horses had been shot out from under us."

✦

In late April, Allied armies were hurtling across Germany, the Americans and British from the west, the Russians from the east. On April 25, U.S. and Soviet advance units met at the Elbe River, an event Hottelet was the first to report. "There were no brass bands, no sign of the titanic strength of both these armies," he said in one broadcast. "The Americans who met the Red Army were a couple of dust-covered lieutenants and a handful of enlisted men in their jeeps on reconnaissance. . . . That's just the way it was, as simple and untheatrical as that. Just some men meeting, shaking hands."

After spending two hours with Red Army soldiers, talking and singing, drinking vodka and champagne, this tough-minded young journalist, as anti-Communist as anyone, fervently espoused the need for brotherhood. "On the Russian side, there is the same unspoken realization that we don't know each other very well but that we ought to get to know each other much better," Hottelet told his listeners. "One Russian captain summed it up to me when he said, 'This is the end of one road and the beginning of a much more important one. We've got to travel it together.' . . . It looks, from here at least, that these Russians are going to be good, practical friends."

✦

On May 4 Hottelet collected some journalist buddies, including John MacVane of NBC, grabbed an army jeep and set out unescorted . . . for Berlin. They knew they were breaking SHAEF regulations, for American and British correspondents had been barred from the German capital. The Russians had captured it the previous day, and no one knew what the situation was there. Hottelet and friends went anyway.

A thick pall of smoke enshrouded the old city as they arrived at the outskirts. Hottelet was astounded at the devastation. Allied bombs had turned the center of Berlin into a wilderness of smoking rubble, dotted by the hulks of burning and burned-out buildings. The Chancellery, above the Führerbunker, in which Hitler had committed suicide only four days earlier, was a shambles. The Propaganda Ministry across the street, where Hottelet, Smith, Shirer, and many other Berlin-based correspondents had had to endure Joseph Goebbels' tirades, was ablaze. The house where Hottelet had lived after arriving in Germany in 1937 was severely damaged and deserted. He and the others spent the night at a Russian command post and headed out on the autobahn the next day to return to camp. They had almost reached the Elbe when the road abruptly ended, destroyed by shells. They sought help at the nearest Red Army headquarters but were told very politely that they would have to be detained until their identities could be verified.

The correspondents' hearts sank. "We could see our war correspondent credentials taken away and ourselves, perhaps, sent as privates to Alaska," MacVane later wrote. For three days they were wined and dined as honored guests, serenaded by Russian renditions of "Yankee

Doodle" and "Dixie," while machine gun–toting sentries guarded the doors, making sure they did not try to escape. On May 8 they were finally escorted to the Elbe.

After they had crossed the river, MacVane called the First Army press camp. "I don't know where you have been," said the officer on the other end. "But if you have been to Berlin, don't tell anyone. Two correspondents who just came back saying they had gone to Berlin got their credentials taken away, and they were sent home. . . . I thought you ought to know all this before you come back to camp. SHAEF is plenty sore."

Those two other correspondents later claimed to be the first American reporters into Berlin. The likelihood is that Hottelet and his pals were there first, but they decided a little discretion was called for and kept their accomplishment to themselves. It was just as well. If they had filed their scoop, it certainly would have been buried by an even more momentous story — the formal announcement that day of Germany's surrender.

✦

On the second floor of a drab red brick schoolhouse in Rheims, Charles Collingwood watched as General Alfred Jodl, the ramrod-straight chief of operations of the German armed forces, signed the surrender documents in SHAEF's war room on a scarred wooden desk. Collingwood noted in his broadcast that a week earlier Jodl probably would have traded one of his armies for a peek at the maps on those walls. But now, at 2:41 in the morning on May 7, Jodl, his monocle firmly screwed in place, stared only at the papers before him. After signing, he stiffly rose and addressed General Walter Bedell Smith, Eisenhower's chief of staff. "Herr General," said Jodl in a choked voice, "with this signing, the German people and the German forces are, for better or worse, delivered into the victor's hands. . . . In this hour, I can only express the hope that the victors will treat them with generosity."

It was a solemn moment, and Collingwood, one of seventeen reporters chosen to cover the ceremony, captured it vividly. He also revealed the zoolike atmosphere surrounding this great event; the news photographers "ran around at top speed, all around the room, up and down ladders, flashbulbs going off all the time." He continued, "The generals are clearly annoyed, but still the photographers dash about, getting in the way of generals handing around documents to be signed. . . . To get a good shot of the Russian interpreter, a photographer leans over the

Germans, elbowing Jodl out of the way, and flashes a bulb at the Russian. The Germans sit there through it all, stiff, unbending."

It was pack journalism at its worst — at least up to that point in history.

◆

Two days later the Russians staged a separate surrender in Berlin, and Howard Smith was present for that event. He reported the tense face-to-face meeting of General Georgi Zhukov, the Russian military chief of staff, and General Wilhelm Keitel, his German counterpart. Smith described them as "perhaps the two bitterest enemies since Rome fought Carthage." Their faces, he said, "were frozen into hard, unmelting frowns. . . . Keitel looked as though he had taken a swig of aged bilgewater and was waiting to spit it out as soon as nobody was looking."

After Keitel was escorted from the room, the Russians threw a victory party to end all parties, with caviar, salmon, and strawberries, and speeches and toasts with vodka, white wine, red wine, and Russian champagne. "I can't tell you how many toasts there were to the Allies and to Stalin," Smith said in his broadcast. ". . . I lost count after twenty-four toasts with white-hot vodka." The only other thing Smith could remember was that "Zhukov was as happy as a kid on Christmas Day."

◆

On V-E Day in London, Ed Murrow sat in a van with Dick Hottelet's wife, Ann. Microphone in hand, he described for Americans the sight of thousands of Londoners streaming out of their flats and offices, shouting, laughing, and singing. Murrow had been there from the beginning and before the beginning and had seen it through to the end. He, Shirer, and the early Boys had created a new form of journalism, and in the time it took to fight a war, had set the standard for radio and, later, television reporting. To a certain extent Murrow must have been talking about himself when he noted in his broadcast that many people were not joining in the celebration. "Their minds must be filled with memories of friends who've died in the streets or on the battlefields. Six years is a long time. I've observed today that people have very little to say. There are no words."

In Paris, Charles Collingwood reported, "the people . . . are physically too tired and emotionally too exhausted to throw themselves into the wild and uproarious celebration one might have expected. . . . Today most people are just content to stroll in the sunshine and feel good. [Paris] never looked more beautiful."

Most citizens of Europe had been too close to the war for too long to feel much more than numbness. Murrow understood that, and so did many members of his team. Most of them had been barely out of school when they arrived in Europe, inexperienced and eager. Now Eric Sevareid, thirty-two years old, had "a curious feeling of age, as though I had lived through a lifetime, not merely through my youth. . . . Like so many others at this moment, I was simply tired — tired in a way I had never known before."

Sevareid, who had returned to the States a month before the end, was in San Francisco, covering the United Nations conference on V-E Day. In his broadcast he offered a sober, cautionary note:

> The strange truth is that when the first sense of relief has gone, men and women will find themselves uncertain, afraid for a time of peace, so completely has war conditioned the pattern of their brain. I feel it in San Francisco among men of state. They do their work in a curiously mechanical spirit. One has the feeling they dread the moment when they must lift their eyes and face an incoming tidal wave of human problems, social, economic and political, which will not wait.

Already there was foreboding about the postwar world. In San Francisco, Soviet Foreign Minister Vyacheslav Molotov had made pointedly clear that after the war his country would rely first on its own military forces for peace and security, next on "friendly neighbors," and only third on the infant UN. The peace that was ratified in Rheims and Berlin, Sevareid reported, is "not the true peace which men have dreamed of, the unworried brotherhood of men."

Immediately ahead lay the nuclear infernos at Hiroshima and Nagasaki, the surrender of Japan, and the beginning of the Cold War.

✦

As they reported on the uncertain future, the Murrow Boys were unsure about themselves as well. Where would they go? What would they do? Would they remain a team? Would their wartime brilliance translate into success in peacetime? In sorting out their futures, they relied, as they had for so much else, on Murrow. He was their touchstone, the author of their careers, the man they loved and revered above all others, their hero.

He had no intention of surrendering leadership of this extraordinary group of journalists. In a letter to Janet toward the end of the war, he wrote, "This is now the best group of reporters in Europe and I hate to see it collapse." And he wrote a few months later to Collingwood:

> For a few brief years a few men attempted to do an honest job of reporting under difficult and sometimes hazardous conditions and they did not altogether fail. Maybe it is a combination of age and little faith in the future, but I cannot believe that I shall again have the high privilege of working intimately and harmoniously with a crew such as the one we gathered together in Europe.

1945 ✴ 1961

18

The Hour of
the Centurions

C HARLES COLLINGWOOD was back from the war!

The word flashed like lightning among the young CBS staff members on the seventeenth floor at 485 Madison Avenue. One of them, a news writer named Ed Bliss, hired just two years earlier, peeked eagerly into one of the tiny cubicles that served as offices for the network's newscasters and commentators. There he was, "wavy-haired, poet-profiled" Bonnie Prince Charlie himself, only twenty-eight years old — five years younger than Bliss — still wearing his perfectly tailored correspondent's uniform. He had arrived from Europe that very morning aboard the aircraft carrier U.S.S. *Enterprise,* and Bliss was pleased to note that he was "actually typing [a story about his homeward voyage], just like one of *us.*"

Winston Churchill described victory in war as "the beautiful, bright-colored flower." It was all of that for the Boys as they, like the soldiers who had done the fighting, came home to hear their praises sung, their accomplishments glorified. This was the hour of the centurions. For the nation it was time to honor those who had defeated the Axis abroad and helped turn America into the greatest superpower in history. And at CBS it was time to honor Murrow and his Boys, who had given their network its identity. Before the Boys, CBS was, as Eric Sevareid said, simply "a collection of leased phone lines and cables, contracts with a lot of scattered actors and others. They had nothing of their own. But suddenly the news people became . . . the personality of the network."

"We regarded all these guys as heroes when they came back," Bliss said. But he thought "there was a little more glamour associated with Collingwood . . . all the stories about him — how he dressed, how he knew Hemingway, and then, of course, we'd had his outstanding reports during the war."

The Murrow Boys who were still with CBS when the war ended — Eric Sevareid, Larry LeSueur, Charles Collingwood, Winston Burdett, Howard K. Smith, Bill Downs, Richard C. Hottelet, and William L. Shirer (who had come home to make his own way at CBS four years earlier) — had achieved a status beyond what any of them could have imagined. They were, said publisher Michael Bessie, who knew them well, "*the* class act" of American journalism — "golden boys!"

They tried, some far more successfully than others, to resist the worst temptations of stardom. But they were in great demand, and to help them manage the demand and profit from it, they hired agents — lecture agents, literary agents, business agents. Neither the Boys nor Murrow himself would ever make the extravagant amounts of money that are common in television news today. But they helped plant the seeds of the broadcast news industry that began to grow in the late fifties and that burst into full, dark blossom in the eighties and nineties — with its extreme commercialism, its hyperinflated top-level salaries, and the increasingly blurred distinction between entertainment and news. For all the Boys' integrity, it was doubtless asking too much that they be above cashing in on their wartime successes. Most of them, at any rate, were not above doing so.

The Murrow team was so popular and respected that Murrow feared it might be broken up. A number of competing news organizations — the *New York Times, Time, Life*, the other networks — tried to lure away one or more of the Boys after the war. Murrow, for professional and personal reasons, wanted to keep the group together under the CBS umbrella, or, more accurately, under *his* umbrella. He gained the power to do so by moving from London to New York in 1946 and accepting a job that Paley had been urging on him since before the war ended: he became vice president for news and public affairs. In effect, Murrow would be in charge of CBS News, which had only just become a separate division. He would outrank news director Paul White and have direct control over the Boys' destinies.

By promoting Murrow to upper management, Paley had all but guaranteed that White would leave the company. How could the proud and competitive White work for a man whom he considered his greatest rival and who until a few months earlier had been, on paper at least, his subordinate? "White had run the show, and he just didn't like this guy coming back and telling him what to do," said Frank Stanton. "You could have written it down in stone that this was not going to work."

For CBS News it was a sad situation. Notwithstanding White's constant sniping at Murrow, his mulishness, and his run-ins with the Boys, he was a radio news pioneer in his own right. He had made many important contributions to the building of CBS into the nation's premier broadcast news organization, and in 1945 had accepted a Peabody Award for the overall excellence of CBS News. Indeed, some at the network felt that White deserved more credit than Murrow.

After Murrow's elevation, White "went to pieces," a newsroom staffer said. A heavy drinker in the best of times, he was hitting the bottle almost constantly now and taking pills as well. More and more, his behavior seemed out of control. In May 1946 the issue came to a head as CBS was about to introduce a brand-new fifteen-minute evening news program, featuring Robert Trout and painstakingly planned and crafted by Murrow. Drawing on the expertise and reporting of thirty-five correspondents and stringers worldwide, *Robert Trout with the News Till Now* was to be the showpiece of the CBS News lineup. Not just a rehash of wire-service reports, it was Murrow's first major project as vice president and would be the most expensive daily news program produced up to that time.

White, however, was not going to let Murrow have all the credit. Determined to carve out a role for himself, he insisted on being allowed to introduce the premier program on the air. White was not, to put it kindly, a natural broadcaster. He had done only a few programs during the war and had developed an extreme case of stage fright each time. Hoping to quiet his nerves for the Trout program, he drank steadily through the day. By the time he went on, he was obviously and thoroughly drunk, slurring his words so badly they could barely be understood. Murrow, who had so much riding on this program, was thunderstruck.

According to one account, often repeated but unconfirmed, when the broadcast was finished, Murrow strode into White's office and unceremoniously fired him. However it came about, two days later CBS formally announced that after all the years and all the fights and all the glory, after all the disagreements about objectivity and who should and should not be hired, after the triumphant return of the Boys and Murrow's promotion to vice president — after all that, Paul White had resigned.

It was for the best. Once removed from the rivalry with Murrow that had so consumed him, White picked up many of the pieces of his life. He and his wife moved to San Diego, where he wrote *News on the Air*, a classic text on radio journalism, and became the editorial writer and news director of KFMB, the local CBS affiliate. It wasn't long before he and Murrow became good, if long-distance, friends. Realizing, finally, how much they had in common, how much each had contributed to the development of radio news, they exchanged frequent letters until 1955, when Paul White, fifty-two years old and suffering from emphysema and heart disease, died.

Less than a decade before Murrow took over, CBS news had consisted of White, Bob Trout, H. V. Kaltenborn, an assistant, and a secretary, with Murrow and Bill Shirer in Europe struggling to become members of the team and get on the air. (Boake Carter worked under contract outside the CBS news structure.) When Murrow assumed control in early 1946, the network's global news organization rivaled those of the major newspapers and wire services. There were correspondents in Washington and all the major European capitals, as well as in Asia, Latin America, and the Middle East. In New York, Murrow presided over platoons of newscasters, commentators, writers, editors, and directors.

The Boys were part of a large and growing bureaucracy now, but they had the best friend a correspondent could have at the top. Murrow persuaded all of them to stay with CBS, saying, "We've seen what radio can do for the nation in war. Now let's . . . show what we can do in peace." His first priority was to make sure the Boys were well placed within the network.

Initially, he had wanted Bill Shirer to replace him in London as chief European correspondent. London was the plum, both because it had been Murrow's base for so long and because Britain still enjoyed a lingering reputation as a great power. Just as Shirer had refused to go to London to spell Murrow during the war, however, he refused to replace him afterward. He and his family loved New York, and he was also loath to give up his Sunday evening broadcast and his weekly column in the *Herald Tribune*, plus the money, celebrity, and social life that came with being a network star.

Murrow then approached Eric Sevareid, who also begged off, citing personal reasons. There may have been more to it than that. According to David Schoenbrun, who knew most of the Boys during the war and who went to work for CBS shortly afterward, Sevareid and Collingwood used to talk about the great opportunities and big money waiting for them in postwar America. "Charles and Eric knew that they would become highly paid stars and could not wait to get to 485 Madison and the CBS studios there," Schoenbrun wrote.

Both men, however, had some other things to take care of first.

✦

Since the early forties, Sevareid's marriage had been in trouble, damaged by his frequent absences, his womanizing, his emotional paralysis, and now by Lois's mental problems. During the war she had exhibited severe mood swings: exuberant excitement and a fierce determination to get her own way, alternating with listlessness and deep melancholy. Now it was clear that she was suffering from manic depression.

Her friends were terribly saddened to watch the slow decline of a woman so intelligent and so full of life. During the war, while Eric was covering the Italian campaign, Lois had left her sons with her mother in the States and moved to Cairo to work for the United Nations Relief and Rehabilitation Administration. Said Janet Murrow at the time, "[Lois] has a wonderful mind and is a trained lawyer. Of the two of them, she's the better brain and the stronger person." But Lois's work in Cairo was one of the few times — and one of the last — when she was able to emerge from her husband's towering shadow. When they were reunited near the end of the war, her mental condition was clearly deteriorating.

Shortly after the UN conference in San Francisco, Sevareid, on leave from CBS, took Lois and the twins to the beautiful California seacoast town of Carmel, where they rented a house and where he wrote — at the age of thirty-two — his autobiography. Always the most thoughtful of the Boys, he had not taken time out during the war to pound out a quickie bestseller about his experiences, as most of the others did. He needed time — time to put the war and the world in perspective, time to figure out who Eric Sevareid was and what had happened to him.

In Carmel he wrote of an odyssey that had begun in Velva, gained purpose in his radical college days, and carried him on to Paris, London, Washington, Burma, China, Italy, Germany. Both the odyssey and his account of it were extraordinary. If he failed to write honestly about his relationship with his wife and others, he wrote with amazing honesty about himself, his insecurities, his fears. But he was also writing about his generation: "young, liberal-minded, well-meaning Americans, who were born around the time of the first war; whose minds grew up and were obsessed with the craving for peace, and yet whose bodies *and* minds were at length possessed by war." It was a generation struggling to find meaning, hope, and brotherhood in the carnage, corruption, and bungling that surrounded them.

In a radio play CBS dramatist Norman Corwin had described the hope of a better, radically changed postwar world as "not so wild a dream." Sevareid liked the phrase and made it the title of his book. In its eloquent soul-searching, *Not So Wild a Dream* struck a deep chord throughout America. After it was published in 1946, hundreds of people — including a young mustered-out army sergeant named Henry Kissinger, about to embark on his undergraduate career at Harvard — wrote to Sevareid to say that he had described *their* feelings, had told *their* story.

But the book affected no one more deeply than Lois Sevareid. One night during their sabbatical in Carmel, she went to Sevareid's desk while he was asleep, slipped from the drawer the first few chapters, and sat down to read them. Her husband's soul was on those pages, all the feelings and emotions, the fears and insecurities he had not been able to share with her directly. She rediscovered the man she had married, and in turn she opened herself up to him.

"It was she, not I, who found the courage to speak, and the second miracle of love occurred," Sevareid wrote movingly in the preface to his book when it was reissued in 1976. "The walls of glass between us dissolved. Her very face altered in my vision. The vibrant young college girl I had met at a party reappeared." Their happiness, however, did not last. Lois's mood swings intensified. "It was the beginning of the doctors, the drugs, the psychiatrists, the sanatoria, the endlessly differing theories and conjectures and advisories," Sevareid wrote.

In the midst of all this, Murrow appointed Sevareid chief of the CBS bureau in Washington.

◆

When Charles Collingwood returned from the war, he was set to marry his London love of seven years, Gracie Blake, as soon as she could obtain her divorce. But by the time she arrived in the States, unencumbered, in 1946, Collingwood had fallen in love with someone else. With atypical boorishness he didn't even bother to arrange a meeting with Gracie. He merely sent word from Los Angeles that he had decided to marry Louise Allbritton, a tall, blonde movie actress whom he had met on a blind date in 1943 during his stateside lecture tour. Gracie was devastated. "We all thought it was so awful," said Janet Murrow. "We were amazed by the fact that he let her come over. Charles was really a dear person. It was incredible that he did that to her."

Collingwood, always a romantic, was bowled over by Allbritton, whose glamour and comic flair in movies reminded some of Carole Lombard. She had set her cap for him after their first date, and when he came to Los Angeles in late 1945 for a vacation, she focused all of her formidable charm on him. Five months later they were married. "I think Charlie was swept off his feet by Louise," said Larry LeSueur. "She represented Hollywood to him. I don't think he could help it." The Collingwoods spent a year in Los Angeles, where Louise played major roles in the movie comedy hits *The Egg and I* and *Sitting Pretty*, and Charles did a daily news and commentary program for CBS affiliate KNX while occasionally reporting for the network.

✦

Having failed to get either of his first two choices for London bureau chief, Ed Murrow came up with a surprising third choice, a correspondent he barely knew, who had spent less than a year covering the war firsthand for CBS. Although Murrow clearly considered him one of his Boys, Howard Smith always remained aloof from the others. Soft-spoken, courtly, and reserved, he did not share in the jocular bonhomie that bound the war correspondents together. His closest friend and confidante, then and later, was his wife, Bennie. "If I have extra time to spend, I'd rather spend it at home, and not with the boys," Smith said years later. "I don't play poker. I don't know how to." Sniffed Larry LeSueur, "Howard was never really part of our little group."

The only one with whom Smith really *had* to get along was Murrow, and in that he was successful. Murrow was impressed by Smith's aggressiveness and clear thinking, by his outspoken and optimistic liberalism. He was also impressed by Smith's stalwart job of covering the Nuremberg trials after the war. When the first round of trials was over, Smith met with Murrow in London and told him he had been offered a job by *Life* and was inclined to take it. Murrow roared, "Harry Luce is not going to raid my staff! You're going to stay [in London], and you're going to take my job, and I'm going to pay you what it takes!"

Joining Smith as European correspondents were Winston Burdett, based in Rome, and Dick Hottelet in Moscow. Sevareid was in Washington, Collingwood in Los Angeles. Larry LeSueur started out as chief correspondent, based in Washington, but soon moved to New York to replace Collingwood at the UN.

The remaining Boy, Bill Downs, did not fare as well as the others. Although he and Murrow had been close personally during the war, Murrow did not seem willing or able afterward to work the same magic for him. Perhaps Downs — with his stocky frame, hot temper, and growling voice — had too many rough edges for the new corporate structure and image of CBS News. After the German surrender he was reassigned from Europe to the Pacific. While his colleagues were enjoying a rest at home, settling into their postwar lives, and taking up their new peacetime assignments, Downs was entering Tokyo with the occupation forces and covering the Japanese surrender. In the immediate postwar period he traveled to assignments in China, Burma, India, Indochina, Singapore, and Java.

It was not until 1946 that he finally made it back to the States. He was first given the turbulent labor beat, working out of New York, an assignment that required a great deal of travel in the Midwest and South. In 1947 he was asked to open a new CBS bureau in Detroit. He grumbled that he wasn't being treated as well as the other Boys, but, like the good scout he always was, he accepted the assignment.

✦

The next item on Murrow's to-do list was hiring more men for his rapidly growing empire. Each of the new correspondents was from the same scholar-journalist mold that produced the original Boys.

For the new Vienna bureau, Murrow brought in Alexander Kendrick, an acerbic Eastern European expert and veteran reporter for the *Chicago Sun*, whose steel-wool voice, Coke-bottle glasses, twisted ties, and rumpled suits indicated there was life yet in the iconoclastic Murrow hiring tradition.

George Polk, an aggressive and handsome young former *New York Herald Tribune* reporter, was assigned to Cairo as the network's Middle East correspondent. Polk, who reminded Howard Smith of a blond Errol Flynn, idolized Murrow and sought to emulate him not only in his writing and broadcast delivery but in what Polk viewed as Murrow's uncompromising adherence to principle.

For the much-coveted job of Paris bureau chief, Murrow chose David Schoenbrun, a short (five foot two), dumpy, and mustachioed former army correspondent whose arrogance was exceeded only by his knowledge of France and his unparalleled contacts among that nation's top leaders. Like the other new men, Schoenbrun was ecstatic at joining CBS. He had known most of the Boys during the war and "admired them enormously." "I just thought they were the greatest bunch of guys I've ever worked with in my life," he said. "They were gay, and sophisticated as hell, and profound students and well read." They were, in short, everything David Schoenbrun had always hoped to be.

◆

Even with the new hires, the eight wartime Boys remained a class apart. They knew it, liked it, and expected to be treated that way. "We not only got special privileges but we were upset if we *didn't* get them," Larry LeSueur said. "Our noses would get out of joint. We considered ourselves special because we'd been associated with the war and Murrow and Paley. People knew who we were. Everybody else were Johnny-come-latelies." Such attitudes caused resentment among the less well connected at CBS. "I sensed jealousy, but it rolled off me like water off a duck's back," LeSueur said. "I *deserved* [the privileges]." He thought for a moment. "They probably hated me."

The tight, closed nature of the Murrow fraternity resulted in considerable complaining and grumbling on the seventeenth floor. "There were exceptions, of course, but some of the new hands felt that if you weren't a member of the 'family,' there was no proving you were just as good," an unnamed CBS staffer told a *New York Post* interviewer. A 1953 *New Yorker* profile of Murrow quoted Wells Church, who had replaced Paul White, as declaiming, "Ed Murrow has collected the goddamnedest bunch of camp followers, and not one of them is worth a damn!" (Church denied he made the comment and demanded a retraction from the *New Yorker*, which he did not get.) In the view of correspondent Ned Calmer, who was hired by Paul White, the Boys "worked for Murrow first and CBS second."

To counter the Murrow clique, some non-Boys in New York organized what they called the "Murrow-Ain't-God Club" and had lapel buttons made with those words printed on them. It was meant as a joke, the organizers said, but some at CBS, who found Murrow pompous and self-important, took it seriously. When Murrow learned of the club's existence, he immediately put in for membership.

As vice president of news and for some time afterward, Murrow worked hard on behalf of his team. There were a few lapses and one major crisis that pitted him against his old pal Bill Shirer, but in general, prior to the age of television, he was quick to challenge anyone who attempted to interfere with the Boys or their reporting. "There's not one of us who doesn't go and cry on his shoulder the minute something goes wrong," one of them told the *New Yorker* writer. "And Ed will pick up the phone and get the right person on the wire [often Bill Paley himself] and say, 'Hey, wait a minute! We can't do this to this guy.'" Many years afterward, Howard Smith said, "He always represented us to the company. When we needed vacations, he made sure we got them. He stood up for me on occasions when I got into controversies; he would do anything for his Boys."

When a Boy dropped in at his office, Murrow would stop what he was doing, pull a bottle of Ballantine's from his bottom desk drawer and pour two drinks. Then they would settle down for a talk, Murrow looking for all the world like a father giving counsel to his son. Eric Sevareid was a frequent visitor. "I remember so many times seeing Eric in there, just the two of them talking," said Ed Bliss, who later became a writer for Murrow. "Eric had different things that would come up in his life and career, and he'd talk them over with Ed. It was obvious he was getting Ed's advice on what he should do."

Where the Boys were concerned, Murrow's generosity seemed unbounded. In 1950, when Bennie Smith contracted tuberculosis and was confined to a Swiss sanitorium for several months, the Murrows offered to take care of the Smiths' small son, Jack. "You know, I am sure, that if there is anything we can do you need only command us," Murrow wrote Smith.

Clearly Murrow regarded the Boys more as members of the family than as subordinates. He was godfather to Sevareid's twin sons. Janet Murrow was godmother to Shirer's second daughter, Linda, and to Larry LeSueur's daughter, Lorna. In turn, LeSueur was godfather to the Murrows' son, Casey. While Murrow shied away from socializing with most of the people at CBS News, he and Janet went out with his correspondents when they came through New York and invited them and their wives to spend weekends at the country house the Murrows had bought in upstate New York, near Pawling.

After Larry LeSueur moved up from Washington to cover the UN, he and Priscilla rented a country house in Brewster, New York, close to Pawling. Murrow and LeSueur spent a great deal of time together on weekends and in the summertime, fishing and hunting, as well as doing a "terrific amount of talking and joking."

Even though the wives were included in Murrow's invitations, he and the Boys focused most of their time and attention on one another. In their world women took second billing. Lois Sevareid, for example, "was noncompetitive with Eric," said old friend Bill Walton. "She knew her place." So did Janet Murrow. "Ed is the master of our house," she once told a reporter. "He doesn't always ask my opinion on big decisions. He says, 'This is the way it's going to be.'" Smith, one of the few Boys who didn't share that macho ethic, recalled, "Janet was kind, compatible with everybody, while Ed was very much wrapped up in Ed and the empire of men he had hired. He was too dominant for Janet."

Murrow loved masculine banter and what he thought of as masculine pursuits, particularly hunting and fishing. He assigned nicknames to several of the wartime correspondents. Sevareid was "the Gloomy Dane." Collingwood was "Bonnie Prince Charlie." LeSueur was "the General" because of the extensive military knowledge he acquired during the war. (LeSueur mischievously dubbed Murrow "Flash," which Murrow hated.) Downs, for some reason, was "Wilbur" (and to Downs, Murrow was "Doctor"). When Murrow first met Bill Shadel, whose family name is pronounced Sha-*dell*, he decided it ought to be pronounced in the German fashion — *Sha*-dul — and that's the way he pronounced it from then on.

When Murrow wasn't using the nicknames he'd assigned to his pals, he would call them "Brother Eric" or "Brother Smith" or would use the family name alone, as a football coach does. Indeed, he often affected a kind of locker-room attitude when dealing with other men. His jokes (practical and otherwise), his use of nicknames, his rather awkward attempts at offhand collegiality — all were meant to display affection even as they subtly established who was boss.

Sometimes, too, there was a hint of towel-snapping sadism. In 1947 Murrow stepped down as vice president and returned, with great relief, to broadcasting, replacing Robert Trout as the anchor of the nightly news program. Arriving in Paris one day during a European swing, he was scheduled to do the program live that evening from the network's Paris studio. Before going to the studio, he invited the new CBS bureau chief, David Schoenbrun, to his hotel suite for a drink. After a couple of Scotches each, they left the hotel for the broadcasting studio, arriving about half an hour before Murrow was to go on the air.

At that point Murrow asked if there was a bar nearby. Told there was one right across the street, he took Schoenbrun in tow and headed for it. Schoenbrun was amazed. Murrow hadn't written a word for his broadcast, and here he was, settling into a bar and ordering his third Scotch of the afternoon!

With only ten minutes to go, the two of them — Schoenbrun more than a little woozy by now — returned to the studio. Still no sign of concern from Murrow. Schoenbrun could hardly believe it. "There's Ed, no script, no nothing, not a worry in his head. I've never admired a man more in my life. Totally relaxed and at ease, such an elegant man."

With the clock ticking down to airtime, the two of them took their seats at the studio table. Schoenbrun put his headphones on, heard the New York announcer's introduction of Murrow, and wondered what in the world Murrow was going to say. Then he heard: "This is Ed Murrow in Paris. I've just flown in from Berlin, and obviously, in such a short time, I'm not any expert on Paris. In fact, I'm not an expert on Paris at all. The reason that CBS News is strong is that we have experts everywhere in the world. My Paris expert is sitting right beside me. Here now is David Schoenbrun."

Murrow pushed the microphone in front of Schoenbrun, sat back, and relaxed. Schoenbrun couldn't believe Murrow was doing this to him! Stunned and half-drunk, he tried to pull himself together. Then he just started talking. No notes. No preparation. Just a stream-of-consciousness summary of everything he knew about French geopolitics. On radio, he knew, nothing was worse than silence, so he kept right on talking until his time was up, then stopped. He could not afterward recall a single word he had spoken.

As they took off their headphones and rose from the table, Murrow said, "Let's go back to that pub." Still in a state of near-shock, Schoenbrun tagged meekly along.

In the bar, drinking more Scotch, they sat for a while, Schoenbrun growing more and more furious. "I may admire him, he may be my god," he said to himself, "but I'm not *nobody*." At last, after many minutes in which neither man spoke a word, Murrow took a drag on his cigarette, knocked back a slug of Scotch, and said, "Well, Brother David, you did not disgrace yourself tonight."

Schoenbrun started to laugh. "You know, Ed, there's a Jewish word. Have you ever heard of the word *chutzpah?*"

"Yeah, it means gall."

"You are a galling bastard. What did you *do* to me tonight?"

It was a test, Murrow explained, a test of Schoenbrun's cool. "One never knows what's going to happen in a radio studio. . . . You might get a bulletin flash from downstairs that de Gaulle had just been assassinated, you might get a bulletin flash on the air from New York, saying, 'David, cut off. The president has just died.' You just don't know when that's going to happen to you. My men have to be calm, cool, and prepared for anything. Now there's no way to train a man to do that, and there's no way to find out whether a man has that quality. . . . Tonight you've earned your job."

He extended his hand. "Welcome to the staff," he said, squinting through his cigarette smoke.

◆

Schoenbrun wasn't the only correspondent to be ambushed by Murrow on the air, although his experience was perhaps the most extreme. According to Vienna bureau chief Alexander Kendrick, Murrow delighted in changing signals on his program, asking his men questions about subjects he knew they were not prepared for, questions about "Yugoslavia, for instance, to the Central European correspondent who believed he would be talking about Czechoslovakia."

But the correspondents didn't seem to mind. When they reported for *Edward R. Murrow and the News,* now broadcast at 7:45 P.M., they knew they were appearing on the most popular news program on radio. "The country damn near stood still when Edward R. Murrow went on the air," said Schoenbrun. He was exaggerating, but not by much: millions of Americans did rely on the Murrow program as their major source of news.

In the fifteen minutes allotted him each night, Murrow summarized the major stories of the day, called on correspondents for eyewitness reports, and delivered a commentary. Like the television networks' evening news programs twenty years later, the Murrow show was CBS's news showcase. Murrow gave the correspondents more exposure, time, and credit for their stories than the anchors of the other newscasts, painting them as the experts and himself as a mere amateur. "Listen, Dave," he'd say on the air to Schoenbrun, "I don't understand what de Gaulle is talking about. Why does he say America is trying to dominate France? Is that what he really thinks?" Then Schoenbrun would hold forth.

It was, said Alex Kendrick, "the fullest and most satisfying professional expression that any news staff has ever had." This was not anonymous, homogenized group journalism. "The Murrow collective was composed of identifiable individuals, who possessed differing, sometimes discordant, points of view," Kendrick said. "It was in its diversity that the strength and appeal of the program lay."

In addition to the exposure, correspondents received a seventy-five-dollar fee each time they were on the program. Not surprisingly, there was ferocious competition to sell stories to Murrow and his editor and writer, Jesse Zousmer. So intense was the competition that the correspondents often neglected the network's other daily news broadcasts, including the popular morning and evening news roundups, which became a major source of irritation for network news executives.

Bill Shadel, who had been hired after the war as a full-time CBS correspondent in Washington, was appalled at the politicking and infighting that went on among his colleagues to get on *Edward R. Murrow and the News*. Part of Shadel's distaste stemmed from his own inability to play the game — or anyway to play it as well as Collingwood, Sevareid, LeSueur, and some of the others. "I wasn't into their socializing," Shadel said. "I wasn't brown-nosing Zousmer and Murrow. I wasn't fighting for the shows." Murrow, who had peremptorily moved in to replace Trout as anchor of the show without so much as an apology, told Shadel, "You're so damn naive. You're such a nice person."

19

"Years of Crisis"

For the boys, the years just after the war were a sweet time. They enjoyed high salaries and lavish expense accounts and, for better or worse, were friends and frequent dinner companions of leaders of government and society. They were experts, authorities; important people both at home and abroad sought them out and paid close attention to what they broadcast. "It was," Charles Collingwood mused later, "a hell of a good life."

The foreign correspondents among them were especially fortunate. In an era when the dollar ruled the world, they ruled their foreign fiefdoms like princes. "Everybody knew the Murrow Boys," said Sandy Socolow, a veteran CBS writer and producer. "They were famous stars in the U.S., but they were also stars wherever they were based."

For generations, foreign correspondents had been the personification of glamour, excitement, and intrigue, trekking off to dark and distant places and reporting back to the untraveled and uninformed. Murrow and the Boys were foreign correspondents to the core and at heart always would be. They could and did report and analyze American issues and politics — sometimes brilliantly — but they usually seemed a little uncomfortable, a little off-key in the domestic arena. Even in peacetime their focus remained overseas. Of the group only Larry Le-Sueur and Bill Shirer were not based abroad for a period after the war, although LeSueur, as UN correspondent, continued to concentrate on international developments.

Most of the CBS foreign correspondents in those days were fluent in the language of the country to which they were assigned and were expert in its culture, history, and politics. "It's amazing how they seemed to fit the environment to which they were sent," said former NBC correspondent Sander Vanocur. "Ed Murrow must have been the great-

est casting director since Louis B. Mayer." Smith, for example, was the
very picture of a tweedy, reserved, pipe-smoking English gentleman;
Hottelet (assigned to Bonn in 1951), the upright, tradition-bound Jun-
ker; Schoenbrun, the dapper little mustachioed Frenchman; Burdett,
the courtly, ethereal Italian cardinal.

Sig Mickelson, the first head of television news at CBS, was impressed with the correspondents' thorough mastery of their foreign
assignments (notwithstanding the many differences he would have with
them and Murrow during his years at the network). "They were on
top of the story. . . . They understood their [assigned] country's government, understood the roles and personalities of individuals in the government, and saw clearly what impact a move by the government would
have elsewhere." They could do these things because they stayed in
their assignments for long periods and because, before and during the
war, they had met and befriended most of Europe's future leaders, not to
mention the people who would govern the United States. "That whole
crowd had cultivated contacts in London and in the trenches that they
were able to transform into sources after the war," said former CBS and
ABC news producer Av Westin.

In the States they moved in the same circles as the country's politi-
cal Establishment; were members of the same clubs, like New York's
Century Club and Washington's Metropolitan Club; belonged to the
Council on Foreign Relations. They shared the Establishment view that
America's leadership role in the world was part of its moral destiny.

The Boys' slow, steady acquisition and husbanding of knowledge
and sources gave them a clear advantage over competitors and colleagues who moved quickly from assignment to assignment, bureau to
bureau. Winston Burdett, based in Rome for twenty-five years altogether, was without peer as a Vatican correspondent. David Schoenbrun, Paris bureau chief from 1947 to 1961, had known Charles de
Gaulle and those around him since the war and was the best-connected
foreign correspondent in Paris. So, too, with Howard Smith, London
bureau chief for eleven years. As president of the Labour Club at Oxford
in 1938, Smith had helped stage marches and demonstrations with the
young Labour Party radicals who would take over from Churchill and
the Tories after the war and seek to revolutionize British social and
economic structures. Smith remained close to several of these future
Labourites, in particular Denis Healey, the ex-Communist who would
become, in time, an influential member of Parliament, chancellor of the
Exchequer, and a lord of the realm.

In the late forties and early fifties, the London flat on Hallam Street that Howard and Bennie Smith inherited from the Murrows was a favorite gathering place for Britain's political, social, intellectual, and artistic leaders. The Smith flat, near the old BBC building, "was the closest thing to a political-literary salon that you could imagine," recalled Sander Vanocur, who as a graduate student at the London School of Economics had been befriended by Smith during his years in London. "You met just about everybody there."

Thanks to their contacts and knowledge, the CBS correspondents often were first with key stories and sometimes developed information that surprised and informed even diplomats and intelligence agents. CBS's reputation was so good that key U.S. government officials, including many in the White House, the Central Intelligence Agency, and the Joint Chiefs of Staff, made it a policy to begin their day with a transcript of the morning CBS *World News Roundup* as well as the *New York Times*. "When you heard me at eight o'clock in the morning speaking from Paris, you knew that's what was happening," said the never-modest Schoenbrun. "Newspapers were already eight hours behind us." So were the reports of CIA agents and American embassies abroad, because "many of their reports were coded . . . and long, and these guys were not fast writers and reporters like we were."

The CBS foreign correspondents operated with an extraordinary degree of freedom. "The desk had no idea what was going to come in," said Perry Wolff, longtime CBS documentary producer. "They just knew it was Schoenbrun or Smith or Burdett on NATO or the Vatican or whatever. These guys did pieces in their own style, pieces that stamped them as philosopher kings."

No one exulted in the dominance of the CBS correspondents abroad more than Schoenbrun. "For a few brief years, the Murrow team was nonpareil," he recalled. "There was CBS and then the others. Our day did not last more than a decade before the producers, managers, book-keepers, and lawyers took over. But while it lasted it was dazzling." Their pride, their sense of being a breed apart, lured an impressive new generation of correspondents to CBS. "We all felt that we worked for the best broadcast news organization in the world, that there was nobody who could touch us," said a member of that generation, Bob Pierpoint. "When CBS was really riding high in news, it wasn't because of ratings. It was because of the reputation of the Murrow Boys, because of the Murrow legacy."

The Boys were so good and so knowledgeable that they felt frustrated at not having more time on the air to tell their stories. Their usual allotment of one and a half to two minutes on Murrow's program or *World News Roundup*, as important and sought-after as those outlets were, was not enough to provide the kind of interpretation and background for which they were noted. As 1950 approached, news writer Ed Bliss and Don Hewitt, the young director of CBS's fledgling television newscast, separately had the same idea: why not bring the foreign correspondents together with Ed Murrow and Eric Sevareid for a lengthy look at where the world was at this midcentury point and where it was going? Thus began an annual event, the CBS year-end roundups.

✦

On the afternoon of New Year's Day, 1950, Ed Murrow and the correspondents sat around a small cloth-covered table in a CBS radio studio. Murrow, in shirtsleeves, opened the program with a line that seemed to reflect how happy he was to have the old gang, or most of it, together again: "I should like some friends of mine to introduce themselves to you," Murrow said, and one by one they did — Eric Sevareid, Howard K. Smith, Winston Burdett, Larry LeSueur, Bill Downs, David Schoenbrun, and a newcomer, Bill Costello, a college friend of Sevareid's who had been hired by CBS as a correspondent in Asia.*

For forty-five minutes the correspondents engaged in a freewheeling, erudite discussion of the parlous state of the world halfway through the twentieth century. Liberated from tight time restrictions and the network's strict objectivity rules, the correspondents showed off their knowledge, displayed their personalities and their skill with words, and expressed their opinions.

Sevareid was tersely eloquent, if rather Eurocentric, in his summary of America's last fifty years:

> We conquered our continent, we saw our absolute physical security and, therefore, our political isolation, disappear. We flirted with imperialism, gave it up because we really didn't care for it. We fought two world wars, took the initiative for world government with the League [of Nations],

---

*Bill Shirer had left CBS by this time. Charles Collingwood and Dick Hottelet, the only other Boys not at the table for that first broadcast, were excluded because both were based in the United States at the time — Collingwood in Los Angeles, Hottelet in New York (between assignments in Moscow and Bonn). The emphasis in this program was to be on foreign news. Only Sevareid was to talk about America.

gave it up, took the initiative a second time, and now find ourselves, rather unwillingly, one of only two great powers in a bisected world. And upon our shoulders is the terrible responsibility of preserving free civilization that Western man has developed through laborious centuries.

Howard Smith was more concise in his summary of modern European history: "The story of Europe these fifty years can be quickly told. Europe declined."

They discussed the big issues, the rise and fall of Hitler among them, but, prompted by Murrow, they also talked about little things, as they had in their wartime broadcasts. For example, Murrow asked the correspondents to name some items that had become luxuries in the countries they covered.

Smith: In Britain, darn near everything British-made is a luxury. Everything is for export.
Downs: Well, in Germany, it's doorknobs with houses on the other end.
Schoenbrun: In France, hot tap water or a cake of fat soap.
Burdett: In Italy, an orange or a clean, unfrayed shirt.
LeSueur: At the United Nations, I guess, the only luxury is just one kind word.

With such small details, the correspondents sketched a vivid picture of an unharmonious world still prostrate from the effects of the war.

The program, heavily promoted by the network before it was broadcast, was an enormous critical and popular hit. Perhaps even more important, it won raves from the big boss himself. "I thought that the broadcast was one of the most distinguished I had ever heard," Bill Paley said in a note to Murrow, copies of which were sent to the other correspondents. Their remarks, Paley said, "sounded like pieces which might be written 50 years from now by top historians, certainly not by guys who have lived through most of the period."

Capitalizing on the broadcast's success, CBS decided to make it an annual event, dubbing it *Years of Crisis*. For the next eleven years, an afternoon between Christmas and New Year's was designated, and the network's top foreign correspondents and sometimes a domestic correspondent or two would sit down with Murrow to discuss what had happened in the world over the previous twelve months. To historian William Manchester those year-end roundups "became as much a part of the Christmas holidays as Lionel Barrymore playing Scrooge."

John Crosby, the television and radio critic of the *New York Herald Tribune*, called the roundups "a splendid, meaty hour" marked by the "tremendous depth and range of the talk and . . . truly surprising literacy of expression." When *Years of Crisis* moved to television, Crosby applauded Murrow for resisting the temptation to make this annual event a "show" — "no film, no dancing girls, only ideas." Nowadays show business seems to be the hallmark of television news discussion programs, where the decibel level of the participants' voices takes precedence over serious, informed examination of important issues. Yet with all their verbal fireworks, they can't compare to the yeasty, provocative experience of hearing Ed Murrow and a few of his "friends" discuss the shape of the world. Their sense of history, their intellectual depth, their ability to conjure up *le mot juste*, an apt metaphor, a memorable phrase, made the program a significant national event. Said Sandy Socolow, "If you were interested in world affairs, the conversation was absolutely brilliant."

On television the roundups were, in the parlance of modern network programmers, sixty minutes of "talking heads." But the heads were so smart and experienced, and the talk so interesting, that millions tuned in every year. One of those millions was a young University of North Carolina student named Charles Kuralt, who found his heroes in the correspondents on the roundup. "Such a tour de force of scholar-journalists," recalled Kuralt, who later became a star of the next generation of CBS correspondents. "Even then, I hoped to be like them someday, but knowing in my heart that I could never measure up."

◆

It did not come easily for them. They worked hard at what they did, and the effort exacted a heavy toll on their nerves. That may be one reason why many of them drank so much. Korean war correspondent Bob Pierpoint remembered his first appearance on a roundup, in 1954, not only because he was sitting at the same table with Edward R. Murrow and the legendary Boys but also because it gave him an understanding of just how heavy the toll could be. With only seconds to go before airtime, he looked around the table at his heroes — men who for years had seemed to him so cool and rational in crisis after crisis, from the Nazi invasion of Poland to the Berlin blockade — and most of them looked like basket cases!

Sweat poured down Murrow's face, and his leg jiggled furiously under the table, as if he were some gland-tormented teenage boy. Sevareid's face was bone-white, his fingers frantically drumming on the table. And Schoenbrun, perched on a pillow to make himself look taller for TV, suddenly jumped up to go to the men's room. Pierpoint was nervous too — it was, after all, his debut in the biggest league in electronic journalism — but he wasn't as nervous as the others. These people seemed positively *ill*. Later Murrow told him, "If you're not really nervous, you don't do a job well." Many years after that, when Pierpoint had retired from CBS, he reflected, "I think one reason I was never a really great broadcaster was because I never quite got up to that degree of tension and nervous energy."

The lineup of correspondents shifted from year to year — newer people like Pierpoint, Daniel Schorr, and Marvin Kalb were occasionally brought in — but the original Boys remained the linchpin of the program and the ones to whom the others paid court. Schorr, hardly a shrinking violet and a remarkable journalist and broadcaster in his own right, never felt part of the inner circle. A frequent participant in the later roundups, Schorr — who once swiped Schoenbrun's pillow just before airtime to break the tension — saw World War II as the great dividing line. He said, "The group that went through danger together, went through the war, had some alumni standing in common that wasn't fully shared by the others."

They hadn't collaborated much during the war, hadn't been particularly close, but when the Boys united for the annual roundups, they treasured their special status, their identification as the Murrow Boys. Murrow was the nucleus of the atom, the force that kept all the other parts in their respective orbits. Most of the Boys had had a personal relationship with him but not with one another. Yet the year-end roundups helped foster the feeling that they really were a band of brothers and always had been. In old age, when Larry LeSueur remembered the war, he remembered team spirit, not rivalry. He welcomed the roundups for renewing "the collegial feeling of working together," a feeling he said he greatly missed. But, he admitted, "we were trying to recreate something that could never be recreated." Or that never really existed in the first place.

The Murrow Boys, as much as or more than anyone else, wanted to believe in their own myth. An elaborate social routine soon grew up around the year-end broadcast. The correspondents would arrive in New York two or three days in advance of the show for discussions and a dress rehearsal — and for considerable socializing, including a lunch with Paley and Stanton. Palmer Williams, a producer on the Murrow television program *See It Now*, recalled the group, in town for the year-ender, hanging out in Murrow's office, sharing his Scotch, "rehashing this incident, that time and place — just a bunch of old war buddies."

Underneath all the conviviality and jocularity, however, the correspondents' old competitiveness still simmered. Inevitably it would boil over, usually during the roundup itself. "It really was a circus to watch all these guys and their rivalries," Palmer Williams said. "You had a popinjay like Schoenbrun, who was so insecure that he was always madly scrambling to get on top. Then you had the more dignified people like Smith, who were above the fray."

Schoenbrun, the defender of France, and Dick Hottelet, the champion of France's historic archfoe, Germany, could be counted on for especially pointed exchanges — all the more so because their antagonism was as much personal as nationalistic. The liberal Schoenbrun considered Hottelet an arrogant right-winger; Hottelet regarded Schoenbrun as a monomaniacal blowhard. On one show Schoenbrun, in his opening remarks, turned to Hottelet and said, "Where I come from, they say you can't trust a German." On another program Hottelet shouted during an especially intense argument with his balding bête noire, "Schoenbrun, if you had any brains in that hairless head of yours . . ."

Although the feud was firmly based in reality, it was also good theater, which the always theatrical Murrow recognized early and encouraged whenever he could. At the end of one debate between the two correspondents, a clearly delighted Murrow said, "You two have been arguing about this to my knowledge for ten years and seven minutes now." He introduced them that same year as "Hottelet and Schoenbrun, who come from France and Germany and who have never yet agreed on anything."

Despite such heat, the prevailing attitude at the year-end roundups was one of deep mutual respect. Marvin Kalb, the last correspondent recruited by Murrow for CBS, understood that the first time he appeared. Kalb studied these men he so deeply admired, watched their eyes, their demeanor. "They'd sit back and listen very closely," Kalb said, "because they wanted to know what each person said, because they thought what was being said was very important. They thought of themselves as a team. There was a generosity of spirit they all seemed to have, a decency, a collegiality, and an incredible degree of professionalism and pride. They knew they were the best, the absolute best."

The man to whom they listened most attentively sat at the head of the table, presiding over it all, holding it together. "This was a twenty-mule team and Ed Murrow was the driver," said Ed Bliss, who served for four years as associate producer of the year-end show. "His presence, his command at those things was absolute."

The debates that characterized the programs, once they got rolling, were real enough, but prior to each broadcast there would be one or two rehearsals to work out the broad outlines, and the correspondents often wrote down their formal remarks in advance and memorized them. (They did not use cue cards, but some of the younger correspondents did bring in personal notes now and then.) Murrow, the paterfamilias, was clearly in charge; the correspondents usually played his respectful sons. "When Ed spoke, everyone else went silent," Kalb recalled. "[At rehearsals], if someone came up with an idea and Ed said, 'Yes, let's go in that direction' or 'No, I think we'll do something else,' no one ever stood up and said, 'That's a terrible idea.' They all bowed to his leadership."

Dan Schorr was also struck by the reverence the Boys showed for Murrow, even in their off hours. When they'd take breaks in their planning sessions and rehearsals, the correspondents would not speak to Murrow unless he spoke to them first. As Schorr watched, he would go from one man to another, engaging him in conversation. Perhaps they thought so much of him because he thought so much of *them*. "What conditioned our relationship with him was his way of expressing enormous respect for journalists," Schorr said. "He'd say, 'I'm not a real journalist. I just drifted into this thing. You guys are the real journalists.' He always made you feel that he was addressing you as somebody who was in some way superior or more knowledgeable or more experienced than himself."

That spirit came through on the year-end broadcast itself. Murrow was in command, but it was the correspondents' show, not Murrow's. He asked the questions and at the end summed up what had been said. But that was it. For the rest, he sat back and let his team shine.

For the correspondents, the most anticipated event associated with the roundup each year was the postbroadcast buffet dinner at the Murrows' Park Avenue apartment, followed by a poker party that usually lasted until dawn or later. "Outsiders were never allowed in," said Dan Schorr. "If Paley had called and said he wanted to come, Murrow would have said, 'Bill, some other time. This is Murrow and his Boys tonight.' Murrow would not violate the integrity of that. It was tradition."

At the Murrows' apartment the correspondents would help themselves to plenty of liquor and to the abundant buffet that Janet Murrow always set out. Still on an adrenaline high, they would burst in, chattering about who had been better on the show, who had outsmarted whom. One correspondent might say to another, "What you said wasn't quite right. You should have said . . ." The other would respond, "Oh, but I did say . . ." To Dan Schorr they were like football players in the locker room after the game, reliving the highlights.

They would laugh about unexpected events like Schorr's theft of Schoenbrun's pillow, or the time that Bill Downs had gone nervously to the men's room before the show and had been in such a hurry to get back that he pulled the zipper out of his trousers. He returned to the table, crossed his legs, and tugged at his jacket to make certain it covered his fly. But in the course of the debate that followed, the exuberant Downs, forgetting about his mishap, uncrossed his legs and gesticulated expansively. After the show went off the air, Don Hewitt's voice boomed from the control room: "A fine show, gentlemen, and you, Bill Downs, really put on a spectacular show. Just look down at your crotch." Downs glanced down, then looked around at his colleagues, who by then were in hysterics. "Well," he said, "for the first time in the history of television, the public can legitimately ask, 'Who *was* that prick?'"

At the Murrows' postbroadcast bash, the telephone rang repeatedly, friends and acquaintances calling with reviews — all highly favorable, of course. Sometimes Murrow would answer the phone, but more often Janet did. Either way, the message would be taken and passed on: "That was Frank Stanton. He said it was wonderful." As the evening progressed and the pall of cigarette smoke thickened and the liquor flowed more and more freely, the ties and jackets came off and the poker game began.

Murrow, the ever-present cigarette dangling from his lips, was a terrible poker player. "He was almost deliberately bad," said Schorr. "It was as if he felt that since he was the host, he should lose. He'd bet on hands he shouldn't have bet on, he always stayed in. After a while, it became embarrassing to play poker with him because he was financing the rest of us."

Murrow didn't seem to mind. He gloried in the game. And in the night.

20

Brother Against Brother

To THE WORLD it might seem that Ed Murrow and the Boys were in command of CBS News, but Bill Paley knew better. The wartime chairman — the drinking and poker-playing buddy who dined out on the excellence of his news outfit — had disappeared. In his place was an aloof and secretive man who tended more and more to manipulate his top people, including Murrow. For the rest of his life, Paley would look back wistfully on the war years. "Life," he said, "had never been so exciting and immediate and never would be again." But he was a practical man, a *business* man, and he moved on, retailoring his life and his network for the postwar era.

Profits and ratings — those were what Paley wanted from his company. He had taken CBS public in 1937. Now the stockholders expected better performance. It was well and good to have Murrow and this big news organization that everyone respected, but news didn't generate enough revenue in a peacetime economy and probably never would. Without the drama of a world at war, there simply wasn't that much demand for news.

To keep people listening, you had to have big-time, big-name entertainment, and in that area NBC had always enjoyed a substantial advantage. Hoping to break NBC's entertainment stranglehold, Paley decided his network would develop its own mass-audience shows, as well as offer more money to lure away NBC's top stars — including several whom NBC earlier had stolen from *him*. It worked. By 1950 Paley's entertainment roster included the most popular entertainers in America — Arthur Godfrey, Jack Benny, Bing Crosby, Burns and Allen, ventriloquist Edgar Bergen and his dummy, Charlie McCarthy. In 1949, for the first time ever, CBS was number one in overall audience ratings. News may have carried Paley in the direction he wanted to go, but it wouldn't bring him all the way home. And Bill Paley was never one to put much stock in loyalty for old time's sake, as William L. Shirer was the first to find out.

◆

After leaving Berlin in December 1940, Shirer returned to the war only twice, for a total of two months. Even then he had broadcast from London and Paris rather than venturing to the front. "It got to be a joke with us," said Bill Shadel. "The big war correspondent — where the hell is he? He'd come over on these tours, these thirty-day wonders."

After the war Shirer was still on friendly terms with Murrow, Le-Sueur, Smith, and some of the other Boys, but the ties had loosened considerably. "The real thing that bound the others together was that they were all working in the war," said Eric Sevareid's New Zealander friend Geoffrey Cox, who also knew several others in the CBS crew. "[Even during the war], I was aware that Bill was no longer one of the Boys."

That was just fine with Shirer. As far as he was concerned, his star shone separately in the firmament, not as just another point in the Murrow constellation. He had a following, a reputation, a position of his own. He did not try to hide this attitude. Never one to mix or chat or play cards or drink with the rest of the staff, he had a personal secretary who, as retired CBS correspondent George Herman recalled, "encapsulated and protected him from the rest of us." At times Shirer played the bully. He once upbraided Rosalind Gerson, the news desk's eighteen-year-old, fourteen-dollar-a-week assistant (and Bill Downs's future wife), because someone had read his copy of the *New York Times* before he did. "I want my *New York Times* pristine!" he shouted. Gerson wasn't in charge of Shirer's *Times*, but from then on she made it a point to come in early each morning and place a "pristine" copy of the paper on his desk, thinking as she did so that Shirer was "a nasty old man."

He wasn't old, only in his early forties, but he had come to expect a certain level of comfort and deference wherever he went. After the war, in Nuremberg with Howard K. Smith to cover the Nazi war-crimes trials, Shirer became preoccupied, almost to the exclusion of the trials themselves, with how badly he felt he was being treated. In a letter to Murrow, Smith reported that Shirer "raised hell because the army didn't provide him with special transportation, grumbled constantly at meals and accomodations [*sic*], and always managed to be ailing whenever I asked him to help me with the load of daily shows."

Years later Shirer acknowledged that he had been insufferable in those days. "It was easy," he said, "with the notoriety and the constant publicity that radio brought, to get puffed up about yourself." With his Sunday program and his newspaper column and his frequent appearances on the lecture circuit, he was one of New York's most noted and best-paid journalists. His broadcast alone provided him with "all the money I needed or wanted." He and Tess were fixtures on the New York social circuit. Their Beekman Place townhouse — in the same neighborhood where Bill Paley once lived — was the scene of many a lively party. And Shirer's affair with the ex-ballerina Tilly Losch continued unabated.

It was a very good life, and if he and his best friend, Ed Murrow, had grown more distant, that was an unfortunate but perhaps unavoidable price of his success. He was no longer in Murrow's sphere, no longer willing to pay court to a man who was, really, his boss in name only. Sometimes the Shirers got together with Ed and Janet for old times' sake, but the spark just wasn't there anymore.

It did not seem to occur to Shirer that Murrow might still harbor a lingering resentment for his refusal to return to Europe to cover the war — really *cover* it — instead of coming in on whirlwind tours like a VIP. On one such tour Shirer had attended a dinner given by Murrow at the Connaught Hotel in London. Shirer was holding forth about Germany when Murrow interrupted him, turned to another guest, and said, "Now let's hear from someone who *knows* something about Germany." Sevareid, who was present, later said, "You could watch Shirer's face turning red."

After the war Murrow and Shirer traveled together from New York to London on the *Queen Mary*. Murrow was agonizing at the time over whether to take the CBS vice presidency Paley had offered, and Shirer was on his way to cover the Nuremberg trials. When the ship docked, they went into Southampton for dinner and had more than a few drinks before setting out by chauffeured car for London. Murrow was drunk, according to Shirer. As the two of them sat in the back seat of the car, Murrow suddenly began cursing and punching his colleague.

Shirer, astonished, could think of no reason for the attack. Murrow, he said, never made clear the reason for his sudden violent outburst. Later Shirer speculated that he may have been jealous that Shirer's book

Berlin Diary had been a much bigger success than an anthology of Murrow's broadcasts published at about the same time. Unable, apparently, to think of any other motive, Shirer said, "I'm still trying to figure it out."

◆

As vice president for news and public affairs, Murrow added another grievance against Shirer to his growing list. "Goddammit, Bill's getting lazy," Murrow complained to John G. "Jap" Gude, his former agent, who was now representing Shirer. Murrow told Gude that Shirer was neglecting to do any reporting to back up his news analyses and was devoting too much of his program to reading quotes from newspapers and magazines. If you went on the air to discuss public events, Murrow believed, you had an obligation to your listeners to participate in those events, either directly or by interviewing people about them.

Murrow was particularly incensed that Shirer had done all his broadcasts during the summer of 1946 from the New York resort town of Lake Placid. "Whatever the benefits of Lake Placid might be, it is not considered the ideal place from which to report and interpret world affairs," Murrow wrote to his friend Harold Laski in London. Shirer claimed long afterward that his doctor had ordered him to take the entire summer off; he had undergone an operation in January and had not yet completely recovered by summer, he said. Both his sponsor, the J. B. Williams shaving cream company, and CBS had asked him to continue the Sunday program, even if he had to do it from Lake Placid. "I nearly killed myself" doing it, he said.

Shortly after Shirer's Lake Placid convalescence ended, Murrow urged him to get out of New York and do some reporting prior to the 1946 congressional elections. Shirer declined. Murrow was in charge of CBS News, but the man who helped him build it thought he no longer had to obey his orders. "The trouble with Bill is that he thinks, because a million people hear what he says, that he's therefore a million times smarter [when] he is talking to us," Murrow once grumbled to Charles Collingwood. But although Murrow complained to others, he never presented any of his grievances directly to Shirer. According to Jap Gude, Murrow was reluctant to confront his old friend, unwilling to "take Bill for a drink or dinner and have it out with him."

On March 10, 1947, Shirer's lovely world collapsed. He received a telephone call from an executive at the J. Walter Thompson advertising agency, who told him the Williams Company, after three years of sponsorship, had decided to drop his Sunday broadcast. Nothing personal, the ad man said; Williams just wanted to shift from news to entertainment. The company was thinking of trying to appeal to a younger audience. Maybe they'd do a jazz show next.

Shirer was stunned. He'd had no inkling this was coming. His weekly 5:45 P.M. program at one point had received a 6.9 Hooper rating, the highest of any Sunday news program. (More recently, though, the ratings, like news ratings generally, had been slipping.) Moreover, Shirer insisted later, no one at Williams or CBS had expressed any dissatisfaction with his performance. In fact, only three months earlier, his contract with Williams had been renegotiated, with the usual thirteen-week option clause. Now, after the first thirteen-week period, Williams was pulling the plug on him, effective March 30. Shirer immediately suspected that he was being punished for the outspokenly liberal positions he took on the air.

It was not an illogical assumption. As relations between the United States and the Soviet Union started to decline almost immediately after the war, American liberals were more and more on the run. To conservative watchdogs and even many middle-of-the-roaders, liberals had become, on an ascending scale of evil, "fellow travelers," "pinkos," "reds," or "commies." Radio shows, movies, books, magazine articles, and newspaper columns went beyond the reality of the Soviet Union's aggressive new international posture and suggested that Moscow had created a vast fifth column within the United States, abetted, consciously or unconsciously, by American liberals.

In the 1946 congressional elections, the voters chose a Republican Congress for the first time since 1930. Many of the new members, prominently including freshman Republican Representative Richard M. Nixon of California, had campaigned against the domestic "Communist threat." Republican Senator Joseph R. McCarthy of Wisconsin, also a member of the congressional class of 1946, would wait until 1950 before launching his own witch-hunting orgy. But the wave of hysteria and fear that now bears his name may fairly be said to have begun in 1947. And Shirer could hardly be accused of paranoia when he suspected that he might be one of its early victims.

Only two months earlier the *New Republic* had reported that in the previous year CBS, NBC, and local radio stations, under heavy pressure from sponsors, had dropped some two dozen liberal correspondents and commentators. "The networks have been growing more and more worried about 'opinion' on their air," the article reported. ". . . Networks want to avoid 'trouble' — especially with their customers. Pressure to 'tone down' news which is sympathetic to organized labor and to Russia has increased rapidly in the last few months."

When President Truman declared the Truman Doctrine and asked Congress for $400 million in aid for the governments of Greece and Turkey to help them resist Communist-backed guerrilla insurgencies, Shirer, among other liberal commentators, attacked the plan. The government in Athens was the same corrupt, repressive oligarchy that had ruled Greece before the Germans conquered it in 1941, he said. The regime had regained power after the war only through the meddling of the British. Aiding such a government, Shirer argued, made neither moral nor political sense.

His criticisms of the Greek government (and of Chiang Kai-shek's regime in China) were drawing increasing fire from the right. The Williams Company forwarded to him a number of letters from angry listeners objecting to his liberalism. He was also told that the staunchly conservative Catholic archbishop of New York, Francis Spellman, had complained about him directly to Paley. And a vice president of the J. Walter Thompson agency told him point-blank one day that he was too liberal for his own good.

That must be why I am being dropped, Shirer thought. *The ad agency V.P. had gotten to Williams.* Greatly upset, he called Jap Gude and told him what had happened. Why did he have to hear the news from the damn agency? he asked. Why hadn't Ed called him? He was sure Murrow and Paley would never stand for this. They would show Williams who was boss. They would find Shirer another sponsor and keep him in the same Sunday slot. He had built up the audience for that program, after all. The time period really belonged to him!

Next Shirer phoned Murrow. Was the program Shirer's or the sponsor's? Would CBS retain the program if he and the network could find another sponsor? Murrow said he'd get back to him.

Murrow went to Paley. He reminded the chairman of the huge contribution Shirer had made to CBS and argued that he should keep the program and the time. According to Frank Stanton, who was present at the meeting, Paley seemed well aware of Williams's position and wouldn't hear of Murrow's solution. Bill Paley was tired of Shirer and his swelled head. He wanted Shirer off the program and out of the time slot.

Clearly Shirer had crossed the chairman of CBS once too often. The year before, William Wrigley, the chewing gum king, had offered to sponsor a new program of news and analysis featuring Shirer, at a fee of $2,500 a week. But the broadcast would have to originate in Chicago, where Wrigley lived. Shirer, who loved his life in New York and had no desire to return to the city of his birth, rejected the offer. Paley was furious. He summoned Shirer to his office, reminded him what an important advertiser Wrigley was, and ordered him to take the offer. Shirer was adamant. "Are you sure you want to turn this down?" Paley asked. His voice was icy. This was not the Paley who had invited Shirer to parties and dinners in Manhattan and Long Island. This was the powerful head of a network perceiving insubordination on the part of an employee.

Now Paley saw his chance to get even. Murrow, who had had plenty of experience of his own with Shirer's arrogance, went along with the boss. In fact, said Frank Stanton, he "caved quickly." At the same time Murrow was reluctant to be the one to break the bad news. "He said he didn't think [making him do so] was fair," Stanton recalled. "It was a personal relationship, and he hated having to tell an old friend he had to get out of the time period."

Stanton, whom Paley had elevated to the presidency of the network in 1945, was not exactly a disinterested party in this affair. He and Murrow were rivals for Paley's attention, and did not get along. Stanton particularly resented that Murrow could — and often did — bypass him and go directly to Paley on any question. Still, in this case Stanton's account squares with the facts. His description of Murrow's reluctance to carry the bad news to Shirer is borne out by the fact that a week passed before Murrow did so — and then it was only in response to a note from Shirer, asking if a decision had been made. Finally Murrow picked up the phone and called Shirer's office. His voice, as Shirer recalled it, was "crisp and cool — most unlike the Ed I had known": sponsor or no sponsor, Shirer was to be replaced on the Sunday program by another commentator. CBS would try to find him a new time slot and in time a new sponsor. Until then he would be "sustaining" — that is, unsponsored.

That meant Shirer would lose his commercial fees of more than a thousand dollars a week, the money that supported his affluent lifestyle. It was just unacceptable, he told Murrow. Sunday at 5:45 P.M. was *his*. Murrow urged calm. After all, this was hardly the first time a sponsor had dropped a program.

That was true. It had happened to Cecil Brown and others, and in the future it would happen to many more. It had even happened to Shirer before: in 1943 General Foods had canceled sponsorship of his Sunday show, and he was put on a sustaining basis — in the same time slot, however — until Williams picked him up. That was precisely what Shirer wanted the network to do this time: keep *him*, not some cowed replacement, in the time slot until a new sponsor came along. Only then, he correctly argued, could Paley and Murrow legitimately claim that CBS controlled the content and presentation of its news programs.

As it became clear to Shirer that he had lost the battle, his anger increased. He began to consider ways to minimize the damage to himself and, if possible, take some revenge. At the very least, he insisted to Murrow, he had the right to tell his listeners that he was being taken off the air. The two men agreed on a vague statement, which Shirer delivered on March 23. "Next Sunday," he said, "I will make my last broadcast on this program. I have been informed by the sponsor and by the Columbia Broadcasting System of that decision."

This was major news, and when Shirer emerged from the studio after the March 23 broadcast, several reporters were waiting to question him about what was going on. He was being throttled by his sponsor, he said. But that was hardly the worst of it: CBS, by forcing him to give up his regular broadcast time, was making it *easy* for the sponsor. In effect the network was endorsing the authority of Williams — or any other sponsor — to dictate the content of news broadcasts.

"To suddenly change my [time] spot," Shirer declared to the reporters, "seems to me purely because of my editorial position. I certainly consider it a move to gag me." In other words, the gag may have been put in place by the sponsor, but it was the network that was tying the knot. Perhaps not until this moment did Paley, Murrow, and CBS realize that they had a war on their hands and that as far as Shirer was concerned, *they* were the enemy!

WILLIAM SHIRER, LIBERAL COMMENTATOR, GETS AXE said a front-page headline the next day in the liberal New York tabloid *PM*. Other New York papers gave the story similar treatment. At CBS people began to suspect that all the press attention was not exactly spontaneous, that Shirer was doing everything in his power to embarrass the network, which was still his employer. Afterward, and for as long as he lived, Shirer denied the charge. He insisted he had no part in summoning the reporters after his broadcast or in organizing the noisy demonstrations outside the CBS building the following week or in the stream

of pro-Shirer telegrams and letters to Paley and Murrow from prominent writers, editors, actors, and artists. Could Bill Shirer help it if he
had a big following?

Among the protesting telegrams that Murrow and Paley received
was one signed by Dorothy Parker, Arthur Miller, Gregory Peck,
Robert Sherwood, and — most painful for Murrow — several good
friends of *his*, including Archibald MacLeish, John Gunther, and Vincent Sheean. There were even direct attacks on Murrow from others he
respected. Now that he was a CBS vice president, they suggested, he
had turned into just another corporate hack. "What have they done to
you since you came back from England, that you aren't out in front
fighting for him?" wrote Ralph Ingersoll, another friend of Murrow's
and the editor of *PM*.

As the reluctant point man for CBS, Murrow denied Shirer's allega-
tions and issued a statement saying the decision to find a replacement
for the Sunday afternoon program had nothing to do with Shirer's
political views. Moreover, Murrow's statement continued, the decision
"does not involve Mr. Shirer's leaving the network unless he chooses to
do so. The decision to replace Mr. Shirer on the air was the decision of
CBS. Mr. Shirer will have a new spot but what it will be is not yet
known. This is a change of assignment."

Many, if not most, prominent liberals refused to accept Murrow's argument. Even if it was true (as it was) that all the Williams Company had done was end its sponsorship, not insist that Shirer lose his
time slot, the network, by reacting as it had, was sending exactly the
wrong signal at a very sensitive political time. Besides, everyone *knew*
that sponsors were accustomed to calling the shots on the programs
they backed. What about Cecil Brown and Johns-Manville less than
four years earlier? Now Shirer seemed to be heading toward the same
fate, although no one at CBS had told him to tone down his commentaries.

Ironically, it was Shirer who had mounted the most vehement defense of CBS against Brown, denying that the network succumbed to
sponsor pressures. With his own ox gored, however, Shirer saw things
differently. Jack Gould, the influential radio critic of the *New York Times*,
agreed with him. Two months earlier Gould had blasted the networks
for allowing sponsors too much influence over news programming. In
response Murrow said CBS's broadcasters were responsible only to
CBS. Now Gould pointed out that Shirer had been told of the decision

to drop his program by the sponsor's advertising agent, not by CBS. "Mr. Murrow . . . has insisted that the decision to drop Mr. Shirer from the Sunday period was solely that of CBS," Gould wrote. "The fact remains, however, that an advertiser again has figured prominently in a controversy over the presentation of opinion on the air when actually there should be no opportunity whatsoever for him to do so." In other words, in a dispute like this, a network's proper place was *between* a journalist and his sponsor.

✦

Two days after Shirer's press conference, Murrow asked Joseph Harsch to take over Shirer's Sunday program. Harsch, who had a daily news and analysis program on CBS at 11:15 P.M., was as outspokenly liberal as Shirer (though not as prominent), a fact Murrow hoped would help quell the escalating controversy. Harsch agreed to Murrow's request, although as an old friend of Shirer's, he was uncomfortable about doing it. He and Shirer had been colleagues in Berlin, where Harsch had been a correspondent for the *Christian Science Monitor.* At Shirer's request Harsch had even done some broadcasting in Berlin for CBS, which had led to his being hired by the network as a Washington-based analyst in 1943.

After talking to both Murrow and Shirer, Harsch came to the conclusion that Shirer's liberalism had not been a factor in the dropping of his program. His old friend, Harsch said, had "a slight tendency to think that the cause of liberal civilization rested on his shoulders. . . . Eric Sevareid and Howard K. Smith were just as liberal, and they stayed on."

In announcing the shift from Shirer to Harsch, Murrow said, "We believe that Mr. Harsch, with long experience in Washington and abroad and his access to news sources in Washington, will improve Columbia's news analysis in this period." The statement was salt in Shirer's wounds, as Murrow must have known it would be. In a return shot Shirer rather extravagantly insisted to a reporter that what CBS had done to him was reminiscent of what he had gone through in Hitler's Germany. "I worked nine years under Nazi censorship and would hate to see that come to us," he said.

With each new statement, each new charge, the controversy intensified. "It is hard to imagine today the firestorm Shirer's dismissal touched off — thousands of telephone calls to CBS, pickets marching in the streets, mass meetings, front-page newspaper reports, petitions, editorials and articles from coast to coast," Harrison Salisbury wrote long afterward in the *Washington Post*. New York's hothouse journalistic and literary worlds were transfixed; two of the biggest names in radio journalism — the two men who *invented* modern radio reporting — were at each other's throats, and the country's most respected broadcast news organization stood accused of kowtowing to a sponsor.

By taking his complaints public, Shirer had generated a whirlwind, and now he watched helplessly as it spun out of control. Before the world he and his once-closest friend were flaying each other with the most wounding of accusations. Murrow had charged Shirer with not doing his job, and Shirer had blasted Murrow for a lack of integrity. If there was anything Murrow prided himself on, if there was anything he wanted to be known for, it was integrity. To have that questioned in public, to be taken to task by friends like MacLeish and Ingersoll, was a deep humiliation. At one point he phoned Shirer and called him a "lousy son of a bitch" for "getting these liberals down on my back."

Still, Murrow made one last try at patching things up. He and Shirer went back too far, had been through too much together, to have their friendship end like this. Throughout that terrible week he asked Bill Downs and other friends what he should do. "This is an old friend," Murrow said. "And he doesn't understand. He keeps saying, 'This is *my* time; this time belongs to *me*.' I can't explain to him, This time does not belong to him."

Finally, on March 28, Murrow and Shirer met in the bar at the Berkshire Hotel, near CBS headquarters, and agreed they both had been acting like idiots. Over a couple of drinks they worked out a compromise in which Shirer would be given a new, sponsored time slot on Saturday evening (a slot that belonged, coincidentally, to Larry LeSueur). In return the protests against the network would end. Exhilarated, they prepared a statement for the press. All they had to do was run it by Bill Paley. Finally the whirlwind would cease.

But when Murrow and Shirer presented the compromise to Paley in his office, he rejected it out of hand. He was mortified by the onslaught of criticism against his network and was certain Shirer had engineered it. "As far as I'm concerned," Paley told Shirer during the meeting, "your usefulness to CBS has ended."

There was stunned silence. Shirer looked at Murrow. According to Shirer, all Murrow could say was, "We had an agreement. But if you don't like it, Bill, you're the boss."

At that moment, in William S. Paley's office, the Murrow-Shirer friendship ended.

✦

Shirer felt Murrow had betrayed him. But Murrow felt equally betrayed by Shirer. For one thing, he, too, was sure that all the protest and negative publicity had been engineered by Shirer. Even Jap Gude, Shirer's agent, thought so. "[Shirer] did have control," Gude said. "Why, he *called* that news conference." It's not clear that Gude ever told Murrow that, but Murrow did receive from H. V. Kaltenborn another piece of evidence. It was a copy of a telegram Shirer had sent to Kaltenborn, then president of the Association of Radio News Analysts: ANY INTEREST IN ARNA OVER ISSUE WHETHER SOAP MAKER SHOULD DICTATE WHO SHOULD NOT BE HEARD ON AIR[?] INFORMATIVELY HAVE HEARD FROM HUNDREDS PROMINENT CITIZENS, MANY ORGANIZATIONS. BUT ARNA'S SILENCE GROWING ELOQUENT. REGARDS BILL SHIRER.

Murrow exploded at Shirer on the morning of Shirer's final broadcast. "You son of a bitch!" Shirer quoted Murrow as saying. "You better not try anything funny today. You better stick to the script or else."

Shirer said he told Murrow, "No problem, Ed. Look at all the experience I've had in sticking to scripts. In Berlin. Remember?"

According to Shirer, two editors were under orders from Murrow to vet every word of his final script, which in the event proved innocuous. "This is my last broadcast on this program," Shirer said. "The issues involved, which make it my last broadcast, are, so far as I am concerned, important; but I believe this is not the place or the time to discuss them."

On the day of that broadcast, Shirer announced his resignation from CBS. Borrowing some of the words Paley had spoken to him in rejecting the Berkshire bar compromise, Shirer said, "I feel that the Columbia Broadcasting System has brought my usefulness on its network to a sudden end after ten years of regular broadcasting from here and abroad. I am therefore resigning."

That same day Murrow also released a statement:

During the last week Mr. Shirer has stated to us repeatedly his agreement and understanding that our decision to reassign him to another time period was not based on the sponsor's wishes. . . . At no time has he claimed to us that our decision was based on any objection to the content of his broadcast or on what have been called his liberal views. The Columbia Broadcasting System and no one else decided to place another news analyst in the period that has been occupied by Mr. Shirer, and Mr. Shirer doesn't like it, and that's all there is to it.

◆

But the mutual scourging was not yet over.

Two weeks later the Overseas Press Club sponsored a luncheon at which both Murrow and Shirer were invited to speak. Murrow had planned to take the high road, addressing not the personal clash with Shirer but the larger question of commercial influence on broadcast news. "It will be a dangerous day for American broadcasting if we ever reach the point where they who have the most money are allowed to dominate the discussion in the marketplace of ideas," Murrow's prepared text said.

Shirer, however, was given the podium first. A few days before, he began, he had received a Peabody Award for his commentary. If he were as lazy as Murrow and CBS claimed, how had he managed to win this prestigious broadcast award? No, Shirer said, he wasn't shoved out because he was lazy; he was shoved out for political reasons and because CBS and Murrow weren't brave enough to stand beside him, or even behind him, let alone in front of him.

Dick Hottelet, who had walked with Murrow from the CBS offices to the lunch, watched his boss as Shirer held forth. "Ed began to paw the ground. To hell with that speech he'd prepared! He never even took the speech out of his pocket."

When it was his turn to talk, Murrow reminded the audience that he had once won a Peabody himself — in 1944, four years *after* what he considered his greatest achievement, his reporting on the Blitz and Britain's underdog struggle against Germany. "I did my great work long before I got any awards," Hottelet recalled Murrow's saying. "I didn't sit somewhere at some lake, sucking my thumb and thinking deep thoughts." The gloves were completely off now, but Hottelet thought Shirer had it coming. "Ed made the case that Shirer had forced him to make, that it was not Shirer's politics but his work that he had called into question. I never heard Ed more forceful or eloquent than on that day." After the lunch Shirer and Murrow stalked out without saying another word to each other.

◆

The debate over whether Shirer was, in fact, silenced by CBS has been going on for almost fifty years. When Shirer recounted his side of the dispute in the last volume of his memoirs, published in 1990, the furor erupted all over again. Murrow was long dead, but his friends and colleagues sprang to his defense. There were vituperative exchanges of letters to various editors. Shirer told his version over and over again to newspaper reporters, as did Murrow's defenders. Though everyone was old by now, and Murrow was gone, the feelings were still raw, the passions unquenched.

On both sides there were undercurrents and hidden agendas, but the likelihood is that both Shirer's liberal views *and* his journalistic short-comings were factors in his downfall. George Herman, then a CBS news writer, said it was common knowledge around the office that "sponsors were beginning to be afraid" of Shirer's liberalism. "But," Herman said, "it is also true that he was lazy. He did the same piece over and over again in different phraseology. A lot of us felt he was there because Murrow liked him rather than because he was a good analyst." When Shirer resigned, hardly anyone at CBS defended him. "There was not much liking or admiration of Shirer in the newsroom," Herman said.

It is possible that Williams canceled Shirer on political grounds and didn't tell CBS, or anyone else, the reason. That was what CBS's critics had been complaining about — the networks had ceded too much power to the sponsors concerning the content of news program-ming. As in the Cecil Brown case, the key questions really were: would CBS have done anything about Shirer's alleged journalistic transgres-sions as long as he kept his sponsor? The answer almost certainly is no. Then wasn't the sponsor really calling the shots? The answer almost certainly was yes.

Murrow himself was deeply troubled by the implications of sponsor influence on broadcasting even as he continued to deny charges that any such influence played a part in Shirer's departure. Shortly after the Overseas Press Club lunch, Murrow wrote to Edgar Ansel Mowrer, a noted *Chicago Daily News* correspondent who was a close friend of both his and Shirer's (and, poignantly, one of the correspondents who had taken part with Murrow and Shirer in the historic first news roundup after the Anschluss in 1938):

> It seems to me entirely legitimate for Shirer or anyone else to question our editorial judgement in replacing him with Joe Harsch, but when

sinister motives are implied, it seems to me that I have no choice except to state the facts. As we both know, there are very serious problems involved in sponsorship of news and opinions, and they go much deeper than anything involved in the case of Bill Shirer.

Nevertheless, CBS's removal of Shirer from the Sunday afternoon time slot only after the sponsor had dumped him sent a clear signal that the network would not stand firm for its journalists. It was, to put it mildly, an unfortunate signal at a time when Joe McCarthy and others were about to do their worst.

Many years later Shirer contended that his ouster "marked the beginning of a new CBS policy of knuckling under to what it thought was the temper of the times." In fact, CBS had "knuckled under" before. The difference was that this time Murrow was directly involved. In the years ahead political pressure on the network's journalists would increase. Others, Murrow included, would have their time in the dock. On that score Shirer had been prescient, telling Murrow in one of their last confrontations, "You can't possibly imagine it now, Ed, but your turn will come. Someday you'll get just what I'm getting."

✦

Cherished friendships were shattered and old loyalties came unraveled because of the Shirer affair. The other Boys rallied around their mentor and irrevocably broke with Shirer. "It was traumatic," recalled Larry LeSueur. "I was a very good friend of Bill's. But I had to choose, and I chose Murrow. I didn't see Bill after that." From London Howard Smith wrote to Murrow that it "broke my heart" to receive word of Shirer's departure; "I am very fond of old Bill, lascivious and pontifical though he is." After agreeing that Shirer was arrogant and lazy, he continued, "Still, the outfit seems incomplete without the gaffer."

Some people, however, thought the entire crisis could have been avoided if Murrow had sat down with Shirer long before the final blowup and had it out with him over his recent performance; if Murrow, not the advertising agency, had told Shirer that his sponsor was dropping his program; if Murrow had not let his complicated relationship with Shirer cloud his judgment as head of CBS News; if Shirer had kept his head and not tried to manipulate the situation.

But neither Murrow nor Shirer was a man to deal honestly with his emotions and feelings. Neither would reveal his insecurities and faults or confront the other about perceived shortcomings. They were proud, and they had oversized egos, and they found themselves backed farther and farther into opposite corners until the gulf became too great.

After Shirer's departure, Murrow, distraught and haunted by guilt, wanted nothing more to do with what he considered the charade of running CBS News. On July 19, 1947, less than four months after Shirer's last broadcast, Murrow resigned as vice president and returned to reporting and broadcasting. "I have no business in this job," he said. "I can't do this kind of thing to my friends."

✦

After Shirer left CBS, he did a weekly fifteen-minute news and comment program for Mutual until 1949, but he never again found a full-time job in broadcasting. In 1950 he was listed in *Red Channels*, the anti-Communist blacklisting bible of broadcasting, as a Communist sympathizer. With that he became unemployable by anyone. In his scramble to make a living, he lectured and wrote two books of nonfiction, *End of a Berlin Diary* and *Midcentury Journey*, as well as several unsuccessful novels. "Those were very lean years for us," recalled his daughter Inga Dean. "It was very wounding for him to be in that position, to see his name mentioned in 'where-are-they-now' columns: 'Whatever happened to William L. Shirer?'"

Early on in this troubled time, Shirer began work on a monumental history of Nazi Germany. In 1959 *The Rise and Fall of the Third Reich* was published by Simon and Schuster. It became a phenomenal bestseller — more than two million copies sold by the Book of the Month Club alone, the biggest seller in the club's history. *Rise and Fall* won the National Book Award, and quite suddenly money, fame, and prestige, which meant so much to Bill Shirer, were restored to him.

But nothing eased his rage. He was a lifelong collector of injustices — he once claimed that the *New York Times* ran critical reviews of several of his books because he had earlier written for the *New York Herald Tribune* — and the injustice he felt Murrow had done him was the greatest of all. He seemed almost to cherish it, tending it like a newborn baby, until the day he died.

In one of Shirer's novels, a 1954 roman à clef about CBS entitled *Stranger Come Home*, Ed Murrow, thinly disguised as television network executive Bob Fletcher, is a chief villain in the smearing and blacklisting of a courageous liberal commentator named Raymond Whitehead. Says Whitehead in the novel: "Deep down there was the uneasy feeling . . . that for reasons still beyond my grasp, this man I once loved and admired was out to destroy me — or at least to assist in my final destruction." Testifying before a McCarthy-like senator, Fletcher implies, but does not say outright, that Whitehead was a Communist, then oh-so-carefully adds, "Senator, I am not here to pass judgement. That, sir, if I may say so, is your task."

Noting Shirer's routine disclaimer that all the characters in *Stranger Come Home* were imaginary, *New York Times* book critic Charles Poore wrote dryly, "If I hadn't seen it and taken it as a statement of an honorable man, I might have got the impression that Mr. Shirer was hell-bent on skewering the living daylights out of several noted persons now seated in the vulnerable picture windows of television, public power and politics." While Shirer was tough on the Murrow stand-in, Poore thought he was even tougher on the Shirer character, portrayed "as one of those men so wrapped in splendid righteousness that they become insufferable."

21

"A Threatened
Little Band"

The year was 1948. A winter evening in the suburban town of Hawthorne, a little south and east of the Los Angeles airport in the days when the airport was in the country. A dozen or so people were sitting on folding chairs and apple crates in front of a store in the dark. Some had brought popcorn or sandwiches, and they drank coffee or hot chocolate from Thermos jugs. A couple of the older ones, whose bones ached with the dampness of southern California's chill night air, were wrapped in blankets.

They sat on the sidewalk and stared through the store's display window at the merchandise inside. The store and all the stores around it were closed and dark. The only light by which the people could see to pour their coffee and cocoa was the faint blue glow from the window they were peering into, and the warmer glow from a lone streetlight thirty yards to their right and from the marquee on the Plaza theater, half a block to their left (Forever Amber and a second feature, plus cartoons and a newsreel, admission fifty cents for adults, fourteen cents for children). They sat there for an hour, two hours, watching the merchandise in the store window.

What they were watching were television sets. The owner had left them all on, tuned to the same channel. But there were no words, no sound at all. The people on the sidewalk couldn't hear a thing. They just watched the blue pictures dance until sign-off, when they saw the American flag flapping majestically in the wind but did not hear the national anthem. Then they got up, most of them, and went home. Only two or three stayed behind to watch the test pattern.

The next night a similar group gathered, and for many nights thereafter until, in a year, two at most, nearly all the homes in Hawthorne had sets of their own and spidery antennas on their roofs.

The age of television had begun.

◆

Frank Stanton, the president of CBS, was practically on his knees at the 1948 Republican convention in Philadelphia, where Thomas E. Dewey would be chosen to run for president against Harry S. Truman.

Please, he begged Ed Murrow and Eric Sevareid, *just give Doug a few minutes at the end of the evening. All you have to do is sit in front of the camera and talk a little bit about what's going on.*

Television's a waste of our time and everyone else's.

Please.

Oh, all right, Frank, if you insist.

Murrow and Sevareid presented themselves at the appointed hour in CBS's tiny television "studio" — with white bed sheets strung up as walls — to face the hot, blinding lights and chat a bit with Douglas Edwards about what was happening at the convention. They even agreed to put on those ridiculous headsets with two protruding antennas and go down on the floor and do some reporting, even though reporting and television seemed to them a contradiction in terms.

Murrow and the Boys wanted nothing to do with television. They regarded it as inconsequential and inherently demeaning for anyone who wasn't an entertainer or pitchman, for anyone who had been a foreign correspondent and had covered a world war. Besides, there were only a million or so television sets in the entire country, while radio sets numbered in the tens of millions.

Murrow and Sevareid, together with Charles Collingwood, Dick Hottelet, Larry LeSueur, and Howard Smith, had come to the Philadelphia convention to report and deliver commentaries for radio. Their colleagues from CBS television had tagged along like distant, unloved relatives. The network's preparations for radio coverage of the convention had been as detailed as an army battle plan; the preparations for television were so haphazard that Douglas Edwards didn't even know he was to lead CBS's television coverage until he arrived in Philadelphia.

When Murrow and the Boys were pressed into occasional TV service, they made it quite clear they thought they were slumming. It was bad enough to work in Edwards's so-called studio up in the rafters, but it was just about unbearable when you went out onto the sweltering floor. You had to wear one of those headsets and carry a thirty-pound voice transmitter on your back, and in only a few minutes your summer suit was soaked through with sweat.

Portable TV cameras hadn't been invented yet. To get on the air you waved a red-tinted flashlight over your head to show your location and hoped the cameraman in the studio would spot you and zoom in with the long lens. If he didn't, you had to climb all the way up to the studio, perched so high that Doug Edwards was forced to borrow his daughter's binoculars so he could see the blackboard where the roll-call votes were tallied. The only good thing about doing television at the convention was that the studio, unlike most of the hall, was air-conditioned.

Just before midnight on that historic first day of televised convention coverage, a bored and exhausted Ed Murrow, keeping his word to Stanton, slouched in his chair before a camera and carried on a desultory conversation with Eric Sevareid and Doug Edwards. "It must be the heat," Murrow said on the air. "We've been here ten minutes and all we've said is that nothing much happened today, or, if it did, we don't know about it."

◆

No one at CBS, except Frank Stanton, took television very seriously at first, not even Bill Paley. Stanton thought the new medium would dovetail perfectly with the public's growing hunger for entertainment and with advertisers' desire for powerful new methods of reaching consumers. He tried to interest Paley, but the chairman wasn't impressed. "Bill thought TV would hurt radio," Stanton said. "He didn't see any profit. He thought we couldn't afford television, that it was too costly. . . . In fact, I couldn't even get Paley to come to the first [TV] budget meeting. I always felt he didn't want to be a party to the commitments, so that he could step back later and say, 'Hey, I didn't want to do this.' It was kind of a dicey period."

Paley's skepticism was based on business considerations, but Murrow and the Boys were worried about television's effects on the news operation. The Boys were writers before they were broadcasters, and to them radio was just another way of delivering the written word, an ethereal extension of the printing press. Television, on the other hand, was a radical departure, an altogether new medium. It was far more — or far less — than illustrated radio. On television pictures were paramount. What's more, its production costs were so high and its appeal so broad that without government subsidies, commercial considerations would always be paramount.

Radio had been heading toward greater commercialism after the war too, but the stakes were much higher in television, the imperatives stronger, the impact greater. Commercial television was almost by definition superficial. It had little memory, little sense of history, little interest in context, little time for news. In the coming decades the television networks would be home to countless serious and talented journalists, producers, directors, technicians, and researchers. But to the extent that these people accomplished something worthwhile, it was usually in spite of the priorities of commercial television, not because of them. It isn't surprising that until the advent of cable, news took a back seat; the surprising thing is that network news was as good as it often turned out to be.

In the early days television had absolutely nothing to recommend it as far as the Boys were concerned. They made far more money from their sponsored radio broadcasts than they could earn in television, and they hated TV's show-business trappings — the lights, the cameras, the makeup that smacked so much of Hollywood. "We felt it was kind of unmanly to go on TV and perform, just as it was in an earlier era somehow unmanly for newspapermen to go on radio," said Howard K. Smith. To Murrow and the others, said Don Hewitt, "radio was for adults and television was for children. . . . I sort of think they may have been right."

After the 1948 conventions, CBS decided to inaugurate a new nightly television newscast, and Stanton pressured Douglas Edwards into becoming the anchor. In the late summer of 1948, Edwards went on the air with *CBS TV News*, a fifteen-minute report shown only in New York and three other East Coast cities. The program was every bit as bad as the Boys had expected, a mossy throwback to the special-events days of radio news. It had no correspondents or camera crews of its own. The film it showed, purchased from a newsreel company, featured beauty contests, dog shows, sporting events, and ribbon cuttings. (There was no film of breaking news because of the time required to get it processed and on the air.) This *was* illustrated radio — and poor radio at that, poorly illustrated!

Scorning the Edwards show, Murrow and the Boys also looked down on Edwards himself. When Murrow inaugurated his year-end round-ups, he refused to allow Edwards to participate, because, according to Sig Mickelson, "he felt Doug was unable to perform with the Hottelets and Collingwoods of the world." The low-key, mild-mannered Edwards was considered a mediocre writer and a superficial thinker. Above all he suffered from the great disadvantage of having missed most of World War II (after begging for an overseas assignment, he was finally sent to London only months before the end of the war). "Doug was never a part of our group," said Larry LeSueur. "How could he be? Murrow, Collingwood, Sevareid, Bill Downs, myself — we shared tremendously indelible experiences. We shared in the making of history in World War II. We knew what it was like to be scared together."

Don Hewitt, Edwards's exuberant young producer, who was trying to improve the evening news program with livelier, more exciting visuals, was also patronized by the Murrow team. He was an upstart, a kid from Associated Press. He hadn't gone to Oxford, hadn't even graduated from college. When Hewitt later worked with Murrow on the groundbreaking *See It Now* documentary series, he was still treated like an outsider. "I could never really make it with that crowd. I was much too flamboyant for them, not thoughtful enough."

✦

"I wish goddamned television had never been invented," Murrow grumbled. But nothing, certainly not Murrow's grumbling, could stop it. People were buying television sets as fast as they could be built. In 1946 there were six thousand sets in the entire United States. The next year there were a hundred ninety thousand, and the year after that a million. By 1949 there were ten million and counting. And the three TV networks — CBS, NBC, and the ill-fated Dumont (ABC didn't move into TV until 1954) — seemed to be creating new entertainment programming as fast as the manufacturers were turning out sets. On June 8, 1948, *Texaco Star Theater,* starring Milton Berle, was launched, quickly followed by Ed Sullivan's *Toast of the Town, Arthur Godfrey's Talent Scouts,* and, in 1950, *Your Show of Shows,* a brilliant and sophisticated comedy-variety show with Sid Caesar and Imogene Coca.

In 1951 a nationwide coaxial cable system was completed, which made possible live telecasts from one coast to the other. The Nielsen ratings responded accordingly: that year, for the first time ever, more Americans watched television between the peak hours of 9 P.M. and midnight than listened to radio. To keep them watching, more new shows were rushed into production. *I Love Lucy,* with Lucille Ball, first appeared in 1951. Popular radio shows like *The George Burns and Gracie Allen Show, Amos 'n' Andy, Our Miss Brooks,* and *Dragnet* quickly switched to the new medium, while altogether new programs, like *Studio One,* explored its inherent dramatic possibilities.

It had all happened so *fast!* Between 1948 and 1951 the nation was transformed. The postwar letdown was over. The fifties, with their strange mixture of consumerism, conformity, and creative exuberance, had begun. Radio, in its pre-fifties guise, was dead, and no one had time even to think about giving it a decent burial.

Now even Bill Paley could see how monumentally wrong he had been, and Ed Murrow and the Boys, grumbling all the way, were forced to come to terms with television. But Murrow laid down some terms for his settlement and, in so doing, established a benchmark of excellence by which TV news would be judged from then on.

✦

"This is an old team trying to learn a new trade," Murrow said into the camera on November 18, 1951, squinting through his own cigarette smoke, as he began the first broadcast of *See It Now*, the first — and still the most provocative — documentary series in television history. "My purpose," he continued, "will be not to get in your light any more than I can, to lean over the cameraman's shoulder occasionally and say a word which may help illuminate and explain what is happening." The syntax was a little confused (perhaps a reflection of his nervousness on television), but the message came through: as far as Murrow was concerned, the word would still be there to "illuminate and explain."

At the beginning of that program, there was some coaxial razzle-dazzle — the Brooklyn Bridge and the Golden Gate Bridge were seen live on the same broadcast, pretty heady stuff in those technologically primitive days. But then Murrow, sitting in the control room of the studio, got down to serious business. He switched to a report from Eric Sevareid in Washington on Korean War casualties. From London, Howard Smith described the latest nuclear disarmament proposals. There had been a brief "peace scare," Smith said, "but now everything is back to normal [and] mutual ill will is entirely unimpaired." From Korea, Bob Pierpoint introduced viewers to the men of Fox Company — in the chow line, playing craps, reading, shaving, singing, and, finally, on patrol across no-man's-land.

Done in a "magazine" format familiar now to television viewers but new at the time, the first *See It Now* put everyone on notice that the series would not dabble in the mindless trivia of what then passed for television news. *See It Now* was designed primarily to examine important events, using words and imaginative camera techniques to provide depth and insight, with occasional light pieces as diversions. "Television was never the same after the first *See It Now*," said Hewitt, who directed the premier episode and who, a couple of decades later, borrowed bits and pieces of the format to create *60 Minutes*. "Ed Murrow made television respectable. All the big names in radio, Sevareid and Howard Smith and Collingwood, could stop looking down their noses at it."

As novel as the program was for television, viewers who had listened to Murrow and the Boys during the war could recognize its primary concept: focus on the "little picture," explore major events and social issues by telling their stories in human terms. In one historic broadcast, *See It Now* took Americans to Korea in the winter of 1952 and for one hour showed them the human face of war. In snow, rain, and sleet the camera crews and correspondents — Bill Downs, Larry LeSueur, Bob Pierpoint, Lou Cioffi, and Ed Murrow — traipsed up and down wind-swept slopes, interviewing troops and filming them in action. They talked to nurses at a MASH unit, flew in C-47s as they dropped propaganda leaflets over North Korea, and went aboard a hospital ship to talk with the wounded men. Standing in the rubble of a bombed-out, shelled-out village, Bill Downs, who had seen enough of this sort of thing to last a lifetime, spoke as the camera followed an old man and a little girl walking hand in hand down a pulverized street. "This," he said, "is the side of the war we don't see very much of, but probably it's the most important part of all."

The program did not require battalions of producers and writers and assistants. Only the camera and sound crews, plus Murrow, two of his favorite Boys, and the two younger war correspondents. Murrow served as both reporter and field producer, making the assignments for the correspondents and their crews. It was almost like the old days in London, Murrow casually suggesting some stories, inviting suggestions for others. "Every morning we'd sit around a table and plan the day," said Pierpoint. "Murrow would say, 'Okay, Bob, why don't you go over to the air force and do something with the pilots over there? I'll go up to one of the infantry units. Bill, what do you want to do?' It wasn't producers who decided what we should do, it was Ed and the four of us. I think he really felt that the core of this show should be the reporter."

But even on *See It Now* that kind of independence and freedom for the correspondents was rare and would soon vanish altogether. Murrow's producer and partner, the titanic Fred Friendly, would see to that.

◆

A New York native, Friendly was a six-foot-four, two-hundred-pound volcano of a man known for his roisterous enthusiasms and violent temper tantrums. "He explodes with a hundred ideas, of which ten might be good," Charles Collingwood once said. Friendly, who had never been a journalist, first collaborated with Murrow in 1947, producing the record album *I Can Hear It Now*, a compilation of historic speeches with narration by Murrow. A major success, the album spawned several sequels, and led to a weekly radio documentary program called *Hear It Now*, produced by Friendly and anchored by Murrow. With the advent of television, *See It Now* was an obvious next step.

Passionate, abrasive, and domineering, Friendly was the engine that drove *See It Now*. He oversaw the correspondents and the cameramen, writers, and editors, while Murrow focused on the stories. The arrangement didn't suit the correspondents at all. Long accustomed to dealing directly with Murrow, they now found in their way a man who, unlike other CBS executives, didn't hesitate to order them about.

Furious at what he considered Friendly's mutilation of a story he had done for *See It Now*, David Schoenbrun let off steam to Murrow:

> In a decade of work together I never had any such trouble with you on radio. I sent you my cables with confidence in the way you would use them and with pride in the fact that you were using them. Why then do I not have the same confidence and pride in *SIN*? Because we are now working not directly with each other but through intermediaries who do not share our standards, who are producers and technicians but not reporters.

Television's peculiar demands were not entirely new to the CBS correspondents. As early as 1949, New York sent each of them a movie camera and casually instructed them, *Oh, by the way, please learn to operate this thing so you can film your stories for TV, too.* Howard Smith, among others, told them what they could do with their camera. "I frankly think it is about the goddamdest idea I ever heard of," he wrote to Murrow. ". . . [It's] about as absurd as asking a surgeon to fill a few of his victim's teeth after an appendectomy — medicine and dentistry being about the same thing."

By the early 1950s the correspondents were besieged with requests to do stories for both the regular television newscasts and *See It Now* — on top of their continuing work for radio. At one point Smith registered a strong protest with Murrow. He had too many masters. He was fed up with the infighting and the lack of coordination. Everything he and the other Boys loved about working for Murrow and CBS was changing. "Where once we worked for one boss and one organization, we now work for three bosses and three organizations. I am forced to tell you that none of your three units shows much appreciation of the fact that we are equally obligated to the other two.... There is a constant tug-of-war. We live in an atmosphere of constant frictions."

The correspondents preferred to work for the prestigious and consequential *See It Now* rather than for daily television. But they were accustomed to having Murrow always on their side, and now they found he was developing a new set of loyalties and sometimes seemed chummier with the *See It Now* crew than with his old buddies from the war. In fact, Murrow was never as close to Friendly and the others at *See It Now* as he was to the Boys. Yet he was less willing than he had been to go to bat for them, let alone for the other correspondents. "All Murrow cared about then was *See It Now*," complained Larry LeSueur. After a meeting in which Murrow suggested that henceforth cameramen and correspondents would be considered equals, Smith said to Schoenbrun, "David, I think we're through."

The introduction of cameramen and producers and expensive technology clearly undermined the very things that had made Murrow and the Boys so special before and during the war: their individualism; their sense of themselves as an elite unit; their morale-boosting dislike of, and sometimes contempt for, the bastards in New York; their belief that the reporter, and the reporter alone, was the best judge of what was a good story and of how a story should be covered. In radio, as Schoenbrun put it, "you threw a switch and you spoke." But television, like motion pictures, could only be produced effectively by a team working closely together *as* a team.

The more television news sought to explore its technological possibilities, the more oppressive the Boys found the process. In June 1952 Smith was assigned to do a report for *See It Now* on America's continental air-defense system. As he flew from England to New York aboard an air force B-29, he crouched against a bulkhead and took a few notes, utterly ignored by his busy crew of cameramen and soundmen. The following Sunday, in his regular radio commentary, Smith explained that he hadn't had time to prepare an analysis of the week's news, because of the *See It Now* assignment. "I have been far too occupied," he continued ". . . satisfying the requirements of up-to-date, streamlined, jet-propelled, electronically operated, plastic-insulated, modern journalism." The least important piece of equipment, he said, "was the reporter."

The Boys thought they were upholding the best traditions of journalism, but some of the TV executives saw them simply as Luddites. John Sharnik, one of CBS's most talented producers, wanted them to look at television not as words illustrated by pictures but as "a totally third medium, neither word nor picture, but a kind of life form in which both words and images function." It didn't work. "They resented being obliged to constrict their style," Sharnik said. "None of them ever really adapted, ever really made any concessions."

Collingwood and Schoenbrun were considered the best of the group on television. Collingwood was especially good. He occasionally filled in for Douglas Edwards on the evening news and also became host of the 1950s science series *Adventure*, which in its first year won a number of prizes, including the Peabody Award. In a story on the series, *Time* described Collingwood as the "suave guide who has wrestled with a 10-ft. alligator, struggled with an 18-ft. anaconda, plunged into the Atlantic in January, and urbanely commented on undersea matters through a diver's helmet 30 ft. below the surface of the Pacific." But even Collingwood and Schoenbrun resisted the encroachment of television. Once while Schoenbrun was recording the narration of a television documentary about Charles de Gaulle, Sharnik interrupted him from the control room. "David," he said, "the script is just too damn long! You're running a half a minute behind the picture. You've got to cut it." Schoenbrun looked up. "Slow down the goddamn film!" he barked.

Most members of the Murrow team "had no idea of the business we were in," said Sharnik. "There was this idea, 'We will not be demeaned by this medium. We will not be overpowered by the camera or by producers who are masters of the camera.' They saw themselves as a threatened little band. After a while they realized that other people had gotten a foothold in a medium that they thought would never work anyway, and had gotten some of the choice spots. That made them all the more resentful, because now they were subservient to guys that they really felt they were better than — and whom they *were* better than."

✦

In the early fifties, however, the correspondents focused their resentment on one particular bête noire — Fred Friendly. Proud and intensely protective of his partnership with Murrow on *See It Now*, Friendly seemed to want to break up the old Boy network. He placed on the desk in his office a plaque bearing the famous line from *Henry V* — "We few, we happy few, we band of brothers" — which had already been used a number of times in reference to Murrow and the Boys during the war.

But Friendly was trying to expropriate it for Murrow and *himself* and, by extension, for key members of the New York–based *See It Now* crew.

There is no question that Friendly played an important, even crucial, role in helping Murrow develop his postwar career. Friendly's contributions to television news and journalism in general were monumental. His vision was an inspiration to many who followed him into the darker recesses of the network news jungle. But, consciously or not, he seemed to see the Boys as threats that had to be neutralized if his own oversized ambitions were to be fulfilled. He became possessive of Murrow and Murrow's reputation in a way that admitted few others — and none of the Boys.

The idea developed that even Murrow may have begun thinking of the Boys as threatening, that he wanted to keep them in their place. After the premiere of *See It Now*, one of its reporter/producers, Joseph Wershba, asked a CBS colleague for her reaction. "Wasn't Murrow great?" "Yes," she replied, "but I *loved* Eric Sevareid. What sex appeal!" Later, when Murrow heard of her remark from Wershba, he said, "Well, we'll just keep him the hell off the show." He laughed as he said it, but the thought behind the quip was no joke: Murrow wasn't going to tolerate competition from the Boys on *his* program.

During the first six weeks of *See It Now*, Friendly decreed that only Murrow would interview people for the program. But *See It Now* covered the world, and there was simply no way that Murrow could conduct every interview himself. So Friendly worked out a little subterfuge. He instructed the correspondents that when Murrow couldn't be present, interviewees were to respond as if he *were* there by working his name into their answers. Skillful film editing would take care of the rest. Howard Smith found this process "ignominious." "Friendly just wanted to spotlight Murrow," Smith said. ". . . And I'm afraid Murrow accepted that. It got on all our nerves." Eventually the practice was dropped, but the resentment lingered.

In 1993, long after Murrow's death, Friendly insisted he didn't know who the Murrow Boys were or even what the term meant — and whatever it meant, it was a myth. The only *real* special relationship, he suggested, had been between Murrow and *himself.* It may actually have seemed that way to him. Friendly wasn't around CBS during the war years, and as Murrow became a bigger and bigger television star, his relationship with Friendly intensified at the expense of his relationship with the correspondents. For his part, Friendly used Murrow's name to boost his own career and reputation. On this issue, as on many others,

Schoenbrun was the most outspoken and colorful. Friendly, he said, "was building his own empire inside CBS News, riding as the tail to Murrow's high-flying kite. At the same time, he was challenging the power and the bonds of the brotherhood of the Murrow Boys."

As television took over and the network grew, Murrow ignored the tension between the Boys and Friendly. He would not resolve disputes or exert leadership. He may have felt he needed Friendly, needed his energy and ruthlessness, his creativity, his ideas. "Friendly eventually dominated and twisted Murrow," Schoenbrun wrote. "Fred began almost as Charlie McCarthy sitting on Edgar Bergen's lap, and ended with Ed as Charlie McCarthy sitting on Fred's lap." Smith thought Murrow was simply loath to choose among colleagues. "With people he respected working together," Smith said, "he didn't want to tell one, 'You're in charge, the others will obey you.' He did not like friction among those whom he considered part of his club. . . . He simply backed away from hard decisions that might offend one or another of us."

Murrow was unwilling or unable to confront the issue of Friendly versus the Boys, unwilling or unable to talk it out, to *act*. It was one thing to admit, as he frequently did, that he wasn't cut out to be an executive and another thing simply to abdicate responsibility in favor of Friendly. "By not choosing and not putting his hands on the reins, Murrow let us pull in different directions," Schoenbrun said.

◆

If Murrow and Friendly and *See It Now* were the pampered darlings of CBS News, the television news department, run by Sig Mickelson, was the network's neglected stepchild. When Mickelson became head of the thirteen-person TV news staff in 1951, he assumed, not illogically, that his portfolio would include the much larger *See It Now* outfit. Paley and Stanton quickly let him know how wrong he was. There would be two TV news operations: Mickelson's and *See It Now*, run by Murrow and Friendly, who were answerable only to Paley. While Mickelson's people were scattered in small, dingy offices and studios all over town, *See It Now* staffers were ensconced in their own area behind a frosted plate-glass door bearing the initials "S.I.N." on the seventeenth floor of CBS headquarters. "We were a law unto ourselves," said Palmer Williams, one of the producers. "We didn't share any of the same space, we didn't have anything to do with anything or anyone else."

Murrow flaunted his show's special status and prestige and was unapologetic that it was a consistent money loser. Where costs were concerned, he told a *New Yorker* writer, he had thrown down the gauntlet when the series began: "If I wanted more than one camera crew, I'd damn well get more than one camera crew. They come to me now, the vice presidents, and say, 'Look, there's so much going out of this spout and only so much coming in.' And I say, 'If that's the way you want to do it, you'd better get yourselves another boy.'" Declared *The New Yorker*: "Murrow has achieved a position at CBS that is outside, and basically antithetical to, the corporate structure of authority. . . . In doing so, he has achieved a singular amount of freedom from authority of any kind."

✦

In 1952 Sig Mickelson, swallowing his wounded pride at repeated snubs from Murrow, asked him to consider anchoring the political conventions that year. Doug Edwards had done yeoman service at the 1948 conventions and had been anchoring the network's nightly newscasts for the four years since. But Mickelson didn't consider Edwards a star, and this time much more was riding on the conventions. The coaxial cable now stretched coast to coast, linking dozens of stations around the country to the network's live broadcasts. More than a third of all American households owned at least one television set. CBS would be on very public display at these conventions, and Mickelson wanted a dominant figure as its voice.

Murrow said no to the anchor job, as did Sevareid when it was offered to him. In Sevareid's case, it was probably just as well. He didn't stammer and stumble and gulp as often as he used to, but he still had moments of panic and hysteria on both radio and television, moments that became the stuff of legend among his CBS colleagues. On occasion he'd get so nervous his skin would erupt in hives and welts and he'd have to wear white gloves to cover the rashes on his hands. "A lot of people start blooming when that little [camera] light goes on," he said once. "I start to die."

The one Boy who probably would have been happy to anchor, and who by all accounts was best suited for television in the first place, was not at CBS at the time. Charles Collingwood had taken a leave of absence to serve as special assistant to an old wartime friend, Averell Harriman, then director of the Mutual Security Administration in Washington. So Mickelson settled instead on someone who was not a member of Murrow's team at all, was not even a correspondent.

He chose Walter Cronkite.

Actually, if Murrow had had his way earlier, Cronkite would have been one of the Boys. In 1943, when Cronkite was still with United Press, Murrow asked him to join his glamorous band and go to Moscow to replace Bill Downs. Dazzled by the offer and the promise of $125 a week, Cronkite accepted. But the UP bureau chief, Harrison Salisbury, offered to raise his $67-a-week salary to $92. For a skinflint outfit like UP, this was an amazing amount of money, and Cronkite began to have second thoughts. He loved the wire service, loved tearing around after stories, loved the adrenaline rush of beating the competition. So he called Murrow and, with appropriate apologies, told him he had changed his mind.

Murrow couldn't believe it. How could Cronkite prefer the formulaic writing and anonymous existence of a UP reporter to life as a CBS correspondent? As Cronkite himself testified, Murrow promptly wrote him off for missing such an opportunity. It wasn't until 1946 that Cronkite finally decided to leave UP. First he became Washington correspondent for a string of ten radio stations in the Midwest. Then in 1950 CBS hired him to go to Korea. Before he could leave, however, he was pressed into temporary service by WTOP, the CBS affiliate in Washington. Every night on WTOP-TV, he reported the latest developments from Korea, using maps and a blackboard to illustrate his points (as he would later do on CBS for the Vietnam War).

Cronkite was no matinee idol — he was dumpy and wore a rather prissy mustache — but something about his personality worked on television. He grabbed your attention and held it, and something remained in your memory so that the next time you saw him, you felt that you knew him, and, more important, that he knew you. He was so good in front of the camera, so relaxed and natural, that WTOP asked him to take over the entire broadcast. Soon he was also doing war reports for Douglas Edwards's evening news program. At a time when Murrow and the Boys were still deluding themselves that they and radio would always lead the pack, Walter Cronkite was coming up fast on the outside.

Mickelson's selection of Cronkite as TV anchorman for the 1952 Republican convention in Chicago was a fateful decision. Cronkite took to the anchor's desk as if he had been born behind it. He was an instant hit at the GOP convention, and again a month later at the Democratic convention. Thanks to him, CBS scored major victories over its competitors, and television news as a whole began to acquire some muscle.

Murrow and several of the Boys, notably Sevareid and Collingwood, treated Cronkite with the same condescension they had shown Doug

Edwards. But now their aloofness had a defensive quality to it. It represented a kind of circling of the wagons against the new breed of news people, from producers to anchormen, who were making the transition to TV with such ease. Cronkite claimed to understand why he was not accepted by them — "they were the cream of the crop," he magnanimously said. But in truth he deeply resented their attitude.

He and Murrow had an especially strained relationship, which occasionally flared into open hostility. Once, at a dinner party hosted by Bill and Roz Downs, Murrow and Cronkite spent the evening snapping at each other. "They were practically chin to chin," said Roz Downs. "It was dreadful." Late in the party, after considerable drinking, the two men took down a pair of antique dueling pistols from over the Downses' fireplace and pretended to fire them at each other. "I think they're serious," Roz Downs whispered to her husband. After the party he told her, "That was a small disaster. I didn't know they disliked each other so much."

◆

By 1954 even the Boys most resistant to television had to acknowledge that it had totally eclipsed radio as the dominant broadcast news medium. The foreign correspondents among them tacitly admitted their defeat in a meeting with Frank Stanton in Paris that August.

Before the meeting CBS had revealed that a temporary split between the radio and television news operations that had been arranged in 1951 would now be made permanent. The correspondents stationed abroad would continue working for radio; *new* correspondents would be assigned to the CBS bureaus to handle assignments for television. Stanton was in Paris to get the correspondents' reaction to the plan.

The reaction was unanimous and clear: the split was a *terrible* idea. The night before the meeting, Howard Smith, Dick Hottelet, David Schoenbrun, Bill Downs (now assigned to the Rome bureau) and Tokyo correspondent Bob Pierpoint met in Schoenbrun's apartment to plan their strategy. They would tell Stanton that separate bureaus and correspondents would be inefficient and expensive and that both operations would be damaged by the inevitable internecine competition. Of course those weren't the real reasons for their opposition. Rather, they had come to the realization that radio, for their purposes, was dead, that the future belonged to television.

To the correspondents' surprise and satisfaction, Stanton readily canceled the plan. He had won what he probably wanted all along —

the Boys' agreement to move wholeheartedly into TV news. On August 16, 1954, CBS announced that the radio and TV news operations would be merged into a single corporate division. The head of that division, with the rank of vice president, was television news chief Sig Mickelson. His staff, which had consisted of 13 people four years earlier, now numbered 376.

The freewheeling Murrow era was almost over.

22

"The Communist Broadcasting System"

Wᴵᴸᴸᴵᴀᴍ s. ᴘᴀʟᴇʏ was many things. Stupid wasn't one of them. As television revenue poured in and profit margins grew in the early 1950s, he easily abandoned his early antagonism to the new medium. By 1954, thanks primarily to television, CBS had become the largest carrier of commercial advertising in the world. Now Paley was antagonistic to anything that got in the way of the phenomenal and tantalizing new opportunities presented by television.

Controversy, however, kept interfering. Beneath the prosperity and the *Happy Days* conformity of the fifties, beneath the raucous innocence of early Elvis and the tired romanticism of late Bing, beneath the college pranks and the mindless crazes, there was fearful stress in the country. Expressions of it could be seen in films, plays, novels and, above all, in politics.

The demagogues of the Red Scare were in full cry. Congress was conducting manifold investigations of Communists in Hollywood, in labor unions, and in government. Senator Joseph R. McCarthy, having been elected to a second term in 1952 and awarded the chairmanship of the Government Operations Committee's permanent investigations subcommittee, proceeded to make Reds in the executive branch his specialty. McCarthy had announced in 1950 that he had a list (a phantom list, as it turned out) of State Department "known Communists"; now he charged that Presidents Roosevelt and Truman had presided over "twenty years of treason," and he launched a series of public hearings aimed at ferreting out the guilty parties.

During this period all Bill Paley wanted to do was make *friends* — friends for himself and CBS, friends in government, on Wall Street, on Madison Avenue, friends, above all, among America's advertisers. It wasn't easy. CBS, with its core of mostly liberal journalists and writers, had come to be known in certain perfervid right-wing circles as the "Red Network" and the "Communist Broadcasting System." In June 1949 an internal FBI memorandum on "Communist infiltration of [CBS]" had been sent to Director J. Edgar Hoover himself, outlining "derogatory subversive" information (much of it secondhand gossip) on network employees. Another bureau memo, dated April 4, 1950, dealt with "Edward Roscoe Murrow, CBS News Analyst" and a "group . . . believed to be communistically inclined or fellow travelers" that worked with Murrow at CBS. That same year the booklet *Red Channels* accused 151 prominent entertainers and broadcast journalists — including Howard K. Smith and Alexander Kendrick — of being Communists or Communist sympathizers.

Among their sins, Smith and Kendrick had suggested that the 1948 murder of CBS correspondent George Polk was the work of the Greek government, which was backed by the United States. It was hardly an illogical position. Polk, who had covered the Greek civil war, was an outspoken critic of the corrupt Athens regime. His body had been found floating in Salonika harbor, hands and feet bound, a single bullet hole in the head. An official Greek investigation, and a CBS investigation by Winston Burdett, concluded that unknown Communist guerrillas, aided by an obscure Greek journalist named Gregory Staktopoulos, were responsible. Staktopoulos, after weeks of physical and mental torture, confessed and was given a life sentence. (The only person ever punished for the murder, he was pardoned thirteen years later after protesting his innocence.) Smith, Kendrick, Sevareid, Murrow, and others were sure there had been a cover-up, but the case was closed — an early indication of how rough the "Cold" War could be.

✦

In mid-December 1950, amid growing anti-Communist hysteria, CBS decided on a policy adopted by none of its competitors: all employees were required to fill out a short questionnaire — it was quickly and somewhat inaccurately dubbed a "loyalty oath" — indicating whether they were then or had ever been members of the Communist Party, or a communist front organization, or any other subversive or revolutionary group, communist or fascist. The attorney general's list of such organizations was attached as a guide. The questionnaire was a flagrant violation of the employees' civil and constitutional rights — all the more so since membership in the Communist Party was legal.

Outraged, most of the Murrow Boys refused at first even to consider filling it out — refused, that is, until they discovered something as shocking to them as the document itself: CBS vice president Joseph Ream had shown it to Murrow before he sent it out to other employees, and Edward R. Murrow had not so much as registered an objection! It was a staggering disappointment. Something seemed to have happened to Murrow. He had lost a few fights of his own recently, and now his courage seemed to be gone. Just as Joe McCarthy was taking center ring in the witch-hunting circus, just as CBS was launching a witch-hunt of its own, the man whom the Boys had always relied on to be their champion seemed listless, unsure, burned out. He was forty-three years old, but these days he looked older by at least a decade.

His health was one explanation. At the beginning of the fifties, Murrow's ferocious living and working habits began to catch up with him. He experienced shortness of breath, fatigue, terrible coughing bouts, cold sweats, sleeplessness. Yet he was still chain-smoking cigarettes, drinking heavily, and maintaining his grueling schedule.

Another part of the explanation is that Murrow was now an even more adept player of the corporate game than he had been before. He knew when to fight and when not to, knew whom to anger and whom not to. He considered McCarthyism a scourge, but he seems to have sensed that he did not have the clout to move Paley on the "loyalty oath" question, just as he had been unable to move him during the final act of the Shirer drama. And this time Murrow wasn't even going to try.

His friends could not change his mind. Michael Bessie and Bessie's father-in-law, Morris Ernst, a prominent civil rights lawyer, spent most of one night arguing with Murrow that he should refuse to fill out and sign the questionnaire himself. CBS had no right to ask these questions of its employees, Bessie and Ernst insisted; if Murrow, with his stature, didn't fight, then no one else could or would. Murrow said he didn't really understand what all the fuss was about. This thing didn't really *mean* anything. He had to pick his fights carefully. Bessie thought he had been "beaten down on the subject, that he had been persuaded to go along."

Nor did Murrow change his mind when the correspondents came or wrote to him for advice and counsel. He heard directly from Sevareid, Smith, Collingwood, Downs, LeSueur, Schoenbrun, and Kendrick. To each his advice was the same: "Sign." To Downs, Murrow declared, "You have no choice. If you don't want to sign the oath, there is no way I can protect you." To Schoenbrun: "If you don't sign it, suspicion will hover over you. I'm signing. Do you have more integrity than I do, David?"

No one could understand it. But, angry, sad, and disappointed, they all did as Ed Murrow said. They all signed. Schoenbrun did not think he had more integrity than Murrow. And Eric Sevareid, who continued his own fight against McCarthyism on the air and who loved Ed Murrow like the most devoted of sons, said he accepted his leader's decision. Then he apologized for him: "Nobody, including Murrow, can spend every day of his life slaying dragons."

Paley, Stanton, and Ream still weren't content. In 1951, again with no hint of a protest from Murrow, they adopted a new screening procedure intended to root out employees with suspected Communist leanings and brought in an outsider to administer it. In effect they hired their very own witch-hunter — Daniel O'Shea, a lawyer and former assistant to movie producer David O. Selznick. O'Shea's new title was vice president for security. Within CBS he became known as "the vice president in charge of treason."

O'Shea worked closely with the FBI and certain congressional committees in deciding who could and could not work for CBS. His decisions led to the firing of people against whom the only evidence was rumor and innuendo. Actors, directors, and writers considered too far left were barred from working on CBS's entertainment programs. Even guests on talk shows had to be approved in advance. "CBS and blacklisting became synonymous," said one report.

CBS's hard line emboldened sponsors to adopt strong measures of their own, as Perry Wolff, producer of Charles Collingwood's science show, *Adventure*, soon discovered. After getting word that the most famous scientist in the world, Albert Einstein, was willing to appear on the program, a jubilant Wolff announced the news to the president of New York's American Museum of Natural History, which sponsored *Adventure*. "I won't have that commie on my show," the museum president declared. Wolff was stunned. "It was a very scary time," he said later.

Journalists all too often added to the fear. They would dutifully report McCarthy's reckless charges about "Communists" in the State Department, for example, with little or no analysis or background checking of their own. In the senator's long hit-and-run campaign, he failed to produce persuasive evidence against even one of the people he attacked. Yet each new accusation was reported as if there were no question of McCarthy's credibility, as if his lengthening record of irresponsibility were irrelevant. Many journalists said their job was to report what important people did and said. Let others decide whether what those people did was good or bad, whether what they said was true or false. McCarthy was news, and they were "objectively" reporting the news.

◆

Eric Sevareid, never a fan of bloodless, lifeless, truthless "objectivity," had battled Paul White on the issue in 1941. He renewed the fight with even more vigor now. In a speech at the University of Minnesota, he said: "Our rigid formulae of so-called objectivity . . . have given the lie the same prominence and impact that truth is given. They have elevated the influence of fools to that of wise men. . . . We cannot go on witlessly, helplessly aiding in the destruction of men we know to be honorable."

At the same time Sevareid understood that reporters weren't the real problem. When even Murrow was afraid to fight CBS, Sevareid publicly hinted that the major portion of the blame belonged at the well-shod feet of executives like Bill Paley (although Sevareid didn't mention Paley by name). "I have been impressed," he said in the same speech, "with how timid a million dollars' profit can make a publisher or radio executive, instead of how bold it makes him."

Sevareid was one of a small, resolute group of journalists who from the beginning rarely, if ever, faltered in the impossible task of trying to keep McCarthy and his ilk honest.* In July 1952 he blasted the Republican National Committee for inviting McCarthy to speak to the convention that year:

> The delegates will be listening, remember, to a man who was found by the Wisconsin Supreme Court to have violated his oath as a judge, who was accused of moral turpitude by his state bar commissioners, who took ten thousand dollars from a construction firm, while dealing with legislation concerning that firm, who is now under Senate investigation on a formal charge of unfitness for office, who won the collective vote of Washington correspondents as the worst senator in the chamber. . . . The political party which often denounces "isms" in social thinking will listen to the one American in this generation who

*Others among the crusading journalists were Sevareid's old college friend Philip Potter of the *Baltimore Sun;* Martin Agronsky, formerly of NBC, and Elmer Davis, formerly of CBS, now of ABC; Homer Bigart of the *New York Herald Tribune;* and Murray Marder and Alfred Friendly of the *Washington Post.*

has achieved a unique place in history by having an "ism" named after *him*.

Perhaps Sevareid's most effective thrust against McCarthy came when he exchanged his bludgeon for a rapier, poking sly ridicule at the senator in one broadcast by comparing him to the blundering protagonist of a children's classic:

It's funny how fairy-tale creatures will suddenly resemble living persons. You take the third chapter of *Winnie the Pooh*, where Senator McCarthy, I mean Pooh, and Senator [Bourke] Hickenlooper [another Red hunter], I mean Piglet, go hunting and nearly catch a Woozle. There's Pooh walking in a circle when Piglet says, "What are you doing?"

"Tracking something," says Winnie the Pooh very mysteriously.

"Tracking what?"

"That's just what I ask myself. I ask myself, 'what?'"

"What do you think you'll answer?"

"I shall have to wait until I catch up with it," said Pooh. "Now what do you see there?"

"Tracks," said Piglet. "Paw marks. Oh, Pooh, do you think it's a . . . a . . . Woozle?"

"It may be," said Pooh. "You never can tell with paw marks. But there seem to be two animals now. Would you mind coming with me, Piglet, in case they turn out to be hostile animals?"

Piglet said he didn't have anything to do till Friday, so off they went together, round and round the spinney of larch trees. . . . Pooh sat down and thought in the most thoughtful way he could think. Then he fitted his paw into one of the tracks.

"Yes," said Pooh.

"I see now," said Pooh. "I have been foolish and deluded."

McCarthyites retaliated by labeling Sevareid "Eric the Red." He was attacked often, and by name, on the floor of the House and Senate. His office phone was tapped (by the FBI, he was convinced); he and his family were hounded by threatening and abusive phone calls. Hundreds of critical letters poured in to CBS and his sponsors. "Everyone knows you are a damn communist yourself," wrote one listener. "You are not fooling many thinking people."

In March 1950 Metropolitan Life Insurance canceled its four-year sponsorship of Sevareid's nightly radio broadcast, which only the year before had won a Peabody. The cancellation, which cost Sevareid his $1,200 weekly fee, came a few months after CBS news director Davidson Taylor had warned him that Metropolitan was getting nervous about all the negative mail. After Sevareid was moved to an unsponsored 11 P.M. slot and replaced on his old 6 P.M. program by Allan Jackson (a newscaster who could be relied upon not to make many waves), Metropolitan resumed its sponsorship.

Unlike Bill Shirer three years earlier, Sevareid took his medicine quietly and planned for a better day. Not long afterward his circumspection seemed to have been rewarded. He was made anchor of a fifteen-minute Sunday afternoon radio program of news and commentary, sponsored by Chamberlain Lotion. But by April 1951 he had lost the Chamberlain program, too. The reason was never made clear; CBS simply announced he was leaving the program, and once again he didn't complain.

Meanwhile, Sevareid was fearful that the McCarthyites would discover a "ticking time bomb" in his background that had not yet been discovered. The "bomb" lay somewhere in the State Department's archives in the form of the confidential report he had written after his trip to China in 1943 on the corruption and incompetence of the Chiang regime. His criticisms were similar to those of John Stewart Service and the other young China experts in the State Department, whose careers had been destroyed by witch-hunters who blamed them for China's turning Communist.

As Sevareid drove home from work each night, he would rehearse in his mind what his answers would be if he were called before some committee to answer for his report. No subpoena ever arrived, and as far as anyone knows, the Sevareid report was never found. But in 1955 the State Department mysteriously refused to renew his passport unless he signed an affidavit swearing he had never been a Communist or a member of a Communist front. Sevareid protested to no avail. He finally submitted the affidavit and received his passport.

✦

By the fall of 1953 Ed Murrow had at last begun to emerge from his lassitude about McCarthy — albeit only on radio, which wasn't good enough for many of his friends. When were Murrow and Friendly going to fire their really big gun at the senator? When were they going to use *See It Now*? Bill Downs, known at CBS as "Murrow's conscience," was particularly persistent. Every time he'd see Murrow, he would say, "You're not tackling the real story," and Murrow would reply, "We're working on it. It's not time yet. Fred says, 'Wait.'" Friendly told the story differently nearly forty years later, putting the onus for the delay on Murrow. "I think Murrow felt we had to be careful that we weren't too far ahead of public opinion," Friendly said.

Whoever was responsible, *See It Now* did very little on McCarthyism and blacklisting until October 20, 1953. That night Murrow narrated a major piece on air force lieutenant Milo Radulovich, who had been ordered to resign his commission because his father and sister were supposedly of dubious loyalty. Murrow, contradicting Euripides, said the sins of the father should not be visited on the sons, and he showed Radulovich to be a modest, polite, and evidently loyal young man. In the uproar that followed, the air force reversed itself, and Radulovich remained a lieutenant.

Five months later Murrow and Friendly were finally ready. On March 9, 1954, they confronted McCarthy in a special edition of *See It Now*. It was perhaps the most powerful documentary in the history of television. Murrow devoted the entire program to a skillful indictment of the senator, relying mainly on film footage of his speeches and his chairmanship of committee hearings. The film revealed a sneering, sniggering, browbeating bully. But Murrow concluded by insisting that the bully was successful only because he had help from the American people. Quoting from Shakespeare's *Julius Caesar*, he said, "The fault, dear Brutus, is not in our stars / But in ourselves."

The program was electrifying. Not "balanced" in the accepted sense of the word, it tested the outer limits of advocacy journalism on commercial television. McCarthy wasn't interviewed, and there was no attempt to present the "other side." (When McCarthy was allowed to reply on a later broadcast, he sounded quite deranged.) Murrow had agonized for weeks beforehand about whether he was right to mount such a one-sided assault. He finally went ahead because he had come to believe about McCarthy, as he had about Hitler, that when a journalist was confronted with unmitigated evil, there was no "other side" to present.

The problem, of course, is that one man's evil can be another man's beacon of righteousness. The CBS brass didn't try to deter Murrow and Friendly. They merely cordoned themselves off from the entire production process. Paley was infamous for not committing himself on anything potentially controversial until he had caught the wind. If Murrow and Friendly fell on their faces when they took on McCarthy, or if the public seemed in a mood to lynch someone afterward, Paley, Stanton, and the others could claim innocence. Network executives had not even been willing to review the film clips of McCarthy prior to the broadcast, and Murrow and Friendly had to pay out of their own pockets to advertise the program in the *New York Times*.

"I'm with you today, and I'll be with you tomorrow," Paley told Murrow before he went on the air. He lied. No sooner had Murrow signed off with his usual "Good night and good luck" than Paley began putting distance between himself and the man who had conferred respectability and prestige on his network. "Paley was proud of the McCarthy broadcast," said Friendly, "but he was determined it wouldn't happen again."

Murrow and *See It Now* did not topple McCarthy. The senator was already losing his grip on the country by the time they went after him. Murrow's program did, however, give him an extra and significant shove. By the end of the year McCarthy would be in disgrace, censured by the U.S. Senate. Murrow, in contrast, became the object of a national outpouring of praise and gratitude. He may not have caused McCarthy's downfall, but the broadcast was so good, its dissection of McCarthy so masterful, that it almost seemed as if he had. A day or so after the broadcast, as Sevareid was driving Murrow from New York to Washington in his canary-yellow roadster, people pulled alongside and saluted Murrow. A policeman shouted, "Attaboy, Ed." When they walked into a restaurant on the New Jersey Turnpike, its patrons stood and applauded.

But amid all the hurrahs, there were a few notes of disapproval or disappointment that it had taken so *long* for Murrow to act. Dorothy Schiff, publisher of the old, liberal *New York Post*, one of the first papers to attack McCarthy, wrote in an editorial after the Murrow broadcast, "'This is no time for men who oppose Sen. McCarthy's methods to keep silent,' said Ed as he leaped gracefully aboard the crowded band-wagon." Bill Downs, who had been transferred to Rome in 1953, showed the broadcast to Americans in Rome, who responded with standing ovations. Downs's own reaction was rather more caustic. "About time!" he thought.

An otherwise approving Eric Sevareid, who had been outspokenly critical of witch-hunting since 1947 and of McCarthy himself since 1950, felt that while Murrow was waiting for the right moment to attack, others, including Sevareid, had been forced to take the heat. On the record Sevareid said he always considered it his role to prepare the way for Murrow: "We were trying, on radio, to keep the salient open so that when the time came, Ed and Friendly could drive their big [televised] tank through." In private, though, Sevareid was resentful that Murrow received so much of the glory and he so little.

He let a little of his resentment show in an interview he gave Charles Kuralt in 1978, after his retirement: "Youngsters read back and they think only one person in broadcasting and the press stood up to McCarthy, and this has made a lot of people feel very upset, including me, because that [Murrow] program came awfully late. But in the meantime, the place was strewn with the walking wounded and the bodies of journalists who'd been under fire from McCarthy."

♦

Unlike Downs and Sevareid and others, Charles Collingwood had unqualified praise for Murrow. In a letter to him Collingwood wrote, "You have fought many battles for all the rest of us in the past, but none bigger nor, I suspect, more difficult to join than this one. Because of what you are and what you have done, you can say things that the rest of us may not, and every time you do, you help all the rest of us. By dignifying the profession you dignify all of us." Collingwood may even have drawn some new inspiration from Murrow's broadcast, because the tide of McCarthyism was about to wash over him as well.

In 1949 Collingwood had moved from Los Angeles to Washington, where he was assigned by CBS to the White House beat and soon became one of President Truman's poker-playing buddies. Three years later he took his leave of absence to work for Averell Harriman, who had been appointed to head a new agency in charge of coordinating U.S. foreign aid. By the time Collingwood returned to CBS in 1953, he had become a subject of some interest to J. Edgar Hoover and the FBI.

At first their interest was piqued because Collingwood had, in FBI-ese, been "associating with communists" during his year in Los Angeles. The charge turned out to have no substance, but that didn't prevent subsequent FBI reports from repeating it. Collingwood's real sin, however, was going on the air on June 12, 1949, to characterize the FBI's investigations of alleged subversives as "a bewildering hodge-podge of gossip, innuendo, and rumor." Mild as this criticism was, it created quite a little tempest in Hoover's office. Collingwood's attitude was, Hoover declaimed privately, "typical of CBS's 'fellow traveler' slant." From then on Hoover seemed to take a personal interest in Collingwood and for years afterward maintained a special file on him.

When Harriman nominated Collingwood for government service, the bureau conducted what it described as "a particularly thorough and searching" background check. At one point an FBI agent showed up at the office of former UP reporter Ed Beattie, a wartime buddy of Collingwood's, who had since joined the CIA. Questioning Beattie about Collingwood's affair with Gracie Blake, the agent insinuated that the relationship revealed "moral turpitude" on Collingwood's part. Beattie all but threw the FBI man out of his office. Romantic affairs, he said, were none of the government's goddamned business.

Despite the FBI's interest in him, Collingwood was actually not very active in the fight against McCarthyism. After working for Harriman and rejoining CBS, he moved from Washington to New York and concentrated primarily on his *Adventure* program and the rather hectic social life he and his wife, Louise, were creating for themselves. They had an apartment in Manhattan and a summer house on Fire Island; both places were the scenes of lavish parties. With all that, plus Charles's art collecting and gambling, there was little time for politics or ideology. Or so Collingwood thought — until one day in the summer of 1955, when John Henry Faulk came calling.

Faulk, a neighbor on Fire Island, was a Texas humorist and writer and the folksy host of a popular daily radio program called *Johnny's Front Porch*, carried by CBS's New York affiliate, WCBS. On that summer day on Fire Island, Faulk proposed that Collingwood run for president of the New York chapter of the American Federation of Television and Radio Artists (AFTRA). It was no small proposal. If Collingwood agreed, he would be caught up in the blacklisting issue that was then tearing broadcasting apart and would be placing himself squarely in the witch-hunters' sights.

At the time the local leaders of AFTRA, a union of entertainers and journalists, were in league with Aware Inc., which fingered performers suspected of being Communists or fellow travelers. Many on Aware's list were subsequently blacklisted. Faulk wanted to put together a slate that would oppose blacklisting. The election was to be in December, and Faulk needed a big name — one that hadn't already been tarnished — to run for president. Collingwood was his choice.

Even though he had only recently joined AFTRA, Collingwood understood the dangers inherent in becoming a candidate. Many of the union's members, although opposed to the leadership, didn't dare go public with their opposition for fear of exposing themselves to blacklisting. Actor Tony Randall, for one, said he was so scared he wouldn't even go to union meetings. "I crawled under a rock and stayed there," he said. Although Collingwood had been inclined at first to do the same, he was interested enough to discuss Faulk's idea with some acquaintances. One woman warned him against antagonizing Aware. You don't know what they can do, she said, to people who cross them. The warning brought out Collingwood's combative streak. He hated being pushed around and decided then and there to run.

With considerable difficulty and after long hours of canvassing, he and Faulk managed to identify enough supporters to be convinced there was a good chance of victory. Calling themselves the "middle-of-the-road" slate, Collingwood and the other candidates on his ticket (including his wife) pledged to end blacklisting. They were, Collingwood said, "the doggonedest bunch of political amateurs you ever saw," but when the votes were counted in December 1955, they had won in a landslide. Joining Collingwood as president were comedian Orson Bean as first vice president and Faulk as second vice president.

The results of the election had hardly been announced, however, before the House Committee on Un-American Activities charged that a "militant Communist faction," using what the committee said was a trumped-up blacklisting issue, had taken control of the New York AFTRA. Fulfilling his platform promises, Collingwood fired off a scathing reply:

> If the committee really thinks that the only people in the entertainment industry who are disturbed by the excesses of the blacklisting system are Communists or their dupes, then it is laboring under a misapprehension. Concern over the manifest inequities of the blacklist is shared by the overwhelming majority of the performers and by, one suspects, a large proportion of the employers as well. The blacklist is dying and the present officers and majority of the N.Y. local board of AFTRA intend to do everything they can to assist the process.

Dying or not, the blacklist still had enough adherents to punish the Collingwood-led upstarts. In early 1956 Aware issued a bulletin to advertising agencies, sponsors, and networks denouncing the new AFTRA leadership. The bulletin vaguely questioned the loyalty of Collingwood, Bean, and other members of the slate, but its real target was Faulk, whom it labeled a Communist sympathizer (in fact, he was neither a

Communist nor a sympathizer). The Aware bulletin threatened a consumer boycott of advertisers' products if they continued sponsoring the miscreants, including Faulk.

Several of those under attack felt the pressure almost immediately. Orson Bean, told by his agent that the Aware bulletin had influence with Ed Sullivan, on whose show he frequently appeared, promptly resigned as first vice president. A couple of Faulk's sponsors announced they were withdrawing from his program, and there were indications that WCBS would cave in to the pressure and try to get rid of him. Again Collingwood got his back up. He called on Ed Murrow, and the two of them confronted Arthur Hull Hayes, the general manager of WCBS. They told Hayes that AFTRA "would take a very dim view indeed" if Faulk were fired in the wake of the Aware bulletin. It was an act of great courage: Collingwood had not suffered at the network because of his union activities, but now he, a CBS employee, was challenging the employment practices of a CBS-owned affiliate.

WCBS agreed to keep Faulk on. But only a battle had been won, not the war. In 1957, after Collingwood went to London as CBS's bureau chief there, WCBS dropped the now-unsponsored *On the Front Porch*. Faulk, unemployed, found himself unemployable as well. Soon he ran out of money. His electricity was shut off, and he and his family were evicted from their apartment.

And still the war wasn't over. In 1956 Faulk filed a libel suit against Aware Inc. It would take six years to come to trial. During those years Collingwood, Murrow, and other friends were John Henry Faulk's lifeline. Murrow gave him the money to retain the famed criminal lawyer Louis Nizer, and Collingwood helped persuade reluctant and frightened AFTRA members to testify on his behalf.

Collingwood himself was a key witness at the trial, describing Faulk's character and Aware's campaign of terror. Networks and sponsors, Collingwood said on the stand, lacked the "guts" to hire performers whose patriotism was unfairly under fire; indeed, certain networks and local stations went so far as to hire people to administer the blacklist — an obvious reference to CBS's Daniel O'Shea, among others. Bill Paley was on record as insisting that CBS had never violated anyone's civil liberties, and here was one of his most visible employees contradicting him. "It was apparent from the faces of the jurors that (Collingwood) had scored heavily for us," Faulk later wrote. At the end of the trial the jury found in Faulk's favor and awarded him more than $3 million, a record libel judgment for the time (reduced on appeal to $550,000).

Finally, after heavy casualties, the war was over.

✦

Charles Collingwood was a dramatic and flamboyant man by nature. Sometimes people mistook those traits for shallowness or flightiness. But his bravery in fighting the blacklist was genuine, and his commitment seemed total. Moreover, he fought not in the showy world of television news, but in the dark back alleys of union politics. He risked his career on behalf of his principles and his friends, many of whom showed as much courage as he.

Yet Collingwood's old insecurities still haunted him: he didn't believe his valor measured up to Murrow's. Said his nephew, Harris Collingwood: "He expressed doubt that he would have been able to take the kind of stand against McCarthy that Murrow did. That kind of bearing witness wasn't his style. . . . He would always hold himself against the Murrow standard and find himself wanting." Many years later Walter Cronkite looked back at the McCarthy era and found the invidious comparison unwarranted. Cronkite said, "[Collingwood] became president of AFTRA at the most delicate time in our history, and led the union brilliantly. And I think that, almost perhaps as much as Ed Murrow's famed exposure of McCarthy, Charles's leadership of AFTRA at that critical time was an important factor in bringing down and ending that terrible period."

23

Burdett's Secret

For pure intelligence, Winston Mansfield Burdett was the best of the Boys. Frail and handsome, considered a comer at CBS after the war, he wrote beautifully and had what others described as a "photographic memory." He could memorize a script in a single reading and speak flawlessly on the air, even when he had to ad-lib. "Winston could sit down without a script and deliver a five-minute report on any subject, with a mastery of the English language that left me on the floor in astonishment most of the time," said Marvin Kalb. "He had an extraordinary gift for explaining complicated issues in the most elegant language."

Burdett was an anomaly in the increasingly cutthroat and cynical world of broadcast journalism. A small bird of a man with a silken, resonant voice and the air of a nineteenth-century Romantic poet, he grew up in upper-middle-class New York, the son of a successful civil engineer. His pampering, domineering mother treated him as if he were a fragile jewel. Winston went to Harvard, majored in Romance languages, and graduated in only three years.

Yet despite his many advantages (or perhaps because of them), he was often confounded by life's more mundane aspects. Shortly after the war, he asked Joseph Harsch, with whom he shared an office in the CBS Washington bureau, what it meant to "go on a note for somebody." It meant, Harsch explained, that one became responsible for the other person's debt if it was not paid. Burdett blanched. He had just "gone on" a thousand-dollar note for a colleague who was notoriously lax about his financial affairs. "In the practical matters of daily living," Harsch said, "Winston's head was in the clouds." Howard Smith remarked, "Sometimes when you'd talk to him, he'd have to regain consciousness before he answered."

His rather flamboyant second wife, Giorgina, said many years afterward, "One thing Winston always said to me was, 'Giorgie, you know you're my link with life.' Because I was the reality, you see. I was his contact with the earth."

Yet there was so *much* reality in Winston Burdett's life. He went to work for the *Brooklyn Daily Eagle* when he was only twenty years old. In 1940 he was a war correspondent covering the fighting in Norway and Finland. CBS sent him to the Balkans, where he met and married Lea Schiavi. Less than two years later, after Lea was murdered in Iran, Burdett covered the Allied drive through North Africa and the bloody Italian campaign. Immediately after the war, still in Italy, he married the vivacious and lovely Giorgina Nathan, daughter of a prominent Italian banker and granddaughter of a former mayor of Rome, the first Jew ever to hold the position.

Burdett's first postwar assignment for CBS was in Washington. Transferred back to Rome in 1948, he covered, among other things, the Arab-Israeli war in the Middle East. Eventually he and Giorgina had two children, a son and a daughter, but their marriage became an unorthodox and tempestuous mix of frequent long separations, affairs, and loving reconciliations. Through it all, Burdett showed himself to be brave, incisive, tough, and resourceful.

With all this reality, whence Burdett's aura of otherworldliness? Why did so many people, including his wife, feel they could never quite connect with him? Some said the solution to the mystery of Winston Burdett lay in the murder of his first wife. Others said it was his health — he had a severe ulcer that caused him terrible pain. No one, including his family, knew for sure. The answer, or a good part of it, finally came on June 28, 1955, in a crowded hearing room of the U.S. Senate Judiciary Committee. No one who knew Burdett expected, or for that matter even imagined, that from 1940 to 1942 he had been a full-fledged, paid spy for the Soviet Union.

✦

His story was one of idealism, adventure, disillusion, betrayal, and guilt. Until the early fifties only Burdett knew all the details. Then, in December 1950, an envelope landed on his desk in CBS's Rome bureau. Inside was the infamous loyalty questionnaire all network employees had to fill out and sign if they expected to retain their jobs. Each of the three questions was to be answered by checking "yes" or "no": Was Burdett then or had he ever been "a member of the Communist Party, U.S.A., or any communist organization"? Was he then or had he ever been a member of a fascist organization? Was he then or had he ever been "a member of any organization, association, movement, group or combination of persons" which advocated the overthrow, violent or otherwise, of "our constitutional form of government"? Below the questions was a space for "details or explanations, if any."

Burdett's heart sank. He could honestly answer "no" only to question two, and it would require a great many pages to provide "details" and "explanations" for his "yes" answers. This was the "knock on the door" he had long expected and agonized about. In a way, however, it must also have come as a relief. Burdett was no longer a Communist, let alone a spy. On the contrary, he had gradually become, at least in the privacy of his conscience, a dedicated *anti*-Communist. Now, as he sat in Rome and studied the questionnaire, he decided, after more than a decade of deception, that it was time to come clean. He answered the questions honestly, signed the form, and returned it to New York with a lengthy letter of explanation. Then he sat back and waited.

His response must have landed at CBS headquarters with all the force of a five-hundred-pound bomb. The network that the extreme right was then castigating as the "Communist Broadcasting System" didn't just have a former Party member in its midst, it had a former Soviet *spy!* Doubtless there were many hurried secret meetings among the few top CBS executives privy to Burdett's secret — Bill Paley, for one, must have been beside himself — and there were consultations between CBS and the Justice Department.

The only outward sign of concern, however, was a sudden order to Burdett to pack his family up and move immediately from Rome to New York, an order he obeyed without apparent protest or complaint. Once there Burdett evidently persuaded Paley, Stanton, and Ream (and probably Murrow) not only that his Communist past was behind him and that he was sorry, but that even as a wartime Soviet spy, he had never really been disloyal to the United States. Or perhaps Bill Paley decided that keeping Burdett at CBS, contrite or not, was vastly preferable to kicking him out and explaining why. Either way, Burdett went unpunished, and for four years his secret remained within the CBS family and the investigatory agencies of the U.S. government. (Even today the FBI has 900 pages of unreleased, still-classified material on him in its files.) His career did not suffer at all. In New York he became the anchorman on radio's evening news roundup and was named UN reporter for CBS television. He continued to count Ed Murrow among his patrons, and soon added the name of CBS's new TV news chief,

Sig Mickelson, who later said, "I really admired the man. He was the best."

The fix was in. Burdett would be protected. All he had to do in return was cooperate fully — but confidentially — with the FBI. All things considered, he said, it was a condition he found easy to accept.

And there the matter rested until 1955. That year, for reasons that are still not altogether clear, Burdett decided it was time to go public with his story. He may have been pressured by the Senate Judiciary Committee and the FBI, which had begun looking for Communists in American journalism. But those who worked most closely with him during this period insisted that Burdett needed no prompting and was motivated by a desire to educate others. "I'm quite convinced that Winston made his decision on his own," said Mickelson, "without any pressure." Burdett himself told both *Time* and *Newsweek* that he had volunteered. He didn't think the public understood how all-consuming the Communist Party was, or that the Party, far from being an agent of political and economic reform, as he had once believed, was an abject tool of Soviet foreign policy. Michael Bessie offered another explanation for Burdett's offering himself up. "In some ways," Bessie mused years later, "I think Winston would have liked to have been an early Christian martyr."

In the spring of 1955, Burdett invited Bessie to the Harvard Club in New York for lunch. The two had been friends since their Harvard undergraduate days. Bessie's father-in-law, attorney Morris Ernst, glided easily from camp to camp during the McCarthy era, managing to be both a stalwart of the American Civil Liberties Union and a chum of J. Edgar Hoover's. And Michael Bessie's cousin Alvah Bessie had been a colleague of Burdett's on the *Brooklyn Eagle* staff and, with Burdett, a leading light in the newspaper's very own Communist Party cell. *
Someone as well connected as Michael Bessie could surely help Burdett find his way through the dark and dangerous McCarthyite forest.

When the two of them were settled at their table in the Harvard Club's magisterial dining room, Burdett came right to the point.

"You never joined the Communist Party, did you?" he said.

"No."

"Well, I did."

---

*Alvah Bessie later became a screenwriter and served a prison term as one of the "Hollywood Ten" — a group of alleged Communists who refused to cooperate with congressional Red-hunting in the movie studios.

He needed advice. Would Morris Ernst help him? In short order Bessie put Burdett in touch with Ernst, who, having heard his story, referred him to a New York municipal judge, Robert Morris. Before becoming a judge, Morris, a fierce anti-Communist, had been counsel to the Senate Internal Security Subcommittee, chaired in those years by the rock-ribbed Democratic senior senator from Mississippi, James Eastland. The subcommittee's main business was hunting down and rooting out subversives. At the time Burdett was contemplating public disclosure of his past, Eastland and his subcommittee were especially interested in any Communists who might be lurking in the Newspaper Guild, the journalists' labor union. Impressed with Burdett's sincerity, Judge Morris met with him in his chambers.

"You know," Burdett told Morris, "I'm working with Ed Murrow up at CBS. They're all talking about communism. But they don't know what they're talking *about*."

"You do?" Morris asked.

"Precisely," Burdett answered.

He said he had decided to tell his story publicly and felt that he probably should resign from CBS before he did so. After hearing him out, Morris said he would be glad to help him and would sit with him when he testified — but only if Burdett gave up any idea of resigning. Burdett agreed, and Morris sent him to Jay Sourwine, who had succeeded Morris as chief counsel to the Internal Security Subcommittee.

At some point during this period it became clear that the subcommittee was interested in Burdett's testimony only if he would name other journalists he knew to have been members of the Communist Party. He said he would. His friends inside CBS, including Ed Murrow, always maintained that he did this only under intense pressure from the government. But Morris did not have that impression. In his view, although Burdett was certainly not enthusiastic about naming others, he thought of it as the price he had to pay for getting his story out. Said Morris, "I think at the time the Communists were making a lot of gains, and he thought that was bad. . . . I know he was a little reluctant about naming names, [but] he said, 'That's it. I'm going to do it. I know Communists are a bad influence.' He played it the way [Morris] Ernst wanted him to. If he agonized, he didn't show it to me."

Shortly after his meeting with Robert Morris, Burdett traveled to Washington and met with Sourwine. Arrangements were made for him to go into a closed executive session of the subcommittee and tell the members what he knew, names and all. The executive session was held May 2. Afterward the committee scheduled two full days of public hearings.

This latest wrinkle in the Burdett saga was too much at first for the corporate thinkers at CBS. It had been one thing for their man to confess in secret; it was something else again for him to create a public spectacle that could prove embarrassing for CBS. Burdett had become a liability: pressure began building for him to resign. "They wanted to be in a position to say, 'He's no longer employed,'" recalled Bessie. "Morris [Ernst] and I labored with him very hard, saying, 'Look, [resigning] is the thing you *can't* do. You corrupt your own coin.'" Bessie and Ernst also went to Ed Murrow. "[We] put the matter to him," Bessie said, "that he must use his strength at CBS to see to it that Winston was preserved."

Murrow did what he could. Among other things, he talked with a number of the Boys and the other correspondents, told them what was happening, and insisted that Burdett had been forced into doing what he was doing. Murrow counseled understanding. David Schoenbrun recalled his saying, "Now, look, you know that Winston Burdett is a gentleman, that he's a great reporter. Now Winston has done something that you guys are really going to hate. It's not just that he was a Communist or a Russian spy. It's that in order to get himself off the hook, he gave names. . . . I want you to know that Winston has suffered enormously. And, under that kind of pressure, he cracked. Don't judge him too harshly. And don't be so goddamn sure you wouldn't have cracked, either. Please don't turn your back on Winston."

Whether Murrow sought to intercede with the brass at CBS is not known. He may have. In any case, Senator Eastland did, and by this time Eastland probably had more influence than Murrow with Paley, Stanton, and the other top CBS people. On June 7 Eastland sent the following letter to Daniel O'Shea:

Winston Burdett has rendered a real service by his [executive-session] testimony before this committee, and I believe should be commended for it and encouraged in every way possible. I know that he has some tough times ahead of him, and I earnestly hope that Columbia will stand by him. I think it would be fine if Columbia should publicly commend him for his decision after he has testified in open session. . . .

Eastland sent a similar letter to Attorney General Herbert Brownell, Jr., urging him to go to bat for Burdett with the top executives at CBS. One reason for Eastland's solicitousness was that, with Burdett's testimony, the subcommittee could finally go after the newspaper industry and the Guild, both of which, until then, had largely escaped the witch-hunt. Burdett was ready to tell the world that the *Brooklyn Daily Eagle* had its own Communist cell, to which he and about a dozen other *Eagle* employees — all of them members of the Guild — had belonged. Eastland was willing to go to great lengths to defend and preserve such a source.

The support paid off. The threat to Burdett's job vanished. O'Shea worked out a deal with Paley, Stanton, and Mickelson under which Burdett, following his public testimony before the subcommittee, would go to London for a time and then be transferred back to Rome.

Before that, however, Winston Burdett would at long last tell his story to the world.

✦

The vast and ornate Senate Caucus Room, site of the Army-McCarthy hearings several months earlier and of many other dramatic hearings before and since, was packed with spectators on the morning of June 28, 1955, as Burdett took his seat at the witness table. Judge Morris was seated just behind him. Facing him was the customary senatorial array, elbows on green baize, with Chairman Eastland at the center. Also at the table was committee counsel Jay Sourwine, who would do most of the questioning. After the preliminaries Sourwine wasted no time in getting down to cases.

"Mr. Burdett," he said, "were you ever a member of the Communist Party, U.S.A.?"

Burdett did not flinch. "I was, sir." He had been a member from 1937 to 1942, he said.

Minutes later: "Did you ever engage in espionage?"

"I did, sir."

✦

His remarkable testimony, only part of it in response to Sourwine's questions and much of it in the form of a lengthy narrative, ran all morning and continued after lunch, well into the afternoon. At one point Burdett delivered a statement of purpose in which he sounded for all the world like a voluntary witness:

I have wished to come before this committee because I felt it my duty to do so in order to discharge what I felt to be a very definite obligation. . . . I was not a casual member [of the Party]. I was a very devoted member. I was young; I was enthusiastic; and I was very earnest. . . . I did not join because of any profound conviction of the truth of Marxist theories; I did not join because of any advance indoctrination. The indoctrination, such as it was, came afterward. But I joined, I think, primarily because I was emotionally impelled to identify myself with a larger movement outside myself, a larger cause which I then believed to be a good one.

In that hushed room Burdett spun a tale of naive idealism transformed into righteous fanaticism, of dashed hopes, of loss and discovery. Like many other young people of the period — with the Roaring Twenties just behind them, the Great Depression all around them, and the dark shape of a world war looming dimly ahead — Burdett after Harvard was searching for some new way in which the world might be organized and run. He joined the Communist Party in August 1937, urged to do so by Alvah Bessie. "Most people who join the Communist Party in this country do not know what they are getting into," he told the subcommittee.

✦

In the early and mid-thirties the *Brooklyn Eagle* was a hell-bent, five-edition-a-day, get-the-story-or-bust newspaper. It was presided over by a massively unpopular publisher named Preston Goodfellow, who came to work each morning with his large dog and paid himself $52,000 a year, his secretary $26,000 a year, and his brother (whose job was rather vague) $25,000 a year. Members of the *Eagle*'s staff, meanwhile, earned between $17.50 and $22.50 — a week. The workday began at 8 A.M. and continued until an editor said you could go home. The workweek was six days. In 1936 the paper's staff went on strike, and on the first day of picketing, management had the New York police arrest eighty of them, including Winston Burdett.

Burdett had been assigned to the culture department with Alvah Bessie and a few other writers and critics whose work appeared mainly in the Sunday supplement. He was young and eager but not very well suited to the *Eagle*'s "Front Page" style of journalism. When he was given a tryout as a beat reporter by the paper's city desk, his editors found him too slow and ponderous for their taste, and back he went to the culture department, where he wrote about and reviewed movies.

In general *Eagle* staffers had a hell of a good time in those days. They called strikes. They joined the Guild. Some became Communists. They covered the city of New York, Brooklyn, and the waterfront like a blanket, with time for love affairs on the side. At one point Burdett and one of his fellow Communists, Victor Weingarten, were courting the same woman, a lovely, lively young reporter named Violet Brown, also a member of the Party. She would eventually choose, and marry, Weingarten, to whom she confided that Burdett had "sweaty hands." (Burdett named both of them in his Senate testimony as having been members of the *Eagle*'s Communist cell.)

By his own account the Party became Burdett's life. He spent two nights a week for two or three months at a "section school" in Communist theory. Afterward he often volunteered his apartment for cell meetings, at which he was "fanatical and hotly dogmatic." Not even the 1939 nonaggression pact between Stalin and Hitler — the cause of bitter disillusionment to so many other American comrades of the day — cooled his ardor. When a fellow *Eagle* reporter stood up at a cell meeting to declare he was resigning in protest against the pact, Burdett by his own account cruelly denounced him.

A Party member so dedicated could not go unnoticed by his superiors. Burdett had been a Communist about two and a half years when he was instructed to make contact "on a matter of some importance" with a correspondent for the Communist *Daily Worker* named Joe North. As directed, he went to North's Greenwich Village apartment on a Sunday afternoon in January 1940. North told him the Party wanted him to go to Finland. "We have an assignment for you there in which you can be useful." The record does not indicate whether Burdett responded to this news with any nervousness. He might well have. Finland had been invaded by the Red Army four months earlier and was at that moment engaged in a brave defensive war. And the twenty-six-year-old Burdett — a movie reviewer — had no experience as a foreign correspondent, let alone a war correspondent.

Still, he was the Party's to command.

A few days later North introduced Burdett to a brawny, thick-necked, slightly balding man with sad, intelligent eyes, who provided more details. He instructed Burdett to go to his editors and make the following proposal: if they would assign him to Europe as a correspondent, he would work free of charge — no salary, no expenses. Predictably, the penny-pinching editors of the *Eagle*, which had never had a foreign staff, jumped at the deal, evidently persuaded that Burdett, a young man of some means, was eager enough and wealthy enough to pull it off. (In fact, the U.S. Communist Party had promised to provide him with whatever money he needed.)

In later clandestine meetings, the brawny man with sad eyes gave Burdett more detailed instructions for his trip. At the time Burdett had no idea who this man was, except that he obviously spoke for the Party and with considerable authority. During Burdett's collaboration with the FBI in the early 1950s, he was shown a 1937 passport photograph of one Jacob Raisin. He recognized Raisin as the man who had been his contact in 1940 and learned that he was really Yakov Golos, the Kremlin's main organizer of espionage for the American Communist Party.

The night before Burdett was to sail for Europe, he met, as directed, with another man on a street corner near Columbia University, where he received his final orders and a bit of reassurance. "You will not be asked to risk your life," the contact told Burdett. "You will not be asked to risk anything." Then he added, "rather sourly," Burdett felt, "[but] plenty of other people *are.*"

Following orders, Burdett went first to Stockholm, where he was contacted by a "Mr. Miller," who gave him some money and told him to report back from Finland on the state of military and civilian morale — especially on the strength of the Finns' "will to resist" the Soviet invasion.

In Finland, Burdett visited the still-frozen front as well as various cities and towns, talking to soldiers and civilians alike. He had been there only two weeks when the Finns were finally crushed by the Red Army's superior force. On March 13, 1940, the government capitulated. Burdett remained another week or two in Helsinki, then returned to Stockholm for a prearranged meeting with "Mr. Miller," whose only question for him was: "Well, how did the Finns take the end of the war?" They weren't prepared for it, Burdett said. They were shocked. The Finnish army wasn't prepared for it either, and would probably have gone on fighting if their government had let them.

After hearing his report, "Mr. Miller" handed Burdett another wad of money — enough for his return passage to New York, plus incidentals — and said, "Well, Mr. Burdett, thank you very much. That's everything."

In effect he had been patted on the head and told to go home.

✦

It was so peremptory, so anticlimactic. "I was surprised that it was all over," Burdett said, "that this was all there was to it. But then I realized that their interest in this business had been Finland, and the Finnish war was over, and, whatever I was able to tell them was, for the purposes of that trip, too late." But he had money of his own, plus what "Mr. Miller" had given him, so for once he decided to disobey the Party's orders. He would stay in Europe and seek his fortune as a freelance correspondent — a much more exciting prospect than returning to the *Eagle*'s culture department.

As the tension of impending war with Germany gripped Scandinavia, Burdett remained in Stockholm, writing stories for the *Eagle* and making occasional radio broadcasts as a part-time correspondent for Transradio Press. One of the few reporters who managed to slip into Norway after the German invasion on April 9, 1940, he was recruited there by Betty Wason to replace her as CBS's stringer.

After the Germans vanquished Norway, Burdett and many other Western correspondents decided to shift their base to Rumania, reckoning that the Balkans would be the next hot spot of the war. Before Burdett could leave, however, "Mr. Miller" paid another call on him. He was not angry that Burdett had stayed in Europe. Indeed, he said, the Party had a new assignment for him in Rumania. Instead of going directly to Bucharest, Burdett should stop off first in Moscow, where he would receive instructions.

At the Metropole Hotel near the Kremlin, Burdett was met by two Russian intelligence officers, a man and a woman, who told him how to make contact with his new case officer in Bucharest. Nothing came of that assignment; the person who was supposed to contact Burdett never did. So Burdett stuck to journalism, working primarily for Transradio Press and doing occasional reports for CBS. And he met and married Lea Schiavi.

Following the Nazis' occupation of Rumania in November, most of the foreign community, Burdett and Schiavi among them, moved on to Yugoslavia. Burdett was beginning to revel in his life as a foreign correspondent. But just as he was thinking that the Party and the Kremlin might have forgotten him, they got in touch again. He and Lea had been in Belgrade only a couple of weeks when he was contacted by a Soviet intelligence officer and told to go to a certain street corner and wait to be approached by a man carrying a single gray glove.

This time the connection was made. The one-gloved man gave Burdett a list of names of Yugoslav government officials and instructed him to cultivate them. Then, after one clandestine follow-up meeting, Burdett never heard again from the one-gloved man. He was beginning to conclude that Soviet espionage wasn't all it was cracked up to be.

From Yugoslavia he filed several stories about resistance in northern Italy to the government of Benito Mussolini. These stories did not sit well with the Fascist government of Yugoslavia, and in mid-March of 1941 Winston and Lea were once again forced to move on. This time they settled in the Turkish capital of Ankara, where Burdett, now a full-time CBS correspondent, did his most serious espionage work.

Paradoxically, it was also during his stay in Ankara that Burdett lost his faith in Communism. Away from the doctrinaire atmosphere of the *Brooklyn Eagle*'s Party cell, associating with older and more experienced foreign correspondents who "saw the world not through blinders but through free and sophisticated eyes," he began to think that the international Communist movement was organized solely to do Moscow's bidding and that the Soviet Union was a cynical and ruthless nation, "willing to throw anyone overboard."

He didn't much like his handlers, either — from Yakov Golos to "Mr. Miller" to his Ankara contact, a woman in the Soviet embassy whose last name was Zhigalova. He didn't like their manners, their lack of culture, their style. He was being "used as a tool by people whom I did not trust for a cause of which I was no longer sure." In New York and Stockholm and Moscow and Belgrade and Ankara, the Party men and women he had dealt with were rude and sullen and treated him, he thought, with "considerable contempt." These grubby people weren't at all romantic or idealistic. They had nothing in common with Burdett. They lived their lives on dank street corners and in harshly lit cafeterias and squalid hotel rooms. Yet they seemed to take themselves so seriously, even when they trafficked in the most trivial information. It was dawning on Winston Burdett that spies almost never get a chance to save the world.

Habit, however, pushed him along a while longer. Under the guidance of Madame Zhigalova, the second-highest-ranking official in the Soviet embassy, he befriended top Turkish officials and well-informed Turkish journalists, pumping them for information about their government's policies and plans. After the Germans invaded Russia in June, Madame Zhigalova was especially interested in whether or not Turkey would remain neutral. Every two or three weeks Burdett would meet with her, either in the Soviet embassy, where he would pretend to be interviewing her for CBS, or at some clandestine location. Each time he would hand her a typewritten report on what he had learned since their last meeting.

He continued in this way until November 1941, when Britain and the Soviet Union occupied Iran and divided it between them — the British in the south, the Soviets in the north. The idea was to provide a safe overland route for U.S. Lend-Lease assistance to the Soviet Union, and CBS immediately sent Burdett to Iran to see if the plan was working. He made occasional quick trips back to Ankara to report to Madame Zhigalova; but that winter, while he and Lea were living and working in Tehran, the Japanese attacked Pearl Harbor, and the United States entered the war. It was then that Burdett decided he wanted nothing more to do with either the Party or spying. He returned to Ankara in February 1942 (Lea remained behind) and told Madame Zhigalova he was through.

She was not pleased. "This obviously came as a shock to her," Burdett told the Internal Security Subcommittee. ". . . She acted like a child that is suddenly deprived of something which it is enjoying." She urged him to reconsider.

"No," Burdett told her. "That is my point. I want you to understand that I have *done* all my reconsidering, and that this is final."

"That," he told the subcommittee, "was the last I ever saw of her, or of them."

Almost immediately after his final meeting with Madame Zhigalova, CBS ordered Burdett to go to India on a brief political reporting assignment. He had hardly arrived in Delhi when he received the terrible news that his wife, while reporting in the Soviet zone of northern Iran, had been shot and killed. Burdett rushed back to Iran to find that the case was already closed and that no one wanted to reopen it. A Kurdish road guard had been arrested and charged with Lea's murder. It seemed clear that he had been ordered to do it.

But by whom? For some time Burdett suspected the Italian Fascist government. After the war, however, he was told that the U.S. Army's Counterintelligence Corps had evidence that Lea had been murdered on orders from Moscow, "because she knew too much" about how the Red Army was training Yugoslav partisans, under Tito, to fight the Germans. The theory was that Moscow did not want anyone to know — least of all, its new allies in Washington and London — about its close involvement with Tito's resistance movement. When Lea found out about a secret Soviet training base in Iran for Yugoslav guerrillas, she had to be killed.

Possibly. But another explanation also fits the facts, namely that Lea was shot in retaliation for her husband's defection from the Party and its cause. Burdett never seemed even to consider that explanation — except, perhaps, during his many sleepless nights. But for the rest of his life he was convinced that, for whatever reason, Moscow had ordered the murder of his wife.

◆

Gripping as Burdett's tale was, the members of the Senate Internal Security Subcommittee did not show much interest in it. What they wanted were names — names of reporters and editors at the *Brooklyn Eagle* and other papers who were members of both the Newspaper Guild and the Communist Party in the late 1930s. Burdett had already provided these in executive session, but the senators wanted the names on the public record as well.

In the afternoon, when Burdett had finished his narrative, Jay Sourwine said, "I want to run through this list to be sure that each name is that of a person whom you identify as a member of the Communist Party at the time when you were a member of the *Brooklyn Eagle* unit."

Then, one by one, under Sourwine's questioning, Burdett handed up his former colleagues and fellow Party members:

Sourwine: Nathan Einhorn?
Burdett: He was a member of the Communist Party of the *Brooklyn Eagle*, yes.
Sourwine: Victor Weingarten?
Burdett: He was also.
Sourwine: Violet Brown, subsequently Violet Weingarten?
Burdett: She was also, sir.
Sourwine: Charles Lewis?
Burdett: Yes.
Sourwine: Hyman Charniak?
Burdett: Yes.
Sourwine: Herbert Cohn?
Burdett: Yes.
Sourwine: Melvin Barnett?
Burdett: Yes.
Sourwine: David Gordon?
Burdett: Yes.

Sourwine: Charles Grutzner?
Burdett: Yes. . . . Yes. . . . Yes. . . .

✦

In all, there were twenty-three names, twenty-three persons at the *Eagle* and elsewhere whose lives were forever changed, many ruined, by Winston Burdett. In the spectators' section, Giorgina Burdett, pregnant with their second child, sat paralyzed in horror. How could Winston *do* this? She wanted to get up and run out. If she could have died at that moment, she said, she would have welcomed it.

Shortly after they were married, Giorgina had learned that her secretive husband had been a Communist. So what? No one in Italy at that time thought being a Communist was such a terrible thing. She didn't know about the spying until she and Winston had moved to New York, and FBI agents started coming to their apartment for what seemed like interminable interrogations. He had told her he planned to testify, to get all of this off his chest. But she didn't know about the names. *My God, the names!* Nearly forty years later, Giorgina Burdett's voice choked when she talked about that dreadful day. "It was the worst moment of my life, the worst moment of our marriage."

During his testimony Burdett tried to soften the blow. At one point he said to Sourwine, "These are persons who went into the Party utter, honest idealists, and there was no other and there could be no other compelling motive." He was sure, he added, that most of them had left the Party, just as he had.

Many had actually left the party long *before* he did. Indeed, Hyman Charniak was the man Burdett had denounced for quitting the Party in protest against the Soviet-Nazi pact. Even so, on the same day Burdett testified, the subcommittee sent subpoenas to all the people on Sourwine's list. Later that summer, during seven days of public hearings on alleged Communist influence in the newspaper industry, thirty-eight witnesses, most of whom Burdett had named, were summoned to testify. Twenty-two took the Fifth Amendment. Six, including three from the *New York Times*, were fired from their jobs.

It was a show trial, nothing more. The idea was to discredit the "liberal press," especially the Newspaper Guild and the *New York Times*. Senator Eastland's subcommittee provided no evidence that any of the thirty-eight people had subverted the Guild, the *Times*, or any other news organization — or had even wanted to. "Hell," said Victor Weingarten, "at the *Eagle*, we were all John Steinbeck communists — defined as any son of a bitch who wants twenty-five dollars a week when [the employers] are paying eighteen."

✦

And what of Winston Burdett? In early 1956 CBS sent him off to the Rome exile that Daniel O'Shea had arranged for him. Even this had an adverse affect on others. It meant that Bill Downs, who had taken over the Rome bureau in 1953 and who for once was enjoying himself, would have to leave. He wrote an anguished letter to Murrow: "I returned from a Middle East swing to find that Georgina [*sic*] had the whole town gossiping about how Winston is replacing me in Rome in January. . . . I wondered if you could kind of keep an ear open and if possible let me know just what the hell is going on."

Replied Murrow: "I don't know what's happening around here anymore."

Although some of Burdett's colleagues — Eric Sevareid and Charles Collingwood, in particular — remained on friendly terms with him and continued to believe that he had only testified under duress, others never forgave him for naming names. Larry LeSueur and Downs, in their early wire-service days, had worked with some of the reporters who lost their jobs because of Burdett's testimony. "These men were great idealists," LeSueur said, "and they got it in the neck." Ernest Leiser, one of CBS's top producers, had two friends whose careers were ruined and whose lives were shattered because of Burdett.

Said Daniel Schorr, who remained a friend, "Winston's colleagues regarded him as a traitor."

24

"Not His Thing Anymore"

IN LATE 1957 Bill Paley casually mentioned to Ed Murrow that he wouldn't be hosting his traditional lunch for the correspondents when they all gathered in New York for the year-end roundup. He was sorry, but he and Mrs. Paley had decided to go to Jamaica for the holidays instead. The chairman, having witnessed the spectacular rise of television and having had his fill of controversy, was losing interest in Murrow and the correspondents. Gone were the days when Paley welcomed CBS journalists into his home and introduced them to his socialite friends. "It's not his thing anymore," said a wistful David Schoenbrun.

The truth was that Paley had never felt as strongly about Murrow and the Boys, or their calling, as they had imagined. "He wasn't in the news business, as the Hearsts, the Luces, the Grahams were," said Don Hewitt. "News was his hobby. He collected Murrows and Sevareids and Smiths the way he collected Picassos and Manets and Degas. They were his icons." But now the icons had served their purpose, and new ones were replacing them. By the mid-fifties Paley's priorities were clear. Television news programs were generally relegated to late nights and the Sunday afternoon "cultural ghetto."

Even there they weren't safe. The network's executives noticed in 1955 that whenever local channels in New York and other large cities carried professional football games on Sunday afternoon (there was no national coverage in those days), their ratings soared at the expense of "ghetto" programs like *Face the Nation*. A New York Giants–Pittsburgh Steelers game in October of that year drew an 8.0 Nielsen rating, compared to *Face the Nation*'s dismal 2.8. Impressed, CBS's executives signed an exclusive contract with the NFL the following year. It was the start of a long and beautiful relationship, and it pushed the "cultural ghetto" back into Sunday mornings, when many people were still in bed.*

See it Now was one of the victims of Paley's new priorities. In 1955 the program lost its sponsor and its scheduled weekly slot. From then on it appeared only eight or ten times a year — "See It Now and Then," wags called it. Content wasn't the problem so much as revenue. Far more money could be made with such programs as *I Love Lucy*, *The Ed Sullivan Show*, and *Gunsmoke*. Even better, for a while, were the high-powered, big-buck quiz-shows like CBS's *$64,000 Question* and NBC's *Twenty-One*. By 1957 the list of the ten top-rated network programs included no fewer than five quiz shows, and four of them were on CBS.

✦

Of all the Boys, none hated and feared television more than Eric Sevareid. He didn't even *own* a set until the mid-fifties. It was a miracle that he not only survived in TV news but actually became a figure of some consequence. "I would guess that Eric was as far over on the anti-television side as one could get," Frank Stanton said. "He just wanted no part of those engineers running around, putting mikes in front of him, changing the lights. It drove him crazy."

In fact the shy, reserved Sevareid was plunged into the world of television cameras before overcoming his fear of the radio microphone. When he did his nightly radio commentaries, he couldn't stand to be watched from the control room window, so he faced the opposite way; instead of having someone signal him by hand, a three-colored light, like a traffic light, was installed on the desk: amber for "stand by," green for "you're on," and red for "you're off." Even with this support, he occasionally panicked before going on the air. Twice Bill Shadel, who delivered a newscast from Washington just prior to Sevareid's commentary, had to rush in to read Sevareid's script for him.

As a rule, his five-minute radio commentaries were well worth hearing. He crafted and polished each script, and many — particularly the more whimsical ones — were memorable. Critic Gilbert Seldes called them "small works of art"; author Theodore White said they were akin to "doing needlepoint on a matchbox."

Sevareid developed a large following with his radio commentar-

---

*The relationship lasted thirty-eight years, but in 1994 CBS was outbid by Fox for its share of the modern NFL contract.

ies and in 1954 was chosen to host a new Sunday-evening TV news program called *American Week*. Like *See It Now*, *American Week* was an early newsmagazine, whose stories were designed to offer insight into the past week's events. But from the beginning, viewers could see how uncomfortable Sevareid was with both the camera and the pictures it produced. In the first installment he said, "I expect to use some words here and there, for old times' sake if nothing more." Later he wrote to Howard Smith, "This program is either going to make me rich and famous or send me to the hospital with ulcers and a breakdown."

Still, he often did first-rate work on the program (which would change names and format several times in the next four years). In the summer of 1954 his interview of a young black law student named Frank Brown produced what was perhaps *American Week*'s most memorable story, a profoundly moving illumination of the pain suffered by blacks as they intensified their struggle for equality. Brown, his pregnant wife, and two small daughters had recently moved into Trumbull Park, a predominantly white federal housing project in South Chicago, and were under constant siege by hostile whites. At one point in Sevareid's interview with Brown, a bomb exploded nearby. But Brown, unruffled, vowed to remain, and Sevareid's report became an important milestone in the development of a new racial consciousness in America.

It was just such programming that Paley by 1957 had decided was getting in the way of his latest vision for the network. More and more he seemed to be looking for ways to cut his journalists down to size. Sevareid gave him an opportunity that same year by several times using his radio program to take on the Eisenhower administration's foreign policy — especially the State Department's refusal to allow Americans to travel to the People's Republic of China. At one point news director John Day ordered a Sevareid script killed. Furious, Sevareid gave a copy of it to Senator Michael Monroney, who took the Senate floor, declared that Sevareid had been muzzled by CBS, and inserted a summary of the script into the Congressional Record.

A barrage of criticism of CBS followed — from *Time* on the right to the *New Republic* on the left — and Bill Paley ordered Sevareid to New York to have it out. Before leaving Washington, Sevareid set out in an internal memo all his feelings of frustration and resentment over the chairman's objectivity policy, which he had always thought hypocritical and unworkable. The memo said:

Speaking for myself, I have been conscious of this policy every broad-casting day for several years and have, on the whole, been too cautious and guarded for the good of my own sense of integrity as a writer. . . . It is not possible to say things worth being heard without at least indicat-ing a personal point of view. To "analyze" without suggesting the results of the analysis is like researching any problem without revealing the findings. . . . Pure, cold "analysis," in the sense of merely listing facts and arguments on each side of a question, could not possibly hold an audi-ence over any period of time. . . . It is corruptive of the writer, forcing him to resort to wording devices to appear to be impartial when at heart he is not. . . . The whole public reputation of persons such as Murrow, Howard Smith or myself rests upon our individual approach to events and our individual manners of expression. People simply do not turn on the radio at appointed periods, saying, "Now I will hear an impartial elucidation of facts and issues." They say, "Now I'll hear what Murrow (or Smith or Sevareid) have to say about it. I may not agree with them, but they will be informed and fair about it." . . . The official network policy of analysis without personal opinion has not been closely fol-lowed. Were it so followed, CBS would discover that it had lost a vital human element that has been intimately connected with the success of CBS News over many years. It would immediately begin to lose its special standing with the press, the critics and its faithful listening public.

Sevareid's arguments did not persuade Paley. The "human element" — the cause of so much grief for Paley in his dealings with the govern-ment and his friends — was precisely what the chairman *wanted* to be rid of. If there was to be a voice at CBS, it was to be Paley's voice and no one else's. When Sevareid arrived in Paley's office for the showdown, the chairman was adamant. Finally Sevareid declared, "Maybe I've been too long with CBS!" For some time he had been telling friends that he was thinking of quitting. Now he had all but offered his resignation. And Paley, on hearing Sevareid's outburst, said . . . absolutely nothing.

Sevareid panicked. *My God*, he thought, *he* wants *me to resign!* That knowledge — the terrible realization that he had lost all leverage with the boss — shocked him. He had only two choices now: leave, or stay and play by Paley's rules. Sevareid sat there, and Paley sat there, and Sevareid decided to play by Paley's rules. "We never talked about it again," Sevareid said later.

They didn't have to. Eric Sevareid had been broken. In the years ahead there would be flashes of his former self, but by and large he hewed to the network's objectivity policy.

◆

Sevareid became an extremely unhappy and difficult man in the late 1950s. His son Michael saw "despair and anger — all the time." Sevareid's 11:10 P.M. radio commentary was abruptly shifted to 10 P.M., then to 9:25 P.M. — changes that confused and frustrated loyal listeners. On television he was named host of a science series called *Conquest*, but his weekly news program was a ratings failure and was canceled, along with *See It Now*, in 1958. As he felt his influence ebbing, he grew more and more sensitive to perceived slights, more insistent on being regarded with respect, more determined to protect his perquisites.

Some wondered if he was on the verge of a crackup. At a party in a Park Avenue apartment to celebrate the premiere of *Conquest*, Sevareid managed to get into a fistfight with his producer. Another CBS producer grabbed him and hustled him into a bedroom, hoping to calm him down. Later a young CBS man named Don Kellerman absentmindedly walked into the bedroom and found Sevareid sobbing convulsively.

Kellerman never learned what had caused the fight or the crying, but, he said, "We had the feeling it was yet another example of Sevareid's unease, his inability to move from being the star, the foreign correspondent in war, to this thing in television news. It was an expression of this guy's readiness to explode out of frustration. What he did that night was really to disgrace himself. He was the *reason* for the party. He was the star they were celebrating, having put this show into the can. There was a terribly self-destructive element in Sevareid's behavior, and not only that night."

Besides his professional problems, Sevareid was trying to cope with a marriage that was basically in ruins. Lois's manic depression had grown more severe since the war. Sevareid felt trapped. Some acquaintances thought he had been extremely supportive of Lois and had worked heroically to keep the marriage together. "He was marvelous with her," said his old friend Geoffrey Cox. "He looked after her very carefully." Others felt he was insensitive and even cruel. "He was not a kind husband," said CBS producer Ernie Leiser. "He was rude to her, ignored her." In the view of many who knew him, Sevareid was a selfish man, absorbed in his own problems, his own interests. "He would let you down personally," said Michael Bessie. "He was an evader of other people's problems. I don't think he ever worked at friendship."

Women always found Sevareid's anguished demeanor to be, in the words of an acquaintance, "sexy as hell." Years later Larry LeSueur mused, "Eric was so popular with women that I was content to follow in his wake, picking up stragglers." Over the years Sevareid had had a number of casual affairs, but with the decline of his marriage, he seemed to want something less casual. Back in 1950, at a party in New York, he had been smitten with a beautiful nineteen-year-old college student named Belèn Marshall. The daughter of two opera singers (the mother Spanish, the father American), Marshall was a talented singer in her own right, as she demonstrated at the party; Sevareid, thirty-eight years old at the time, asked her to join him for a midnight supper at the Sherry-Netherlands hotel. After consulting with her mother, Belèn accepted.

Sevareid was then broadcasting from New York on weekends. During the next year he asked Belèn out whenever he came to Manhattan. The vivacious, fun-loving Barnard student accepted his invitations but limited their encounters to dinner. She was the sheltered product of strict convent schools and fervently believed that sex must wait until marriage. After a year of this, Sevareid, whether out of frustration, flagging interest, or a feeling that he was becoming too emotionally involved, stopped calling. Heartbroken, Belèn, on graduating from Barnard, moved to Italy with her mother.

But Sevareid did not forget her. He wrote occasionally, and in 1954 asked her to join him in Anzio, where he was shooting an *American Week* segment commemorating the tenth anniversary of World War II's Italian campaign. The conservative college girl had matured and was now a worldly and successful songwriter and professional singer. She knew very well what Sevareid had in mind, and she accepted his invitation. "I thought by that time we were grown up enough to try something," she said. But when they sought to check into a hotel as husband and wife, they were turned away by a suspicious desk clerk. It is unlikely that Sevareid ever had a more frustrating affair.

In 1957, when Belèn moved back to the United States, the relationship was finally consummated and became serious. "It was soon understood," Belèn said with a certain Latin finality, "that we would be married." There was one major obstacle: Sevareid was still married to and living with Lois. Typically, he decided to duck the problem by leaving both Lois and the United States. In 1959 he persuaded network officials to give him a four-month leave of absence and then assign him to London. Sevareid asked Belèn to come with him. Hopelessly in love, "spellbound by his talent and his mind and his knowledge," she agreed. "I guess, to him, I represented his last chance for happiness or romance," she said. "But for me he was everything."

Trying to justify his abandonment of Lois, Sevareid wrote later, "The fantasy grew in me that her last chance for health lay in my own departure as well as my own last chance to feel again, to see again with the poet's eye and perhaps, one day, to write something that would be more whole than the writer." But Lois never recovered. She was devastated by Sevareid's leaving and for some time would just sit in a chair in their house all day without saying a word. She finally retreated to a rustic cabin that she and Sevareid had bought a few years earlier near Warrenton, Virginia. And Sevareid, with *Not So Wild a Dream* behind him, never again wrote anything that was more whole than the writer.

Sometimes, when he was alone with Belèn, he would break down in tears.

"Don't you feel guilt?" he said once.

"No," she answered. "About what?"

Years later she thought about those days and said, "I suppose, if I had been older, I might have shared the fact that we both were the cause, but for some reason I didn't include myself. I wasn't grown up enough to take his heartache and make it a part of me."

◆

During Howard Smith's time in London as chief European correspondent, he had become a top CBS star on both radio and television (although he, like Sevareid, didn't much care for the new medium). He had roamed the continent, reporting various upheavals and commenting on them in a fifteen-minute news analysis every Sunday afternoon. Many considered him a better analyst than even Murrow and Sevareid. Paris bureau chief David Schoenbrun, not normally given to self-deprecation, was intimidated whenever he was asked to fill in for Smith. "Substituting for Howard Smith," he said, "was like being asked to pinch-hit for Babe Ruth."

Even though Smith adopted the look and style of an English gentleman during his years in London — right down to his jewel of a house overlooking Regent's Park — at heart he was still the young Oxford radical. His radio commentaries were often scathing rebukes of U.S. foreign policy and its fixation on propping up corrupt anti-Communist regimes. For *See It Now* he held apartheid up to the light in South Africa and got CBS banned in Pretoria. In another memorable *See It Now* broadcast, he and Murrow took opposite sides on the Middle East crisis. Murrow thought Israel, which he equated with England in the days when it stood alone against Nazi Germany, could do little wrong; Smith, for the first time on a major U.S. program, explained the Palestinian question from the Arab perspective. *Variety* called it "electronic journalism at its best."

Occasionally Smith was chastened by New York for his bluntly expressed views, but he was never really curbed: Americans had far less concern about foreign affairs then, and Smith's superiors didn't worry much about his flouting the ban on opinion from more than three thousand miles away. But in 1957, after living in Europe for almost twenty years, Smith decided to give up the freedom of his London post and return to the States as chief Washington correspondent. Even though he and Bennie loved London, he did not want to become a permanent expatriate. He made the decision with "dreadful trepidation": the closer he got to New York, he thought, the more likely he was to get into trouble for his outspokenness. He didn't know the half of it.

✦

After Sig Mickelson took over the combined television and radio news operations at CBS in 1954 and subsumed Ed Murrow's proudly independent fiefdom, Murrow seemed lost. He still had *Person to Person*, his lighter-than-air, split-screen celebrity interview show, and his nightly radio broadcast. But he was beginning to think he might be finished at CBS.

When Murrow learned that *The $64,000 Question* and other quiz shows had been rigged almost from the beginning by their producers, he found it just too much to take. In October 1958 he lashed out at his own bosses in a scorching speech to the Radio and Television News Directors Association in Chicago. He denounced recent cutbacks at CBS News and said the hunger for profits by network executives had turned television into little more than a medium of "decadence, escapism and insulation." "This instrument can teach," he declared. "It can illuminate. Yes, and it can even inspire. But it can do so only to the extent that humans are determined to use it to those ends. Otherwise, it is merely wires and lights in a box."

Paley was livid. He thought, quite rightly, that the speech was a "direct attack" on him. Murrow had embarrassed the chairman in public, just as Shirer had in 1947. Murrow would not be dumped as Shirer had been, but he would soon know what it felt like to be a pariah. On the night of the 1958 elections, instead of doing commentary he was put in charge of the eastern states' returns, chalking up the latest numbers on a blackboard and reporting them to anchor Walter Cronkite. He accepted the assignment without protest, but, said Howard Smith, "He had been number one for so long that it was quite a blow."

Even when CBS tried to undo some of the damage of the quiz-show scandal by unveiling a new documentary program called *CBS Reports*, under Fred Friendly, it was made clear that Murrow was to be kept at arm's length. He would be permitted to do occasional reports for the program, but under no circumstance was he to be the anchor. Instead the job was to be rotated among several of the Boys, Howard Smith preeminent among them: the most renowned broadcast journalist in history was being replaced by his protégés. Friendly had argued in favor of Murrow, but when the decision went the other way he dropped the subject.

Murrow was floundering now — bitter, depressed, purposeless, perpetually exhausted. In the summer of 1959 he decided to take a year's leave of absence and travel around the world with Janet and their son, Casey. While they were in Europe on the first leg of their journey, CBS's president, Frank Stanton, still trying to clean up the quiz-show mess, announced that the network was taking a hard look at all its programs to make sure each was "exactly what it purports to be." One that wasn't, Stanton said in an interview with the *New York Times*, was *Person to Person*, because the guests knew the interview questions in advance. This was a direct shot at Murrow, then in London, and he fired off to the *Times* a plainly insubordinate cable:

> Dr. Frank Stanton has finally revealed his ignorance of both news and the requirements of production. . . . Surely Stanton must know that cameras, lights and microphones do not just wander around a home. . . . The alternative to a degree of rehearsal would be chaos. I am sorry Dr. Stanton feels that I have participated in perpetrating a fraud upon the public. My conscience is clear. His seems to be bothering him.

On reading this in the next day's *Times*, Paley immediately demanded a retraction by Murrow. After some negotiations Murrow came up with a statement that was far less contrite than what Paley wanted. If

CBS's reputation had not already been so badly tarnished, Fred Friendly said later, Paley would have fired his old friend then and there. Instead, orders came down to the producers of *Person to Person*, now presided over by Charles Collingwood, to run a disclaimer every week acknowledging that the program had been planned in advance with its guests. That ended the matter for the moment, but Paley and Stanton were in no mood to forgive or forget.

When Murrow returned to New York a couple of months early, in May 1960, he found there was no longer any real work for him to do. He said to Collingwood, "You're only important around here as long as you're useful to them, and you will be for a time. And when they're finished, they'll throw you out without another thought."

✦

In January 1961 the great Edward R. Murrow–CBS epic — which had begun in 1935 and swept through World War II, the postwar era, the Cold War, the advent of television, and McCarthyism — ended. Murrow accepted an offer from President-elect John Kennedy to become director of the United States Information Agency — "a beautiful and timely gift," said Janet Murrow. On January 31 Murrow appeared on a closed-circuit CBS broadcast to say goodbye to his network colleagues throughout the country. His eyes swimming with tears, his voice breaking, he tried desperately to keep his composure. "For many years, I have received credit for what other people have done," he said. ". . . There is in this CBS organization a crew . . . Smith, Collingwood, Cronkite, and all the rest, who will do a much better job than I ever did. It's naturally a little difficult to leave this shop after twenty-five years. But I would think it's fair and honest to say that some part of my heart will stay with CBS."

1961 ✴ 1992

25

Three Resignations

EDWARD R. MURROW and the Boys had created something brand-new out of thin air, but the age in which they did their greatest work lasted less than twenty-five years. As much as they may have wished otherwise, CBS News was not, after all, a higher calling; it was just a business. After Bill Paley took the company public in the late thirties and thus had to cater to the profit demands of his shareholders, too much was at stake for the age to survive — too much money and too much power. The end was already in sight by the time Murrow made his McCarthy broadcast in 1954. With his departure from CBS in 1961, the golden age was over.

Even the news division, which for so long had done things Murrow's way, was now heading in new directions. There was a plan to turn the CBS evening news program, hitherto little more than a headline service, into the division's showcase. (The same thing was happening at the other networks, but they didn't have anything like CBS's distinguished traditions.) Here both money and content were involved. It was not only safer to read the day's news than to go around attacking senators or criticizing U.S. foreign policy, it was also potentially more lucrative.

Murrow and his correspondents had built their careers and CBS News's reputation on thorough reporting and informed analysis — and on the assumption that the network's schedule would remain flexible and expansive enough to make room in prime time for their kind of journalism, the kind that went beyond the latest bulletins. That had been the whole idea ever since Murrow and Shirer first teamed up in 1937. But in the late fifties and early sixties, the nightly news, which the Murrow Boys had long ridiculed as more show business than journalism, was laying claim to most of the news division's human and financial resources.

An internal CBS memo, written just before Murrow resigned in

1961, confirmed their worst fears: "We want, where practical, to use the electronic camera as our reporter [on the evening news]." To underscore the point, the author deigned to add that the camera would be "backed up by the skills of our excellent correspondent staff." But the message and the future were clear: the word was dead; long live the picture. The correspondent was dead; long live the camera and the producers and executives who control it.

✦

One of Murrow's last official acts at CBS had been to ask Howard Smith to take over a *CBS Reports* documentary that Murrow and producer David Lowe had been preparing on the racial violence then tearing apart the city of Birmingham, Alabama. Having spent a few days watching Birmingham police commissioner Bull Connor's reign of terror, Murrow did not want the project to languish after he left. Would Smith do it?

Smith would. Of the things he felt passionately about, and there were many, none came before civil rights. From his early boyhood in Louisiana, he'd had a keen sense of the injustice of Jim Crow. When he had taken Bennie to New Orleans shortly after the war to introduce his new Danish wife to his family, he did so with some hope that the South, out of the annealing experience of fighting a war for freedom and the rights of man, would have begun to rid itself of the racist vestiges of slavery. He was disappointed. Even in relatively liberal New Orleans, discrimination was as prevalent as ever. Smith and the equally horrified Bennie could not wait to leave.

On his return to the United States from London in 1957, Smith's first major assignment was to cover the school integration battle in Little Rock. The segregationists of Little Rock were wrong, Smith thought, and his stories and commentaries on Douglas Edwards's evening news program often said as much. Paley, more than ever in a "whose-network-is-this-anyway?" mood, was growing unhappy with Smith's outspokenness. Nothing much came of this during the Little Rock crisis, but Paley and Smith would clash again and again over the next four years — ironically, the same period in which Smith was gaining a reputation as the heir to Murrow's mantle. For Smith had been chosen to do commentaries on Douglas Edwards's program and had been selected as moderator of the first Kennedy-Nixon televised debate in 1960. He anchored several highly praised installments of *CBS Reports*, including one for which he and producer Av Westin won a George Polk

Award and an Emmy. And in early 1961 Smith was promoted to Washington bureau chief.

Rapid advancement did not, however, make him less outspoken — just the opposite — and Paley finally ordered that all Smith's television commentaries be scrutinized in advance. Smith caught considerable hell during this period, and his scripts were often hacked to pieces. His editors were so worried about incurring Paley's wrath if they failed to detect some unacceptable thought that one of them approached Smith as he was writing a particularly sensitive commentary and said, "Our wives and children are counting on you, Howard. Please go easy on this."

In January 1961, the same month that Murrow left CBS, Smith took a stand. He would cease doing news analysis for the Edwards program unless they gave him more editorial slack. They refused. Smith quit the program, and no one was assigned to take his place.

Four months later he went to Birmingham, which Martin Luther King later called "the most segregated city in the United States." Smith had not been in town long before he was told by the grand titan of the local Ku Klux Klan that if he wanted "to see some action," he should be at the Trailways bus station the following day. Smith knew that a small band of Freedom Riders — young black and white civil rights activists from the North — were to arrive in Birmingham that day; virtually every newspaper in the South had been carrying stories about their expedition. When he staked out the terminal, he saw some thirty or forty beefy men in sport shirts standing on the sidewalk nearby. A local reporter told him they were Klansmen. As a bus approached, the men converged on it. They dragged off six Freedom Riders, pushed them into a nearby alley, and clubbed them with lead pipes, brass knuckles, key rings, fists, and feet. Smith and other reporters followed. One of the passengers was so badly beaten that he was paralyzed (for life, as it turned out). Another fell at Smith's feet, his face a bloody, unrecognizable mass. "They . . . just about slaughtered these kids," Smith said later.

After a time one of the thugs glanced at his watch and evidently decided enough was enough. The melee ended, and the mob dispersed. Only then did Bull Connor's police officers — whose station house was just three blocks away — arrive at the bus station. Later Smith saw some members of the gang standing in front of Connor's office, laughing and talking. Badly shaken, Smith felt he had witnessed another Kristallnacht. His eyewitness account, broadcast by CBS Radio, was also carried the next morning in the *New York Times*. Reporting on the aftereffects of the violence on both radio and television over the next few days, Smith and his crew received several death threats and had to hire an armed bodyguard to protect them while they were filming.

Smith wanted to make listeners and viewers feel some of the impotent rage he had felt as he watched the Freedom Riders being beaten. He used his Sunday radio commentary that week to vent his anger, managing to get the script past his editors only because radio didn't count for much anymore. He laid the ultimate blame for the incident at the feet of two men, the Klan's grand titan and a local chiropractor who Smith said had "gained a certain fame for writing and distributing hate literature directed at Jews and Negroes." He compared the "panting and exhilarated" thugs he had seen to Julius Streicher, "the vilest of the Nazi Jew-baiters, who used to . . . beat prisoners with a bullwhip . . . [and] seemed, it was said, to derive an almost perverse exhilaration from the brutality." Unless America provided justice to its black citizens, he said, it was in danger of "becoming a racial dictatorship, like Nazi Germany, or reverting to barbarism, as has happened . . . in Alabama."

Smith wanted to end his television documentary with a quote from the eighteenth-century British statesman and philosopher Edmund Burke: "The only thing necessary for the triumph of evil is for good men to do nothing." This was strikingly similar to the quote from *Julius Caesar* with which Murrow had concluded his McCarthy broadcast — "The fault, dear Brutus, is not in our stars / But in ourselves." But Murrow was gone from CBS — and so was Bill Paley's patience.

The real issue as far as Paley was concerned wasn't racial justice. As usual it was money. Because of Smith and other CBS correspondents covering the civil rights struggle, some of the network's southern affiliates had jumped to NBC and ABC. Others were threatening to do so. What was worse, the city of Birmingham was suing CBS for one million dollars over Smith's reports.

At that point Dick Salant, who had recently moved from the corporate side to replace the fired Sig Mickelson as president of CBS News, issued an edict: Smith was not to quote Burke or to do any "editorializing." In a rage, Smith went to see Salant, and they had a lengthy argument. "We won't allow opinions!" Salant said. "We won't allow you to adopt causes!" Smith countered that there was right and there was wrong, and he for one absolutely refused to believe that "right is an equidistant point between good and evil."

Many people consider Salant to have been the best president CBS News ever had, and in later years he would stoutly resist editorial interference from management. But in 1961 he would not let Smith have his way. "Who Speaks for Birmingham?" would be broadcast without the words of Edmund Burke. Smith then decided on passive resistance. At the point during his final standup where he would have quoted Burke, he stood in silence while the camera ground away. (Film editors later deleted Smith's several seconds of insolence.)

A few days later Jack Gould took a shot at CBS in the *New York Times* for not allowing Smith to be as forthright on the documentary and the nightly television news as he had been in his radio commentary:

> Mr. Smith's talk, delivered last Sunday evening over radio, painted an exceptionally vivid picture of the forbidding atmosphere of extremists taking over the center of a community while police looked the other way. In fact, it was a description not excelled by any of the newsreel films shown on television. . . . It is precisely such a display of conviction, of determination to influence society's course for the good, that builds respect for the world of broadcasting. Yet the policy of CBS News with respect to commentary does seem ambivalent. . . . Nighttime video, with its large audience, heard a diluted Smith, while Sunday night radio, with a very much smaller potential audience, heard Smith at his best.

Yet again Bill Paley's network was being chastised for throttling one of its correspondents, and Paley blamed Smith. The pattern was familiar from Shirer's case and again from Murrow's: there was a line you didn't dare cross with Paley. If you did, regardless of how big you were in the wider world, you were finished at CBS. ("It doesn't matter how much you like [journalists]," Paley said years later to CBS News executives Van Gordon Sauter and Edward Joyce. "There'll come a day when they'll want to [express their opinions on the air], and you've got to stop them.") Word came down from New York to the Washington bureau that Smith's future was being reconsidered. If he thought there was a case to be made for the kind of pointed commentaries he preferred, Salant told him, he should make that case in writing and send it directly to Paley. Smith did so, and in October he was summoned to New York for a showdown.

It took place over lunch in the executive dining room at CBS headquarters on October 29. Present were Smith, Paley, Frank Stanton, Salant, and Salant's deputy, Blair Clark. A former CBS Paris correspondent, Clark had known Smith well in Europe and was angry with him for forcing the issue. As Clark recalled it, Smith was "extremely offensive" to Paley during the lunch: "He was absolutely rigid on his right to do commentary. He said in effect, 'Murrow could do it, why can't I?' He just bore down on it, and Paley got angrier and angrier and said, 'Are you saying I can't determine the editorial policy of this enterprise?' Smith said something like, 'Not with me around'."

Frank Stanton was appalled as Paley and Smith lashed at each other. Stanton was no stranger to corporate power plays, but he didn't like this kind of face-to-face display of anger. In his view the confrontation was unnecessary and inappropriate. He thought Paley and the others had greatly overreacted to the Birmingham documentary; he himself didn't find the Burke quote at all offensive. Besides, he had learned to be philosophical when dealing with journalists. "It's inevitable, just as sure as God made little apples, that you're going to have differences between the front office and the editorial side," he said. "It just has to happen, and you've got to roll with the punches. Bill just wouldn't roll. They were both stubborn."

Midway through the lunch, Paley took Smith's long memo from his inside coat pocket and hurled it across the table. "If you want to report like this," he shouted, "then go somewhere else!" Smith got up and, without another word, strode from the room. In that instant, less than a year after Murrow's departure, Smith's twenty-year career with CBS came to an end.

The next day CBS issued this brief statement: "CBS News and Howard K. Smith announced today that their relations are being terminated because of a difference in interpretation of CBS news policy."

After he left, Smith sought Ed Murrow's advice. Murrow, still bitter at the way *he* had been treated, urged Smith to sue. "I'll testify to anything you say," Murrow told him. But Smith was in no position to do that: in his fury he had demanded that the network cancel his five-year contract, a demand CBS was only too happy to meet, for it meant that Smith was releasing his employer from all financial obligations. Bennie, who had been urging Smith to resign, couldn't believe the high-minded, self-destructive way he went about it. "You're not going to get any compensation," she told her husband. "We had complete security for the rest of our lives. Now we have nothing."

They had recently bought a large old house in Maryland, set on four and a half acres overlooking the Potomac River, and had embarked on its loving — and expensive — renovation. Bennie was set on redoing part of the interior to duplicate as nearly as possible the interior of their cherished Regency house in London. When the break with CBS came, the only money Smith received from the network — the settlement of his pension — was barely enough to pay off the painters. Work on the house was stopped, with the renovation only half completed.

Smith then began negotiating with the president of NBC News, William McAndrew, for a job. The contract was almost ready for signing when McAndrew abruptly called the deal off. "I can't tell you a thing about it," he said to Smith. "It's just business." Smith thought he detected the malicious interference of William S. Paley, probably working through NBC's founder and head, David Sarnoff.

Just when Smith began to worry that he might have to become an anchorman for some local news program, "a large hand reached out and arrested my fall." Ironically, the hand belonged to a sponsor. Murray Lincoln, a dedicated liberal who also happened to be president of the Nationwide Insurance Company, offered to sponsor Smith on a news-and-commentary TV program. All Smith and his agent, Bennie, had to do was find a network willing to carry him. Two of the three networks had already sent him packing, so Howard K. Smith, hat and sponsor in hand, went to what was then TV's bargain basement, ABC. Smith had to provide his own libel insurance, but in exchange the network agreed to a remarkable clause in his contract preventing both sponsor and ABC from interfering with Smith's "independence of mind and spirit."

Once hired, he set out to bring to television the same kind of news commentary that radio had featured. *Howard K. Smith — News and Comment* made its debut on ABC on February 14, 1962. The program was a mélange of filmed interviews and news footage, with Smith in the studio, discussing such disparate subjects as illegitimacy, disarmament, a do-nothing Congress, baseball, and the state of television. From the beginning it was pure Howard Smith — tough, insightful, highly opinionated. Said *Newsweek*: "He has displeased practically everyone, including the business community, conservatives, liberals and [President] Kennedy. . . . He is now producing the most stimulating news show on television." When ABC polled New Yorkers in the summer of 1962 to find out their favorite ABC program, Smith's show came in first, higher even than the network's hit medical drama, *Ben Casey*.

Then Richard Nixon was defeated in his 1962 bid for the governorship of California. In a broadcast entitled "The Political Obituary of Richard M. Nixon," Howard Smith interviewed several key figures from Nixon's past, including former senior State Department official Alger Hiss, the alleged Soviet agent whom Nixon had investigated in the late forties. Overall, Smith's program was a balanced assessment

of Nixon, but the inclusion of Hiss brought a firestorm of protest —
a firestorm ignited, Smith and ABC were convinced, by the right-
wing John Birch Society. ABC's switchboards were jammed. Telegrams
poured in. Sponsors of other ABC shows threatened to cancel. Smith's
own sponsor received more than eighty thousand anti-Smith letters.

Eight months later Nationwide Insurance quietly ended its sponsorship of *Howard K. Smith — News and Comment*, claiming it could no
longer justify the expense. Within days ABC dropped the program from
its schedule. Smith remained at the network but wasn't given enough
work to keep him fully engaged. Months became years, and by 1966 he
felt abandoned. "I have been wasted at ABC for three years," he complained. "I am walking around with nothing to do and no particular
function. I am in limbo and I am tired of it."

Another three years would pass before he was rescued by Av Westin,
an old CBS colleague and admirer of the Murrow Boys. Westin, hired to
be executive producer of ABC's floundering evening news program,
decided that if it was to be saved, Howard Smith had to play a major
part. In March 1969 he made Smith commentator and coanchor with
Frank Reynolds.

Smith lost no time in stirring up new controversy. He remained a
liberal on many domestic matters but, to the bewilderment and disappointment of many friends and colleagues, became an outspoken hawk
on Vietnam. Some speculated that he had been influenced by the near-
fatal wounding of his son, Jack, an army enlisted man, in the war. Smith
denied it. He was more influenced, he said, by his experiences in Europe
during the thirties, by watching Hitler swallow up Czechoslovakia and
Poland. Whatever his reasons, he was said to be the only TV journalist
whom President Nixon — whose 1962 political obituaries, including
the controversial one by Smith, had turned out to be premature —
could stand.

But not for long. As the Watergate scandal unfolded, Smith, more
and more dubious about Nixon's denials of guilty knowledge, kept ham-
mering away with his doubts. Finally, in a commentary on October 31,
1973, he called for the president's impeachment or resignation. "President Nixon has put a strain on the nation's trust that is nearly unbearable," he declared. ". . . I think it not excessive to say we have been put
through too much."

Whether they agreed with him or not, viewers responded to Smith's
independence and outspokenness. By early 1974 ABC had a 23 percent

share of the national audience, just a point or two behind second-place NBC. Smith was teamed in this period with former CBS correspondent Harry Reasoner as coanchor, and the combination of the prickly, opinionated Smith and the easygoing Reasoner had clicked with the public. In some major markets, including New York and Philadelphia, ABC was actually in first place.

But there was trouble just ahead. The two CBS News alumni, both with huge egos, hated sharing the anchor job. Reasoner, however, had more clout with the ABC boardroom brass. When his contract came up for renewal in 1975, he demanded that he be made sole anchor and that Smith be limited to commentaries. Reasoner took over the program that fall, and within weeks ABC's entry in the evening news sweepstakes was again far back in third place. Without Smith's weight and authority, Reasoner seemed too airy and insubstantial. "He just couldn't hold it," said Av Westin. "He needed Howard, who had substance."

The following spring ABC's executives made a bad situation worse by hiring Barbara Walters of NBC's *Today* show to be coanchor with Reasoner — at an unprecedented one million dollars a year. Reasoner fumed until June 1978, when he gave up in disgust and returned to CBS. By then ABC News had a new president, Roone Arledge, who soon dropped Walters and created a troika of anchors: Frank Reynolds in Washington, Peter Jennings in London, and Max Robinson in Chicago. At the same time he dumped Howard K. Smith's commentaries.

It was now clear to Smith that ABC no longer had a place for him. On April 20, 1979, he strode to the bulletin board at the network's Washington bureau and posted a single sheet of paper — the announcement of his resignation. As he left the ABC office that day, he knew that his long and turbulent broadcasting career was over.

✦

When Smith left CBS in 1961, a great fissure seemed to open under the feet of the correspondents who remained. "We realized that, in this new era, the act of challenging management, however slightly, had become a cardinal sin that would not be tolerated," wrote David Schoenbrun. "The era of Murrow and the Murrow boys, freewheeling, making all the decisions, had definitely come to a close." In 1962 Schoenbrun quit (some knowledgeable people said he was fired) after a short, disastrous run as Smith's successor as Washington bureau chief.

Next to tumble into CBS's memory hole would be two of the network's best combat reporters from World War II — Bill Downs and Larry LeSueur. The one assignment Downs had really enjoyed after the war — his posting to Rome — had come to an abrupt end in 1956 when he was yanked back to the States to make room in Rome for the exiled Winston Burdett. Downs was then assigned to Washington, but no one seemed to know quite what to do with him there. In 1957 he was named anchor of a daily five-minute radio news summary. The commercial fees were good, but for a man who loved the excitement of reporting, there wasn't much satisfaction in merely reading the news. (Besides, he was a *terrible* reader.) As his frustration and bitterness mounted, his temper and drinking started getting the better of him. He would rail at the "pygmy" editors, producers, and executives who he felt were ruining the network, occasionally punctuating his anger by picking up some object — a telephone, for instance — and hurling it across the newsroom. Among those feeling the brunt of his temper was Washington bureau chief Howard Smith. "Downs was so apoplectic all the time, I found it hard to get along with him," said Smith. "It got to the point where I gave up on him. I didn't see him anymore."

Eventually Downs lost his radio show, and Smith assigned him to cover the State Department. But New York hated the way Downs, with his glasses, growling voice, and paunch, came across on television. Downs could report from the State Department, but only if Smith did the on-air reports for him. It was the ultimate insult. Downs (and many others at CBS) thought he had been a good soldier who had been treated shabbily for most of his career. He wasn't going to put up with it any longer. He exploded at Smith, screaming and hurling insults.

In March 1962 Downs resigned, intending to spend the rest of his life writing novels. Difficult though he may have been, he was regarded as a generous, thoughtful, caring friend by most of his colleagues. Larry LeSueur, Eric Sevareid, and fifteen others gave him a silver cigarette box with their names engraved on it when he left the network. In a letter of thanks to Sevareid, he talked about how happy he was to be out of television: "At least I can shout to the world this — I'm my own midget. The mistakes will be my mistakes — the failures will have my fiat — the successes, if any or none, will not be subject to people who worry about thick lenses, long noses, or advertising agency or affiliate bias."

For a year and a half Downs worked hard at writing fiction, but publishers weren't interested. In November 1963 he ran out of money and was forced to return to broadcast news. Hired by ABC, he remained a second-echelon reporter in its Washington bureau for the rest of his life.

✦

By the time Ed Murrow left CBS, Larry LeSueur had long since grown bored with his UN beat, bored with the interminable hours of listening to high-flown rhetoric and interviewing stuffy, long-winded diplomats. His radio coverage of the UN had earned him a Peabody Award, and for a time in the fifties he had his own UN-based Sunday TV interview program called *Chronoscope*. But the sense at CBS was that LeSueur was on automatic pilot. In 1960 the network offered to assign him to Moscow, and LeSueur, recalling the exciting year he had spent in the Soviet Union during the war, eagerly accepted. Divorced from Priscilla Bruce in 1951, he had gotten married for the third time in 1957, to Dorothy Hawkins, the fashion editor of the *New York Times*. Three years later the two of them, with their toddler daughter, were preparing to leave for Moscow when word came from the Soviets that LeSueur was persona non grata. Stunned, he protested, but a Soviet official tersely replied, "You've been there before, Mr. LeSueur."

So Larry LeSueur languished in New York a while longer, then was transferred to the Washington bureau. In 1963, sensing that he was no longer very much wanted at CBS, he took an unpaid leave of absence and approached Murrow at the United States Information Agency about a job there. Regretfully, Murrow said, civil-service regulations being what they were, there was nothing he could do. But LeSueur applied to the Voice of America, an arm of the USIA, and was hired as a news analyst. Later he became White House correspondent. Perhaps Murrow helped, perhaps he didn't. At least Larry LeSueur and he were, in a manner of speaking, together again. But not for long.

26

"Good Night, Sweet Prince"

Edward r. murrow, after all those cigarettes, was dying of cancer at the age of fifty-seven.

His left lung was removed in October 1963, and a few months later he stepped down as USIA director. He tried recuperating in La Jolla, California, then returned East to friends and his beloved farm in Pawling. But the cancer soon metastasized to his brain, and he had to undergo surgery again. As he struggled to live, several of the Boys, including Charles Collingwood, Larry LeSueur, Dick Hottelet, and Howard K. Smith, visited him in New York. The Hottelets sent books; LeSueur, Collingwood, and Bill Downs wrote chatty letters, using their pet nicknames for him.

In one of his letters Collingwood said, "We're all a dispirited lot, your correspondent as much as anyone." It was hard not to be able to talk things over with Murrow, hard not to have his advice. Collingwood expanded on the theme in a separate letter to Janet: "CBS these days is almost more than I can stand. I often think that if [Ed] were around or if we could just hoist a couple and curse the panjandrums the way we did in the old days, it might stir up a fresh breath of reason that would make it bearable."

In the spring of 1964 Murrow was supposed to give the commencement address to his son's graduating prep school class, but he was too weak to do it. At the last minute he asked Howard Smith to step in for him. Late that summer, despite his rapidly failing health, Murrow and Janet drove hundreds of miles to attend the wedding of one of Eric Sevareid's twin sons, a trip that "pretty well flattened me out," Murrow wrote later to Collingwood. Then a discordant note of mild rebuke for Sevareid: "Eric," Murrow wrote, "seemed to me to continue his preoccupation with Eric."

Murrow knew Sevareid all too well and the ways he had of warding off life. By focusing on himself, Sevareid didn't have to confront the many things that terrified him, including his certain knowledge that the person he loved and respected above all others was now a frail and weak shell of a man, who would surely die soon. Smith and LeSueur and some of the others visited Murrow after his brain surgery that autumn. Sevareid could not bring himself to do so. He would not have known what to say to this thin, hairless man with the pathetic red cap on his head. So Sevareid the writer instead sent notes and telegrams to Janet to buck her up and to thank her for all *she* was doing for Ed. He would offer to help, in that way people have when they don't really want their offer accepted. Yet the pain Sevareid felt as his hero declined was surely as acute as any he would feel in his long, pain-filled life.

If Sevareid's aloofness was a disappointment to Murrow, Bill Shirer's was staggering. Murrow and Shirer — proud and talented men who had pioneered broadcast journalism together — had barely spoken since 1947, the year of Shirer's bitter fall from grace at CBS. Murrow, however, had hoped all along to repair their shattered friendship, and by the summer of 1964 he knew that time was running out. Janet Murrow called Tess Shirer one day and invited them to lunch in Pawling. Tess, who was very fond of the Murrows and who had been upset when her husband and Ed became estranged, said she would do her best to persuade Bill. For his part, Shirer made clear to Tess that he wanted no part of any sentimental reconciliation. But he finally, grudgingly, agreed to go.

Over lunch the two couples laughed and reminisced about the years before the war when two young men, best friends, traipsed about Europe and did things no one thought could be done. It was wonderful to talk that way again, almost like old times. Then Murrow, impossibly emaciated, asked Shirer to ride around the farm with him in his Jeep. Shirer did not want to be alone with Murrow and protested he didn't think Ed was up to the drive. Murrow insisted. They climbed into the Jeep and drove slowly over the Pawling hills, with Murrow at the wheel. He was coughing and sweating, in obvious pain.

Twice in the circuit around the farm, he stopped, pointed out the view, then tried to turn the conversation to the hows and whys of Shirer's departure from CBS and its devastating effect on their friendship. Both times Shirer cut him off and changed the subject "as quickly and gracefully as I could." After trying again to breach the wall, Murrow, defeated, fell silent. He started the Jeep and drove back to the house. Everyone chatted amiably enough over a civilized pot of tea. Then the Shirers rose to leave, and the Murrows walked them out to their car and thanked them for coming. It had been, Murrow said with a weak smile, "much too long a time."

After that sad and unyielding reunion, William L. Shirer and Edward R. Murrow never saw each other again.

In late 1993, when Shirer, almost ninety, had only a couple more months to live, he still had not forgiven or forgotten, was still trying to get even. "Ed cast his lot with Bill Paley, who wasn't worth a hundredth of Ed Murrow," he said. "I remember saying to Ed, 'You'll get just what I got.' And he did in the end." So why didn't he reconcile with Murrow in Pawling, knowing how desperate Murrow was to end their feud before he died? "I thought [being forced out at CBS] was a lousy deal for me," Shirer said. "Ed didn't have to do what he did to his best friend. I just didn't want to make up after twenty years." The old man paused and peered with his one good eye at some distant point. "I may have been wrong," he said softly, "but that's the way I felt about it."

◆

On April 27, 1965, Eric Sevareid received a call at CBS's Washington bureau. Ed Murrow was dead. Sevareid's large body sagged. His head drooped. He hung up the phone, went into his office without saying a word, and shut the door. He did not come out for a long time.

He had known this day was coming but had been unable to prepare himself for it. A few days before, when he learned that the old *See It Now* crew was preparing a news special to be aired after Murrow's death, he insisted on taking part. In a screening room Palmer Williams showed him some of the footage they were planning to use — an excerpt from the McCarthy broadcast, an interview with Murrow, still shots from London of a somber, elegant young man in a homburg and mackintosh, with perfectly creased trousers and perfectly shined shoes. When the lights came up, Sevareid's face was crumpled, his eyes glittered with tears.

Shut away in his office on the day of Murrow's death, he did more than grieve; he sat down at the typewriter and poured out his feelings. That evening on Walter Cronkite's news program, Sevareid, the one true poet of the Boys and their experience, read what he had written:

> There are some of us here, and I am one, who owe their professional lives to this man. There are many, working here and in other networks and stations, who owe to Ed Murrow their love of their work, their standards and sense of responsibility. He was a shooting star; we will live

in his afterglow a very long time. . . . He was an artist, passionately alive, living each day as if it were his last, absorbing and radiating the glories and miseries of his generation; the men, the machines, the battles, the beauties. The poetry of America was in his bones. He believed in his family, his friends, his work and his country. Himself, he often doubted. . . . I will presume to use the words of England's greatest poet about another brave and brooding figure who also died too young — "Now cracks a noble heart. Good night, sweet prince."

Three nights later Sevareid and Collingwood coanchored a special prime-time program on Murrow. The idea for the program, and its scheduling, had come from Fred Friendly, who had been promoted to president of CBS News a few months earlier. Bill Paley at first was reluctant. It wasn't that Paley was still mad at Murrow. On the contrary, after Murrow left CBS, he and Paley resumed their friendly relationship. Paley even visited him while he was in La Jolla recovering from surgery and again while he was recuperating in New York. No, the objection by Paley and other CBS executives was purely financial. "It was Friday night at eight o'clock, and they just didn't want to give up the airtime," Friendly said. But they finally gave in, and Paley insisted on appearing on the program himself, a rare tribute. Summing up Murrow's career, he singled out for praise Murrow's recruitment of the Boys: "The originator of an overseas reporting organization unequaled anywhere, Ed Murrow set standards of excellence that remain unsurpassed. His death ends the first golden age of broadcast journalism. I shall miss him greatly, as will all of us at CBS."

The funeral was held at St. James's Episcopal Church in midtown Manhattan. The Boys watched as the coffin was borne down the aisle. The man who had created this team was gone, the team itself irrevocably splintered, its members bereft. Howard Smith felt like "a planet whose sun had gone." Charles Collingwood mused, "I loved him as much as I did any man except my father and brother." Sevareid mourned the loss of Murrow's "incandescence," that quality that drew, "like moths to the light, friends, strangers, the curious, the hangers-on, all those who need light and magic in their lives."

27

"Writing Captions for Pictures"

O F THE EIGHT BOYS who were with CBS at the end of World War II, only Eric Sevareid, Charles Collingwood, Winston Burdett, and Dick Hottelet were still there in 1965, and their prospects were uncertain. They were in or near their fifties, and the world was turning beneath their feet. John F. Kennedy had been assassinated. The Vietnam war had escalated. Ahead lay the killings of Robert Kennedy and Martin Luther King, urban riots and student demonstrations, LSD, the "credibility gap," Kent State, the 1968 Democratic convention in Chicago, Woodstock, Altamont. This was a world for which the Boys, from a different, more gallant epoch, were not prepared. It confused and alienated them, all the more so because of the ever-growing influence of television. The Murrow Boys were growing old. The future was no longer theirs, so they looked back to where they had been.

On a bitingly cold day in January 1965, Charles Collingwood watched as Winston Churchill's casket was solemnly borne into the nave of St. Paul's Cathedral in London. He recalled the excitement and terror, the overwhelming satisfaction and pride, of being in London a quarter of a century before, of being with Murrow. As CBS anchorman for the Churchill funeral, Collingwood struggled to find words for what he was feeling. Shortly afterward he wrote to the dying Ed Murrow, "The whole thing is a flood of memories and I find myself thinking constantly of you and of those days and of those people. . . . I really have missed you like hell these last days."

In August of that same year, Eric Sevareid, fifty-one years old, went to Saint-Tropez on a pilgrimage. Sevareid stood on the beach, gazing out to sea, and remembered how, twenty-one years earlier, he had bobbed there in a landing craft, smelling the wonderful, clean scent of pine forests, waiting for the invasion of southern France. Now the beach was carpeted with refreshment stands, tents, gas stations, and hundreds of sunbathers who had no idea what had happened there in 1944 and probably little interest. "The new generation worships today, brown skin and hot sun," Sevareid wrote later. "The old gods in their old temples are willfully forgotten as an encumbrance on what is. No place for the middle-aged, Saint Tropez. To the swarming brown-skinned young we are, as they contemptuously put it, *les croulants* — 'the crumbling' — along with our hollow gods, our dusty, crumbled shrines."

✦

When Ed Murrow died, Charlie Collingwood had been chief European correspondent for CBS for one year, his second postwar foreign assignment. He had worked in London for a couple of years in the late fifties, but when Murrow went on sabbatical in 1959, Collingwood had returned to New York to take over as host of *Person to Person*. Finally, he thought, he would come into his own on television. But *Person to Person* was canceled in 1960, and two years later, when CBS was looking for a new evening news anchor to counter the popular, dynamic NBC team of David Brinkley and Chet Huntley, Collingwood, who desperately wanted the job, didn't get it.

According to former CBS news manager Blair Clark, both Collingwood and Sevareid had shown interest in replacing Douglas Edwards as anchor. Neither correspondent approved of the trend away from analytical journalism and toward the evening news headline service, but both apparently calculated that if their further fame, fortune, and power depended on sitting on a newsroom set every evening and reading from a TelePrompTer, it was a price they were now willing to pay. Sevareid, with his fear of the camera, never had a chance at the job, but Collingwood was a serious contender. In 1962, though, the CBS executives passed over him in favor of the man who had hitched his star to CBS television after the war and for whom the word "avuncular" seemed to have been coined: Walter Cronkite.

Collingwood was devastated. As far as he was concerned, Cronkite was just a "marionette" who didn't even write his own copy. As a consolation prize, Collingwood was selected to replace Cronkite on *Eyewitness*, a half-hour review of the major news story of the week. Then, in July 1963, *Eyewitness* was canceled, along with a number of other news programs.

Collingwood's frail ego could not stand much more battering. His position at CBS had become tenuous: Harry Reasoner replaced him as the regular substitute for Cronkite on the new thirty-minute evening news, and Collingwood was demoted to utility man — in his words, "to provide pad if the President's news conference runs short, to give voice to interruptions in soap operas, to substitute for your regular broadcasters at a few minutes' notice. . . ." Profoundly disheartened, Collingwood in 1964 persuaded CBS to send him back to Europe as chief foreign correspondent, based first in Paris, later in London. It was a good move: Collingwood loved Paris and London, and they returned the favor. He could swirl his cape and swing his walking stick and whip down the Champs-Élysées in his white Rolls Royce and be appreciated as the flamboyant, larger-than-life bon vivant he truly was.

Sometimes, however, he went a little over the top. During the student-led leftist uprisings in Paris in 1968, for example, he showed up in the CBS Paris bureau one day wearing what London correspondent Morley Safer described as "the most absurd coat I'd ever seen — a Holmesian thing, not a cape, but huge, skirted, with sleeves and flaps and hoods and pockets." Collingwood modeled it for Safer.

"What do you think?" he asked.

Safer laughed. "Charles, this time you've finally gone too far."

"You don't think they'll be impressed on the barricades?"

"I don't think so."

Downcast, Collingwood said, "I *knew* it was a mistake" and never wore the coat again.

Beneath Collingwood's dilettante exterior, however, there still dwelt a top-notch reporter, as he proved time and again in Europe, Asia, and the Middle East. Of the Boys remaining in network television, only he and Winston Burdett were still foreign correspondents, real shoe-leather reporters who frequently showed their juniors a thing or two about how to cover a story.

At a Geneva conference on the future of Laos in the sixties, CBS foreign editor Ralph Paskman assembled his correspondents in a hotel bar one afternoon to discuss the story they would put together for the evening news that night. The meeting had already begun, and no one had much beyond official handouts, when Collingwood strolled in, cigarette holder jauntily clenched between his teeth. Said Paskman, irritated at Collingwood's tardiness, "What we're trying to *do*, Charles . . ."

"I know what you're trying to do," Collingwood said. "I thought this might help." He drew a folded sheet of paper from his inside pocket and began to read the minutes of the closed meeting. Later he explained to his astounded colleagues, "There's a young man in the Laotian delegation whom I used to know at the Sorbonne. He's nothing, the fifth secretary of the delegation. But he did happen to have the minutes."

Said Marvin Kalb, who was in the group that night: "That's the way CBS got this great scoop. I asked Collingwood about it later, because here I was running around after Chou En-lai and obviously couldn't get anywhere near him. Charlie went for somebody like the Laotian fifth secretary, who he *knew* would know what was going on."

During this period Vietnam became one of Collingwood's passions. Between 1960 and 1972 he made seventeen trips to Indochina, collaborating with his producer and pal Les Midgley on a string of superb special reports. Collingwood was skeptical of the official U.S. predictions of incipient victory but was never really a dove. He, like a number of the other Boys who remembered the Munich sellout to Hitler, felt that the United States had an obligation to protect the people of southeast Asia from Communist aggression. "But Charles was no fool," Midgley said. "He saw that what was happening in Vietnam wasn't right, and he came around."

In 1968, over the objections of his superiors, he took what was supposed to be a one-year sabbatical, suffering, he said, "fatigue in the bone, in the mind and in the heart." He and Louise repaired to a vacation home they'd purchased in Puerto Vallarta, Mexico, where their friends and drinking partners included Richard Burton and Elizabeth Taylor. Their idyll was interrupted in March, shortly after the Vietcong's Tet offensive, when Collingwood received a cable from CBS in New York. North Vietnam's government was inviting him to visit Hanoi. The next day he was on his way. *

Collingwood was the first American network journalist to visit North Vietnam. The North Vietnamese, eager to cash in on their political victory during Tet, had decided to use CBS and others to convey the message that they were now willing to begin peace negotiations. According to one version, this information was given to Collingwood informally several days before his scheduled interviews with Premier Pham Van Dong and Foreign Minister Nguyen Duy Trinh. On March 27 Collingwood cabled the peace-talk message to CBS in New York. Very soon afterward the White House was informed, and in May peace

---

*Hanoi's invitation went originally to Walter Cronkite, but Cronkite declined, wanting to avoid any suggestion that he was being rewarded by North Vietnam for his recent negative assessment of the U.S. war effort. CBS and Hanoi agreed on Collingwood as a substitute.

talks officially began in Paris. In 1969 Collingwood won an Overseas Press Club award for his reports from North Vietnam.

Despite such successes, Collingwood, now fifty-seven, stepped down as chief foreign correspondent in 1975 and moved back to New York — in large part because he thought he could take better care of his wife there. The hard-drinking Louise had become a hopeless alcoholic and was suffering from cancer as well.

The Collingwood-Allbritton marriage had always been a combustible mix of mutual love, dependence, and hostility. On their good days they both exuded charm and sophistication — as if they'd just stepped out of a Noel Coward play, cigarette holders and all. Collingwood would baby Louise as his "poor darling" when some small vicissitude of life intruded on their dreamy existence. She, meanwhile, seemed torn between her desire to be someone, or something, other than Mrs. Charles Collingwood and her very traditional ideas about marriage. "He had no sense of a real self, no sense of assurance," said Bill Walton. "Neither did Louise. That was one of their bonds."

Charles was flagrantly unfaithful. She probably reciprocated, though less flagrantly. On their bad days they fought like cats, and during their last decade or so together, both drank heavily. Walton recalled a time when Louise was drunk on opening night of a play in which she was appearing in Washington. "The curtain went up on an empty stage with a staircase, and suddenly there was a great crash," Walton said. "Louise, in making her entrance, fell down at the top of the stairs and came down on her ass all the way. We gave her an ovation."

Don Hewitt and his wife encountered Louise one summer morning on Fire Island. "We're walking along," Hewitt said, "and over a dune comes Louise, with a cornucopia hat, a cigarette holder, a bikini that she really shouldn't have been wearing, because she was coming out of it everywhere, and a martini in her hand. 'Oh, darlings,' she said, 'you've simply got to come to lunch! The Smithfields are coming, and they'll *die* if they don't see you!' I didn't know who the fuck the Smithfields *were!* Then Louise turned and disappeared over the dune with her martini and her cigarette holder."

Louise loved children and was good with them, and she seemed to regret that she and Charles were unable to have any of their own. For years they agonized about adoption but never seemed able to bring themselves to act. "I had the feeling that they just sort of bumbled along in their personal lives," said Nancy White Hector, then married to author Theodore White, one of Collingwood's closest friends. "I don't think they ever thought it out. It was the way they dealt with things: a lot of it got lost in the booze. There was this attitude, 'Let's have another drink. We'll talk about it tomorrow.'"

Watching Louise decline was terribly painful for Collingwood, and his pain was compounded by the knowledge that CBS, his employer for thirty-four years, had little or no use for him anymore. He was told on moving to New York that he would report and anchor news specials, but the assignments were rare. "Once in a while, they'd say to him, 'Stand up on your hind legs and speak or bark. Show us how the dogs used to do it,'" correspondent George Herman said. "He was treated as if he were quaint." The Bonnie Prince was gone; in his place was a man his colleagues now referred to as "poor Charlie Collingwood."

But he would not go quietly. He was angry at what was happening in broadcast journalism — the decline of the correspondents and the rise of pictures and producers; the decline of good writing and the rise of "happy talk" and gimmicks; the loss of integrity. In the seventies and eighties he delivered a number of speeches about what he saw happening. In one he said:

> The serious correspondent is more and more relegated to a back seat, and the public is less and less well informed than it should be. In the old days a correspondent was responsible for what he put on the air. As a result, he knew his stuff or he didn't last long. . . . It was his mug and his voice out there, and what he said was his own work, unsullied by the dirty fingerprints of anonymous producers and writers. Because it was that way, with a few notable exceptions, I think my generation of correspondents did a better job than the present one. . . . Today's correspondents so often are limited merely to writing captions for pictures.

Such complaints were regarded by certain members of the new generation of producers and executives as additional proof, if any were needed, of just how out of touch and out of date Collingwood and his ilk really were. The shunning continued, and Collingwood increasingly turned to the bottle for solace. "It was kind of a truism that if you had to shoot a Collingwood piece, you shot it in the morning, because after lunch he wouldn't make it," recalled John Sharnik. To most of the people he knew at CBS, Collingwood had been a kind, generous friend and mentor, and several of his colleagues now did all they could to help and protect him. But he seemed beyond help. His drinking became worse, and so did Louise's health.

On February 16, 1978, Louise died of cirrhosis of the liver at their home in Mexico, where she had gone to rest. She was only fifty-eight years old. On the day of her death, Collingwood was in New York, working on a half-hour late-night special on Iran. Les Midgley pleaded with him to stop work and fly to Mexico. He shook his head. "No, damn it. They think I can't do this." Only after the broadcast aired the following night did he finally get on a plane, exhausted and beyond sadness.

In Puerto Vallarta he discovered that shipping Louise's body to the States was going to be no easy matter. There were forms to fill out, bureaucracies to satisfy, "fees" to be paid. Louise had said she wanted to be cremated and her ashes buried in the United States. But time was limited, and the Mexican authorities were getting cranky. So in the course of a sodden wake for Louise on the night Collingwood arrived, he, Richard Burton, and a few other friends concocted a plan: they placed the body in a plain plywood box, slid the box into the back of a station wagon, and covered it with luggage. The next day a three-car convoy, each car loaded with luggage, set out for Los Angeles.

Collingwood drove the car with Louise's body in it. The day was hot, the car's air conditioning broke down, and the U.S. customs officials at the border were suspicious. For a while it looked as if they might want to search the car, but finally the conspirators crossed safely into California. It was, said a relative of Collingwood's, "a pretty madcap Keystone Kops caper involving these very drunk celebrities."

The cremation took place in Los Angeles. A memorial service was held February 23 at Saint James's Church in Manhattan. "I tried very hard to comfort him afterward," said his sister-in-law, Molly Collingwood, "but he wouldn't be comforted. It was as if there was no core there anymore."

In 1982 he retired from CBS. Eric Sevareid sent him a telegram so unabashedly emotional that Collingwood dared not read it aloud at his retirement dinner for fear he would break down and cry. "It isn't always that mutual affection and respect survive so much and so long," he wrote back to Sevareid. "I'm awfully glad ours has. I value our relationship enormously."

✦

Eric Sevareid and Belèn Marshall had returned to New York in 1961 after living together in London for two years. At first there wasn't much professional satisfaction for Eric in New York, other than his new nationally syndicated newspaper column. Then in 1963 he was asked if he'd like to do commentaries on Walter Cronkite's evening news program, which was being expanded from fifteen to thirty minutes. Sevareid said yes.

The executives at CBS believed that all commentary should be as inoffensive as possible, but Sevareid was no longer likely to give them much trouble. His world-view had changed dramatically over the years. The passionate young idealist of *Not So Wild a Dream* had become a world-weary pragmatist — more like Henry Kissinger now than Thomas Paine.

Yet he was still capable of surprises. In the spring of 1966 he embarked on a five-week trip to Vietnam, Laos, Cambodia, and Thailand. When he returned, Dick Salant gave him a half-hour in prime time — "Eric Sevareid's Personal Report on Vietnam" — to tell the country what he had learned. "I propose to sit here for the next thirty minutes and talk about America in Asia, about war, and about troops," Sevareid began, adding a typical backhanded slap at the medium he was using: "This may set television back a long way. We'll find out."

There were no fancy graphics, no dramatic war footage — just Eric Sevareid, uncomfortable as always before the camera, sitting at a desk, offering images, opinions, conclusions — and becoming the first prominent television journalist to challenge U.S. policy in Vietnam. He was not an authority, he admitted, but he felt he had learned enough in five weeks to dismiss the Johnson administration's "domino theory" and to conclude that the United States was being sucked deeper into the morass of what was essentially a civil war. At the same time, he had no prescription for ending American involvement except optimism and faith: "This reporter, like most, even those who fear and doubt, still believes that God and the stars will again indulge their notorious weakness for Americans, and bring us through this unhappy Vietnam transaction in safety and peace."

In 1962 Sevareid had finally divorced Lois; he married Belèn the following year. In 1964 the couple, with their two-month-old daughter, Cristina, moved to Washington. He had once contemptuously referred to the capital as "that leafy, dreaming park" but this time seemed more than pleased to be there. He and Belèn bought a large stone house just across the city line in Chevy Chase, Maryland, and Sevareid quickly rejoined the inner circle of the political and journalistic elite.

Belèn never became part of that world. She had no friends in Washington, no existence she could truly call her own. She didn't know how to drive a car and thus felt trapped and isolated in their great stone house. She was also intimidated by her husband's many powerful and influential friends, especially those she called "the cool blue ladies" — Katharine Graham, Marietta Tree, and others — who she thought looked down on her and resented her for taking Lois's place. One day while Belèn was gone from the house, Sevareid took Cristina, still an infant, to introduce her to *New York Times* columnist James Reston and his wife, Sally. According to Belèn, the Restons had made clear to Eric that they were not interested in meeting Cristina's mother.

Indications of problems in the Sevareids' relationship were evident even while they were still living in New York. Three days before their wedding, Sevareid had panicked and gone into hiding. None of his friends knew what had happened to him or whether he would even show up for the ceremony in Teddy White's New York apartment. Several months later, when Belèn became pregnant, Sevareid was so fearful that she might have twins, as Lois had, that he asked her to get an abortion. She refused, and he, in a rage, moved out of their apartment for several days. (From the day Cristina was born, Sevareid doted on her and continued to do so for the rest of his life.)

It was in Washington that the marriage collapsed. The many differences between Eric and Belèn — age, interests, temperaments — that had intrigued him in the beginning soon became insurmountable emotional barriers. He complained about the loud Latin music she played and sang so much at home, about her mother's constant presence and the frequent visits by her many relatives. Eric and Belèn fought often, and both had affairs. Belèn started drinking and eventually admitted she was an alcoholic.

During this period Sevareid would sometimes hang out in seedy clubs. There was a rather disreputable bar near CBS's Washington bureau to which he enjoyed taking younger producers for lunch. Once in L.A. he insisted on going to an especially raunchy joint with two CBS colleagues. One of them, Sandy Socolow, recalled the evening: "[The place] had what I can only describe as ladies doing continuous, gynecological dances on top of a piano and then coming over as waitresses. One came over with almost nothing on and wound up sitting in Sevareid's lap. She asked him what he did for a living. He answered, 'I'm just rich.'"

While Sevareid was becoming estranged from Belèn, his first wife, Lois, still coping with manic depression, was slowly and painfully reconstructing her life in the Virginia town of Flint Hill, some seventy miles from Washington. She built a house on the summit of a hill and went to work in the town's library, playing a leading role in its development. Sevareid supported her financially, according to her brother Eben Finger, but "he was the one who remained dependent. He kept leaning on her, kept going to her for emotional help, telling her constantly about all his problems."

In August 1972 Lois suffered a massive stroke, and three days later, only fifty-nine, she died. That November Sevareid announced that he and Belèn had separated. He would have custody of Cristina, an arrangement Belèn agreed to because of her drinking problem. She returned to Italy, still — always — in love with him. It was, she thought, "the end of my life, my dreams, my everything."

✦

After the divorce some of Sevareid's least attractive traits seemed to become more pronounced — his gloom, his self-absorption, his irritability. A lifelong hypochondriac, he was forever complaining about a variety of real and imagined ailments, from gout to stomach problems to bursitis to back pains to rheumatoid arthritis. Several times in the sixties and seventies, he took to his bed with what he called nervous exhaustion. "It was a very dangerous thing to ask him 'How are you, Eric?'" Howard Smith said. Not that his ailments were all imaginary. He suffered constant pain from arthritis and a bad back, which slowed him down and made him tired and cranky.

During his years as nightly news commentator, there was constant tension between Sevareid and Walter Cronkite. "Eric didn't feel Walter had any brains," said former CBS president Bill Leonard. Sevareid also thought Cronkite monopolized the airtime when they worked together. For his part, Cronkite would have been happy if Sevareid's commentaries had been dropped entirely. One night Cronkite fumed after going off the air, "We could have gotten another item on tonight, but Eric had three swallows. Goddamn, I counted them! Without those swallows, we could have gotten that story on." When Howard Smith watched his old network, he thought that Cronkite seemed "a little derogatory" about Sevareid's pieces. "Walter always looked as though he wanted to say, 'I'm being interrupted now. Eric Sevareid has some thoughts.'"

By the late sixties many of Sevareid's colleagues thought he was spending too much time ruminating and not enough time learning the facts to support his ruminations. There also was grumbling that he was repeating himself, that his commentaries were too dense, that he was out of touch with popular culture. In East Coast journalistic and literary circles, denigrating him came close to being a fad. He was belittled as "Eric Severalsides" or "Eric Everyside." Philip Roth satirized him in his novel *Our Gang* as Erect Severehead. And Gloria Emerson wrote in *New York* that "his most memorable trait seemed to be the manner in which he could blunt and make boring the most unforgettable moments of our lives." Sevareid rejected the criticisms. "There's always the clamor of praise for more outspoken people," he said. "Well, it's easy to blow your own opinions all over the place. I always thought there ought to be a little more *in*spokenness."

As it turned out, he had one really good fight left in him. The Watergate scandal in the early seventies aroused his old fervor; he took on President Nixon and his men in commentary after commentary, charging them with "subversion, moral decay, and bankruptcy." He was even more passionate in private. When his friend Teddy White once tried to defend something Nixon said, Sevareid erupted: "You're a damn fool! You just don't understand the evil of the man. He is evil!" Sevareid pounded his fist on the table. "Evil! Evil!"

For his passion Sevareid was excoriated by Nixon's defenders and repeatedly denounced by Vice President Spiro Agnew and various White House aides, including Charles Colson and Pat Buchanan. Under pressure from the administration, Frank Stanton recommended to Dick Salant that a conservative commentator be brought in to alternate with Sevareid on a regular basis. Indeed, according to Tom Rosenstiel in his book *Strange Bedfellows*, Ronald Reagan was offered the commentator's position after leaving office as governor of California. But Reagan turned it down, and, faced with strenuous objections from Salant, CBS dropped the whole idea. Bill Paley, however, did impose a ban on "instant analysis" by CBS commentators after a presidential address — a ban for which Nixon administration officials had lobbied. Ironically, Paley's move was supported by Sevareid, who had always disliked "instant analysis" because he hated going on the air without considerable time to ponder what he was going to say. In any event the ban was short-lived: Paley dropped it a few months later after hearing from several friends that they no longer watched presidential speeches on CBS because of the absence of analysis.

Sevareid soon had reason to wish Paley's ban had been permanent. In his comments after Nixon's resignation on August 9, 1974, Sevareid had nothing but kind words for the man he had earlier denounced as "evil." Nixon's farewell speech, Sevareid said, was "as effective, as magnanimous a speech as he ever made. . . . Some would say that nothing became him so much as the leaving." Although Sevareid wasn't alone in going easy on the disgraced president, he was hit with a storm of criticism from CBS viewers. Later he claimed he'd been tired. Besides, he said, "I felt sadness for [Nixon], for the country."

◆

As Sevareid's long career approached its end in the mid-seventies, his attitude toward television in general and CBS in particular seemed almost schizophrenic. On the one hand he decried multi-million-dollar contracts for journalists and warned that TV news was degenerating into show business. "In the radio days," he said, "two men with a microphone, a typewriter and a telephone could put more substance on the air at one-hundredth of the cost." On the other hand it rankled this celebrated man — who, when he wasn't worrying about his health, was worrying about money — that he hadn't been able to collect one of those mega-salaries himself.

For all his criticisms of TV news, Sevareid also could be quite defensive of it and of CBS, almost as if he were trying to justify to himself his forty years as a broadcaster. In a vitriolic speech at the Washington Journalism Center in June 1976, he denounced the critics and journalists who pushed a number of "myths" about CBS: the myth that Ed Murrow had been forced out of CBS. The myth that the news division "has been somehow shoved out to the periphery of the parent corporation." The myth that "since the pioneer, groundbreaking TV programs of Murrow and Friendly, CBS News has been less daring, done fewer programs of a hard-hitting kind." Above all, the myth that an ogre named William S. Paley "sits at the remote top of CBS Inc. . . . keeping the news people nervous if not cowardly." Many of Sevareid's friends and colleagues were astonished by the speech — not least because every one of his "myths," with due allowance for complexities and exceptions to the rule, was true.

In September 1977 CBS announced that Sevareid was taking mandatory retirement at age sixty-five. He would give his last commentary on November 30, four days after his birthday. Despite all the grumbling about him around CBS, the announcement came as a shock and a disappointment. Losing Sevareid would be like losing Murrow all over again.

In his last broadcast Sevareid paid tribute to Murrow, "the man who invented me," and to the other Boys. All of them, and not least Sevareid, had pursued their own lives and careers without much thought for what a unique group they were. Now, though, Sevareid was giving it more and more thought: "We were like a young band of brothers in those early days with Murrow," he said, expressing an idea that would resonate with the other surviving Boys. He continued:

> I have found that [the public] applies only one consistent test: not agreement with one on substance, but the perception of honesty and fair intent. There is in the American people a tough, undiminished instinct for what is fair. Rightly or wrongly, I have the feeling I have passed that test. I shall wear this like a medal. Millions have listened, intently and indifferently, in agreement and in powerful disagreement. Tens of thousands have written their thoughts to me. I will feel, always, that I stand in their midst. This was Eric Sevareid in Washington. Thank you and goodbye.

For all the carping about Sevareid, he had a large following in the country — viewers who thought of him as the last bulwark of thought and reflection and, yes, even wisdom in a business that was increasingly devoted to sensationalism and stark simplicities. Wrote the *Washington Star* after his retirement: "He has probably touched the minds of more Americans and touched them more often than any journalist in the history of the profession, and his words have probably been taken more seriously than those of all but a few politicians, poets and preachers in this century."

From the day his retirement was announced, thousands of letters flooded into his office. A lawyer wrote that in his youth he had searched for older men to respect and consult. "I found a few personally. But in the media you were the single individual who approached filling that need." Said a sixteen-year-old: "You started me thinking about the world. . . . I have not always agreed with you, but I have always admired you and will miss your evening talks greatly." Wrote another viewer, "Together, you and Ed Murrow helped us to steer a sane course through the hectic and rather hysterical McCarthy, Nixon, Agnew, Vietnam era." And another: "I felt silly sitting there saying goodbye to you with tears in my eyes."

✦

Now only Winston Burdett and Dick Hottelet remained.

Burdett had returned to Rome in 1955, and despite illness and his guilt about his testimony to the Senate Internal Affairs Subcommittee, he performed brilliantly over the next twenty-three years. He spoke several languages, and the scope of his knowledge was encyclopedic. He was an expert on Israel (where for several years he kept a mistress) and the Middle East. In 1969 his book, *Encounter with the Middle East*, was published by Atheneum, a house cofounded by his old Harvard classmate and confidant Michael Bessie.

In 1973, when word came to the CBS bureau in Rome that Egypt's president Gamal Abdel Nasser had died, Burdett was alerted at home by bureau staffer Diane Quint. She also managed to locate Eric Sevareid, who was in Rome covering a state visit to Italy by President Nixon. As soon as Burdett and Sevareid arrived at the studio, they were rushed onto the air and promptly gave a demonstration of what being one of the Murrow Boys was all about. Quint, the wife of CBS correspondent Bert Quint, could barely contain her admiration: "They just arrived there and had to go right on, live, and they sat down and had all these things to *say!* They didn't have time to look over notes or put on makeup or anything. . . . They just gave these interesting insights about what might happen and what did this mean and who was Nasser — and they never once had to go to a computer for a fact."

As much as he knew about the Middle East, however, Burdett's real specialty — odd as it might seem for a former Communist — was the Vatican. He had educated himself on canon law and had developed contacts at the highest level of the Curia. He was so knowledgeable that when he spoke on the air it was almost as if he were speaking ex cathedra. Once, during the election of a new pope, Gordon Manning, a former CBS hand who had moved to NBC and was coordinating his new network's coverage in Rome, joked to his reporters: "Go out and count the cardinals going into the conclave. If there are a hundred and twelve, we're fine. If there are a hundred and thirteen, Burdett's in there, and we're going to get beaten."

But the growth of television and the decline of CBS News, plus his continuing gastrointestinal ailments, began getting the better of Burdett in the early seventies. Said his wife, Giorgina, "In the end, he hated his work. They had him seeing Sophia Loren off at the airport and things like that. But when he could go and do his reporting — oh, he adored that. . . . Getting on a plane. Off to India. Off to Australia. In Yemen with [legendary CBS cameraman] Joe Falletta. That was what he really loved!"

Burdett's son, Richard, saw profound disappointment: "My father was not proud of his career. If someone he respected happened to say something nice about it at dinner, he might raise a tiny little smile. But he wouldn't pursue it in any way. . . . He resented being — quote — in the media — unquote — during the last years of his life. He'd get calls from some twenty-five-year-old editor in New York who'd say, 'Reuter has a story about an Italian politician's homosexual brother. Can you cover this?' He'd say, 'Look, that's really not very important.' But the editor would insist: 'It's a good story. It'll fill at least three minutes here.' Dad thought it was all so low grade. It wasn't worth it to him."

In 1970 Burdett, suffering from a bleeding ulcer, had half his stomach removed. From then on he was in almost constant pain, unable to eat more than a few mouthfuls of food at a sitting. His melancholy deepened. "He was a fundamentally unhappy person," said Dan Schorr. "When he was sitting alone, you knew he was not thinking joyous thoughts." Burdett's son once asked him about what had happened in the fifties; Burdett gave him a brief, tortured answer. "I knew that I should not ask him again because it hurt him so much," Richard Burdett said. "I just saw this enormous pain." Burdett had begun his adult life as a dedicated, radical Communist. Over the years, like an oyster protecting itself from a grinding grain of sand, he accreted layer on layer of protective covering until, near the end, it was almost impossible to see the real man. Said Sander Vanocur, "I always thought Winston might have ended up in the secretariat for the Curia, moving around in dark shadows in the Vatican, like the man who walked across a field of fresh snow and never left any tracks."

✦

When Winston Burdett retired in 1978, the only Boy still on the air was Richard Hottelet — and he wasn't on very much. As far back as 1956, shortly after Hottelet's return to the United States from Germany, news chief Sig Mickelson and others had decided — on the basis of one rather wordy live report by Hottelet on the sinking of the passenger liner *Andrea Doria* — that he didn't have much of a future in television. In the late fifties he anchored an early-morning daily TV newscast called *Richard C. Hottelet with the News*, and in 1960 he was assigned to replace Larry LeSueur on the United Nations beat. Still, Hottelet knew as much about world affairs as anyone at the network, as Gordon Manning discovered after war broke out in the Middle East in 1967. Still, Winston Burdett was on the scene in the Middle East, but neither Walter Cronkite nor any of his regular substitutes was available in New York.

The only CBS journalist Manning could find to anchor a special on the war was Hottelet.

As Manning recalled it, "Hottelet is in the anchor seat, I'm in the control room, Winston Burdett is in Israel — and we are *killing* the competition! It was Hottelet and Burdett, two of the Murrow Boys, at their very best." They ad-libbed for hours, smoothly interweaving details of the war with historical perspective about past Mideast conflicts and the formation of Israel. "Dick had this fund of knowledge that was just amazing," Manning said. "There's no question we should have used him more."

But they didn't, and when a new generation took over the running of CBS News in the early eighties, it became clear there was no room anymore for Hottelet and the complex international stories he specialized in.

◆

In 1981, after Dan Rather replaced Walter Cronkite as anchor, Van Gordon Sauter, former general manager of CBS's Los Angeles affiliate, KNXT, was named president of the news division, and Ed Joyce, former news director at New York's WCBS, became Sauter's deputy. The proud operation that Ed Klauber, Paul White, and Edward R. Murrow had built was now controlled by experts in what made local television news tick.

Over the previous two decades, local news programs had become cash cows for their owners. Many of them, particularly in the larger "markets," unabashedly adopted the view that news was, first and foremost, entertainment. "In city after city," grumbled Eric Sevareid before he retired, "the news is delivered by newsmen turned actors — very bad actors. They grin, they laugh, they chuckle or moan the news. . . And any day now, one of them will sing the news while doing a buck-and-wing stark naked."

Local anchors were increasingly chosen for their looks and charm. "Happy talk" among the members of the news team became the norm. Crime, the gorier or more heart-rending the better, was the favored "top story." Weather, sports, and features on everything from pets and celebrities to blatant plugs for network movies received more airtime than serious news. Reports on the workings of government, except when there was some sensational angle, were dismissed as boring "process stories."

During Sauter's term as CBS News president, he railed against "elitists" who declined to cater to popular tastes. He wanted fewer process stories, fewer talking heads, less pontificating, more features. He was especially fond of what he called "moments" — human-interest pieces of no particular news value that evoked an emotional response from viewers. The trivialization of the news turned out to be good business, at least for a while. Sauter had been brought in to shore up Dan Rather, whose ascension to the anchor's chair as Cronkite's replacement — following a blatant campaign for the job — had resulted in sharply lower ratings for the CBS evening news. By October 1981 the program had fallen for the first time into third place, behind NBC and ABC. But after Sauter assumed control, the ratings slide was halted. CBS regained first place and remained there for the next two hundred weeks.

Under Sauter's reign the CBS News staff was divided into two categories: "yesterday" people and "today" people. Yesterday people were the correspondents, producers, and writers identified with Cronkite and Murrow. "Murrow's ghosts," they were sometimes also called by network executives. Today people were, for the most part, younger correspondents and producers whom Rather liked. They received the good assignments, while yesterday people were elbowed aside or laid off or fired — victims of the massive cost-cutting under way as all three broadcast networks were taken over in the eighties by outside investors. The bottom line was paramount now, and network news divisions were for the first time required to be "profit centers," a policy that resulted in layoffs and firings, the closing of many domestic and foreign bureaus, pressure to produce more income with less staff, and lower salaries (except for the anchors and star correspondents).

In 1985 a new wave of cutbacks rocked CBS News: seventy-four staffers were fired, fifty others "encouraged" to retire, and the *CBS Reports* documentary unit gutted. On the list of people that management wanted to be rid of was Dick Hottelet. That October he retired.

The last of the Murrow Boys had left CBS.

28

"So Long Ago"

IT WAS A GATHERING of old men.

In the spring of 1985, to commemorate the fortieth anniversary of V-E Day, they sat around a table in London's Café Royale and recalled "their war," a time when Ed Murrow was their King Harry, they his devoted band of brothers. Statesmanlike Eric Sevareid was present, and Charles Collingwood, grown thick and puffy, and Winston Burdett, frailer than ever, and Dick Hottelet, always professorial, always "on." Even Bill Shirer was there, the oldest of them all at eighty-one, thoroughly bald on top, with a wild fringe of shoulder-length white hair and a wispy goatee. This was his first formal reunion with the other Boys since his break with Murrow in 1947.

Missing were Tom Grandin, Mary Marvin Breckinridge, Cecil Brown, Bill Downs, Howard K. Smith, and Larry LeSueur. Grandin, who forsook CBS to accompany his wife to America after the fall of France, had died in 1977. The next year death claimed Bill Downs, the great and loyal trooper, whose family and friends buried his ashes in his own backyard and drank a champagne toast to his memory. Breckinridge and Brown were still alive, but CBS had long since forgotten them.* Howard Smith was deliberately not invited, because Bill Paley had never forgiven him for storming out in 1961. And Larry LeSueur, who had worked at the network for a quarter of a century and whose coverage was so much a part of its history and the war, was simply overlooked.

The Boys who *were* at the Café Royale that day were joined by three other CBS men who also covered the war but not for CBS: Walter Cronkite, Andy Rooney of *60 Minutes*, and producer Ernest Leiser. And then there was Dan Rather: he had been all of thirteen years old on

---

*Cecil Brown died in 1987 in Los Angeles.

V-E Day, but he was now CBS's top news star, and the network executives wanted him to take part. He readily agreed: the Boys were his heroes.

And now, their bitterness toward CBS momentarily set aside, the old men told their best war stories. Burdett recalled how Italian women had thrown themselves at Sevareid, "so very splendid in his army uniform," as he drove through Rome in his jeep on the day the ancient city was liberated. Cronkite remembered being pinned down in a ditch with Downs during the battle of Arnhem. And Charles Collingwood, fighting the cancer that would kill him before the year was out, happily recalled the day Paris was reclaimed from the Nazis.

"Oh, we had a splendid liberation," he said.

"We were a privileged lot, gentlemen," added Eric Sevareid.

It was Cronkite who generously noted their accomplishments. "These men made broadcast journalism what it is today," he said (a compliment that may have caused some of them to wince). "Nobody else was doing it; nobody else had realized the potential then. Murrow put together this team who were wordsmiths and could graphically, on radio, tell you what they were seeing. It was better in some ways than television today. It was descriptive, it had emotion, it had the realism of the event."

CBS was celebrating the *word* during those few hours in London — not the evocative pictures and whiz-bang graphics of modern television but the simple and unvarnished word. Afterward, when Sevareid complained to the news division's executive vice president, Howard Stringer, that they hadn't used a tape of him reading one of his famous World War II broadcasts, Stringer replied that the producers had found it "too literary and reflective." Defensively and rather disingenuously, Stringer continued, "Producers now spend more time worrying about limousines and hairstyles and less about editorial content. It is sadly true that many of today's stars have twice the ego for half the reason. I'm coming to the reluctant conclusion that your golden age may be the last of its kind."

◆

In 1982 Bill Paley had helped arrange a post-retirement CBS contract for Charlie Collingwood, according to which he would carry the title "special correspondent" and work for the network several months a year. The trouble was that they gave him little or nothing to do. He would arrive every appointed day at his office, impeccably dressed as always . . . and just sit. One day a good friend, former *Time* chief of correspondents Dick Clurman, casually asked how he was doing. Clurman was stunned by the vehemence of the reply. "Some days I can't get off the floor," Collingwood said.

He had never fully recovered from Louise's death, but being put out to pasture by CBS seemed to trouble him almost as much. "He was such a disappointed man," said his nephew, Harris Collingwood. "I think the sense of rejection and betrayal and disappointment that Charles felt — well, it didn't sound like it happened in a professional sphere. It sounded like a family thing, like his CBS family had betrayed him."

Collingwood, who often threatened suicide, was drinking almost nonstop now. He began with bloody marys in the morning and ended with Scotch or cognac at night. He would often adjourn from his office to the Century Club at noon and spend the afternoon downing martinis. After his retirement dinner, as on many other nights, his loyal friend and sometime producer, Bernie Birnbaum, gently led him to a cab and saw him home.

Collingwood, who as a teenager had so hated baby-sitting for his siblings, now lamented not having children of his own. He seemed to regard his nephew, Harris, and niece, Kate Spelman, as his surrogate son and daughter. He and Harris, a journalist then in his early twenties, were especially close and would often dine and drink together in Collingwood's penthouse apartment. One summer weekend Collingwood invited Harris and his girlfriend to dinner at his house on Fire Island. When the couple arrived, Collingwood answered the door drunk and stark naked. Furious, Harris whisked his girlfriend away and for several years refused to have anything more to do with his uncle. (They finally reconciled just before Charles's death.)

Fantasies were becoming a symptom of Collingwood's depression and alcoholism. When Ann Sperber interviewed him for her biography of Murrow, he implied that he had been present during Murrow's famous visit to Buchenwald at the end of World War II: "Well, it was one of the concentration camps," Collingwood said during the interview, "and — it sticks in my mind that it was Buchenwald, but I'm not sure." Later in the same interview, however, he began a sentence by saying, "When we went into Buchenwald . . ."

It was an assertion that surprised former CBS newsman Bill Shadel when he read it in Sperber's book. For it was Shadel, not Collingwood, who had been at Buchenwald. Nor could Collingwood have been with Murrow at some other Nazi death camp and confused them. Murrow never visited another camp, and, as far as anyone can recall, Collingwood, based mostly in Paris during this period, never saw one of them.

Why would he lie about such a thing? Shadel gave him the benefit of the doubt, speculating that Collingwood, in an alcoholic haze forty years after the fact, had simply confused a story he had heard — Shadel remembered telling him about the visit a few days after it occurred — with something he had experienced. Other former CBS colleagues weren't so charitable. They thought Collingwood knew perfectly well he hadn't been at Buchenwald. As one of them said to Shadel, Collingwood "was trying to find something to hang onto and build himself up, because he was so shattered."

In 1984 he became reacquainted with an old girlfriend, a Swedish singer named Tatiana Angelina Jolim with whom he had had an affair back in the late 1940s. After the affair ended, she married and became known as "the Swedish Snow White" for dubbing Snow White's songs into Swedish for the Disney film. More than thirty years after that, a widow now with two grown daughters, Tatiana came to New York and looked up her old lover. They soon embarked on another affair, and Collingwood seemed happier for a while. Tatiana even persuaded him to check into a rehabilitation clinic for alcoholics.

In the summer of 1984 they were married, but the marriage was over almost before it began. Collingwood began drinking again and found Tatiana to be, in his words, "cold, unresponsive, downright insulting." In a letter he wrote to her (but that he apparently never gave to her), he acknowledged that he sometimes drank too much. But, he continued, "the repulsion [from you] on these infrequent occasions . . . was so far beyond anything I had done to cause it that it should have given me cause to wonder about the depths of your professed love."

According to a family member, Collingwood felt "badly tricked" by Tatiana. Deciding she was more interested in his money and property than in him, he considered writing her out of his extensive and complex will, only to discover that, under New York law, a widow was entitled to not less than 51 percent of her husband's estate unless there was a prenuptial agreement. Nevertheless, they remained married.

The issue was more than academic. In late 1984 Collingwood was diagnosed as having colon cancer. He underwent surgery and chemotherapy. At first the prognosis was hopeful, but the cancer soon recurred, and Collingwood knew he was dying. The death sentence seemed to jar him back to a semblance of his old grace and insouciance.

It was his final performance as the Bonnie Prince. On the day his doctors told him the situation was hopeless, he said to a friend, "The bad news is that I'm dying. The good news is that it has nothing to do with drinking or smoking. Imagine all those years I would have wasted if I'd quit."

In late September 1985 Collingwood collapsed and was rushed to Lenox Hill Hospital. The end was near, and friends rallied around. At Ernie Leiser's request, Bill Paley wrote a letter full of reminiscences, which Leiser read to Collingwood in the hospital. When Collingwood complained to his close friend and agent, Richard Leibner, that the doctors would not let him have alcohol or tobacco, Leibner smuggled in both. Leibner remembered watching Collingwood sitting contentedly in the hospital solarium, a drink in one hand, a cigarette in the other, and the racing form on his lap. Joe Wershba paid a visit and asked if he had been able to place any bets. In a weak, barely audible voice, Collingwood said, "Sure. I won a hundred dollars yesterday. The nurse sneaked the bet out."

The day before he died, Teddy White came to see him. "Is there anything I can do for you, Charles?" he asked.

"Oh, no, Teddy," Collingwood said, "there's nothing anyone can do. Just make me young again."

✦

On October 3 Richard Leibner called Eric Sevareid in Washington. It was almost over; if Sevareid wanted to say goodbye to Collingwood, he'd better come quickly. Sevareid took the next plane to New York. By the time he reached the hospital, Collingwood was already in a coma. Forlorn, Sevareid sat for two hours at his bedside, looking at the wasted, sixty-eight-year-old body of the extraordinary person he'd first met in Paul White's office in 1943, the "beautiful young man with golden curls" who had so dazzled everyone with his coverage of North Africa and with his patented, careless ease. As if he would remain CBS's golden boy forever. As if those fine days with the wind at his back would never — could never — end.

Collingwood did not awaken. Finally Sevareid telephoned a cab, returned to La Guardia and flew back to Washington on the shuttle. At 5 P.M. that same day, just as Sevareid's plane was landing at National Airport, Charles Collingwood died.

More than a thousand people — a fair number of whom would find themselves named to receive some special memento or gift in Collingwood's meticulously thought-out will — crowded into the vast sanctuary of St. Bartholomew's Episcopal church on Park Avenue to say farewell. Bill Paley and Frank Stanton were there. So were Janet Murrow, Eric Sevareid, Dick Hottelet, Walter Cronkite, and the other big names of CBS News. So, too, were the cameramen, soundmen, lighting technicians, makeup artists, and other network employees who had come to regard Collingwood as their friend.

One by one his friends got up and shared their memories of his charm and grace, his generosity and talent. Said Sevareid, "There was a kind of glow about the man, just in his person — that curious magic of personality that he possessed." When Morley Safer rose to speak, he looked down at Paley in the front row, his face drawn and gray, "just shattered." "Twenty years ago, Ed Murrow left us," Safer said. "It was Murrow and Charles and a few others who made the mere business enterprise of CBS into a proud and vital moving part of the American democracy. They spoke up, when others chose the ugly, prudent path of silence. And I pray we have men and women of that stern stuff today, not to honor their memory, but to honor ourselves."

As heartfelt and occasionally eloquent as the speeches were, some in the audience were getting restless. "Just another damn corporate funeral," thought Collingwood's old pal Bill Walton. "Nobody speaking but the CBS guys, and they're all vying for the spotlight. No mention of Louise or Charles's brothers and sisters. Awful!"

Bill Moyers began to bristle, too, listening to the master of ceremonies, Dan Rather, go on about Collingwood's loyalty to, and love for, CBS, about how "blessed" Collingwood had felt to work for the network and its executives. Moyers couldn't believe it. Here were Rather and others talking about what a terrific correspondent Collingwood was and never mentioning that this network he supposedly loved so much had long since turned its back on him, as it had on Murrow and the rest of the Boys. Moyers got to his feet and strode angrily from the church. As he rushed up the aisle, he passed Sandy Socolow, who heard him mutter, "Hypocrites! If he was so great, why didn't they put him on the air?"

The final speaker that afternoon, Charles Kuralt, also knew how badly Collingwood had been treated by CBS and decided this was no time to keep quiet about it. "There came those years," Kuralt said, "when Charles was the most honored of all of us, and the most respected, and not on the air very much. He accepted that puzzling turn of events with great dignity, as he accepted everything in life, but not with much happiness. He was alone a good deal, and he was a good deal unhappy, I think."

◆

In contrast to Collingwood, Eric Sevareid actually found some happiness in his last years. Once he was away from daily deadlines, he learned to relax more and enjoy life. He gave up a fifty-year smoking habit and spent more time at his beloved cabin near Virginia's Blue Ridge mountains, fishing for bass and bluegills in the pond and hunting quail and ruffed grouse in the nearby woods.

By all accounts the main reason for Sevareid's new contentment was his third marriage. In 1970 he had met Suzanne St. Pierre, then a researcher on a CBS News special in which Sevareid had played a key role. St. Pierre, who later became a *60 Minutes* producer, thought Sevareid "very warm and courtly and kind." But he was still married to Belèn in 1970, and, according to St. Pierre, their relationship didn't begin in earnest until 1972, when he came to New York and invited her to dinner. They were married on July 4, 1979. Sevareid was sixty-six; his bride, who had been married once before, was forty-two. "We had both built walls around our hearts," said St. Pierre. "Eric's definitely melted. You can see it in his photographs. In some of his earlier pictures, he looks older than he did ten years later — his face drawn, circles under his eyes. . . . I think we had a very good marriage."*

But Sevareid wouldn't have been Sevareid without something to worry about. While happy in his personal life, he "agonized about a lot of other things," St. Pierre said. He was upset, for example, that CBS, having given him a post-retirement consultant's contract, with a part-time secretary and a small, windowless office several blocks from the CBS bureau, basically ignored him after that.

Sevareid conceived his post-retirement role as that of elder statesman, adviser, conscience. He shot off memo after memo to Rather, to Stringer, even to Laurence Tisch, the chairman of Loews Corporation, who took over CBS in 1986. In his memos Sevareid urged these men, in effect, to return to the standards that he and Murrow and the other Boys had established. "It was the creation of the news division, nearly fifty

---

*After Sevareid's death St. Pierre brought a lawsuit against other members of the family over what she claimed was her rightful share of the estate. In 1995 the suit forced an auction of some of Sevareid's personal effects — an auction conducted over interactive cable television.

years ago, that gave the network its identity, its 'personality,'" he wrote Tisch. "I think I embody the basic values of those early days as conceived by Ed Klauber, Ed Murrow, Paul White, Elmer Davis, and supported through so many years by Bill Paley and Frank Stanton." He urged Tisch to call a halt to the "glitz" and the "hype" that had "crept into our news operations," to bring back commentary, to revive the year-end roundups. None of it happened.

To Dan Rather, Sevareid wrote to warn against the "star system": "Learn to detest that goddam word 'image,' and that goddam word 'celebrity.'" Rather had been Sevareid's protégé, but the warning seemed to have little effect: the protégé reveled in being a star. A former local television reporter from Houston, the aggressive and talented Rather had swiftly ascended the network's ladder. Some of his colleagues came to regard him as a brazen opportunist and self-promoter, but the Boys he cultivated — especially Charles Collingwood and Winston Burdett in Europe and Sevareid in Washington — did not hesitate to help him, as they had not hesitated to help many others. A line about Rather that circulated around CBS went: "Collingwood taught him how to dress, and Sevareid taught him how to think."

When he was assigned to CBS's Washington bureau during the Johnson administration, Rather, according to former CBS News vice president Edward Fouhy, "attached himself to Sevareid like a barnacle." Insecure about his own intellectual prowess, Rather saw in Sevareid a perfect model for what he wished to become. "If there could be such a thing as a guru in television," Rather said, "then Eric would qualify as mine." Sevareid once advised Richard Leibner to "watch this kid. He's uneducated, but he's good." Leibner did watch and soon became Rather's agent, an association that would make both of them rich.

No one at CBS during the Rather era paid more lip service to the Murrow tradition than Rather himself. He wrapped himself in it, even to the point of exaggerating his association with the Boys. One of his favorite stories was about how Sevareid had counseled him on his career when both were on assignment in Vietnam and had recommended that he read the works of, among others, Montaigne and Herodotus. "A man isn't educated until he reads Montaigne," Sevareid was supposed to have said. Rather also maintained that it was on Sevareid's advice that he always carried with him *The Elements of Style*, the classic handbook on writing by William Strunk, Jr., and E. B. White.

Unfortunately, according to Sevareid, not a word of this charming tale was true, and in 1987 he wrote to Rather telling him so. "I do not recall discussing your career in Saigon amid the rockets' red glare. . . . I could not have discussed Herodotus in relation to the Vietnam war. . . . I have scarcely looked at Montaigne since college. . . . [and] Strunk and White remain alien to my experience."

As far as the "star system" went, however, Rather may have found Sevareid's advice a bit hypocritical. The Boys were hardly unfamiliar with the world of celebrity journalism. They had agents and went on lecture tours, some had special tables at glitzy restaurants and clubs, they had autobiographical bestsellers (although, unlike Rather, they wrote the books themselves). In TV and radio the siren of success was ever present. The Boys' personal strength and integrity may have helped them keep her at arm's length, but they were by no means immune to her charms.

After Sevareid's retirement, Frank Stanton took him to lunch at the Harvard Club. When they were seated, Stanton noticed that Sevareid seemed a little more glum than usual. "Is something wrong?" he asked.

"I walked through this whole room and nobody recognized me," Sevareid said.

Recalling that story years afterward, Stanton shook his head. "That's a hell of a thing for a newsman to say. But that's what television did to those guys."

As if to reassure the new generation on that score, Eric Ober, who became president of CBS News in 1990, decorated a wall of his office with a framed magazine advertisement that featured Murrow plugging a brand of cigarettes. The ad was there, he said, as "a reminder that things weren't so wonderful in the so-called golden age, either."

✦

CBS News had promised to use Sevareid on the air occasionally, but he was hardly ever called. When Ronald Reagan's inauguration as president in January 1981 coincided with the release of American hostages in Iran, Bernie Birnbaum had to remind his bosses, who were screaming that they didn't have enough bodies to cover the stories, that they were overlooking a valuable resource. "I said, 'Sevareid is in town here and he's sitting on his ass doing nothing, and he's great.' So they brought him in, and he *was* great." But once the day was over, Sevareid was put on the shelf again.

He had other ventures: he narrated independently produced documentaries, had cameo roles in several movies, was in demand on the lecture circuit. A television documentary was made of the first part of *Not So Wild a Dream* and shown as a segment of the Public Broadcasting System's program *The American Experience*, with Sevareid narrating. As always, money was a major concern. In his negotiations with those who sought his services, Sevareid tried to get the largest possible fees. Yet when he was offered one million dollars to do testimonials for a major investment house, he rejected the deal. He asked himself whether he should "leave my children a name with no tarnish on it, or a name with a little bit of tarnish and some sustenance." Later he wrote to a friend, "I don't know whether I feel good about it or lousy."

Before Sevareid retired, he was asked repeatedly if he intended to write books again. Probably, he said. In his pre-retirement days, he had always given "no time" as an excuse for not writing a sequel to *Not So Wild a Dream*, despite the many requests from friends, colleagues, and fans, not to mention agents and publishers. "I begged him to write his memoirs," said Sandy Socolow. "I said he owed it to me, he owed it to my children." Now that Sevareid was retired, there were no more excuses.

But, although he considered *Not So Wild a Dream* his finest achievement, he did not return to writing. "I think he was just too lazy," Socolow said. "I also think he didn't want to face the truth about a lot of things." About himself and the way his life had turned out. About his relationships with his first two wives and his children. About what had happened to him and Murrow and the rest of the Boys at CBS. But there was also the fear that he wouldn't be able to live up to the brilliance and eloquence of the younger Sevareid, the suspicion, as Suzanne St. Pierre put it, "that he had lost the touch of poetry that was in him." He once told an interviewer, "I don't know if I can write well anymore. I don't know why; maybe it's hardening of the imagination."

In the depths of his soul, he seemed to have the feeling that perhaps he had taken a wrong turn after *Not So Wild a Dream*. Perhaps he should have left CBS and opted for the uncertainties of a writer's life. When Bill Shirer's daughter, Inga Dean, paid a call on Sevareid after he retired, he told her, "Your father did the right thing. He got out and wrote books."

"You did all right," Dean said.

Sevareid shook his head. "I should have done what he did."

Still, he cherished his early association with Murrow and the Boys. "To this day," he once said, "I and others who were once called the

Murrow Boys receive letters from listeners who assure us, because of some performance of ours, that Ed Murrow would have been proud of us or ashamed of us. And nothing in the daily mail so pleases or wounds me."

In 1988, after hearing Janet Murrow praise him during a dinner in his honor at the Museum of Broadcasting in New York, he sent her a brief thank-you note: "I was moved to tears listening to you the other night at my beatification; it was all so long ago, and we were all so young and you were so beautiful. I will never forget the evening as I will never forget you and Ed for so much that was so good in my life."

Sevareid also did his unselfish best to ensure that history would not forget any of the Boys. When a broadcasting magazine ran a photograph of Murrow and Tom Grandin, with a caption calling Grandin an "unidentified man," Sevareid immediately wrote to the magazine to set the record straight.

This picture has appeared with those words before, even in a book or two. The man is Thomas Grandin, American. . . . Grandin's role in those pioneering radio days has been overlooked by historians. I have been troubled, too, by the relative neglect of Larry LeSueur, who also covered the London blitz with Murrow, who made the perilous convoy voyage through the Arctic to Russia and who was our man on [Utah] Beach.

As Sevareid aged, he seemed to draw more and more consolation from his own history and the nation's — and in particular from his growing up in the little town of Velva. "He never let go of his Middle Western roots," Belèn Sevareid said. "He was absolutely true."

When he was little, his favorite book had been *Brite and Fair*, the fictional diary of a boy growing up in eighteenth-century Andover, Massachusetts. Near the end of his life, when he was seventy-nine years old and thinking hard about where he had come from and who he had been and what he had become, *Brite and Fair* was his favorite book again. In the spring and summer of 1992, as he lay dying of stomach cancer, he asked Suzanne to read it to him over and over again. It reminded him of his own growing up — of turning over outhouses on Halloween night with his gang of friends, of stealing watermelons from Doc Ritchie's garden, of opening Mr. Anderson's pasture gate and letting his cows wander all over Main Street. "He loved that book," said St.

Pierre. "He remembered whole parts of it. He laughed. He was very, very weak then, but it was the one thing that pleased him."

Arnold Eric Sevareid, Ed Murrow's truest son, was going home.

✦

A few days before his death on July 9, his son Michael visited him at his home in Georgetown. Sevareid, who had been lying on the couch, decided to go upstairs to bed. He was so weak he could barely move. But he made it to his feet and limped to the stairs and then began slowly to climb,with Michael ahead of him and Suzanne behind to help.

At one point Sevareid paused and gasped, "I don't know if I can make it."

But Michael saw him set his famous jaw and knew he was determined to do it, just as he had been determined, despite pain and self-doubt, to make that 120-mile trek out of a Burmese jungle in 1943. "One step at a time," he had told himself back then, "just one step at a time." And now, on carpeted stairs in Georgetown, Michael heard him mumble the same words again:

"One step at a time."

This memory of his father remained with Michael for years afterward: one step at a time, one slow step at a time. Up the stairs.

Epilogue

They had emerged from the Great Depression and World War II with an irresistible enthusiasm and an expansive sense of the possibilities open to them and to their country. They were among the best of their generation yet also typical of it. For they were American to the core, no matter what part of the country they sprang from. In their day their influence was enormous. But their true medium was radio, and their day was short.

That thought may have been on Eric Sevareid's mind near the end of his life as he lay in a hospital after surgery. One afternoon he awoke suddenly from a nap and mumbled to his son Michael, "I had the most terrible nightmare."

"What about, Dad?"

"Television," said Sevareid.

◆

Commercial television at once trivialized and corrupted what they did. Then it tired of them and tossed them aside. Perhaps, given the dynamics of the medium, there could have been no other result. But it is discouraging nonetheless that CBS tilted the balance so quickly and now so completely away from a commitment to news and public affairs and toward lowest-common-denominator programming.

By the nineties the things that had distinguished CBS News were gone — its worldwide coverage, its commitment to the highest standards of journalism and to serious commentary and documentaries, its impressive libraries, its army of researchers. One by one the network's proud foreign bureaus were closed, until only four remained — London, Tel Aviv, Moscow, and Tokyo. On CBS, as on the other networks, there was now a proliferation of prime-time "newsmagazine" shows, some of them no better than televised tabloids — entertaining to watch, relatively inexpensive to produce, and highly profitable.

The gutting of CBS News meant a new ratings slide for Dan Rather's evening news broadcast, and by 1990 it had been knocked out of first place by ABC. Three years later, in a desperate attempt to reverse the program's precipitous decline, CBS selected former correspondent and popular Los Angeles news personality Connie Chung as coanchor. Jon Katz, who'd once been executive producer of CBS Morning News, wrote in *Rolling Stone*, "Rather has now been reduced to playing the serious male in one more happy anchor-couple, the format [that] market researchers keep telling executives viewers want, though in fact fewer and fewer are watching."

At the press conference announcing Chung's new job, Rather said he and she would be offering "the new news . . . more modern, more exciting, and more relevant" — a far cry from Murrow's instructions to Sevareid in 1939 to "just provide the honest news." Predictably, the "new news" didn't work either. The pairing of Rather and Chung proved a disaster, and CBS sank to a dismal third place in the ratings. In May 1995 Chung was removed from her anchor position, as she and Rather, in an unseemly public squabble, blamed each other for the failure.

The real problem was that CBS and most of its competitors were ignoring the basics. Said a top current CBS correspondent, "I have this old-fashioned idea that people turn on the set to find out what's going on. You will not find out if you watch most networks, although you still do if you watch ABC."

In the nineties ABC's *World News Tonight* with Peter Jennings was the top-rated evening news program and the standard for commercial television. ABC was hardly immune, however, to the pressures and stupidities that were ruining CBS (and NBC). In 1992 Jennings was given an almost unbelievable five-year, $35-million-dollar contract — the most lucrative in the history of television news. Yet only a year earlier, Jennings's news division had been ordered to cut costs. As it was preparing to make Jennings the richest anchor of all time, the division laid off about a hundred people, including some of its most experienced correspondents, and closed bureaus in St. Louis, Rome, Frankfurt, and Hong Kong.

The closing of three foreign bureaus meant that ABC, like its competitors, would have less original reporting from abroad. On many foreign stories (and sometimes even on domestic ones), the U.S. networks bought videotape from freelancers or foreign networks, then dubbed in voice-overs by their own people, who had not even covered the story. It was the ultimate victory of the camera over the correspondent, the picture over the word. Said Tom Fenton, CBS's veteran chief European correspondent, who did a great deal of this sort of thing from London and didn't care for it: "When I was working with Winston Burdett in Rome in the seventies, we still had one of the world's best news-gathering organizations, bar none. I have seen it progressively dismantled. . . . Can you *imagine* covering the world from Tokyo, Tel Aviv, Moscow, and London?"

Increasingly, too, the stories that *were* put on the evening news focused on violence and death: bombings and wars and killings provided more compelling pictures than analytical pieces about a country's political and economic and cultural life, pieces that once were the Boys' specialty. "Crazed gunmen, serial killers, psychopaths and mad bombers are characters in a very gloomy landscape that television news too often presents," former NBC anchor John Chancellor said. "What makes it worse is that we know this is not an accurate picture of the world around us."

With few exceptions (like PBS's *MacNeil/Lehrer NewsHour* and National Public Radio, where, said Roger Mudd, "the flame still burns"), broadcast news seemed to have little interest in helping viewers and listeners make sense of the bits and pieces of information it put on the air, in providing illumination or explanation or context. For broadcast reporters it was more important to know about satellites and stand-ups than about history and economics and literature. Frank Stanton recalled watching a network news broadcast one night and being appalled at the lack of knowledge of the young correspondent reporting from the Middle East: "He had the technology, he had the pictures, he had the people to interview, and he asked the stupidest questions in the world. That didn't happen with the Shirers, the Howard K. Smiths, the Sevareids, the Murrows. They had a sense of history. They knew what was going on."

In Tom Fenton's view, "The first broadcast journalists were the best. None of the later generations came near to [the Boys'] professional skills." Said Fenton's former CBS colleague, Charles Kuralt, "They brought a tone of scholarship. They knew their subjects and they were able to refer easily to the past and draw conclusions for the present. . . . I think you can safely say there's no one like that in broadcasting today."

For Kuralt and Fenton and many others, the Boys weren't just good examples. They acted as mentors, with a selflessness that is increasingly lacking in an egomaniacal business. "For us who would eventually succeed them," said Roger Mudd, "they showed the way. They infused the profession with a seriousness and a professionalism that influenced me a lot. Now, when you're hired, nobody helps you at all. I think it's because an awful lot of people don't want you to succeed — because if you succeed, they're diminished."

Shortly after his retirement in 1994, Kuralt said he didn't "detect much mentoring going on around the CBS office anymore. . . . The bookkeepers are really in control. . . . I decided to leave before they could invite me to leave."

It is almost axiomatic that the more an institution breaks faith with those who built it, the more it sanctifies them. When it suits their purposes, CBS News's modern executives and journalists pretend that theirs is still the network of Edward R. Murrow and the Boys. It isn't. Said former NBC and ABC correspondent Sander Vanocur, "It drives me up the wall when I hear people at CBS invoking the name of Murrow. Most of them couldn't carry his typewriter. . . . CBS is now like a cult. They're pagans praying to idols. They invoke these deities to justify their present base claims. In a funny way, they're schizophrenic — they both want to illuminate and erase the tradition."

✦

At the time of Eric Sevareid's death in 1992, six of the eleven correspondents who at various times were included among the Murrow Boys were still living: William L. Shirer, Mary Marvin Breckinridge Patterson, Larry LeSueur, Howard K. Smith, Winston Burdett, and Richard C. Hottelet. They took pride in what they and Murrow had achieved and looked with jaundiced old eyes on the disarray at CBS and in modern television news generally.

It is inevitable, perhaps, that in a young person's business the older ones will leave, burned out and bitter. To one degree or another, all of the Boys left CBS that way. Yet they kept working, kept struggling, kept faith with what they had been. Even Patterson, who was with CBS for only a brief period in her long life and who rarely looked back after she left, enjoyed reminiscing about her experiences in London, Amsterdam, and Berlin with Murrow and Shirer, covering the rising Nazi tide.

As for the others . . .

✦

Winston Burdett remained in Rome the rest of his life, ill and more and more isolated. His great professional passion after he retired was a book he was writing on Italian culture. There was to have been a chapter on Alessandro Manzoni, the nineteenth-century poet and novelist, a chapter on Leonardo da Vinci, a chapter on Renaissance painting. But he never completed the book. His frail physical condition and acute emphysema from years of heavy cigarette smoking took an ever greater toll. In the last year of his life he was rarely out of bed and had to wear an oxygen mask constantly to breathe.

On May 19, 1993, he died of heart failure at seventy-nine.

✦

William L. Shirer — the original Boy, the disappointed journalist, the amazingly successful author of nonfiction books — eventually moved to Lenox, Massachusetts, where one of his two daughters lived. He bought a large, rambling old house, furnished it carelessly, and continued to write. Among his books were three volumes of autobiography, a major purpose of which was to settle old scores with the many people he felt had done him wrong, especially Ed Murrow. Nevertheless, when Shirer was eighty-nine years old and suffering from "a bum leg, a heart condition, a lung condition and, on top of everything else, being deaf and blind," he admitted that few days in his life went by when he didn't think fondly of Murrow and their pioneering years together.

Shirer's marriage to Tess finally ended in divorce in 1970. Two years later he married again, this time to a Lenox neighbor, who quickly became disenchanted, filed for a divorce in 1975, and locked him out of their house. Shirer had begun learning Russian about this time, as he prepared to research and write a book on Leo Tolstoy. In 1988 he married his teacher, Irina Alexandrovna Lugovskaya.

He never mastered Russian but went ahead with his Tolstoy book anyway. He called it *Love and Hatred — The Stormy Marriage of Leo and Sonya Tolstoy*. For twenty years after his divorce from Tess, he had tried unsuccessfully to write something about their breakup. By turning to Tolstoy, who deserted his wife at the age of eighty-two, Shirer seemed finally to have found the proper vehicle. When he finished in the summer of 1993, he knew he would never write again. "This is my last book," he wrote in the acknowledgments. "The first one, *Berlin Diary*, appeared in June, 1941, more than half a century ago. Over some fifty-two years my books have been coming out — fourteen in all. That's a long span for a writer. I've been lucky. But I shall be ninety in early 1994. Time to quit."

That winter, on December 28, 1993, two months short of his birthday, William L. Shirer died.

◆

Howard and Bennie Smith presided over their elegant old house and its gardens on the high banks of the Potomac River in Maryland. They rarely went out, although Smith sometimes ventured forth to lecture on politics and the media. Otherwise he worked on what he called "a history of the twentieth century" but which was really a personal memoir. He wrote in his large study, with its shelves of leather-bound books and Wedgwood busts of great English writers.

More than thirty years after he stormed out of CBS, Smith remained bitter about the way he had been treated — all the more so as he saw himself systematically written out of the network's official history. The end of his subsequent career at ABC hadn't been much better, and he and Bennie were bitter about that, too. "We've never been invited to anything at those two networks, which Howard was with for forty years of his professional life," Bennie said. "It's astonishing."

◆

After his own departure from CBS in 1963, Larry LeSueur worked another twenty years for the Voice of America. He finally retired at age seventy-five to a quiet and comfortable life with his wife, Dorothy, in a house in northwest Washington, near where the vice president of the United States lives. Over the mantle in the LeSueurs' living room was an oil portrait of the young Larry, looking snappy in his World War II foreign correspondent's uniform.

LeSueur was CBS News's forgotten man. His reporting during the war had ranked with that of Sevareid, Collingwood, and Murrow himself. His coverage of D-Day and its aftermath alone should have earned him a permanent place in the network's pantheon. Yet whenever CBS staged one of its commemorative extravaganzas extolling Murrow and the Boys, the people in charge always neglected to include Larry LeSueur.

Unflappable as ever, he didn't seem to mind too much. For the fiftieth anniversary of D-Day, LeSueur, then eighty-five, simply booked passage on a cruise ship bound for Normandy, where he and Dorothy attended the official ceremonies on their own, as spectators. Ignored by

Dan Rather and CBS, LeSueur was interviewed by National Public Radio and C-SPAN, where people worked who *did* remember his exploits and accomplishments.

◆

And, finally, Richard C. Hottelet. The youngest of the Boys, he stayed with CBS longer than any of the others. After his retirement in 1985, he worked for a time as spokesman for the U.S. ambassador to the United Nations. When he left the UN, he continued to make frequent forays from his home in Wilton, Connecticut, to his office at the Council on Foreign Relations in Manhattan and to the venerable old Century Club, where the ghosts of Murrow and Collingwood lingered and where Hottelet would have lunch or cocktails with old friends and colleagues.

Then in 1993, at the age of seventy-six, he launched a weekly interview program, *America and the World*, underwritten by the Council on Foreign Relations. Richard C. Hottelet was back on the air, the last of the Murrow Boys to cast his voice broadly over the land.

Not on television, though. Hottelet was on NPR, on radio again. Where he belonged. Where it all began.

NOTES

BIBLIOGRAPHY

ACKNOWLEDGMENTS

INDEX

Notes

PROLOGUE

The material about Eric Sevareid's memorial service came from Lynne Olson's notes and observations of the service, as well as from interviews with Don Hewitt, Dan Rather, and Larry LeSueur. Murrow made the remark about his wartime team to Charles Shaw, who noted it in an unpublished essay. Sevareid's comment to Rather about not being "Edward R. Murrow II" was in a Dec. 18, 1987, letter to Rather, which is in Sevareid's papers at the Library of Congress.

I ✦ THE VOICE OF THE FUTURE

The information about Larry LeSueur's background came from interviews with LeSueur. Irving Fang, *Those Radio Commentators!* and David Culbert, *News for Everyman*, were the primary sources on Boake Carter.

2 ✦ MURROW AND SHIRER

The information about William L. Shirer's early years, his meeting with Murrow, and the beginning of his CBS career came from three of Shirer's books — *Berlin Diary* and *The Start* and *The Nightmare Years*, volumes one and two of his three-volume autobiography. Shirer's explanation of his attractiveness to women came from our interview with Priscilla Jaretzki, Larry LeSueur's former wife.

Two biographies of Murrow — A. M. Sperber, *Murrow: His Life and Times*, and Joseph E. Persico, *Edward R. Murrow: An American Original*, were the main sources for Murrow's background. For accounts of the early days of radio foreign news and Murrow's role as CBS's European director of talks, we also relied on Culbert, *News for Everyman*.

3   ✦   "WE TAKE YOU NOW TO LONDON"

The efforts of NBC and Max Jordan to thwart CBS in gaining access to European radio systems are discussed in Jordan's autobiography, *Beyond All Fronts*, and in NBC internal memos. The autobiography also mentions Jordan's scoops of CBS in Austria and Czechoslovakia.

The description of Shirer's and Murrow's coverage of the Anschluss and their work on the first radio news roundup came from *Berlin Diary* and *The Nightmare Years*, as well as from the Murrow biographies by Sperber and Persico.

The influence of CBS and Murrow were described in "Edward R. Murrow," *Scribner's*, December 1938. Shirer acknowledged in an interview with the *Washington Post*, Aug. 10, 1989, that his marriage had suffered because of his work. Interviews with Shirer and his daughter, Inga Dean, provided other information and insights about him and Murrow during this period.

4   ✦   THE FIRST DISCIPLE

Paul White's antipathy to Tom Grandin is summed up in Persico's biography of Murrow.

The account of Eric Sevareid's meeting with Murrow and his joining CBS came from Sevareid's autobiography, *Not So Wild a Dream*, as did most of the material about his growing up, including his canoeing, mining, and hobo adventures; radical college years; and early days in Paris. Sevareid described his fear of the hills and prairies of Velva in "You Can Go Home Again," *Collier's*, May 11, 1956; he discussed the shame of his father's financial ruin in a 1983 interview with UPI, which is in his papers at the Library of Congress. He recalled his fantasy about returning to Velva in a column in the *Velva Journal* five years after he left his hometown; it is also in Sevareid's papers.

Sevareid commented on the improved equipment of those who recreate his canoe trip in a radio interview with John Dunning (KNUS, Denver), Sept. 18, 1983. He set down his memories of meeting his wife, Lois, and their subsequent elopement in an undated memo, which is in his papers. Murrow's letter confirming Sevareid's hiring is in Murrow's papers at the Fletcher School of Law and Diplomacy, Tufts University, Medford, Mass. (The Murrow papers are also on microfilm at the Library of Congress.)

Janet Murrow's letters to her family complaining about H. V. Kaltenborn and Paul White are in her papers at Mount Holyoke College, South Hadley, Mass. The best account of Sevareid's humiliation at Kaltenborn's hands and Murrow's subsequent anger is in R. Franklin Smith, *Edward R. Murrow: The War Years*. Shirer described his and Murrow's fury at White's pre-Poland power play in *The Nightmare Years* and in an interview with *The* (Chicago) *Reader* (undated). Sevareid recounted his activities on the war's first day in *Not So Wild a Dream*. He mused about the awakening of the French soldiers in a CBS broadcast on Mar. 21, 1941.

Additional quotes and information for this chapter came from interviews with William Shirer, Bill Shadel, Michael Bessie, Mary Marvin Breckinridge, Richard C. Hottelet, Sir Geoffrey Cox, Eben Finger, Lee Loevinger, and Richard Scammon.

5 ✦ PICTURES IN THE AIR

Murrow made his touching comments about his friendship with Shirer in a broadcast from London on Sept. 7, 1939. Shirer described his feelings about being stuck in Berlin and about CBS's refusal to allow recordings in *Berlin Diary* and *The Nightmare Years* and in his interview with us. His broadcasts making fun of false German news reports were aired Sept. 11 and Oct. 21, 1939; his feelings about the German bombing of Gdynia were broadcast Sept. 24, 1939.

The evolution of CBS's objectivity policy and the growth of the network's news operations in New York are well described in Sally Bedell Smith's biography of William Paley, *In All His Glory*, as well as in the Murrow biographies by Sperber and Persico. Sevareid recounted his conversation with Murrow about taking money from sponsors in a speech on Feb. 22, 1988.

In interviews Larry LeSueur told us how he was hired by Murrow and sent to France and how he stayed with Lois Sevareid while her husband went to the "front." LeSueur's broadcast describing the perilous flight of a British pilot was made Feb. 7, 1940. Sevareid talked about the "schoolboys of Europe" in an Oct. 27, 1939, broadcast; his remarks about "a new kind of . . . essay" and his feelings about the "phony war" are in *Not So Wild a Dream* and in his broadcasts of the time.

Mary Marvin Breckinridge Patterson told us of her background and how she came to be hired by Murrow in an interview; other information came from a speech she made at Boston University on Dec. 1, 1976, and from a paper by University of Maryland professor Maurine H. Beasley, "Mary Marvin Breckinridge Patterson: Case Study of One of 'Murrow's Boys.'" Murrow's instructions to Breckinridge about "the little policeman" are found in David H. Hosley, *As Good As Any*, on radio foreign correspondents. Murrow's Dec. 18, 1939, letter praising Breckinridge's work is in Murrow's papers at Tufts. Her broadcast on "Little Red Riding Hood" was Mar. 26, 1940; on the Dutch Nazi party, Apr. 28, 1940; on the newspaper, Feb. 8, 1940; on the Nazi bride school, Feb. 15, 1940.

Murrow and Shirer's joint broadcast from Amsterdam occurred Jan. 18, 1940; the account of their meeting, including the snowball fight, came from *Berlin Diary* and *The Nightmare Years.*

6 ✦ THE FALL OF PARIS

Shirer wrote in *Berlin Diary* about his inspection of the Maginot Line and his broadcast about Allied inaction. His ironic report about Germany's "safeguarding" Norway was aired on Apr. 10, 1940. The information about Betty Wason came from Hosley, *As Good As Any.*

Lois Sevareid's difficult pregnancy and childbirth were described in an interview with Michael Sevareid and in *Not So Wild a Dream.* That book was also a principal source for material about Sevareid's activities before, during, and after the fall of Paris. His broadcast on the demolished refugee train aired May 16, 1940; his doubts that the French would abandon Paris, June 1, 1940; Grandin's report that the French would stand firm, May 31, 1940. Janet Murrow commented on Lois Sevareid's courage in an interview with us.

The Sperber and Persico books on Murrow contain material about Grandin's marriage and his leaving France. Janet Murrow criticized Grandin in a June 1, 1940, letter to her family. Murrow recommended Grandin for a job in an undated telegram to Major Edwin Clark; Grandin's thank-you letter is dated July 22, 1940; both letters are in Janet Murrow's private papers. The information about Grandin's life after he left CBS came mainly from *Who's Who in America.* His Feb. 26, 1948, telegram to Murrow is in Murrow's papers at Tufts.

The account of Mary Marvin Breckinridge's short stay in Paris, her leaving CBS, and her marriage to Jefferson Patterson was drawn from her interview with us and from Beasley, "Patterson," and Hosley, *As Good As Any.* Breckinridge's report on refugees was broadcast May 14, 1940.

In interviews Larry LeSueur described his adventures after the fall of Paris, including his brush with death and Sevareid's reluctance to share broadcasts with him in Tours.

Shirer's reaction to the fall of France and details of his coverage of the armistice are in *Berlin Diary* and *The Nightmare Years.*

7 ✦ CLAPPERLESS BELLS

Sevareid's broadcast about the "clapperless bells" was made Aug. 4, 1940; about the fake war monument, Aug. 21, 1940. LeSueur's broadcast on the aerial shows of the Battle of Britain was made July 4, 1940. The story of Sevareid in the swimming pool came from an interview with LeSueur. Sevareid's account of the first big bombing attack on London was aired Sept. 7, 1940; his broadcasts on Londoners' reactions to the bombing, Sept. 13 and 26, 1940. "London after Dark" was broadcast Aug. 24, 1940.

Sevareid wrote about "the men, the instrument, the moment" and "our Camelot" in his foreword to a collection of J. B. Priestley's wartime broadcasts. Murrow wrote to William Boutwell about "building bonfires" on July 22, 1941. Janet Murrow made the pointed comments about her "second fiddle" role in the lives of Murrow and the Boys in an interview with us. Her Feb. 15, 1943, letter about her husband's reluctance to have her broadcast is in her papers at Mount Holyoke.

Sevareid's late nights with Murrow are described in Persico, *Edward R. Murrow*. Sevareid's wistful recollection of the Murrow-LeSueur friendship came from R. Franklin Smith's biography of Murrow. Interviews with LeSueur, along with Sperber, *Murrow*, and Edward Bliss, Jr., *Now the News: The History of Broadcast Journalism*, provided more details of the friendship. LeSueur also told us about the BBC bombing and his attempt to get on the air that night. Murrow's recounting of LeSueur's adventure was described in a story in the New York *Journal-American*, Mar. 24, 1941.

Sevareid eloquently wrote of his fear during the Blitz in *Not So Wild a Dream*; the anecdote about the hotel bombing came from R. Franklin Smith's book. Sevareid's final broadcast from London was Oct. 4, 1940; he described listeners' reaction to it in *Not So Wild a Dream*.

Shirer's broadcasting problems in Berlin, his decision to leave, and his reunion with Murrow in Lisbon are in *Berlin Diary* and *The Nightmare Years*. In interviews Joseph C. Harsch and Howard K. Smith cast doubt on Shirer's belief that he was being set up by the Nazis. Larry LeSueur told us about Murrow's anger over Shirer's leaving Europe and the war.

8 ✦ A TASTE OF FAME

Sevareid's description of hearing LeSueur's voice in Manhattan came from *Not So Wild a Dream*, as did most of the material about his triumphal return to New York. His Feb. 19, 1941, letter to Robert Sherwood about writing a play and his detailed movie "treatment" are in his papers at the Library of Congress.

Shirer wrote about his return to the United States in *A Native's Return*. His Apr. 16, 1941, letter to Murrow expressing reluctance about returning permanently to Europe is in Murrow's papers at Tufts.

9 ✦ "BONNIE PRINCE CHARLIE"

Helen Kirkpatrick Milbank discussed Murrow's thwarted attempt to hire her in an interview with us; it is also recounted in Sperber, *Murrow*. Charles Collingwood talked about his UP days during the Blitz and his first meeting with Murrow in a radio interview with John Dunning (KNUS, Denver) in May 1984. The Sperber book also provided material on Murrow's hiring of Collingwood and offered Pat Smither's description of Collingwood as looking like a "tailor's dummy." Information about Collingwood's early life and his time at Oxford came from his sister Jean Collingwood Spelman, his brother Tom Collingwood, nephew Harris Collingwood, and another family member. Austin Kiplinger and Bruce Netschert recalled Collingwood at Cornell.

Collingwood's letter to his parents about Armageddon was dated May 14, 1940; about moving to London, May 22, 1940; about his parents' criticism of his lifestyle, Feb. 2, 1941; about his new CBS job, Mar. 3, 1941. Collingwood told the story of his first CBS broadcast in his interview with Dunning; it is also recounted in R. Franklin Smith, *Murrow*. Collingwood described his attempts to learn Murrow's writing technique in a Jan. 8, 1976, speech; the quote about his wanting to "write like Ed" came from Joseph Persico, "On the Air," *Memories*, Apr. 5, 1990. In his biography of Murrow, Persico discusses Sevareid's imitation of Murrow.

10 ✦ CENSORSHIP

Winston Burdett told about his reporting from the Balkans and his marriage to Lea Schiavi in his 1955 testimony before the Senate Internal Security Subcommittee; additional information came from Ray Brock, *Nor Any Victory*; Cecil Brown, *Suez to Singapore*; and interviews with Richard Burdett, Martin Agronsky, and Farnsworth Fowle.

Cecil Brown's early years are described in a short autobiography, which is in his papers at the Mass Communications History Center, State Historical Society of Wisconsin, in Madison. In *Suez to Singapore*, Brown wrote about his reporting in Italy, Yugoslavia, and the Middle East. The story about the mispronunciation of his first name is in Hosley, *As Good As Any*.

The details of Larry LeSueur's adventures in the Arkhangelsk convoy, on the train trip across the Soviet Union, and in Kuibyshev and Moscow came from interviews with LeSueur; from LeSueur, *Twelve Months That Changed the World*; and from Eddy Gilmore, *Me and My Russian Wife*. LeSueur's half-sentence broadcast occurred on Jan. 7, 1942; the cable about his first trip to the front, on Dec. 17, 1941; his Stalingrad broadcast, on Sept. 29, 1942.

11 ✦ LAST TRAIN FROM BERLIN

The primary sources for material on Howard K. Smith's background and his years in Berlin were interviews with Smith and his wife, Benedicte (Bennie), and Smith's book, *Last Train From Berlin*. Denis Healey provided additional information about Smith's time at Oxford.

In *Not So Wild a Dream*, Eric Sevareid wrote about his problems adjusting to wartime Washington and about his difficulties with Paul White. White's July 7 and July 15, 1941, letters criticizing Sevareid's anti-isolationist broadcast are in Sevareid's papers at the Library of Congress, as is Sevareid's undated reply.

The Murrow letters complaining about those profiting from the war, the anecdote about Murrow's destruction of Shirer's hat, and Murrow's conversation with Roosevelt on Dec. 7, 1941, came from the Sperber and Persico biographies of Murrow. Sevareid's coverage of Pearl Harbor was recounted in an interview with Sevareid in *USA Today*, Dec. 21, 1983, and in Roger Burlingame, *Don't Let Them Scare You*, a biography of Elmer Davis. Sevareid wrote about his and Murrow's Dec. 7 conversation in *Not So Wild a Dream*. Paul White's jettisoning of neutrality is discussed in Bliss, *Now the News*.

12 ✦ TRIUMPH AND MISERY

The details of Cecil Brown's adventure aboard the *Repulse* and his difficulties with the British in Singapore came from *Suez to Singapore*, as well as from his broadcasts and magazine articles about the *Repulse* incident. Martin Agronsky discussed Brown's splenetic behavior in an interview with us. Paul White's letter of Sept. 26, 1941, reproving Brown for criticizing British officials is in Brown's papers at the State Historical Society of Wisconsin, as are the cables from White warning Brown about his crusading (Feb. 14, 1942) and telling him what to say when he accepted the OPC Award (Feb. 19, 1942). Murrow's Jan. 25, 1943, letter to Sevareid about Brown's book is in Murrow's papers at Tufts. Sevareid's letter to Brown is in Sevareid's papers at the Library of Congress.

Information about Bill Downs's early years and his experiences with UP in London came from interviews with Adam Downs, Bonnie Downs Shoults, and John Malone. Downs's Aug. 30, 1942, letter to his parents about his new CBS job is in his papers at Georgetown University, Washington, D.C. Murrow told the story of Downs's hiring in a 1951 broadcast (exact date unavailable). Downs's Stalingrad broadcast was made Feb. 8, 1943.

Charles Collingwood made his broadcast about the third anniversary of the war on Sept. 3, 1942. His letter to his parents about art collecting was dated Feb. 9, 1943; his July 30, 1982, letter to Janet Murrow about North Africa is in her papers at Mount Holyoke. The story about Collingwood's and Murrow's night on the town comes from Persico's biography of Murrow. Collingwood's letter criticizing the military's attitude toward radio is undated. He made his first broadcast from Algiers Nov. 15, 1942.

Collingwood recounted the story of his Darlan assassination broadcast coup in a Mar. 28, 1978, letter to Ed Bliss, now in Bliss's papers at American University, Washington, D.C. John MacVane discussed his reaction to Collingwood's success in his *On the Air in World War II*. Much of the information about Collingwood's reporting and his off-hours pursuits in North Africa came from his radio interview with John Dunning and from articles in *Newsweek*, Feb. 1, 1943, and *Time*, Apr. 5, 1943. His broadcasts criticizing Giraud were made Dec. 30, 1942, and Mar. 10, 1943. Collingwood told about Eisenhower's attempt to get rid of him in the interview with Dunning.

The story of Lea Schiavi's murder came from Winston Burdett's testimony before the Senate Internal Security Subcommittee. Morley Safer told us the story of Collingwood's dinner party in Algiers; he had heard it from Burdett.

Tom Collingwood talked about his brother's penchant for betting in an interview with Richard Hornik. The anecdote about Collingwood and Stoneman playing horseshoes was drawn from Drew Middleton, *Where Has Last July Gone?* Collingwood's broadcast about the liberation of Tunis was made May 9, 1943; his letter about the liberation was dated May 12, 1943. Murrow's Jan. 25, 1943, letter to Eric Sevareid is in Sevareid's papers. Ann Sperber told us about Collingwood's gonorrhea; she learned of it from one of the Murrow Boys.

13 ✦ THE SIN OF PRIDE

Many of the details about Cecil Brown's confrontation with CBS over objectivity, including Shirer's quote about Brown, came from Craig D. Tenney, "The 1943 Debate on Opinionated Broadcast News," *Journalism History*, Spring 1980. Gilbert Highet's parody of Brown, "I Was Robbed," appeared in *The Nation*, Nov. 28, 1942. Brown's broadcast criticizing American attitudes toward the war was made May 25, 1942. H. V. Kaltenborn criticized the CBS objectivity policy in remarks to the Association of American Radio News Analysts on Sept. 23, 1943. FCC chairman James Fly made his negative comments about CBS during an Oct. 8, 1943, speech to the Radio Executives Club. Walter Winchell's charge about advertisers' influence on CBS was in his column in the New York *Daily Mirror*, Sept. 27, 1943.

In an interview with us Frank Stanton talked about Paley's ousting of Ed Klauber. Shirer's Sept. 21, 1943, letter to Murrow criticizing Brown is in Janet Murrow's papers at Mount Holyoke. Paul White's telegram renouncing his former views about objectivity appeared in the Letters column of *Newsweek*, Apr. 12, 1954.

14 ✦ RETURN TO BATTLE

Not So Wild a Dream was a primary source concerning Eric Sevareid's discontent in Washington, his airplane jump over Burma, and his reporting of the Italian front. He talked about "the American Dream" on *Town Meeting of the Air*, Sept. 17, 1942; he commented on being "cut off from solid work" in a broadcast on Oct. 2, 1942. His July 20, 1942, letter to Murrow about his frustration and Murrow's Aug. 25, 1942, reply are in Sevareid's papers at the Library of Congress. He mused about Flickinger, about his own fortitude during the hike out of the mountains, and, later, about his surroundings in Chungking, in an unpublished journal, also in his papers. His report about the "Burmese jungle headhunters" was on the front page of the *New York Times*, Aug. 28, 1943. In an interview Sir Geoffrey Cox talked about the effect on Sevareid of his experience in Burma.

Sevareid's interview with the relief worker in China was aired Oct. 2, 1943. He assessed Communist strength in China in an unpublished article, which is in his papers. He wrote about being a celebrity in New York in his unpublished journal. His recollection of meeting Collingwood came in his remarks at Collingwood's memorial service, Oct. 9, 1985.

Sevareid's broadcast about the rear-echelon military's cushy life was reprinted in *Not So Wild a Dream*. He made his broadcast on training films, Apr. 3, 1944; on "living in a bull's-eye" at Anzio, Apr. 23, 1944; on the failure of the Anzio operation, Apr. 30, 1944; on the real reason for taking Rome, May 4, 1944; on "the awesome field of devastation," May 19, 1944; the "dusty pile of masonry," July 2, 1944; on the GIs' exhaustion, June 1, 1944. Winston Burdett recalled Sevareid's triumphal procession into Rome in a *CBS Morning News* broadcast on May 6, 1985, celebrating the fortieth anniversary of V-E Day.

15 ✦ PLEASURES OF WAR

Sevareid talked about being "spoiled" in a Sept. 22, 1962, speech to the Radio and Television News Directors Association. In interviews Andy Rooney, William Walton, and Sir Geoffrey Cox offered their assessments of the Boys. Harrison Salisbury's view of the Murrow team is in Sperber, *Murrow*.

Information about Howard K. Smith's years in Bern came from interviews with Smith and his wife, Bennie. The copies of Smith's scripts, many with doodles and handwritten notes, are in his papers at the State Historical Society of Wisconsin.

The story of Larry LeSueur's brief first marriage and his relationship with Priscilla Bruce is drawn from interviews with LeSueur and Priscilla Bruce LeSueur Jaretzki. Joan Phelps LeSueur's divorce and immediate remarriage were also reported in the *New York Times*, Feb. 11, 1944. Janet Murrow's comments about LeSueur's book were made in an Aug. 27, 1943, letter to her parents; her letters about LeSueur's marriage were dated June 25 and July 6, 1943.

Downs wrote about "more bodies" in a letter dated Apr. 8, 1943, which is in his papers at Georgetown University. He recounted his experience in Rzhev in an undated broadcast. In an interview John Malone described Downs's reaction to coming back to the States.

Walter Cronkite talked about his wartime admiration of Collingwood at Collingwood's memorial service. William Paley's memories of the Collingwood stag party and the hedonism of London are in Sally Bedell Smith, *In All His Glory*. Harrison Salisbury offered his own views on that hedonism in his memoirs, *A Journey for Our Times*. Murrow's affair with Pamela Churchill Harriman is discussed in Christopher Ogden's biography of Harriman, *Life of the Party*, as well as in the Murrow biographies by Persico and Sperber. Collingwood's comment about Harriman came from Persico.

Charles Shaw wrote about his delight in being part of the Murrow team in a proposal for a book that was never written. In interviews Richard C. Hottelet provided most of the material about his background, relationship with Howard K. Smith, stint in a German prison, and hiring by Murrow. Collingwood's December 1943 letter about Murrow's Berlin raid broadcast is in Janet Murrow's papers at Mount Holyoke.

Larry LeSueur and Dick Hottelet told us about their pre–D-Day activities. Hottelet's comment to Shaw about the size of the D-Day armada was noted in Shaw, "D-Day Plus 40 Years," *New Hope* (Pa.) *Gazette*, May 31, 1984.

16   ✦   "HANDFULS OF FRANCE"

In interviews Larry LeSueur talked about his Utah Beach landing and his problems in broadcasting, his march across Normandy, his dental problems and subsequent dash back to Paris, his broadcast from a liberated Paris, and his suspension. His broadcast about his D-Day experiences was finally aired June 10, 1944. Murrow interviewed the U.S. military press chief on May 14, 1944; Murrow's letter about army red tape was written to Ed Klauber on June 5, 1944.

The account of Collingwood on Utah Beach is taken from Persico's biography of Murrow, Collingwood's interview with John Dunning, and Collingwood's June 9, 1944, broadcast. LeSueur's broadcast on hedgerow fighting was made July 16, 1944; on the liberation of Cherbourg, June 29, 1944; on the GIs' renewed confidence, July 2, 1944. In an interview Bill Shadel talked about the dangers facing correspondents in Normandy.

In an interview Bill Walton described Collingwood's advance across Normandy; it is also in Richard Whelan, *Robert Capa*. Collingwood's report from Orléans was broadcast Aug. 17, 1944. His premature broadcast on the liberation of Paris and the broadcast's aftereffects are discussed in detail in Larry Collins and Dominique LaPierre, *Is Paris Burning?* In an interview Dick Hottelet recalled his role in airing the broadcast. LeSueur's broadcast debunking Collingwood's report was made Aug. 24, 1944; his broadcast from a liberated Paris, Aug. 25, 1944. Collingwood's explanation appeared in *Editor and Publisher*, Sept. 2, 1944. Ed Murrow's response came from Dickson Hartwell and Andrew A. Rooney, eds., *Off the Record: The Best Stories of Foreign Correspondents*. In an interview Andy Rooney described his disappointment with Collingwood and told us about Ernie Pyle's "goddamn exhibitionist" remark. John MacVane discussed his post-liberation broadcasting problems in *On the Air in World War II*. Bill Walton gave us the details of his and Collingwood's stay in Montmartre.

Howard and Bennie Smith told us the story of their narrow escape in Annecy; Smith's Aug. 20, 1944, cable to Paul White and Aug. 28, 1944, cable to *Time-Life*, also mentioned it. The Smiths recounted for us their first meeting with Collingwood in Paris.

LeSueur's competitiveness was described by Smith and Dick Hottelet, who also talked about the Boys' egotism and individualism. Murrow recalled his and the Boys' wartime freedom on the CBS radio program *We Take You Back*, Mar. 13, 1958. In an interview Bill Shadel discussed his problems in getting on the evening roundup.

Shadel, Howard K. Smith, and Farnsworth Fowle told us about the technical problems of broadcasting. Murrow mentioned the correspondents' frustrations in a Dec. 28, 1944, CBS publicity release.

Charles Collingwood's letter to his parents about his love of Paris was dated Nov. 15, 1944; about his reluctance to have Gracie in Paris, Mar. 25, 1945; about his poker losses and sale of a Picasso painting, Feb. 18, 1945. Bill Walton recalled Collingwood's life in Paris and his friendship with Robert Capa, which is also mentioned in Whelan, *Capa*.

In *America Inside Out*, David Schoenbrun wrote about Eric Sevareid's leaving the French front. Sevareid described his liberation of Gertrude Stein and his London broadcast about how GIs viewed the war in *Not So Wild a Dream*.

Bill Downs's letter to his parents about covering four armies was dated Jan. 18, 1945; about his experiences in Caen, July 11, 1944; about getting shelled, Aug. 1, 1944; on the liberation of Brussels, Sept. 5, 1944; on his depression over Londoners' indifference, Oct. 9, 1944. Bill Shadel assessed Downs's reporting in an interview; Paul White's view of Downs is in Persico, *Murrow*. Walter Cronkite told the story of how he and Downs were pinned down at Arnhem on *CBS Morning News*, May 6, 1985.

Hottelet's eyewitness account of the battle at Aachen was broadcast Oct. 16, 1944. Smith's broadcast about his return to Germany was made Nov. 5, 1944; his assessment of German artillery, Mar. 9, 1945. In interviews LeSueur told us of his near-disaster in recording a battle, and Hottelet recounted his discovery of the Battle of the Bulge.

Downs's broadcast about Operation Varsity was made on Mar. 24, 1945. Hottelet described his parachute jump in an interview, as well as in an article in *Collier's*, May 5, 1945. On the May 6, 1985, *CBS Morning News*, Sevareid said he gave Hottelet the microphone; Hottelet and LeSueur, in interviews, said he did not, although Hottelet later said he could not be certain. The archival record indicates that no Hottelet broadcast on this subject was made.

Smith's broadcast about his broken-down jeep was aired May 27, 1945. The Persico biography of Murrow was the source for Sevareid's comment about Smith and Hottelet. Murrow's Oct. 7, 1944, letter to his wife about the Boys is in Janet Murrow's papers at Mount Holyoke. Sevareid wrote about the boredom of war in *Not So Wild a Dream*. His broadcast about London was made on Oct. 12, 1944; on British policy in Greece, Dec. 12, 1944. Murrow remarked on the fading of idealism in an Oct. 13, 1944, broadcast. Burdett's broadcast about the Marchesa Torrigiani was July 30, 1944.

In an interview LeSueur told us about Dachau. Murrow's Buchenwald broadcast was on Apr. 15, 1945; Hottelet described Murrow's negativity toward Germans in an interview. Bill Downs's gloomy postwar mood was summarized for us by his son, Adam.

Hottelet told us about his unauthorized trip to Berlin and his coverage of the U.S.-Russian meeting at the Elbe; other details are from his Apr. 27, 1945, broadcast and MacVane, *On the Air*. Collingwood's delayed broadcast of the German surrender at Rheims aired May 8, 1945; that same day Murrow and Collingwood reported on V-E Day celebrations in London and Paris. Smith's broadcast of the German surrender in Moscow was on May 9. Sevareid made his V-E Day broadcast from San Francisco on May 8. He wrote about his sense of exhaustion in *Not So Wild a Dream*. Murrow's letter to his wife about the Boys was dated Oct. 7, 1944. His Jan. 2, 1946, letter to Collingwood about his wartime team is in Murrow's papers at Tufts.

18 ✦ THE HOUR OF THE CENTURIONS

In interviews Ed Bliss described his awe at seeing Charles Collingwood right after the war, and Michael Bessie talked about the Boys' stature in American journalism. Murrow's elevation to CBS vice president and Paul White's departure are well covered in the Persico and Sperber biographies of Murrow. Frank Stanton added further perspective to the Murrow-White struggle.

In *America Inside Out*, David Schoenbrun wrote about Sevareid's and Collingwood's hunger for fame and fortune. Interviews with Priscilla Le-Sueur Jaretzki, Sir Geoffrey Cox, Eben Finger, and Michael Sevareid provided information abut Lois Sevareid's manic depression; Eric Sevareid wrote about it in *Not So Wild a Dream*. Janet Murrow favorably compared

Lois to Eric in a letter to her parents on Jan. 1, 1943. Sevareid's description of his generation came in a Sept. 19, 1946, broadcast interview. The young Henry Kissinger's Sept. 14, 1947, letter to Sevareid is in Sevareid's papers at the Library of Congress. In his preface to the 1976 edition of *Not So Wild a Dream*, Sevareid discussed how Lois found the book's first chapters.

In interviews with us, Janet Murrow, Larry LeSueur, Tom Collingwood, Jean Spelman, and other members of the Collingwood family discussed Collingwood's jilting of Gracie Blake and his marriage to Louise Allbritton. The description of Howard Smith's personality and his replacing Murrow in London came from interviews with Smith and LeSueur and from Persico, *Edward R. Murrow*. The account of Bill Downs's postwar activities was taken from interviews with Adam Downs, Karen Downs, Bonnie Downs Shoults, and John Malone.

Schoenbrun expressed his admiration for the Boys in an interview for the University of Maryland Broadcast Pioneers Oral History project, May 30, 1974. In an interview with us, LeSueur discussed the special status of the Boys at CBS. That subject was also mentioned in profiles of Murrow in the *New York Post*, Feb. 27, 1959, and *The New Yorker*, Dec. 26, 1953. The letter from Wells Church's lawyer to *The New Yorker*, demanding a retraction, is in Murrow's papers at Tufts. Ned Calmer commented on the Boys in an interview with Ann Sperber. The "Murrow-Ain't-God Club" is discussed in the Persico biography. (Sperber called it the "Murrow-*Isn't*-God Club.")

Sperber's biography quotes Howard Smith on Murrow's standing up for the Boys. Further information about Murrow's relationship with the Boys came from interviews with Smith, LeSueur, Priscilla Jaretzki, Janet Murrow, Ed Bliss, and Bill Shadel. Murrow offered to take care of the Smiths' son in an Oct. 16, 1950, letter to Smith, a copy of which is in Murrow's papers at Tufts. In an interview Bill Walton discussed Lois and Eric Sevareid's relationship. Janet Murrow's and Howard Smith's quotes about the Murrow marriage came from the Persico biography. The anecdote about Murrow's on-air sabotage of Schoenbrun was drawn from Schoenbrun's University of Maryland Oral History interview. Alexander Kendrick wrote about Murrow's news program in *Prime Time*, a biography of Murrow. In an interview Bill Shadel talked about the competition to appear on the Murrow show.

19 ✦ "YEARS OF CRISIS"

Most of the information about the Boys' influence and the year-end round-ups came from interviews with Larry LeSueur, Richard C. Hottelet,

Howard K. Smith, Ed Bliss, Sandy Socolow, Robert Pierpoint, Perry Wolff, Sander Vanocur, Sig Mickelson, Av Westin, Don Hewitt, Charles Kuralt, Daniel Schorr, Marvin Kalb, and Palmer Williams. Collingwood's remark about a good life came from Bliss, *Now the News*. Schoenbrun discussed the Boys' influence in his University of Maryland Oral History interview and in his book *America Inside Out*. A copy of William Paley's letter to Murrow after the first year-end roundup is in Bill Downs's papers at Georgetown University. William Manchester's remark about the roundups is in his *The Glory and the Dream*. John Crosby made his assessment in his *New York Herald Tribune* column, Jan. 6, 1956. The story about Bill Downs's problem with his trousers came from Schoenbrun, *On and Off the Air*.

20 ✦ BROTHER AGAINST BROTHER

For the material about William Shirer's departure from CBS, we relied on interviews with Shirer, Inga Dean, Bill Shadel, Sir Geoffrey Cox, George Herman, Frank Stanton, Joseph C. Harsch, Larry LeSueur, Howard K. Smith, and Richard C. Hottelet. The third volume of Shirer's autobiography, *A Native's Return*, and his novel, *Stranger Come Home*, were also important sources, as were the Sperber and Persico biographies of Murrow and *PM*, Mar. 24, 1947. Paley's wistful memory of the war came from his memoirs, *As It Happened*. Roz Gerson Downs told Ann Sperber about her confrontation with Shirer. The story of Murrow's snub of Shirer in London is found in the Persico biography. Murrow's complaints about Shirer and his behavior during the Shirer brouhaha are well described by Persico and Sperber. *The New Republic*, Jan. 13, 1947, reported on the troubles of liberal radio commentators. Paley's anger at Shirer over the Wrigley program is discussed in Persico, *Edward R. Murrow*, and in David Halberstam, *The Powers That Be*. Jack Gould defended Shirer in the *New York Times*, Mar. 24, 1947. Harrison Salisbury wrote about the furor over Shirer's charges in the *Washington Post*, Feb. 9, 1990. Murrow's letter to Edgar Ansel Mowrer about the controversy, dated Apr. 17, 1947, is in Murrow's papers at Tufts, as is Smith's Sept. 24, 1947, letter to Murrow about Shirer's departure. Charles Poore reviewed *Stranger Come Home* in the *New York Times*, May 27, 1954.

21 ✦ "A FRIGHTENED LITTLE BAND"

The anecdote about people watching television in Hawthorne, California, came from Stan Cloud's personal recollections. The coming of television news and the Boys' reactions were described in interviews with Frank Stanton, Fred Friendly, Larry LeSueur, Howard K. Smith, Richard C. Hottelet, George Herman, Don Hewitt, Robert Pierpoint, Lou Cioffi, Sig Mickelson, Ed Bliss, Perry Wolff, Michael Bessie, and John Sharnik. In *The Evening Stars*, Barbara Matusow describes the meager television coverage of the 1948 political conventions. Murrow's quote about nothing much happening came from John Crosby, *Out of the Blue*.

Matusow also recounts Smith's feelings about being on TV and LeSueur's and Mickelson's remarks about Douglas Edwards. Don Hewitt's statement about the influence of *See It Now* on the Boys came from the Persico biography of Murrow. The "Christmas in Korea" segment of *See It Now* was broadcast Dec. 29, 1952.

Charles Collingwood's description of Fred Friendly is in Persico's biography of Murrow. David Schoenbrun complained about *See It Now* in an Apr. 4, 1956, letter to Murrow, and Howard Smith protested the conflicting demands of radio and TV in a Mar. 17, 1953, letter. Smith talked about the reporter as anachronism during his June 29, 1952, radio analysis. The *Adventure* series was discussed in *Time*, July 2, 1956. Murrow's reaction to Eric Sevareid's appearance on *See It Now* was mentioned in a June 22, 1988, letter from Joseph Wershba to Eric Sevareid.

Schoenbrun made comments about Friendly in *On and Off the Air* and to Ann Sperber. Murrow boasted about his independence in *The New Yorker*, Dec. 26, 1953. Walter Cronkite's background and his first and subsequent encounters with Murrow are described in the Persico and Sperber biographies.

22 ✦ "THE COMMUNIST BROADCASTING SYSTEM"

The FBI memos on CBS and Murrow were obtained under the Freedom of Information Act from the files on Murrow at FBI headquarters in Washington. Information about the murder of George Polk came from Kati Marton, *The Polk Conspiracy*. Background on the CBS "loyalty oath" and Murrow's reaction to it was drawn from interviews with Frank Stanton and Michael Bessie, as well as from the Sperber and Persico biographies of Murrow. The network's internal witch-hunt is well documented in the Fund for the Republic, *Report on Blacklisting*. In an interview Perry Wolff discussed the blacklisting of Einstein on *Adventure*.

Eric Sevareid's response to McCarthyism was discussed in interviews with Michael Sevareid, Sir Geoffrey Cox, and Jean Friendly. Sevareid's Oct. 23, 1953, speech at the University of Minnesota about objectivity is in his papers at the Library of Congress. His broadcast attacking the Republican National Committee was made July 1, 1952, and his Winnie-the-Pooh broadcast was included in his collection of broadcasts, *In One Ear.* Sevareid described McCarthyites' retaliation against him in a CBS interview with Charles Kuralt on Jan. 4, 1978; Michael Sevareid and Geoffrey Cox added further details. Davidson Taylor's Sept. 1, 1949, letter warning Sevareid about Metropolitan Life Insurance's nervousness is in Sevareid's papers.

Bill Downs's attempts to get Murrow to confront McCarthy are described in Sperber, *Murrow,* and in an interview by Ed Bliss with Downs and his wife, Roz. Fred Friendly talked of Murrow's caution in an interview with us. Friendly's quote about Paley's reaction to the McCarthy broadcast is in Sally Bedell Smith, *In All His Glory.* Sevareid mentioned his post-broadcast trip with Murrow on a CBS broadcast after Murrow's death. Dorothy Schiff's and Bill Downs's reactions to the broadcast are summarized in Sperber's book. Sevareid's quote about the "tank" came from Gary Paul Gates, *Air Time.*

Charles Collingwood's Mar. 13, 1954, letter praising Murrow for the McCarthy broadcast is in Murrow's papers at Tufts. FBI memos on Collingwood — dated Mar. 31, 1949; May 31, 1949; June 14, 15, and 16, 1949; and Oct. 20, 1951 — are in Collingwood's FBI file, released to us under the Freedom of Information Act. Collingwood mentioned Ed Beattie's ouster of the FBI agent in a letter recommending Beattie for membership in the Players Club. An important source for information about Collingwood's AFTRA activities and his fight on behalf of John Henry Faulk is Faulk's book, *Fear on Trial.* Collingwood's comment about being an amateur came from his January 1956 inaugural message to the AFTRA membership, which is in his papers at the State Historical Society of Wisconsin. The exchange of letters between the House Committee on Un-American Activities and Collingwood was published in the *New York Times,* Jan. 23, 1956. The *New York Times,* May 15, 1962, ran an account of Collingwood's testimony at the Faulk libel trial. In an interview Harris Collingwood discussed his uncle's insecurities. Walter Cronkite praised Collingwood in his eulogy at Collingwood's memorial service.

23 ✦ BURDETT'S SECRET

An important source for information about Winston Burdett's life as a Communist and Soviet spy is the transcript of his testimony before the Senate Internal Security Subcommittee, June 28, 1955. Yakov Golos's position in the hierarchy of Soviet intelligence came from Pavel Sudopatov,

Special Tasks. Additional material about Burdett was provided in interviews with Giorgina Burdett, Richard Burdett, Michael Bessie, Robert Morris, Marvin Kalb, Joseph C. Harsch, Howard K. Smith, Larry LeSueur, Daniel Schorr, Ernest Leiser, Sig Mickelson, and Victor Weingarten. Burdett's statement about his voluntary testimony appeared in *Time* and *Newsweek*, July 11, 1955. David Schoenbrun told Ann Sperber about Murrow's request for forgiveness of Burdett. Senator Eastland's letters to Daniel O'Shea and Herbert Brownell are in the National Archives. The real purpose of the Senate hearing and the consequences of Burdett's testimony are outlined in Ralph H. Johnson and Michael Altman, "Communists in the Press," *Journalism Quarterly*, Autumn 1978.

24 ✦ "NOT HIS THING ANYMORE"

Paley's cancellation of his lunch with Murrow and the Boys is recounted in Sperber, *Murrow*. David Schoenbrun talked about Paley's coolness in his University of Maryland Oral History interview. In an interview with us, Don Hewitt talked about Paley's attitude toward the Boys.

Frank Stanton, Bill Shadel, Ernest Leiser, and Don Kellerman discussed Eric Sevareid's difficulties with television in interviews with us. Sevareid's Apr. 29, 1954, letter to Howard Smith about *American Week* is in Sevareid's papers at the Library of Congress. The story about Trumbull Park and Frank Brown appeared on *American Week*, July 4, 1954. A good source for the furor over Sevareid's commentary on the State Department's ban on travel to China and the resulting confrontation with Paley is Sally Bedell Smith, *In All His Glory*. Sevareid's undated memo about the CBS objectivity policy is in his papers. Belèn Sevareid was the main source for material about her relationship with Sevareid. Michael Sevareid, Sir Geoffrey Cox, Ernest Leiser, Michael Bessie, Larry LeSueur, and Sander Vanocur also provided details about Sevareid's personal life during this period.

David Schoenbrun's remark about substituting for Howard Smith is in *America Inside Out*. In an interview Smith discussed his reporting in the early 1950s, including the *See It Now* broadcast on the Middle East crisis. *Variety*'s review ran Mar. 21, 1956.

Much of the account of Murrow's last days at CBS was taken from the books on Murrow by Persico and Sperber and from Sally Bedell Smith's biography of Paley. Murrow's closed-circuit farewell to CBS was broadcast Jan. 21, 1961.

25 ✦ THREE RESIGNATIONS

The departures from CBS of Howard Smith, Bill Downs, and Larry Le-Sueur were described in interviews with Howard and Bennie Smith, Larry LeSueur, Janet Murrow, Frank Stanton, Fred Friendly, Blair Clark, Ed Bliss, Av Westin, and Adam Downs. Jack Gould's column criticizing CBS for muzzling Smith was in the *New York Times*, May 28, 1961. Paley's comment about stopping outspoken journalists came from Ed Joyce, *Prime Times, Bad Times*. The piece about Smith's ABC program was in *Newsweek*, Oct. 29, 1962. Smith's quote about being wasted at ABC came from Matusow, *The Evening Stars*. Schoenbrun commented on the close of the Murrow Boy era in *On and Off the Air*. Bill Downs's thank-you letter to Sevareid is in Sevareid's papers at the Library of Congress.

26 ✦ "GOOD NIGHT, SWEET PRINCE"

Ed Murrow's last months are described in the Sperber and Persico biographies. Collingwood's Sept. 2, 1964, letter to Murrow and May 6, 1964, letter to Janet Murrow are in her papers at Mount Holyoke. Murrow's letter to Collingwood about Sevareid is in Collingwood's papers at the State Historical Society of Wisconsin. The account of Murrow's and Shirer's last meeting came from an interview with Shirer and from *A Native's Return*. Sevareid's reaction to Murrow's death was drawn from interviews with his then-assistant, Marion Goldin, and Palmer Williams. Fred Friendly told us about Paley's first reaction to the Murrow special. Howard Smith's sense of loss at Murrow's death was expressed in an Apr. 27, 1965, letter to Janet Murrow. Collingwood's quote about his love for Murrow is in the Persico book. Sevareid's comment about Murrow's "incandescence" is taken from his syndicated newspaper column the week of Murrow's death.

27 ✦ "WRITING CAPTIONS FOR PICTURES"

Collingwood talked about his World War II memories in an Aug. 16, 1965, letter to Murrow. Sevareid wrote about his memories of St.-Tropez in his newspaper column on Aug. 16, 1965.

The account of Collingwood in the sixties and seventies is drawn from interviews with Harris Collingwood, Molly Collingwood, another Collingwood family member, Morley Safer, Joseph Dembo, Marvin Kalb, Les Midgley, Blair Clark, Bill Walton, Don Hewitt, Nancy White Hector, Heyden White Rostow, George Herman, Tony Hatch, John Sharnik,

Bernie Birnbaum, Marvin Kalb, and Ernest Leiser. Collingwood complained about being a utility man in a June 3, 1963, memo to Leiser; his comment about his fatigue was in a June 29, 1967, memo to Richard Salant. The material about North Vietnam's timing of its signal regarding peace negotiations came from Lyndon Johnson, *Vantage Point*, and Tom Hayden, "The Impasse in Paris," *Ramparts*, 1968. Collingwood's July 28, 1982, letter to Sevareid is in Sevareid's papers at the Library of Congress.

The descriptions of Sevareid in the sixties and seventies came from interviews with Belèn Sevareid, Michael Sevareid, Cristina Sevareid Kennedy, Eben Finger, Ed Fouhy, Michael Bessie, Blair Clark, Sandy Socolow, Gordon Manning, Howard Smith, and Bill Leonard. Sevareid's report on Vietnam aired on CBS on June 21, 1966. Gloria Emerson complained about Sevareid in "Why I Won't Miss Eric Sevareid," *New York*, Dec. 4, 1977. Sevareid responded to his critics in a 1986 interview with the *Washington Times*. His calling Nixon "evil" was discussed in a *Washington Post* Sunday magazine profile, Dec. 14, 1975. He explained his comments on the day Nixon resigned in a *New York Times* profile, May 2, 1979. Sevareid's remark about radio versus television was quoted in a column by Cecil Smith in the *Los Angeles Times* (date unknown). The letters from viewers about Sevareid's retirement are in his papers.

Information about Winston Burdett's later life came from Richard Burdett, Giorgina Burdett, Bert Quint, Diane Quint, Joseph Dembo, Gordon Manning, Daniel Schorr, and Sander Vanocur.

Material about Dick Hottelet was supplied by Hottelet, Sig Mickelson, and Gordon Manning. Ken Auletta, *Three Blind Mice*, Peter Boyer, *Who Killed CBS?* and Peter McCabe, *Bad News at Black Rock*, were important sources for information about CBS News in the eighties. Sevareid complained about local anchormen in his CBS commentary of Apr. 22, 1974.

28 ✦ "SO LONG AGO"

For background on the Boys' 1985 reunion and those not there, we relied on interviews with Larry LeSueur, Howard Smith, Ernest Leiser, Bill Shirer, Dick Hottelet, and Adam Downs. Other important sources were the transcript of the *CBS Morning News* broadcast, May 6, 1985, and Shirer, *A Native's Return*. Howard Stringer's July 8, 1985, letter to Sevareid explaining why his broadcast wasn't used is in Sevareid's papers at the Library of Congress.

Charles Collingwood's last years, including his second marriage, and details of his memorial service were described by Harris Collingwood,

Molly Collingwood, Tom Collingwood, another Collingwood family member, Richard Clurman, Tony Hatch, Morley Safer, Bernie Birnbaum, Bill Shadel, Sid Offit, Richard Leibner, Robert Pierpoint, Bill Walton, Michael Bessie, Ernest Leiser, Heyden White Rostow, and Charles Kuralt. Other sources on the memorial service were a transcript of the service and Boyer, *Who Killed CBS?*

Collingwood talked about Buchenwald in an interview with Ann Sperber. Bill Shadel's presence at Buchenwald with Murrow is attested to by a 1945 CBS press release. Collingwood's undated letter to his wife, Tatiana, is in his papers at the State Historical Society of Wisconsin. Joe Wershba told Ed Bliss about his hospital visit to Collingwood; Bliss's notes are in his papers at American University. Severeid described seeing Collingwood in a letter to Kate Knull, Oct. 12, 1985.

Severeid's final years were discussed by Suzanne St. Pierre, Belèn Severeid, Michael Sevareid, Cristina Severeid Kennedy, Frank Stanton, Bernie Birnbaum, Sandy Socolow, and Inga Shirer Dean. Sevareid's Dec. 16, 1986, memo to Laurence Tisch is in his papers at the Library of Congress, as is his Feb. 20, 1980, letter to Dan Rather warning about the "star system." Richard Leibner told us about Sevareid's recommendation of Rather. Sevareid's Dec. 18, 1987, letter to Rather about his "advice" is in Sevareid's papers. Eric Ober talked about the Murrow cigarette ad in an interview. Sevareid discussed his million-dollar offer in the *New York Times*, May 2, 1979. His Nov. 9, 1981, letter about the offer is in his papers. He expressed doubts about his writing in a 1983 UPI interview. Sevareid's Mar. 1, 1988, letter to Janet Murrow about the past is in his papers. He commented on Tom Grandin and Larry LeSueur in a letter to the editor of *Communicator*, May 1988.

EPILOGUE

Much of the material in the Epilogue was drawn from interviews with Michael Sevareid, Mary Marvin Breckinridge Patterson, Richard Burdett, Giorgina Burdett, William Shirer, Howard K. Smith, Bennie Smith, Larry LeSueur, Richard C. Hottelet, Tom Fenton, Roger Mudd, Frank Stanton, Charles Kuralt, and Sander Vanocur. Important sources for material about network news operations in the nineties were Auletta, *Three Blind Mice*; Marc Gunther, *The House That Roone Built: The Inside Story of ABC News*; and Jon Katz's article about Dan Rather, *Rolling Stone*, Oct. 14, 1993.

Selected Bibliography

Alterman, Eric. *Sound and Fury*. New York: HarperCollins, 1992.

Auletta, Ken. *Three Blind Mice: How the TV Networks Lost Their Way*. New York: Random House, 1991.

Barnouw, Erik. *A History of Broadcasting in the United States*. Vol. 2, *The Golden Web: 1930–1953*. New York: Oxford University Press, 1968.

———. *A History of Broadcasting in the United States*. Vol. 3, *The Image Empire: From 1953*. New York: Oxford University Press, 1970.

———. *Tube of Plenty: The Evolution of American Television*. New York: Oxford University Press, 1975.

Bliss, Edward, Jr. *Now the News: The History of Broadcast Journalism*. New York: Columbia University Press, 1991.

Boyer, Peter J. *Who Killed CBS?: The Undoing of America's Number One News Network*. New York: Random House, 1988.

Brown, Cecil. *Suez to Singapore*. Garden City, N.Y.: Halcyon House, 1942.

Burlingame, Roger. *Don't Let Them Scare You: The Life and Times of Elmer Davis*. Westport, Conn.: Greenwood, 1974.

Cogley, John. *Report on Blacklisting: Radio and Television*. New York: The Fund for the Republic, 1956.

Collingwood, Charles. *The Defector*. New York: Harper and Row, 1970.

Collins, Larry, and Dominique LaPierre. *Is Paris Burning?* New York: Simon and Schuster, 1965.

Cox, Geoffrey. *Countdown to War*. London: Hodder and Stoughton, 1990.

Crosby, John. *Out of the Blue*. New York: Simon and Schuster, 1952.

Culbert, David Holbrook. *News for Everyman: Radio and Foreign Affairs in Thirties America*. Westport, Conn.: Greenwood Press, 1976.

Desmond, Robert W. *Tides of War: World News Reporting 1940–45*. Iowa City: University of Iowa Press, 1984.

Donovan, Hedley. *Right Places, Right Times: Forty Years in Journalism Not Counting My Paper Route*. New York: Henry Holt, 1989.

Fang, Irving E. *Those Radio Commentators!* Ames, Iowa: Iowa State University Press, 1977.

Faulk, John Henry. *Fear on Trial.* New York: Simon and Schuster, 1964.

Flannery, Harry. *Assignment to Berlin.* New York: Alfred A. Knopf, 1942.

Friendly, Fred W. *Due to Circumstances Beyond Our Control . . .* New York: Random House, 1967.

Gates, Gary Paul. *Air Time: The Inside Story of CBS News.* New York: Harper and Row, 1978.

Gilmore, Eddy. *Me and My Russian Wife.* New York: Greenwood Press, 1968.

Gordon, George N., and Irving A. Falk. *On-the-Spot Reporting: Radio Records History.* New York: Julian Messner, 1967.

Gunther, Marc. *The House That Roone Built: The Inside Story of ABC News.* Boston: Little, Brown, 1994.

Halberstam, David. *The Powers That Be.* New York: Alfred A. Knopf, 1979.

Harsch, Joseph C. *At the Hinge of History: A Reporter's Story.* Athens, Ga.: University of Georgia Press, 1993.

Hartwell, Dickson, and Andrew A. Rooney, eds. *Off the Record: The Best Stories of Foreign Correspondents.* Garden City: Doubleday, 1953.

Hosley, David H. *As Good As Any: Foreign Correspondence on American Radio, 1930–1940.* Westport, Conn.: Greenwood Press, 1984.

Jordan, Max. *Beyond All Fronts.* Milwaukee: Bruce, 1944.

Joyce, Ed. *Prime Times, Bad Times.* New York: Doubleday, 1988.

Kendrick, Alexander. *Prime Time: The Life of Edward R. Murrow.* Boston: Little, Brown, 1969.

Knightley, Phillip. *The First Casualty.* New York: Harcourt Brace Jovanovich, 1975.

Leckie, Robert. *Delivered from Evil: The Saga of World War II.* New York: Harper and Row, 1987.

Leonard, Bill. *In the Storm of the Eye: A Lifetime at CBS.* New York: G. P. Putnam's Sons, 1987.

LeSueur, Larry. *Twelve Months That Changed the World.* New York: Alfred A. Knopf, 1943.

MacVane, John. *On the Air in World War II.* New York: William Morrow, 1979.

Manchester, William. *The Glory and the Dream: A Narrative History of America, 1932–1972.* New York: Bantam, 1973.

Marton, Kati. *The Polk Conspiracy.* New York: Farrar Straus and Giroux, 1990.

Matusow, Barbara. *The Evening Stars.* Boston: Houghton Mifflin, 1983.

McCabe, Peter. *Bad News at Black Rock: The Sell-Out of CBS News.* New York: Arbor House, 1987.

Metz, Robert. *CBS: Reflections in a Bloodshot Eye.* New York: Playboy Press, 1975.

Middleton, Drew. *Where Has Last July Gone?* New York: Quadrangle, 1973.

Midgley, Leslie. *How Many Words Do You Want?* New York: Birch Lane Press, 1989.

Ogden, Christopher. *Life of the Party.* Boston: Little, Brown, 1994.

Oldfield, Barney. *Never a Shot in Anger.* New York: Duell, Sloan and Pearce, 1956.

Paley, William S. *As It Happened.* Garden City, N.Y.: Doubleday, 1979.

Persico, Joseph E. *Edward R. Murrow: An American Original.* New York: Laurel, 1990.

Polmar, Norman, and Thomas B. Allen. *World War II: America at War 1941–1945.* New York: Random House, 1991.

Powers, Ron. *The Newscasters.* New York: St. Martin's Press, 1977.

Rather, Dan, with Mickey Herskowitz. *The Camera Never Blinks.* New York: William Morrow, 1977.

Rosenstiel, Tom. *Strange Bedfellows: How Television and the Presidential Candidates Changed American Politics, 1992.* New York: Hyperion, 1994.

Ryan, Milo. *History in Sound.* Seattle: University of Washington Press, 1963.

Salisbury, Harrison. *A Journey for Our Times.* New York: Harper and Row, 1983.

Schoenbrun, David. *America Inside Out: At Home and Abroad from Roosevelt to Reagan.* New York: McGraw Hill, 1984.

———. *On and Off the Air: An Informal History of CBS News.* New York: Dutton, 1989.

Schroth, Raymond A. *The American Journey of Eric Sevareid.* South Royalton, Vt.: Steerforth Press, 1995.

Sevareid, Eric. *Canoeing with the Cree.* 1935. Reprint, St. Paul: Minnesota Historical Society, 1968.

———. *Not So Wild a Dream.* 1946. 2nd ed., New York: Atheneum, 1976.

———. *In One Ear.* New York: Alfred A. Knopf, 1952.

———. *Small Sounds in the Night.* New York: Alfred A. Knopf, 1956.

Shirer, William L. *Berlin Diary: The Journal of a Foreign Correspondent.* New York: Alfred A. Knopf, 1941.

———. *End of a Berlin Diary.* New York: Alfred A. Knopf, 1947.

———. *Love and Hatred: The Stormy Marriage of Leo and Sonya Tolstoy.* New York: Simon and Schuster, 1994.

————. *Stranger Come Home*. Boston: Little, Brown, 1954.

————. *Twentieth-Century Journey*. Vol. 1, *The Start*. New York: Simon and Schuster, 1976.

————. *Twentieth-Century Journey*. Vol. 2, *The Nightmare Years*. Boston: Little, Brown, 1984.

————. *Twentieth-Century Journey*. Vol. 3, *A Native's Return*. Boston: Little, Brown, 1990.

Slater, Robert. *This . . . Is CBS*. Englewood Cliffs, N.J.:Prentice Hall, 1988.

Smith, R. Franklin. *Edward R. Murrow: The War Years*. Kalamazoo, Mich.: New Issues Press, 1978.

Smith, Sally Bedell. *In All His Glory*. New York: Simon and Schuster, 1990.

Smith, Howard K. *Last Train from Berlin*. New York: Alfred A. Knopf, 1942.

Sperber, A. M. *Murrow: His Life and Times*. New York: Freundlich, 1986.

Westin, Av. *Newswatch: How TV Decides the News*. New York: Simon and Schuster, 1982.

Whelan, Richard. *Robert Capa*. New York: Alfred A.Knopf, 1985.

White, Paul. *News on the Air*. New York: Harcourt, Brace and Co., 1947.

Acknowledgments

This book would not have been possible without the help of the surviving members of Edward R. Murrow's team — Mary Marvin Breckinridge (Mrs. Jefferson Patterson), Richard C. Hottelet, Larry LeSueur, and Howard K. Smith. One has only to chat with them a short time to understand that their greatness of spirit and intellect is no myth. We were also privileged to spend the better part of one sunny fall afternoon interviewing William L. Shirer at his home in Lenox, Massachusetts, not long before his death in 1993 at the age of eighty-nine. And we wish to pay tribute to Janet Murrow, Edward R. Murrow's widow, for her assistance, her elegance, her intelligence, her kindness, and her hospitality to us and to our daughter.

We thank the Boys' extended families — including, in some cases, wives and ex-wives — who were so open to our questions and helpful as we tried to understand who the Boys really were and what motivated them. Space (and, in a very few cases, confidentiality agreements) prohibit our listing all of them here, but we'd like especially to mention Giorgina Burdett, Richard Burdett, Inga (Shirer) Dean, Harris Collingwood, Molly Collingwood, Jean Collingwood Spelman, Tom Collingwood, Adam Downs, Karen Downs, Bonnie (Downs) Shoults, Eben Finger, Belèn Sevareid, Suzanne St. Pierre, Michael Sevareid, Cristina (Sevareid) Kennedy, Benedicte Smith, Dorothy LeSueur, Priscilla (LeSueur) Jaretzki, and Ann Hottelet.

Our appreciation also goes to the friends, colleagues, and acquaintances of Murrow and the Boys whom we interviewed, particularly Martin Agronsky, Michael Bessie, Bernie Birnbaum, Ed Bliss, Jules Buck, Lou Cioffi, Blair Clark, Richard Clurman, Shirley Clurman, Sir Geoffrey Cox, Joseph Dembo, Sara Engh, Tom Fenton, Ed Fouhy, Farnsworth Fowle, Fred Friendly, Jean Friendly, Marion Goldin, Fred Graham, Skyla Harris, Joseph C. Harsch, Tony Hatch, Sir Denis Healey, Nancy White Hector, George Herman, Don Hewitt, Marvin Kalb, Don Kellerman, Austin Kiplinger, Charles Kuralt, Richard Leibner, Ernest Leiser, the late Bill Leonard, Lee Loevinger, John Malone, Gordon Manning, Paul Manning, Leonard Miall,

Sig Mickelson, Les Midgley, Helen Kirkpatrick Milbank, Robert Morris, Roger Mudd, Bruce Netschert, Sid Offitt, Robert Pierpoint, Bert Quint, Diane Quint, Dan Rather, Andy Rooney, Hayden White Rostow, Morley Safer, Richard Scammon, Ray Scherer, Daniel Schorr, Bill Shadel, Julie Shadel, John Sharnik, Sandy Socolow, Frank Stanton, Tom Stix, Emerson Stone, Sander Vanocur, the late Bill Walton, Victor Weingarten, Av Westin, Palmer Williams, and Perry Wolff. These people not only provided us with a wealth of detail; they also suggested other sources we might consult or interview. Any errors, we note in time-honored tradition, are ours and not theirs.

A few words of praise and gratitude for the librarians and archivists who assisted us with our research. They are the preservers of history and civilization, and their selfless approach to the work they do is nothing short of heroic. We'd like to single out Elaine Trehub, the Mount Holyoke College Archives librarian, whose generosity and cheerfulness we greatly appreciated as we examined Janet Murrow's papers. Also helpful were the librarians in the manuscript division of the Library of Congress, which houses Eric Sevareid's papers and microfilm copies of Edward R. Murrow's papers.

Thanks also to the National Archives, which contains recordings of many of the Boys' World War II broadcasts; the Mass Communications History Center of the State Historical Society of Wisconsin, which has the papers of Cecil Brown, Charles Collingwood, and Howard K. Smith; the Museum of Television and Radio; the Academy of Motion Picture Arts and Sciences Library; Georgetown University archives, which has Bill Downs's papers; and American University archives, where Ed Bliss's papers reside.

Our agent, Gail Ross, provided much appreciated — and needed — counsel and support. We're also grateful to Hilary Liftin and Wendy Holt, our editors at Houghton Mifflin, for their enthusiasm and understanding, and to Peg Anderson, senior manuscript editor, for her intelligence and sensitivity — and for her witty comments in the manuscript's margins. These three fine professionals are living proof that good editing does still occur in modern book publishing.

We wish to acknowledge the kindness and collegiality shown us by the late Ann Sperber, author of *Murrow*; Ray Schroth, author of *The American Journey of Eric Sevareid*, and Barbara Matusow, author of *The Evening Stars*. Special thanks also to Richard Hornik of *Time*, who generously volunteered to interrupt his Hawaii sabbatical in order to interview Tom Collingwood for us in Honolulu, and to Ola Kinnander, an American University graduate student of communication, who helped with research.

We acknowledge and thank our fellow journalists and colleagues, past and present, at CBS and elsewhere, including *Time* and the American University. Without their direct and indirect assistance, their encouragement, their example, this book would not have been written and, more to the point, could not have been written. Journalists are in ill repute these days, but those with whom we dealt while researching *The Murrow Boys* were uniformly thoughtful and insightful and often as concerned as the general public about the direction in which their craft is headed.

A special message of appreciation to Jessica and Walter Olson, whose lives and examples have served as touchstones for their daughter. Jessica's support and encouragement of this book and its authors meant more than she ever knew, and the fact that she didn't live to see the book's publication is a source of great sadness. And thanks to Maxine and Wade Cloud, who encouraged their son to be a writer almost from the day he was born.

Thanks, too, to Stan's sons, Michael, David, and Matthew, and to our daughter, Carly, an aspiring teacher and writer herself, who endured with her customary grace and good humor her parents' years of absorption with the Murrow Boys.

Index